TONARI'S FRIENDS

...with Tonari, planning their escape together.

Sandel

Wants to be a doctor
when he grows up.

Mia

Her dream is to be a
famous artist's model.

Uroy

Loves eating poultry.
He dreams of raising
many animals.

Ligard

Tonari's partner, the
three-toed owl. Came to
the island with Tonari.

Oopa

Always wanted to know
where the sun comes from.
Her dream came true.

The Beholder

Created Fushi in order to
preserve the world. Can
only be seen by Fushi.
Can detect the location
of Nokkers.

Hayase

A Yanome official who
killed March and Parona.
Used Tonari to lead
Fushi to the island.

Pioran

Has been with Fushi since
they met in Ninannah.
Taught him words and how
to write them. Currently in
the island's prison.

Nokker

Plots to obstruct the Beholder's plans. Was designed not
only to steal what Fushi acquires, but also to weaken him.
Has the ability to learn. Destroying their core stops them.

CONTENTS

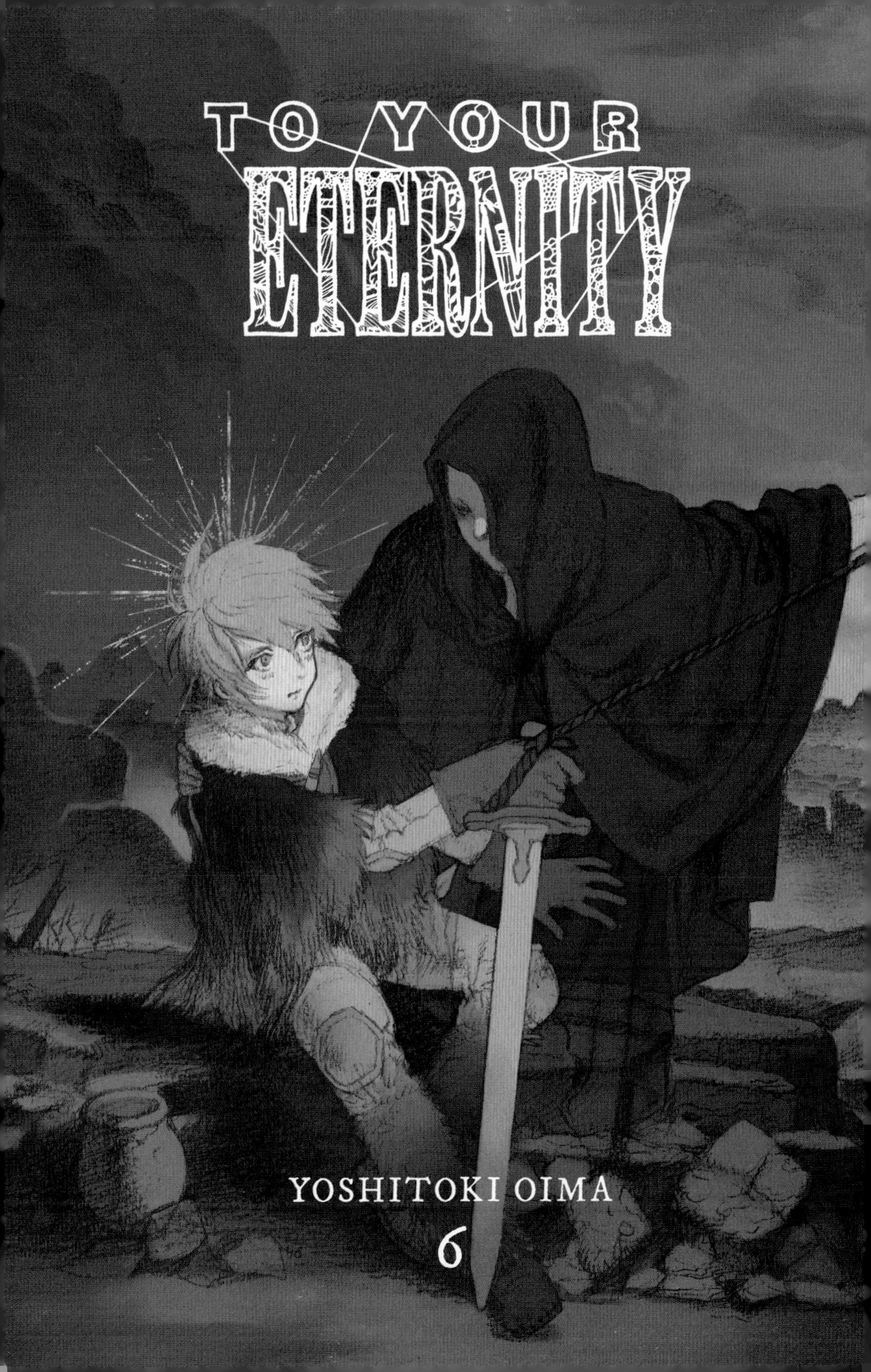
TO YOUR
ETERNITY
YOSHITOKI OIMA
6

THE STORY SO FAR

After Gugu's death, Fushi was awakened—
he began questioning his own existence for the first time.
To distance everyone from the threat of the Nokkers,
Fushi left Takunaha, but Pioran alone followed him;
before long, the two reunite. In order to protect Pioran,
and in order to regain the piece of himself the Nokkers took,
Fushi vowed to grow stronger. The pair was then tricked by a girl
named Tonari to go to Jananda, an island of heinous murderers.
In order to save Pioran after they are separated, Fushi must obey
Tonari, who told him to participate in a tournament to select the
island leader. In the final round, his old enemy Hayase appeared
before him and revealed that she killed Parona. Infuriated, Fushi
attacked Hayase, but she drugs him and drags him away...

CHARACTERS

Tonari

Came with her father, a suspected
murderer, to Jananda island when she was
only seven years old. Received the
position of island leader from Hayase.
Her dream is to surprise her father.

Fushi

Created to preserve the world by
accumulating data. When a vessel he has
acquired is stolen by a Nokker, he loses
his memories of it. Immortal.

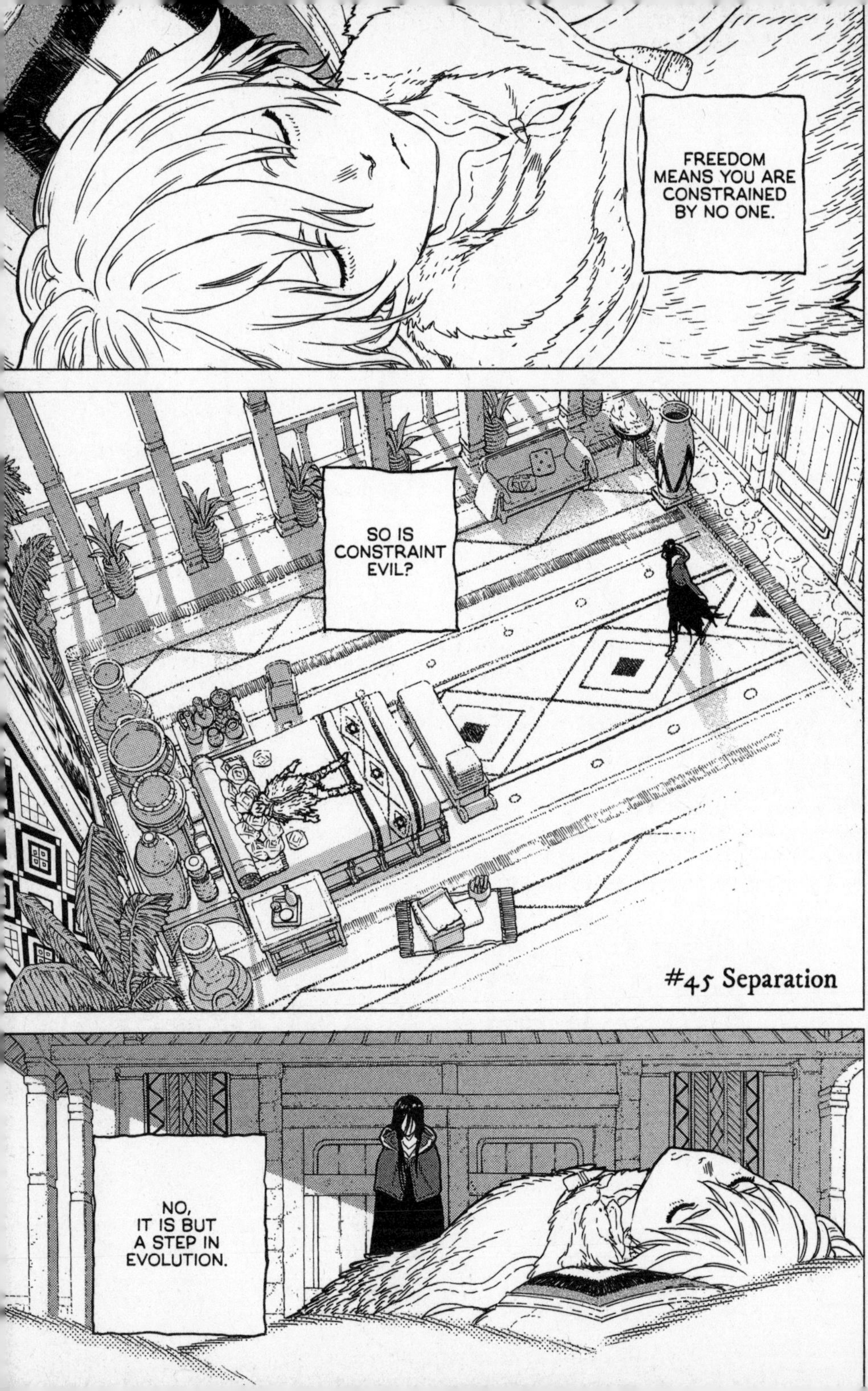
FREEDOM MEANS YOU ARE CONSTRAINED BY NO ONE.
SO IS CONSTRAINT EVIL?
#45 Separation
NO, IT IS BUT A STEP IN EVOLUTION.

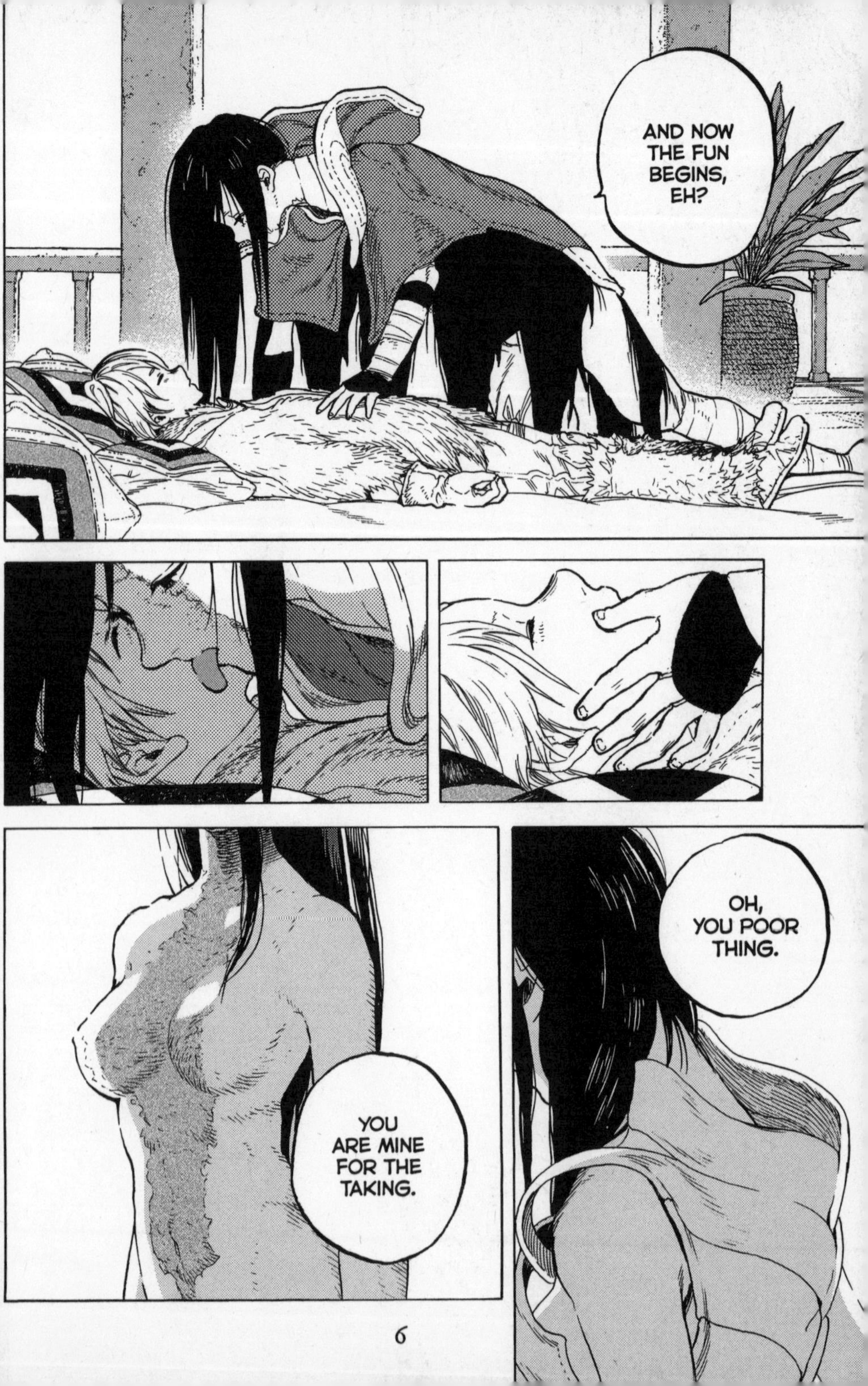
AND NOW THE FUN BEGINS, EH?
OH, YOU POOR THING.
YOU ARE MINE FOR THE TAKING.

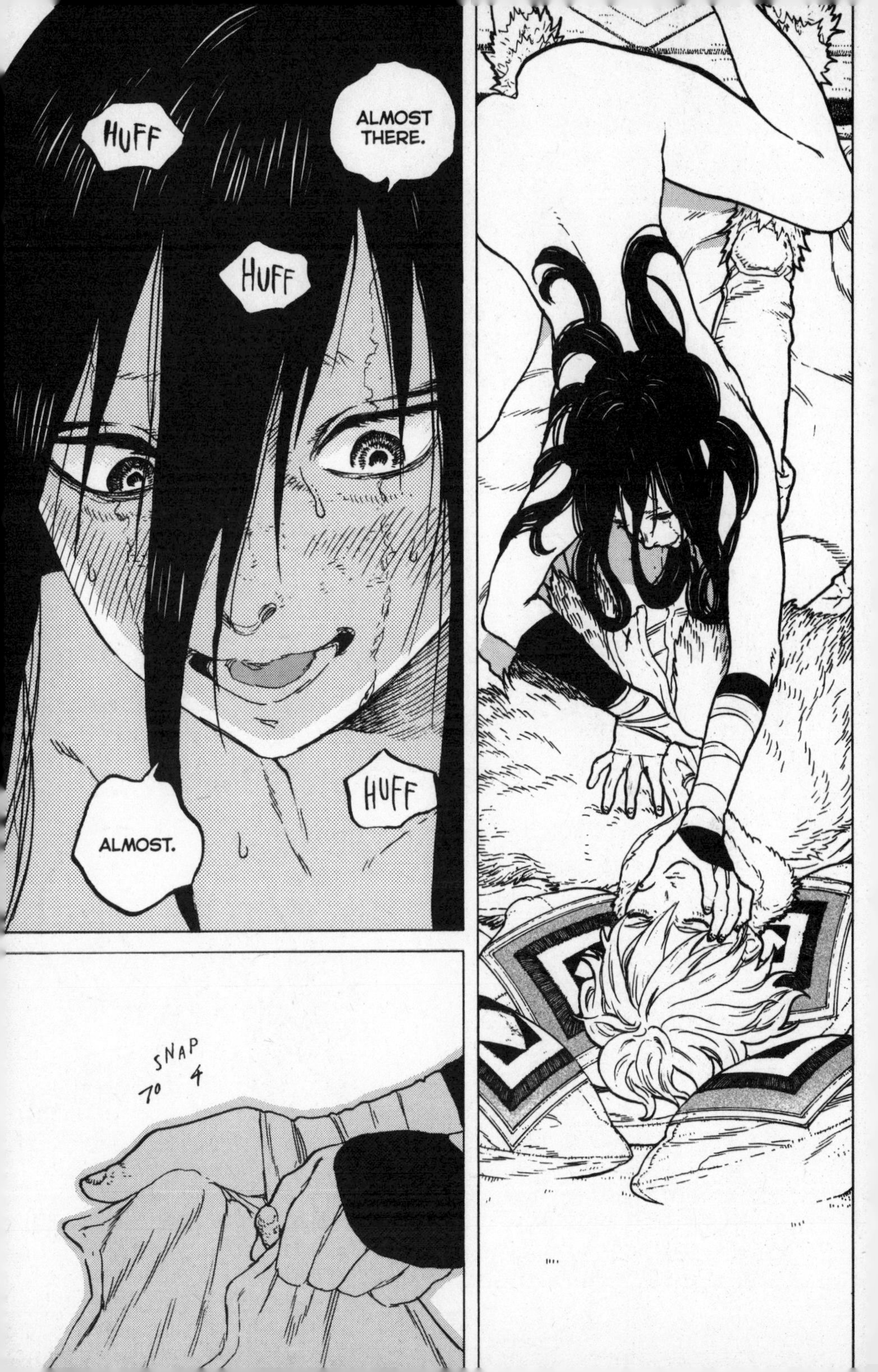
ALMOST THERE.
HUFF
HUFF
HUFF
ALMOST.
SNAP

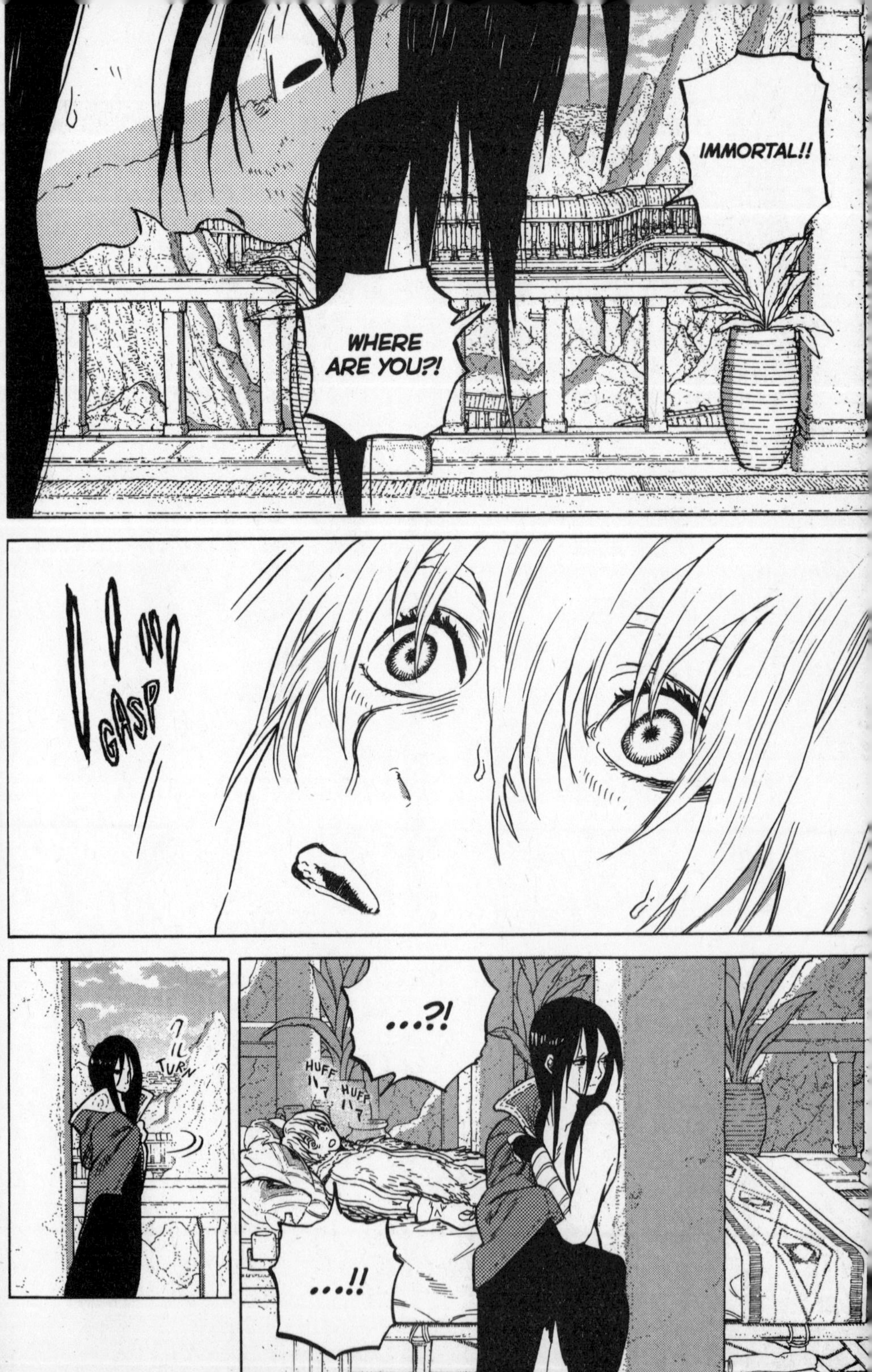
IMMORTAL!!
WHERE ARE YOU?!
GASP
...?!
HUFF ハァ HUFF ハァ
...!!
クル TURN

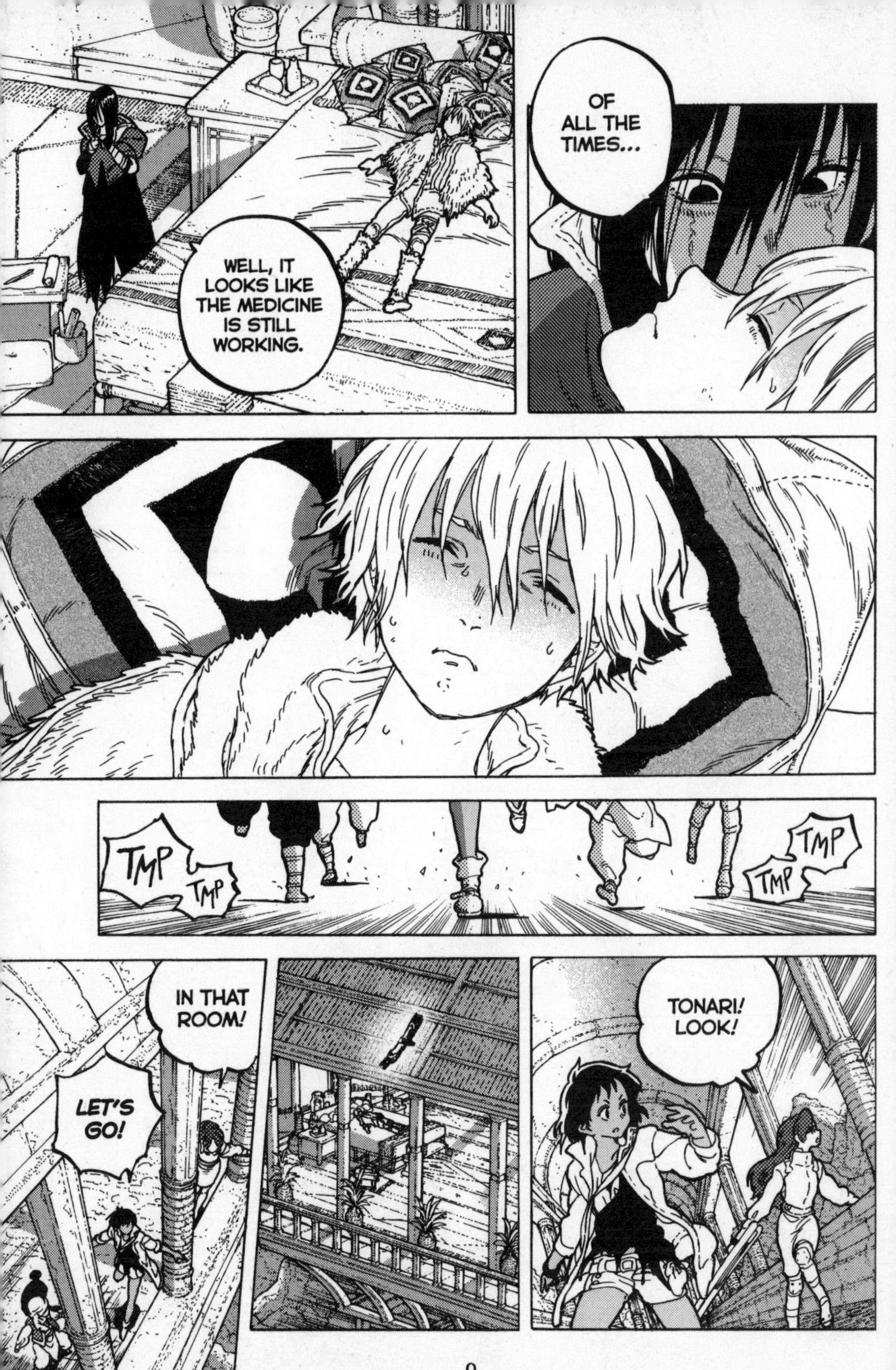
OF ALL THE TIMES...
WELL, IT LOOKS LIKE THE MEDICINE IS STILL WORKING.
TMP
TMP
TMP
TMP
TONARI! LOOK!
IN THAT ROOM!
LET'S GO!

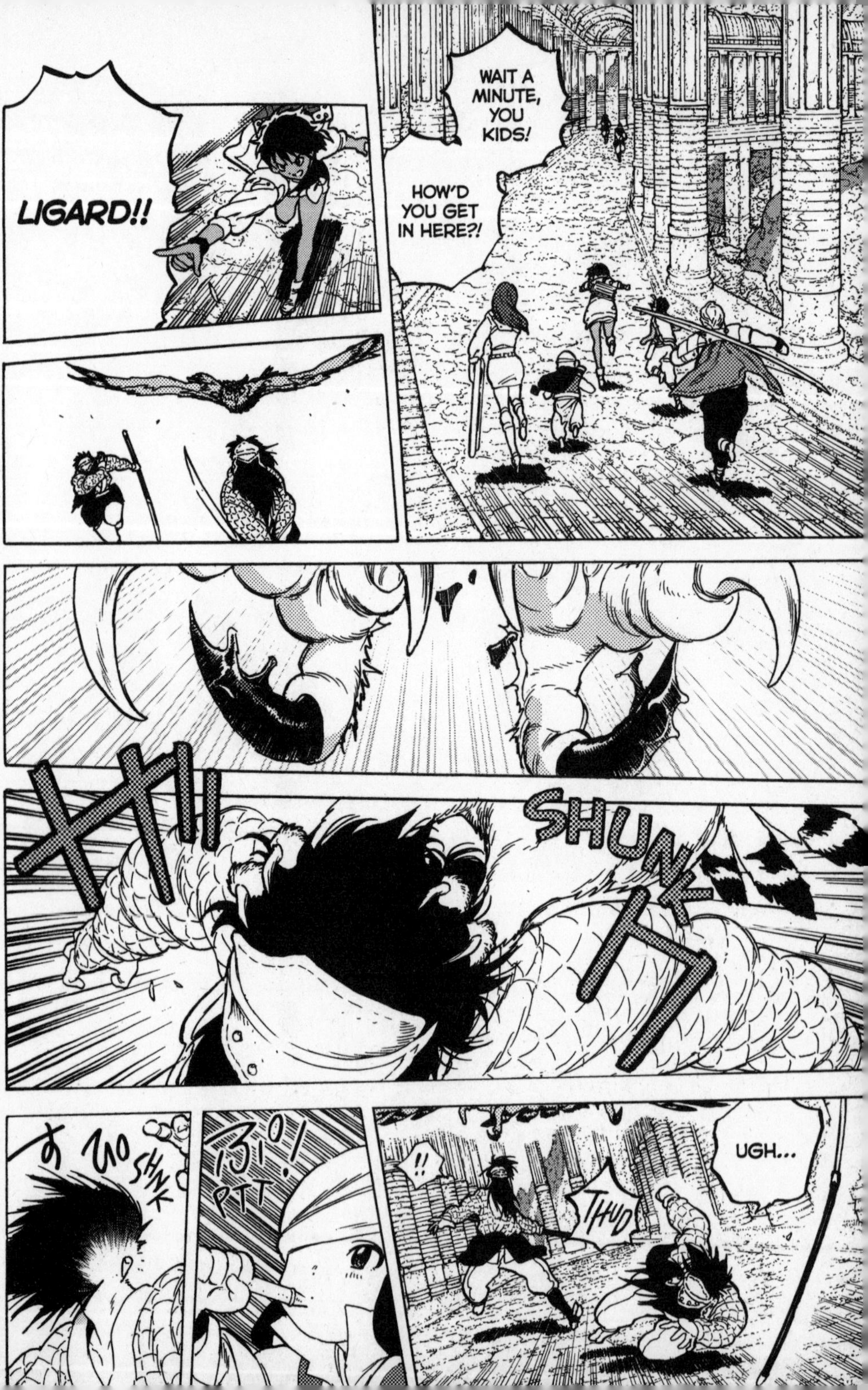
WAIT A MINUTE, YOU KIDS!
HOW'D YOU GET IN HERE?!
LIGARD!!
SHUNK
UGH...
!!
THUD
PTT
SHNK

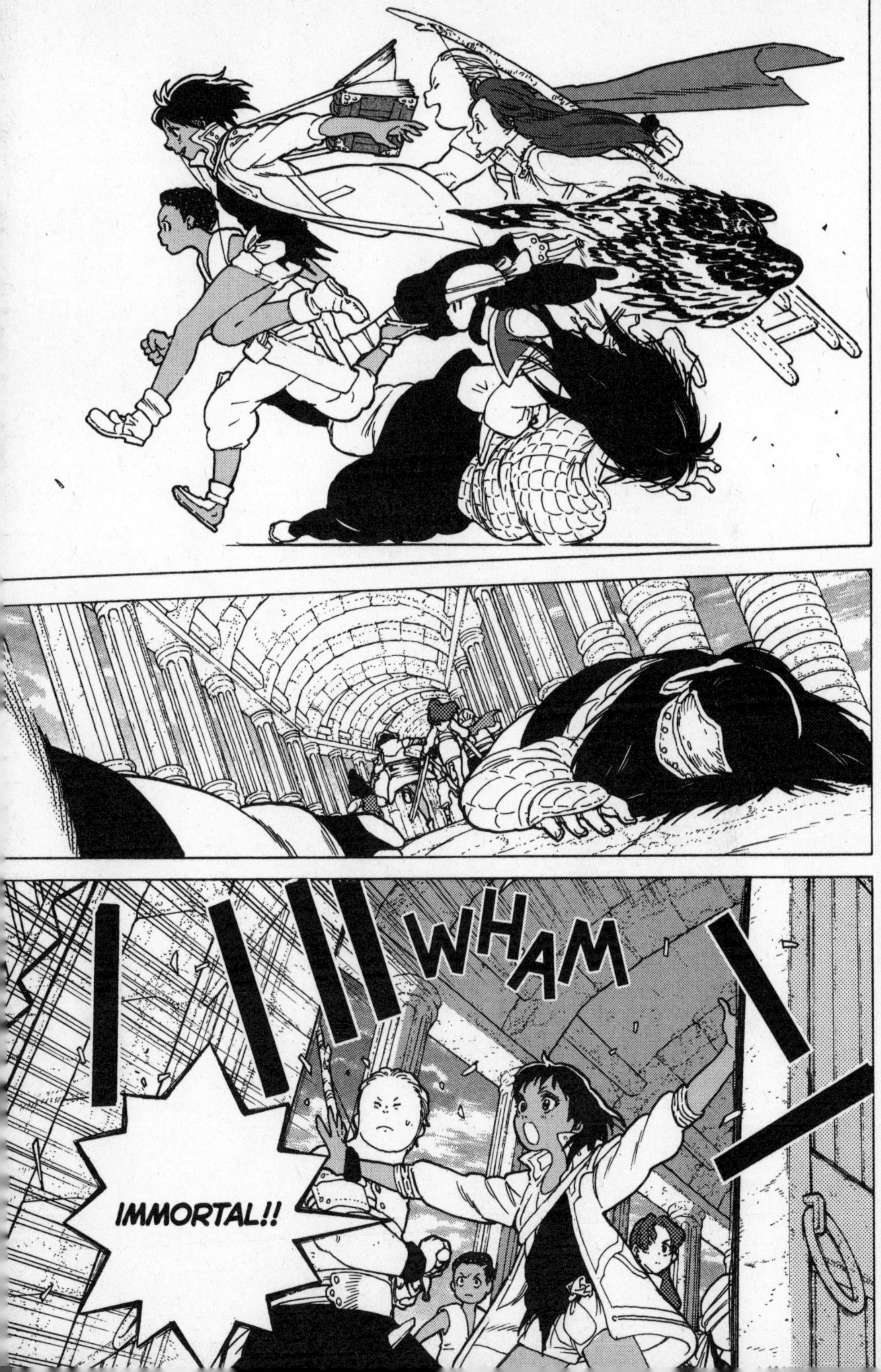
WHAM
IMMORTAL!!

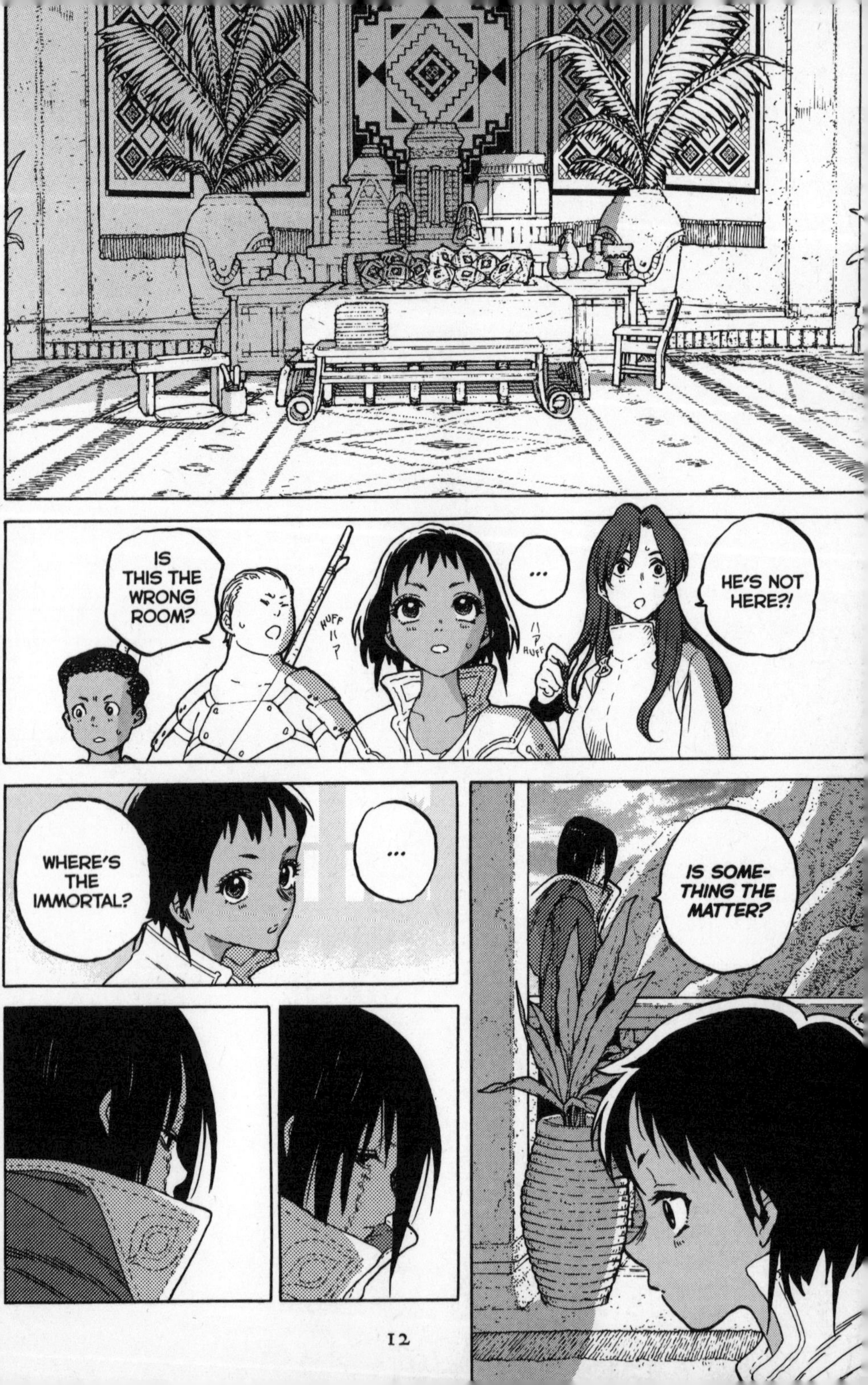
HE'S NOT HERE?!
HUFF ハァ
...
HUFF ハァ
IS THIS THE WRONG ROOM?
IS SOME-THING THE MATTER?
...
WHERE'S THE IMMORTAL?

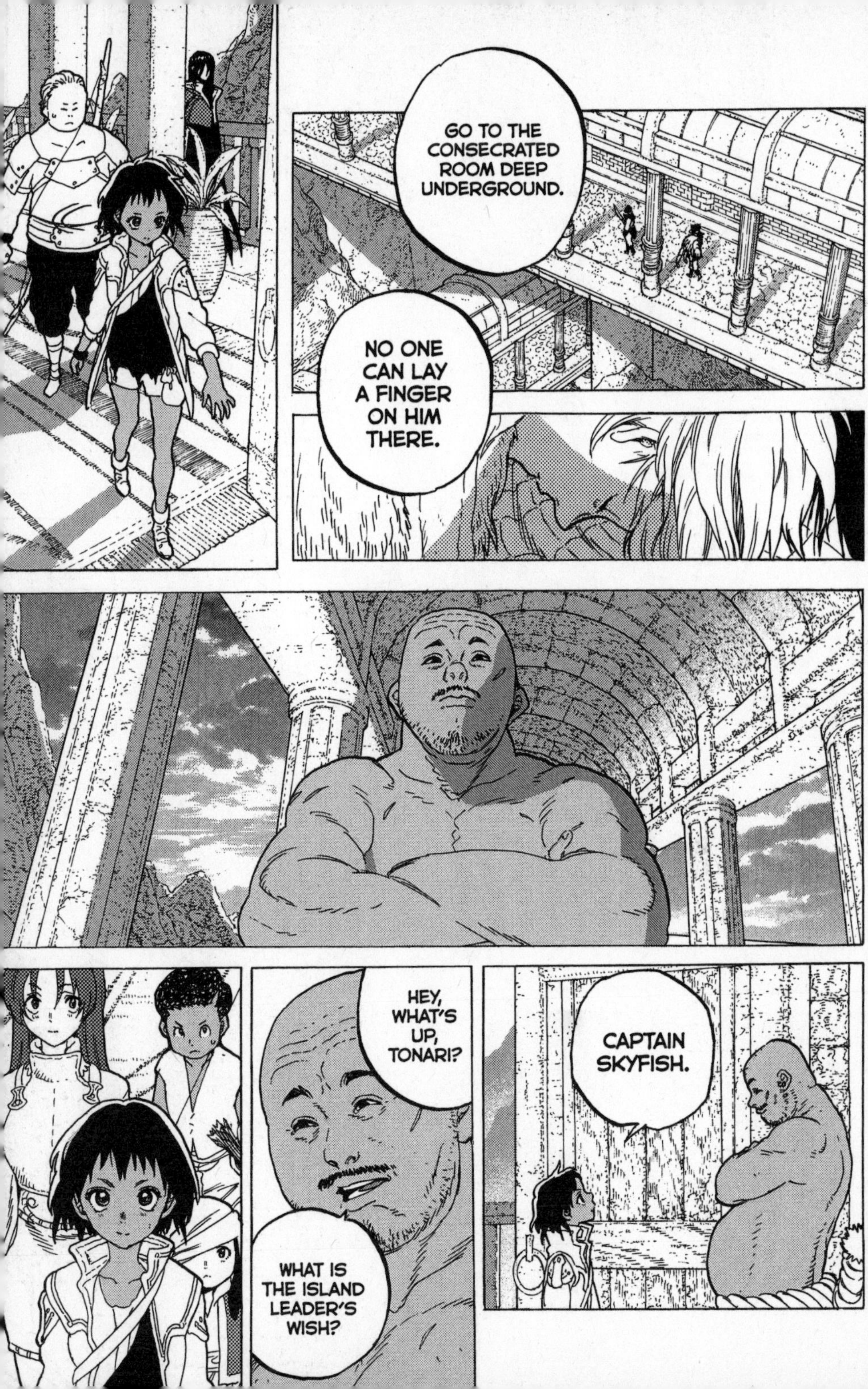
GO TO THE CONSECRATED ROOM DEEP UNDERGROUND.
NO ONE CAN LAY A FINGER ON HIM THERE.
CAPTAIN SKYFISH.
HEY, WHAT'S UP, TONARI?
WHAT IS THE ISLAND LEADER'S WISH?

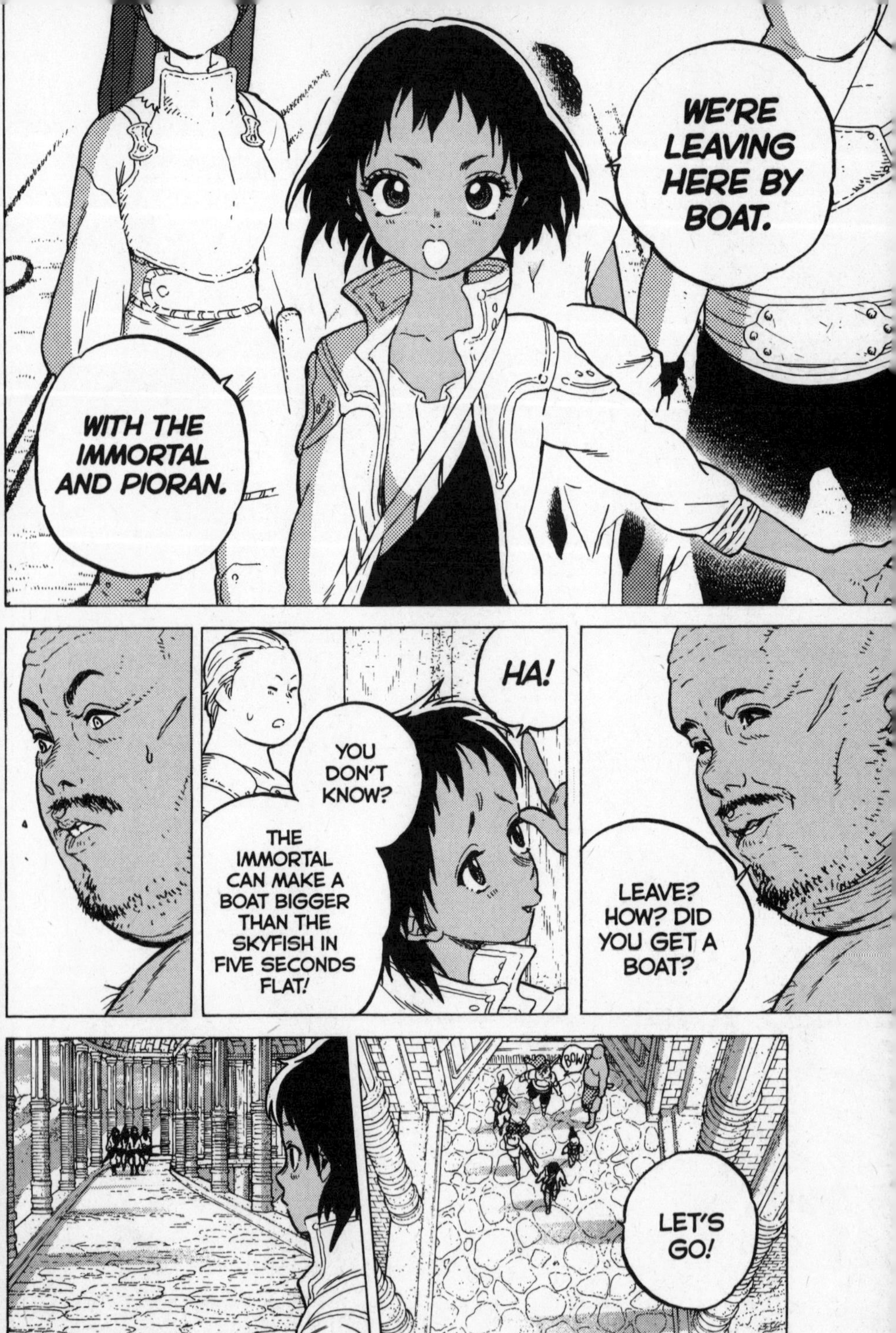
WE'RE LEAVING HERE BY BOAT.
WITH THE IMMORTAL AND PIORAN.
LEAVE? HOW? DID YOU GET A BOAT?
HA!
YOU DON'T KNOW?
THE IMMORTAL CAN MAKE A BOAT BIGGER THAN THE SKYFISH IN FIVE SECONDS FLAT!
BOW
LET'S GO!

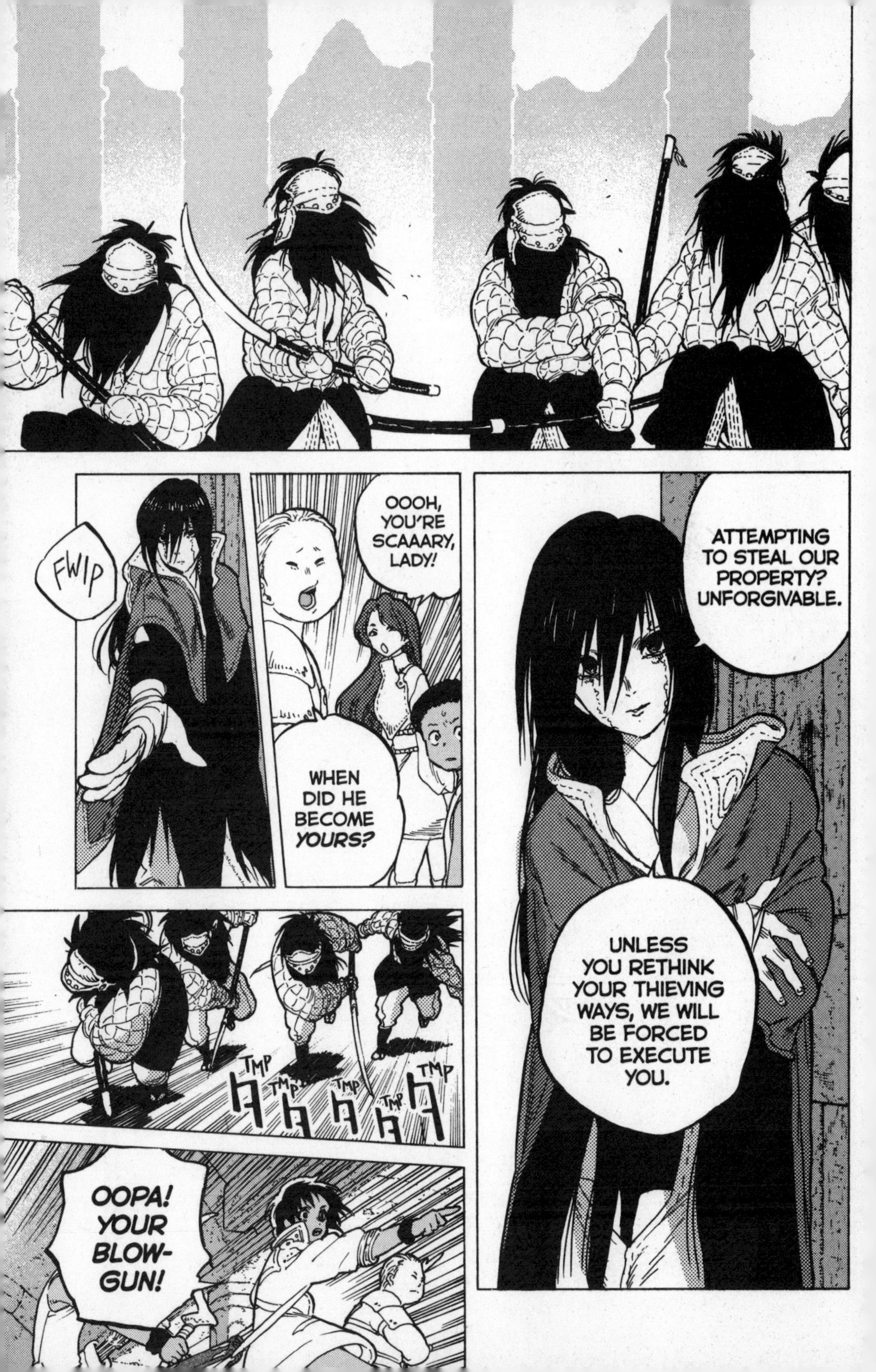
ATTEMPTING TO STEAL OUR PROPERTY? UNFORGIVABLE.
UNLESS YOU RETHINK YOUR THIEVING WAYS, WE WILL BE FORCED TO EXECUTE YOU.
OOOH, YOU'RE SCAAARY, LADY!
WHEN DID HE BECOME *YOURS?*
FWIP
TMP TMP TMP TMP TMP
OOPA! YOUR BLOW-GUN!

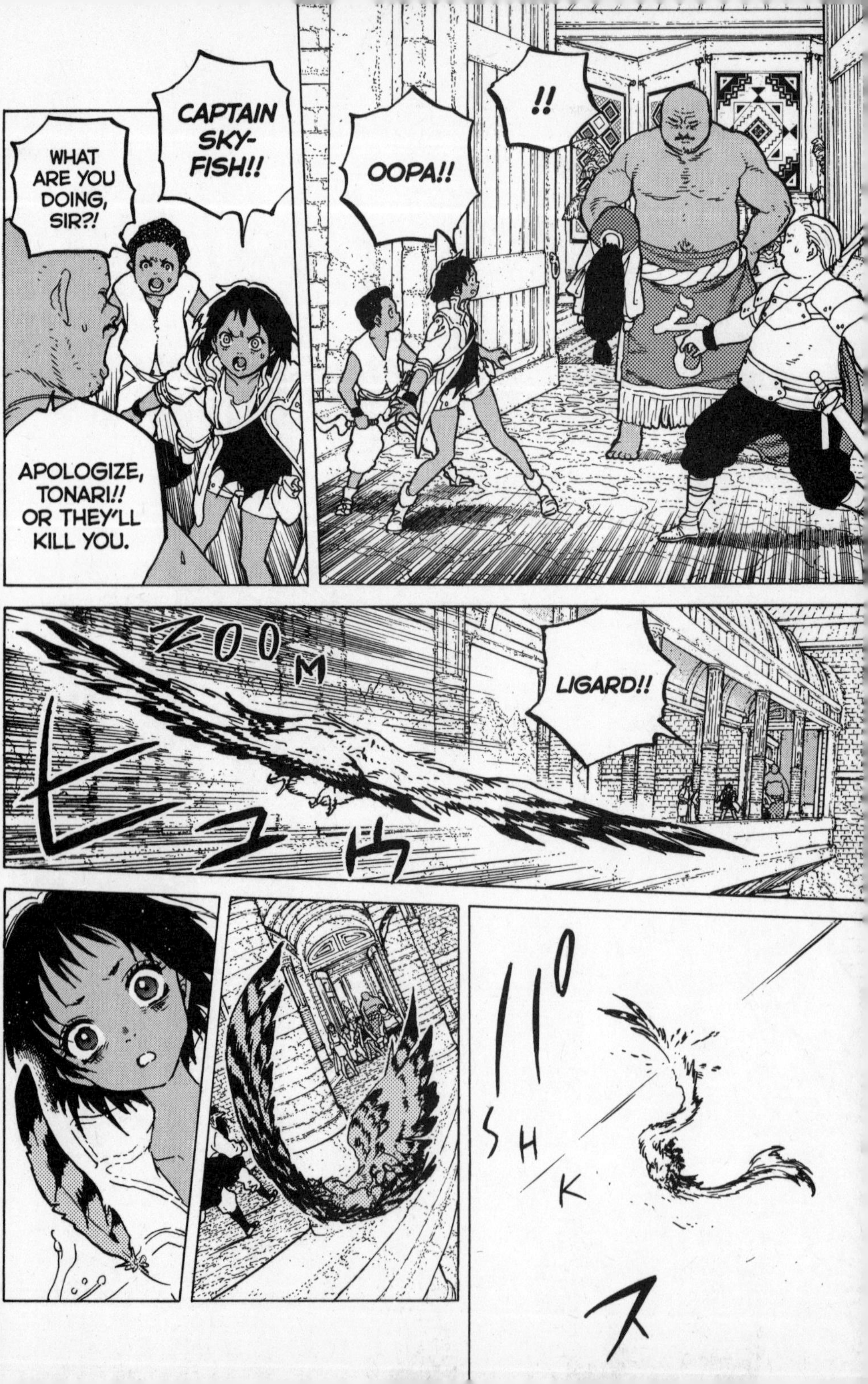
!!
OOPA!!
CAPTAIN SKY-FISH!!
WHAT ARE YOU DOING, SIR?!
APOLOGIZE, TONARI!! OR THEY'LL KILL YOU.
LIGARD!!
ZOOM
SHK

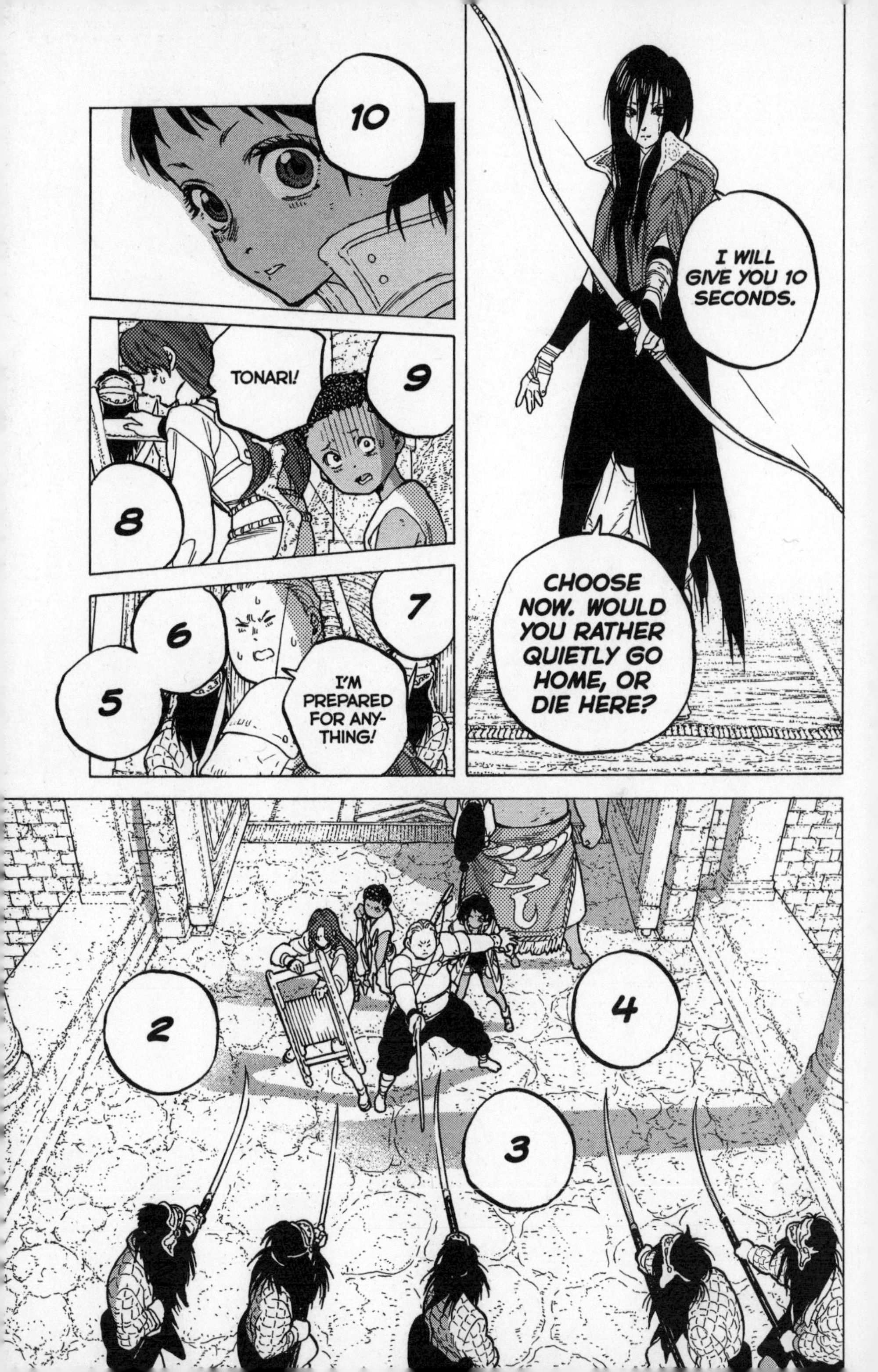
I WILL GIVE YOU 10 SECONDS.
CHOOSE NOW. WOULD YOU RATHER QUIETLY GO HOME, OR DIE HERE?
10
9
TONARI!
8
7
6
I'M PREPARED FOR ANY-THING!
5
4
3
2

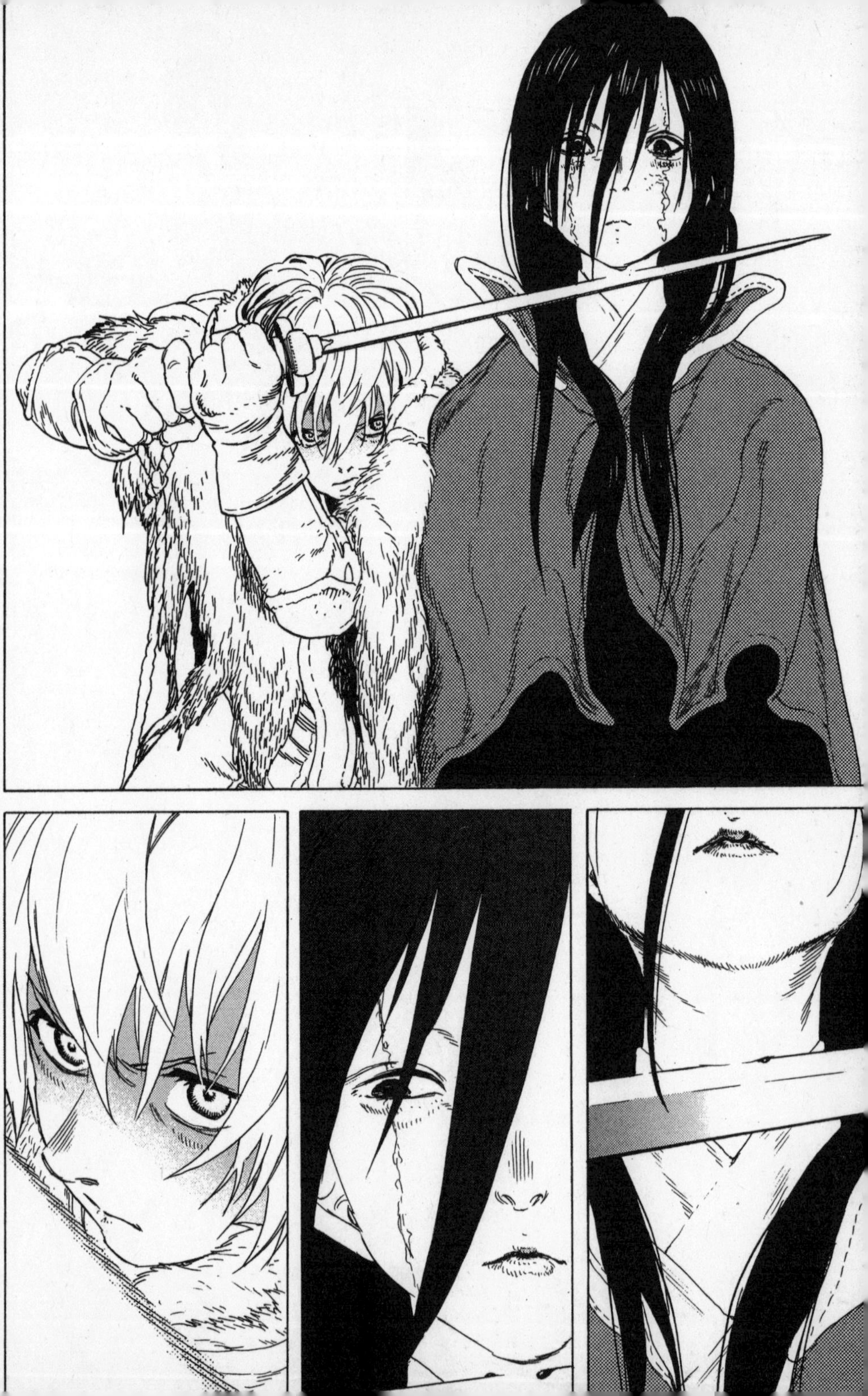

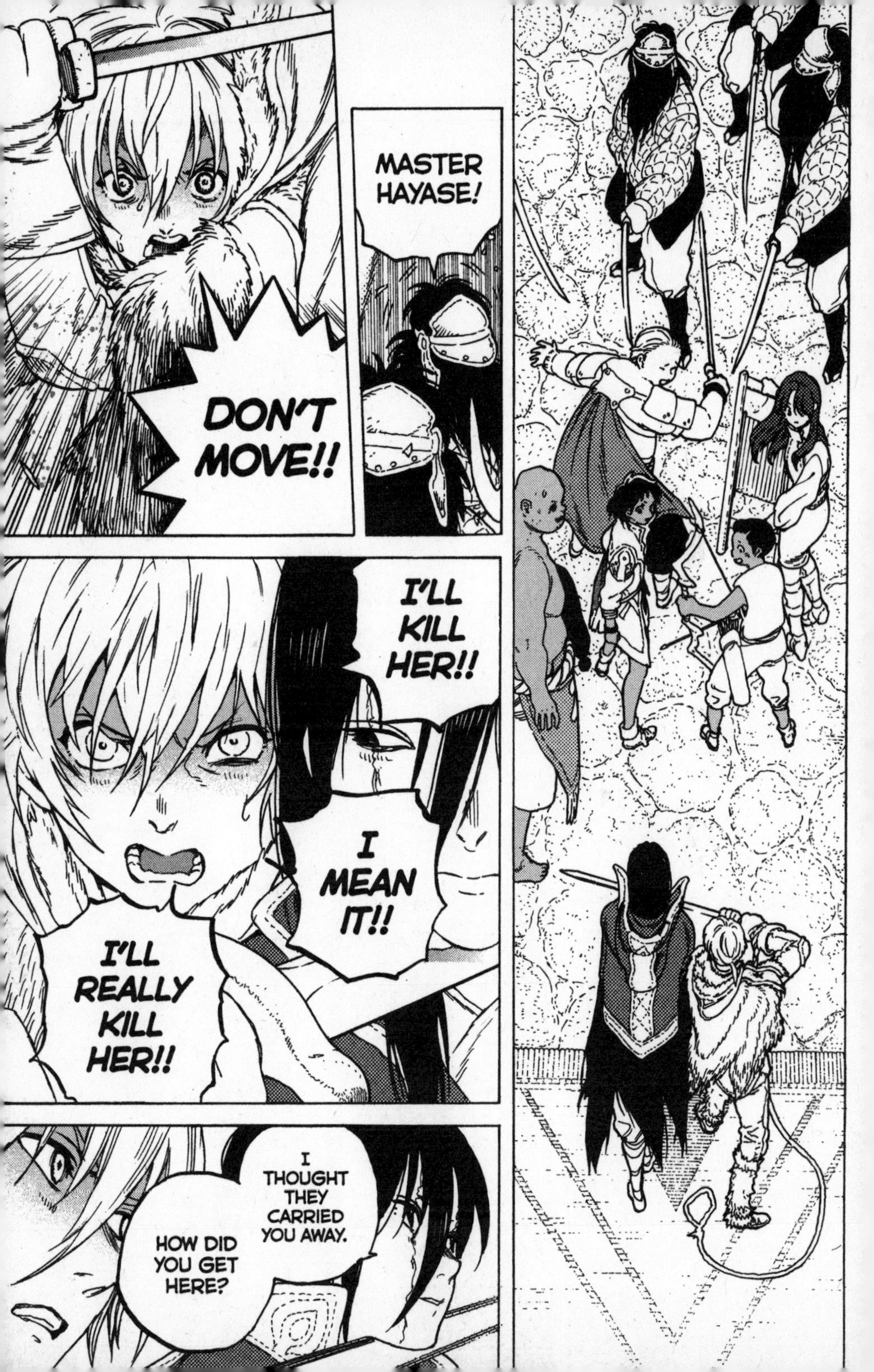
MASTER HAYASE!
DON'T MOVE!!
I'LL KILL HER!!
I MEAN IT!!
I'LL REALLY KILL HER!!
I THOUGHT THEY CARRIED YOU AWAY.
HOW DID YOU GET HERE?

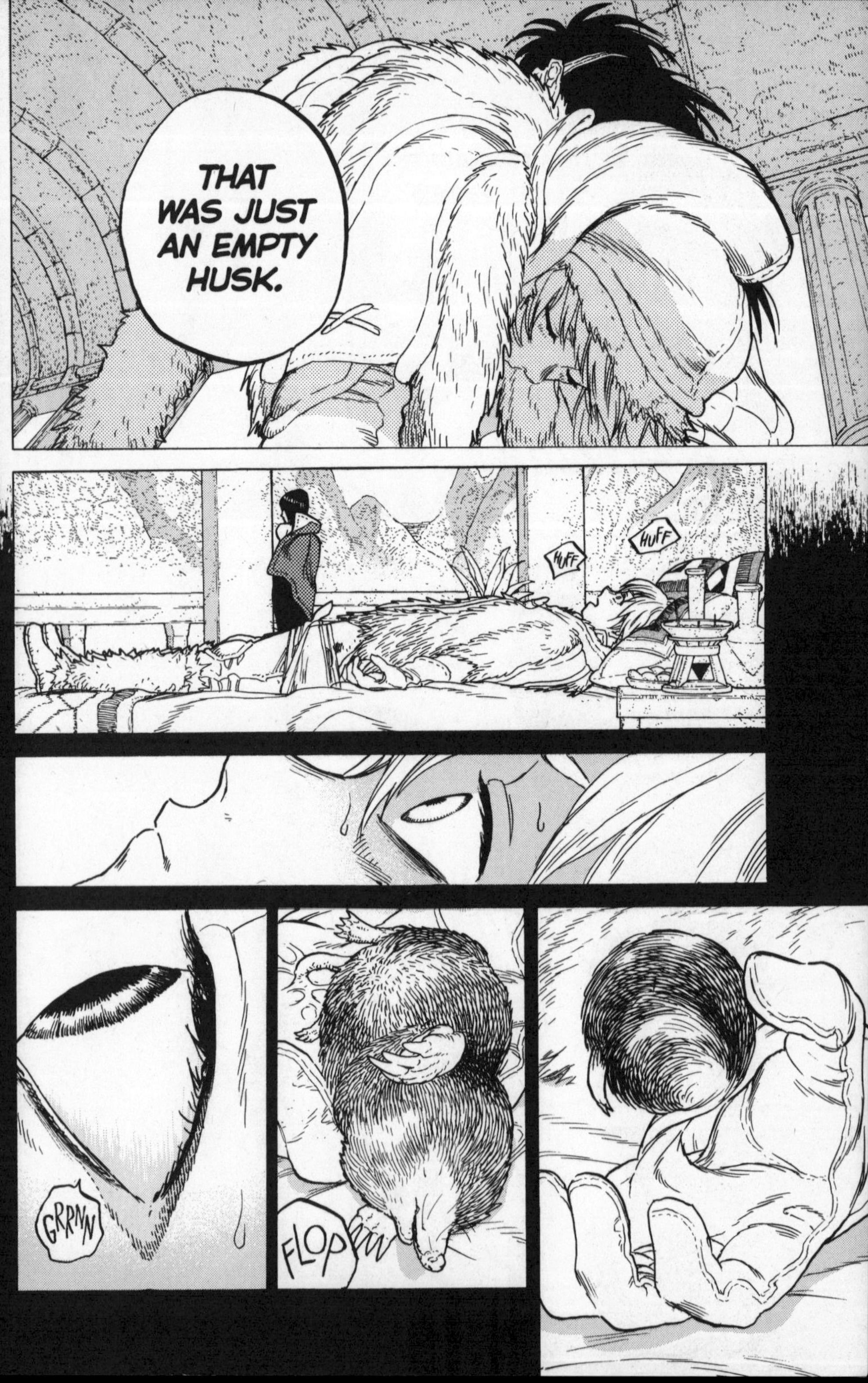
THAT WAS JUST AN EMPTY HUSK.
HUFF
HUFF
FLOP
GRRNN

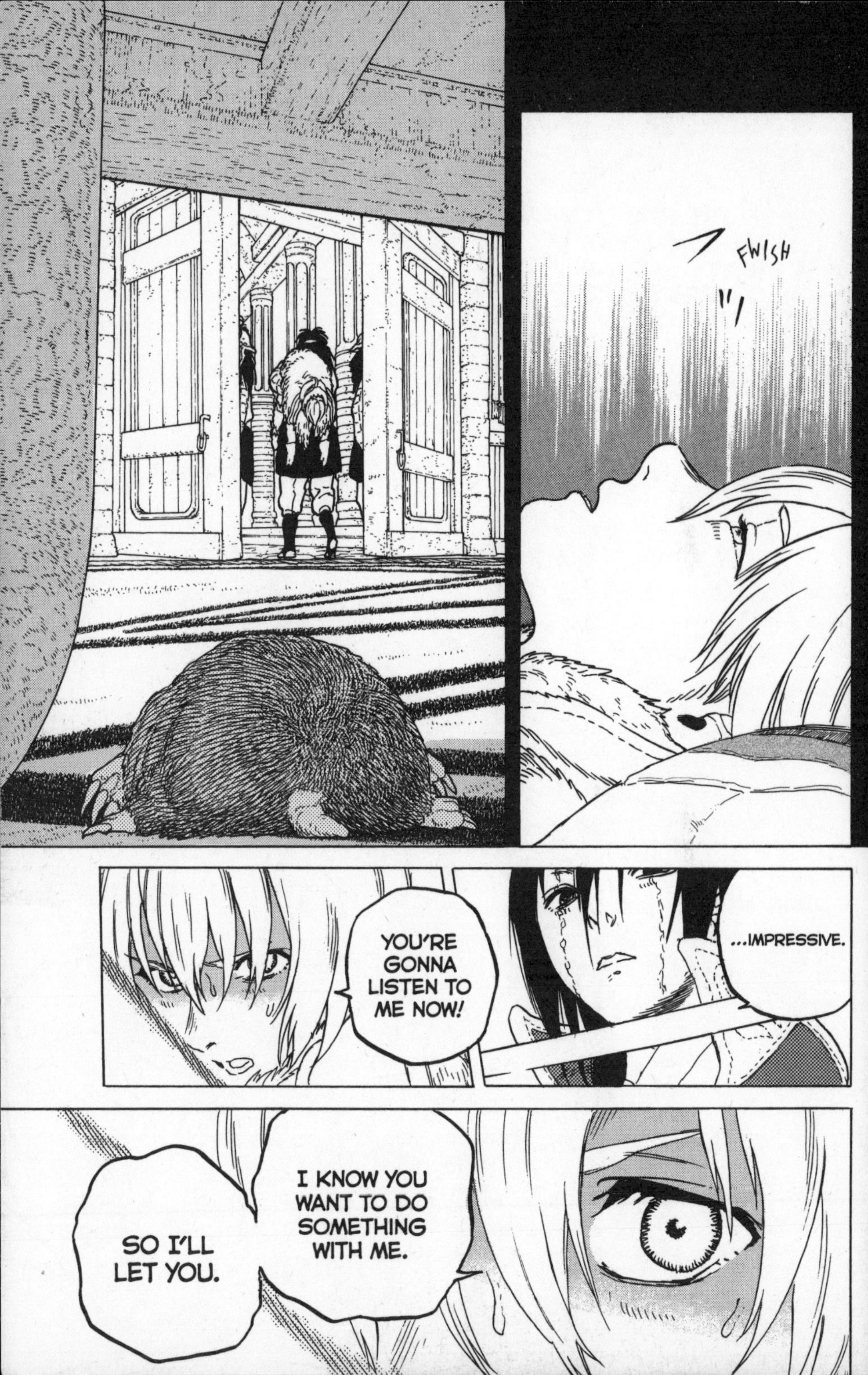
FWISH
...IMPRESSIVE.
YOU'RE GONNA LISTEN TO ME NOW!
I KNOW YOU WANT TO DO SOMETHING WITH ME.
SO I'LL LET YOU.

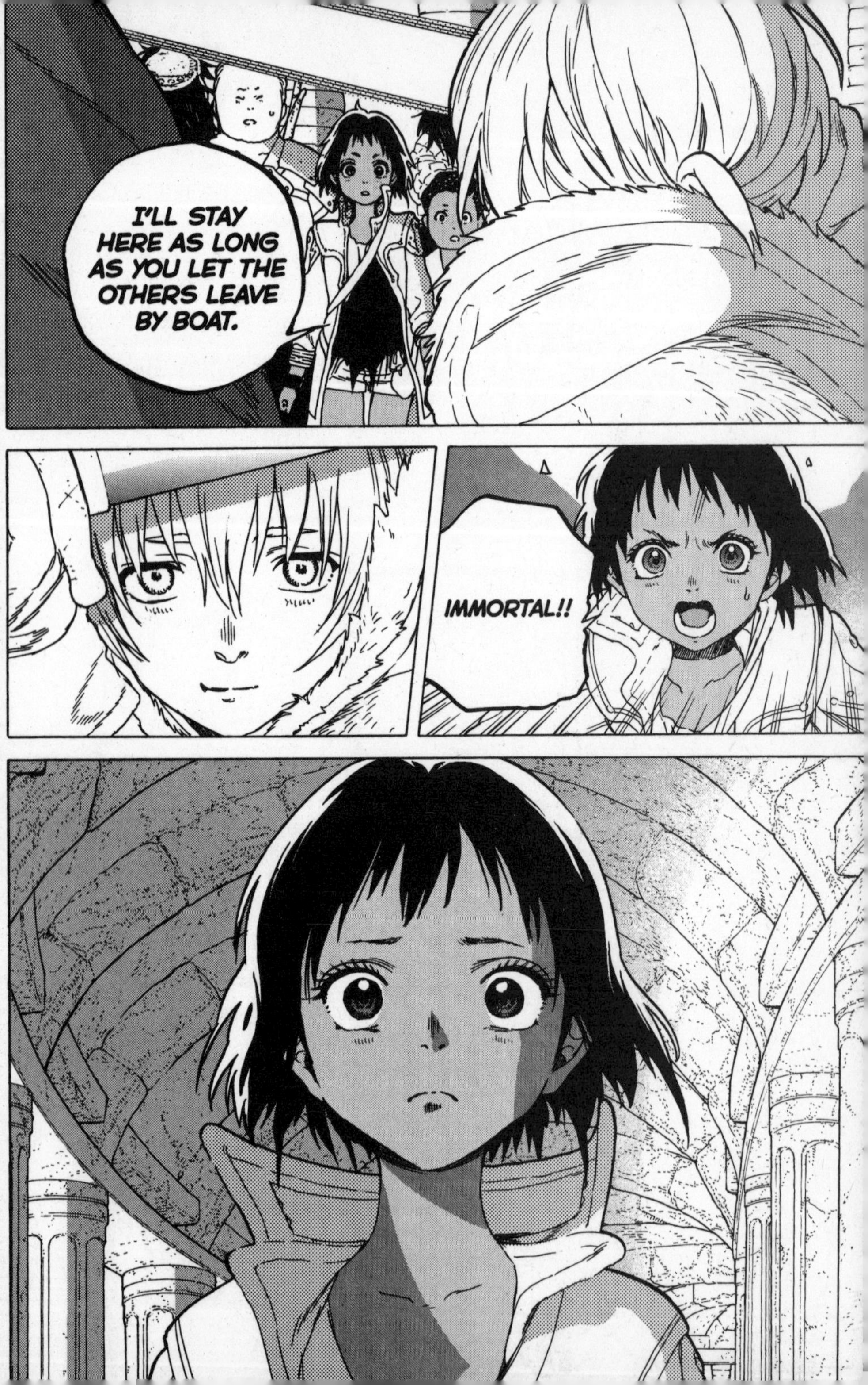
I'LL STAY HERE AS LONG AS YOU LET THE OTHERS LEAVE BY BOAT.
IMMORTAL!!

#46 Setting Sail

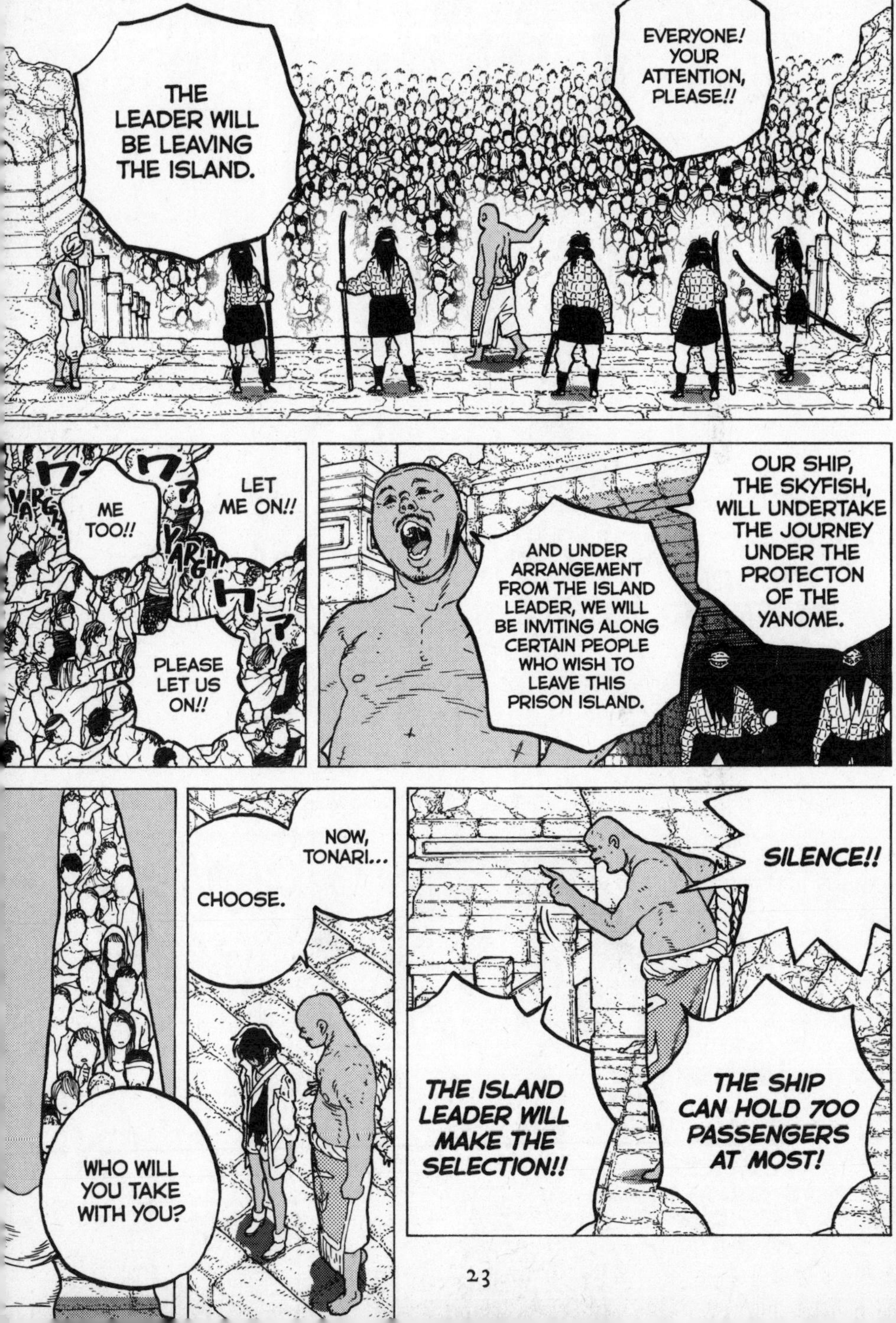
EVERYONE! YOUR ATTENTION, PLEASE!!
THE LEADER WILL BE LEAVING THE ISLAND.
OUR SHIP, THE SKYFISH, WILL UNDERTAKE THE JOURNEY UNDER THE PROTECTON OF THE YANOME.
AND UNDER ARRANGEMENT FROM THE ISLAND LEADER, WE WILL BE INVITING ALONG CERTAIN PEOPLE WHO WISH TO LEAVE THIS PRISON ISLAND.
LET ME ON!!
YARGH!
ME TOO!!
YARGH!
PLEASE LET US ON!!
SILENCE!!
THE SHIP CAN HOLD 700 PASSENGERS AT MOST!
THE ISLAND LEADER WILL MAKE THE SELECTION!!
NOW, TONARI...
CHOOSE.
WHO WILL YOU TAKE WITH YOU?

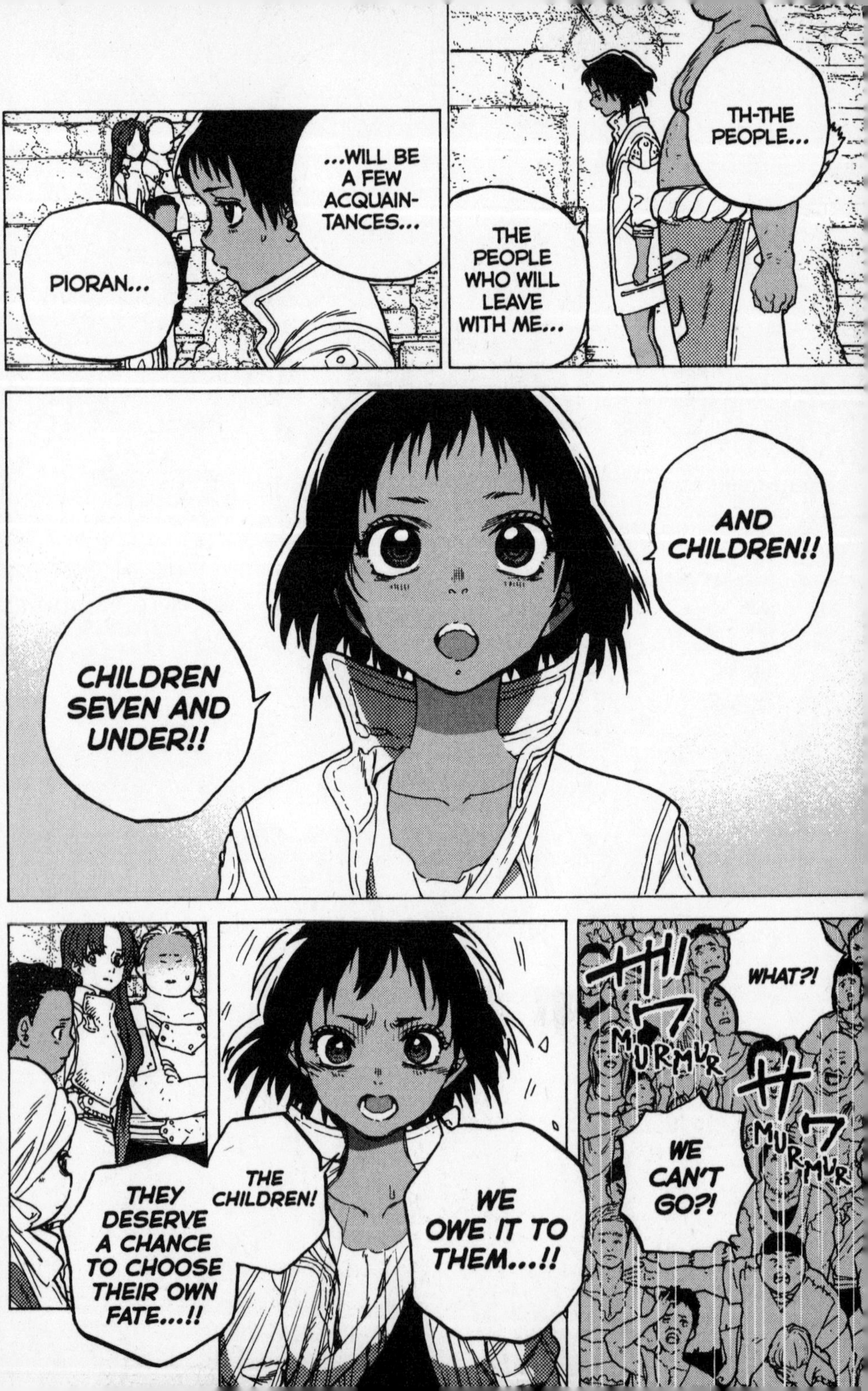
TH-THE PEOPLE...
THE PEOPLE WHO WILL LEAVE WITH ME...
...WILL BE A FEW ACQUAINTANCES...
PIORAN...
AND CHILDREN!!
CHILDREN SEVEN AND UNDER!!
ザワ
MURMUR
WHAT?!
ザワ
MURMUR
WE CAN'T GO?!
WE OWE IT TO THEM...!!
THE CHILDREN!
THEY DESERVE A CHANCE TO CHOOSE THEIR OWN FATE...!!

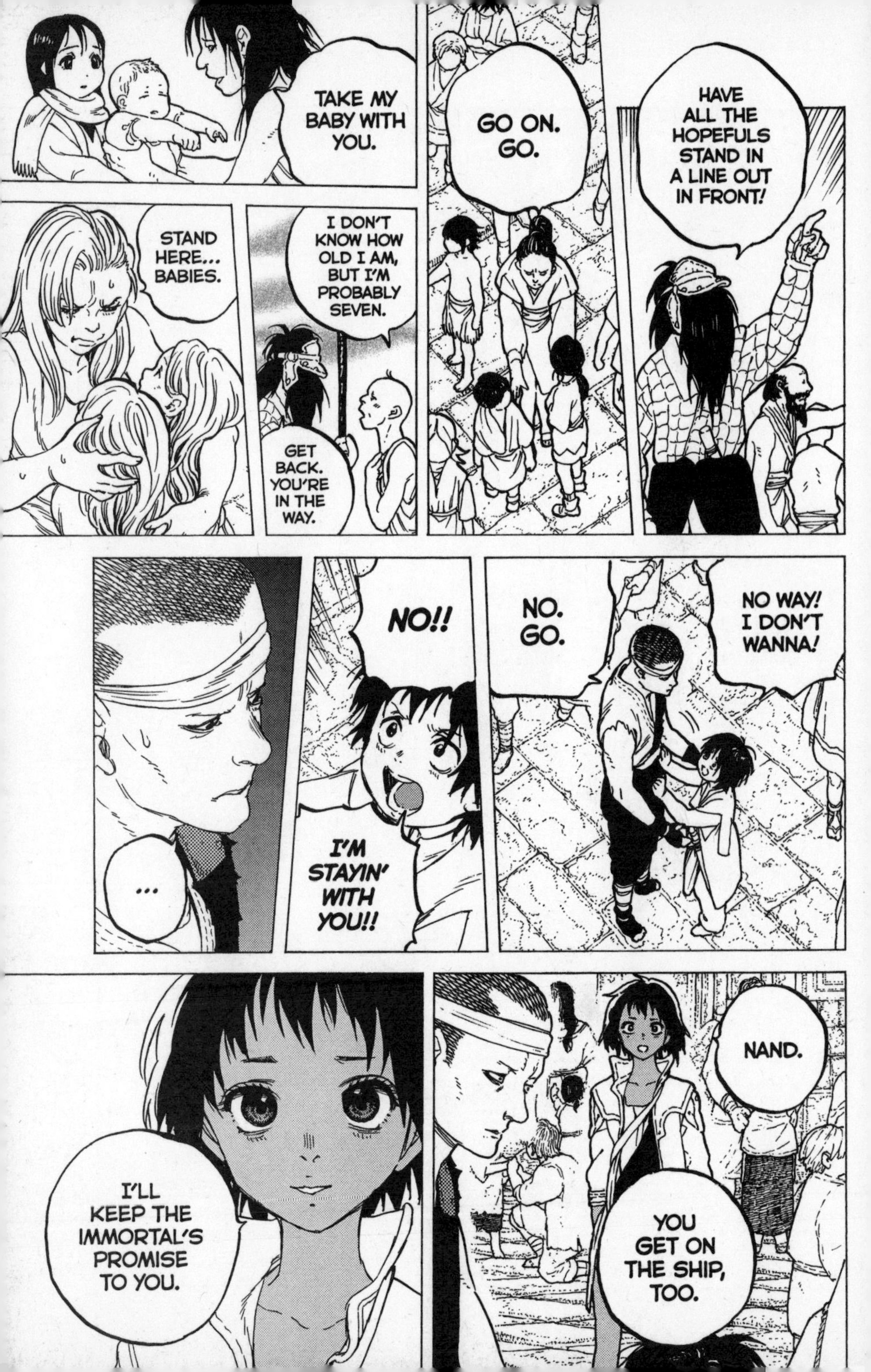
HAVE ALL THE HOPEFULS STAND IN A LINE OUT IN FRONT!
GO ON. GO.
TAKE MY BABY WITH YOU.
I DON'T KNOW HOW OLD I AM, BUT I'M PROBABLY SEVEN.
GET BACK. YOU'RE IN THE WAY.
STAND HERE... BABIES.
NO WAY! I DON'T WANNA!
NO. GO.
NO!!
I'M STAYIN' WITH YOU!!
...
NAND.
YOU GET ON THE SHIP, TOO.
I'LL KEEP THE IMMORTAL'S PROMISE TO YOU.

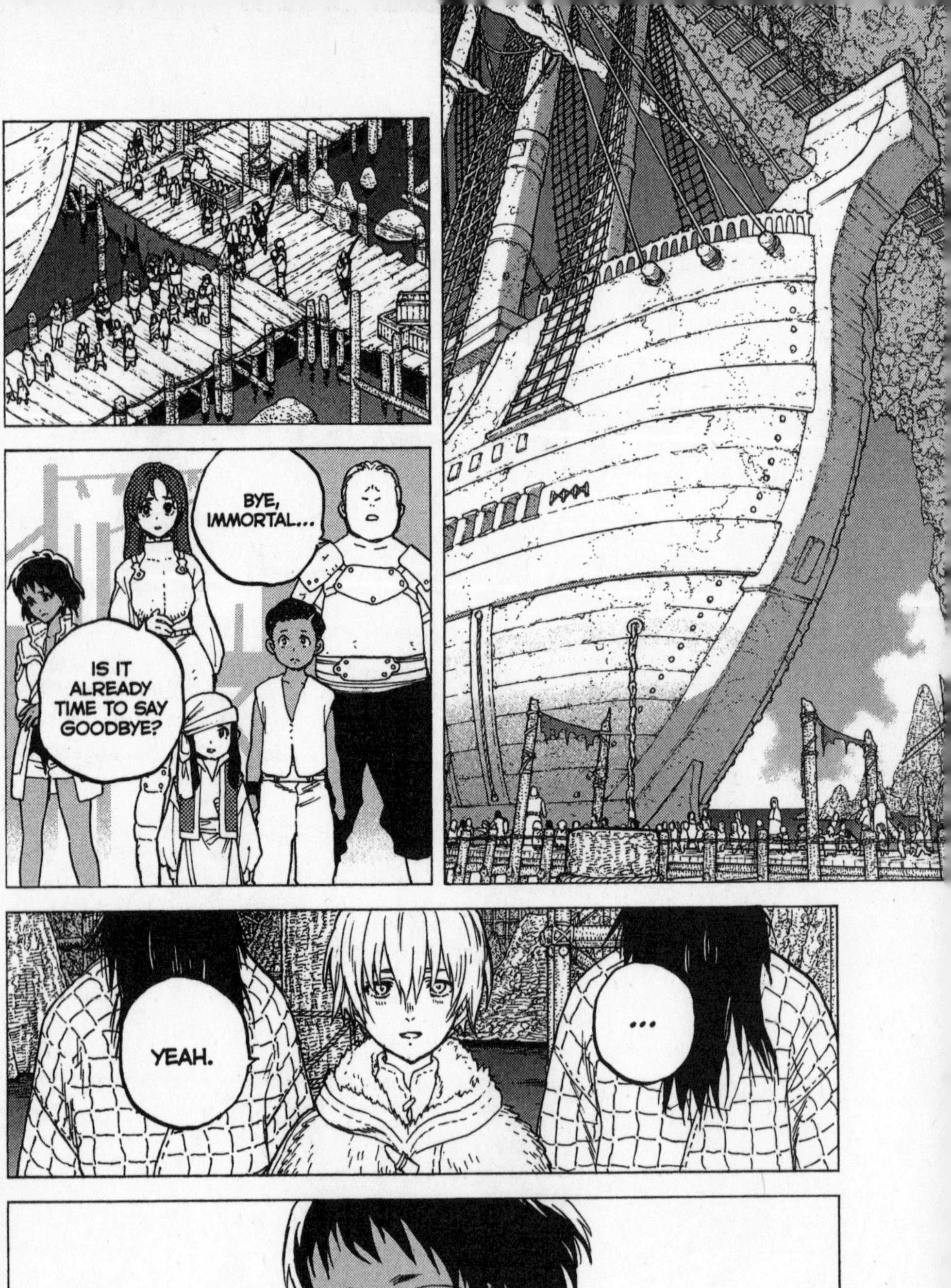
BYE, IMMORTAL...
IS IT ALREADY TIME TO SAY GOODBYE?
...
YEAH.

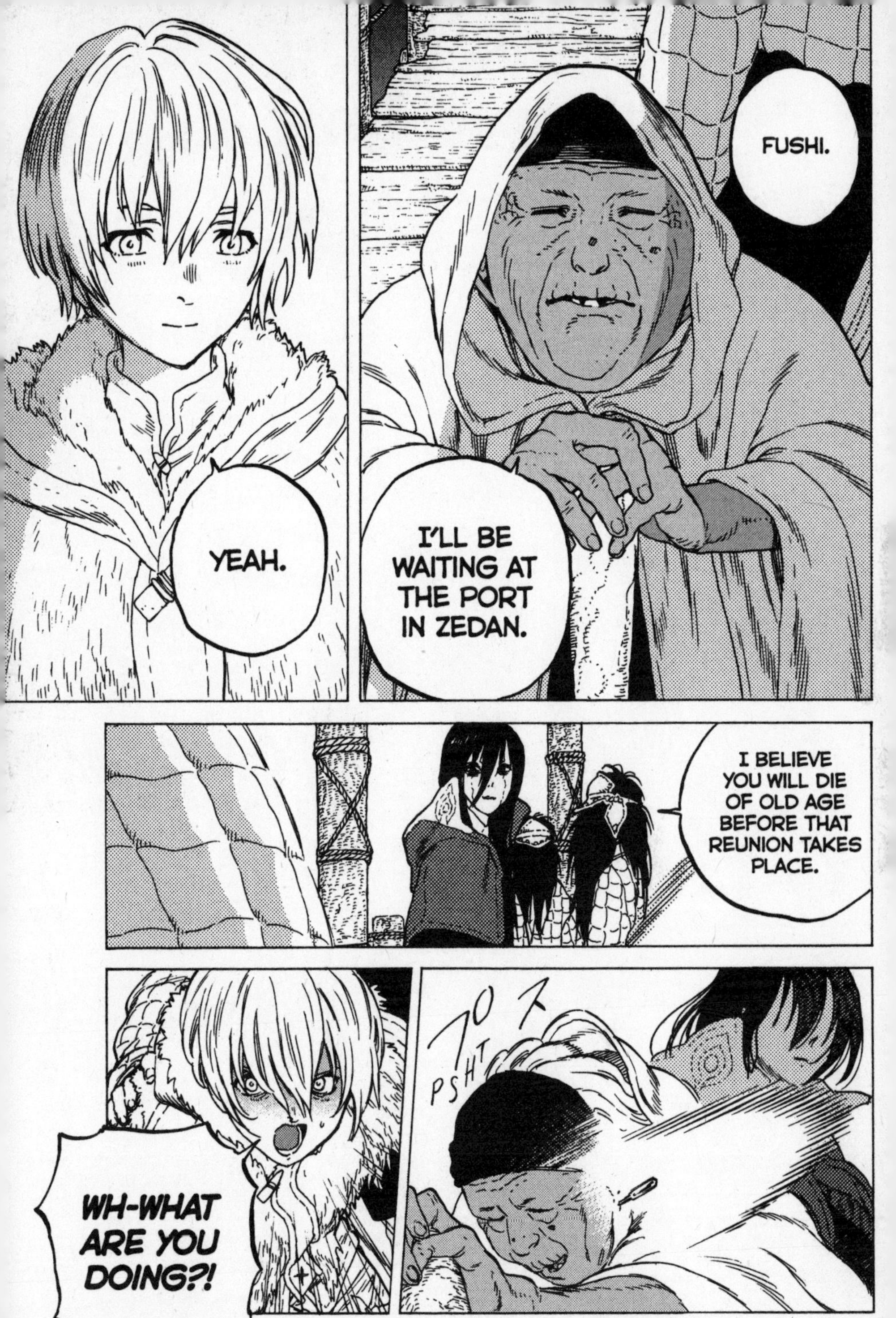
FUSHI.
I'LL BE WAITING AT THE PORT IN ZEDAN.
YEAH.
I BELIEVE YOU WILL DIE OF OLD AGE BEFORE THAT REUNION TAKES PLACE.
PSHT
WH-WHAT ARE YOU DOING?!

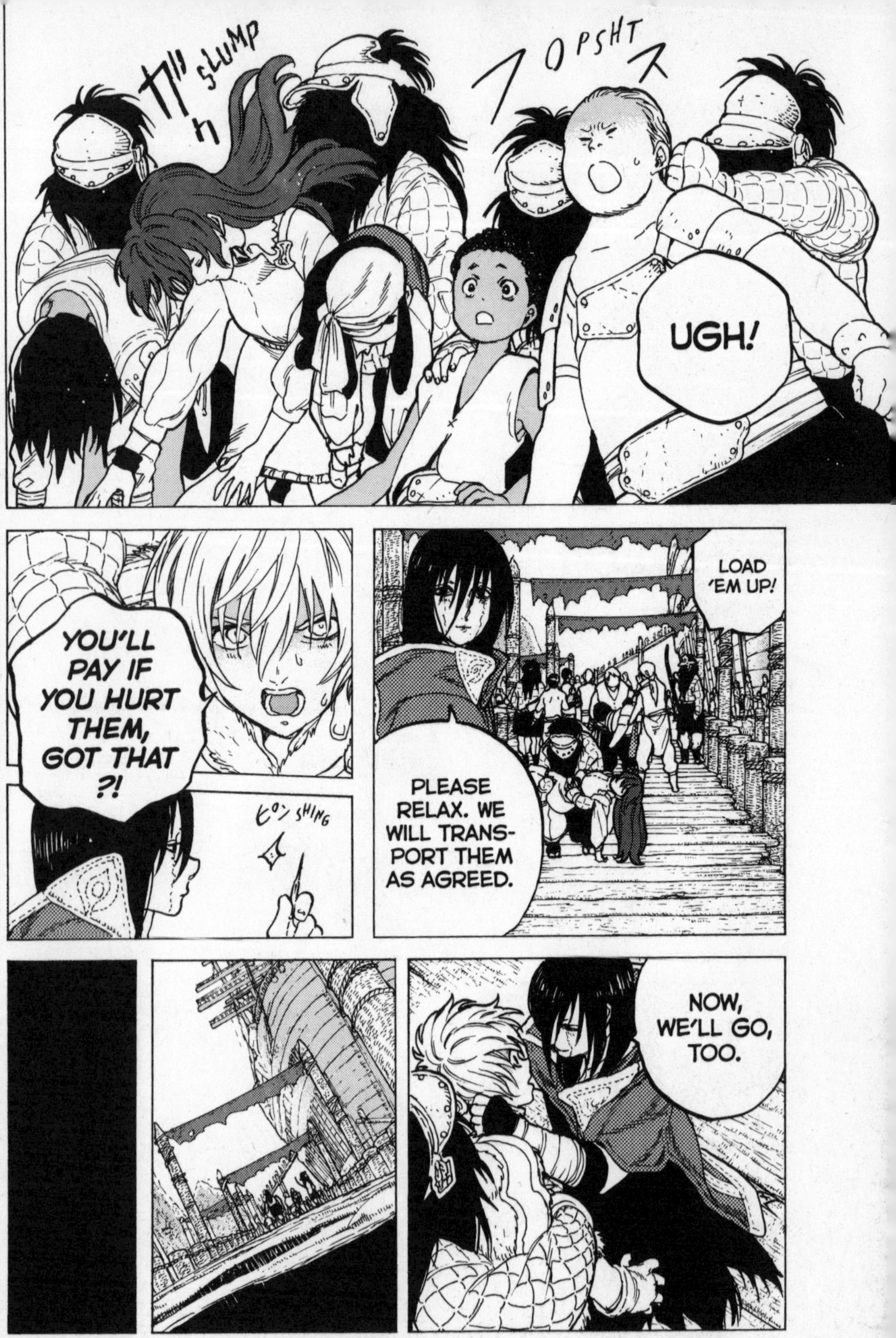
SLUMP
OPSHT
UGH!
LOAD 'EM UP!
PLEASE RELAX. WE WILL TRANS-PORT THEM AS AGREED.
YOU'LL PAY IF YOU HURT THEM, GOT THAT ?!
SHING
NOW, WE'LL GO, TOO.

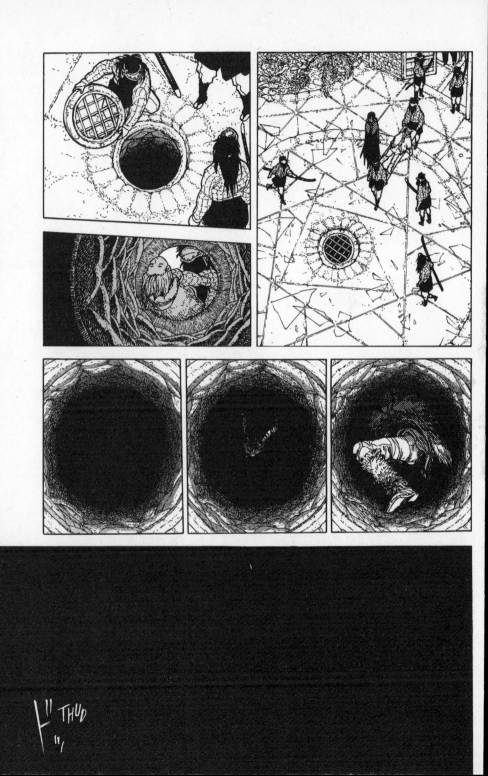

THUD

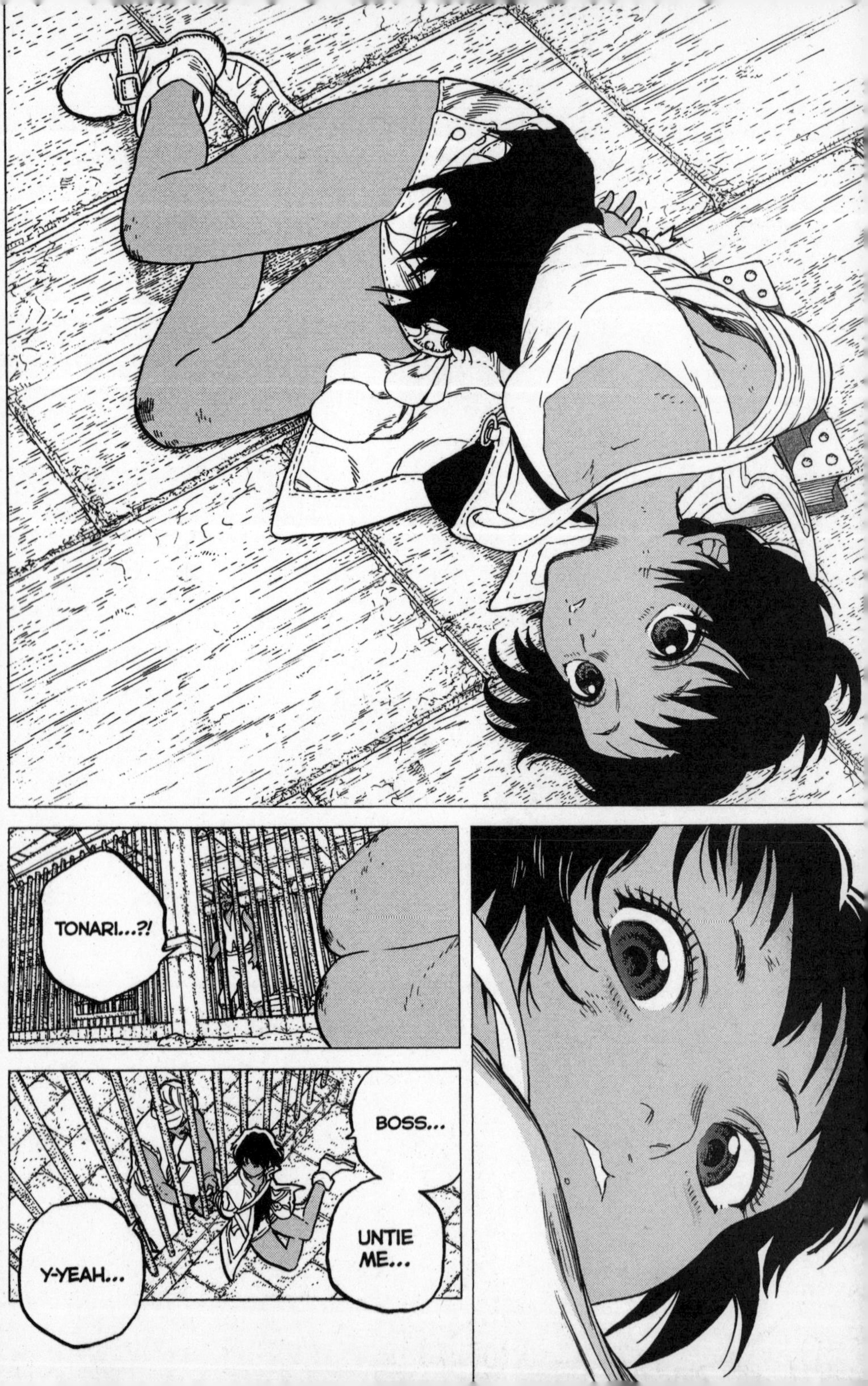
TONARI...?!
BOSS...
UNTIE ME...
Y-YEAH...

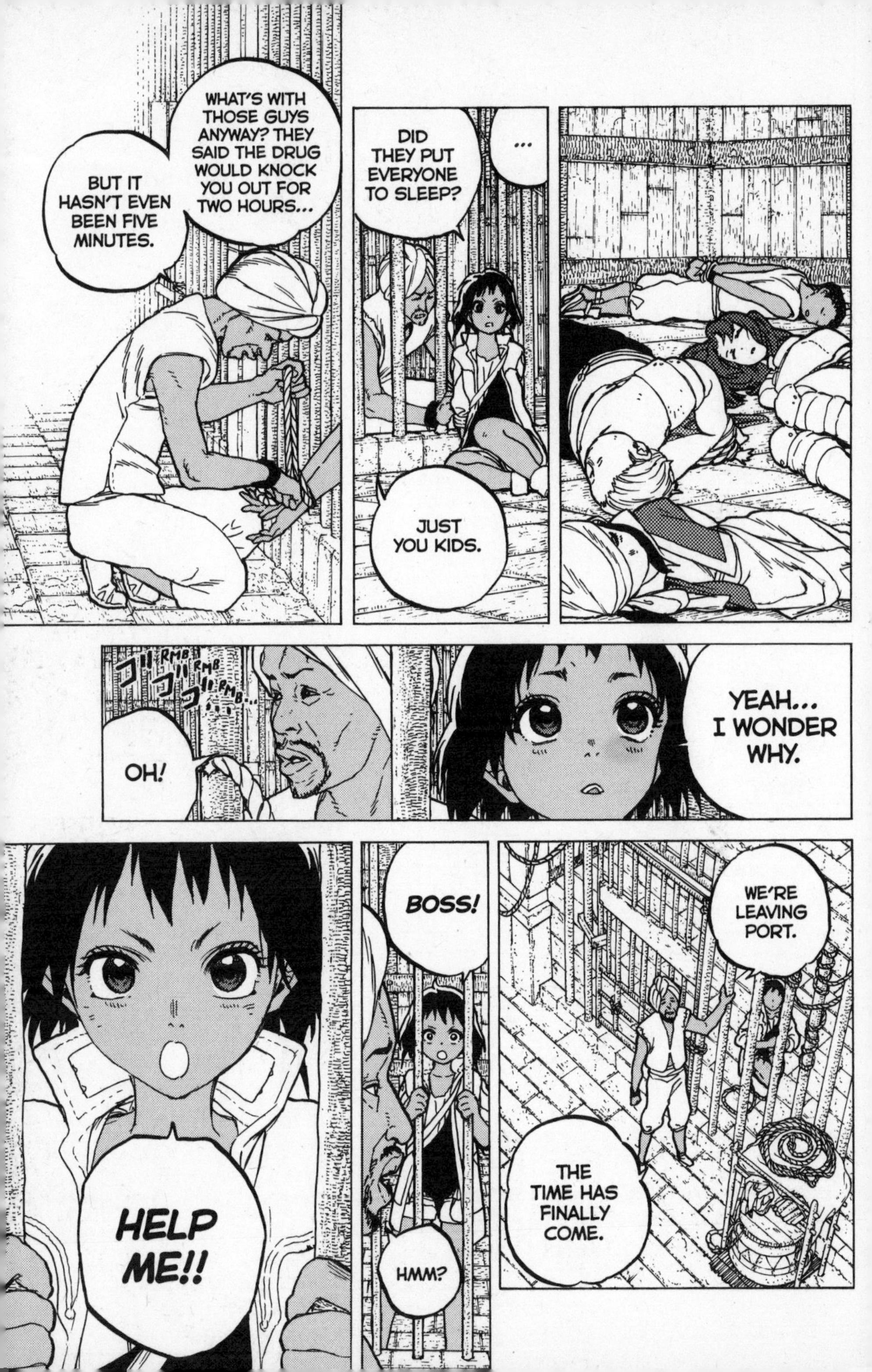
...
DID THEY PUT EVERYONE TO SLEEP?
JUST YOU KIDS.
WHAT'S WITH THOSE GUYS ANYWAY? THEY SAID THE DRUG WOULD KNOCK YOU OUT FOR TWO HOURS...
BUT IT HASN'T EVEN BEEN FIVE MINUTES.
YEAH... I WONDER WHY.
RMB RMB RMB...
OH!
WE'RE LEAVING PORT.
THE TIME HAS FINALLY COME.
BOSS!
HMM?
HELP ME!!

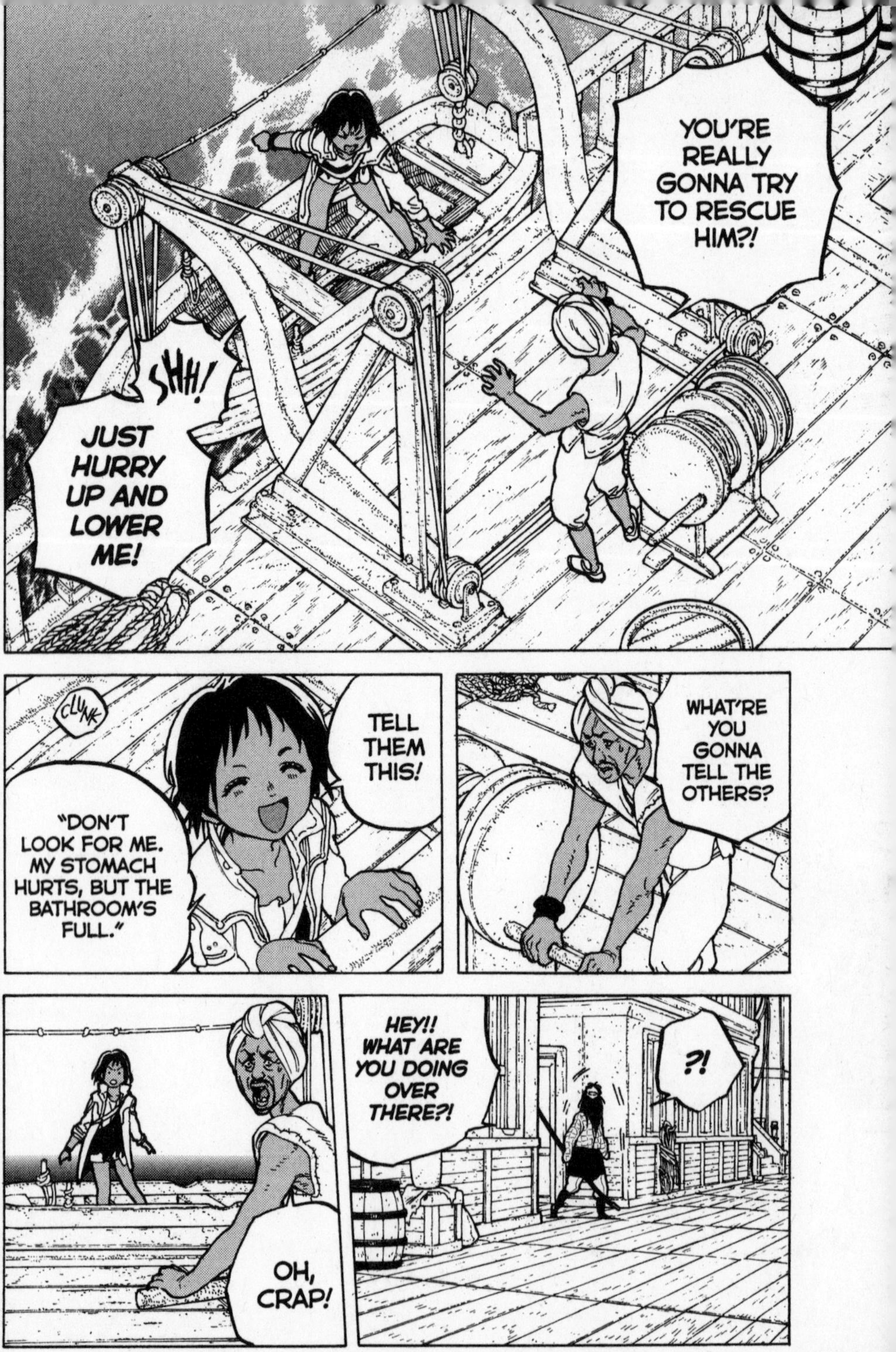
YOU'RE REALLY GONNA TRY TO RESCUE HIM?!
SHH!
JUST HURRY UP AND LOWER ME!
WHAT'RE YOU GONNA TELL THE OTHERS?
CLUNK
TELL THEM THIS!
"DON'T LOOK FOR ME. MY STOMACH HURTS, BUT THE BATHROOM'S FULL."
HEY!! WHAT ARE YOU DOING OVER THERE?!
?!
OH, CRAP!

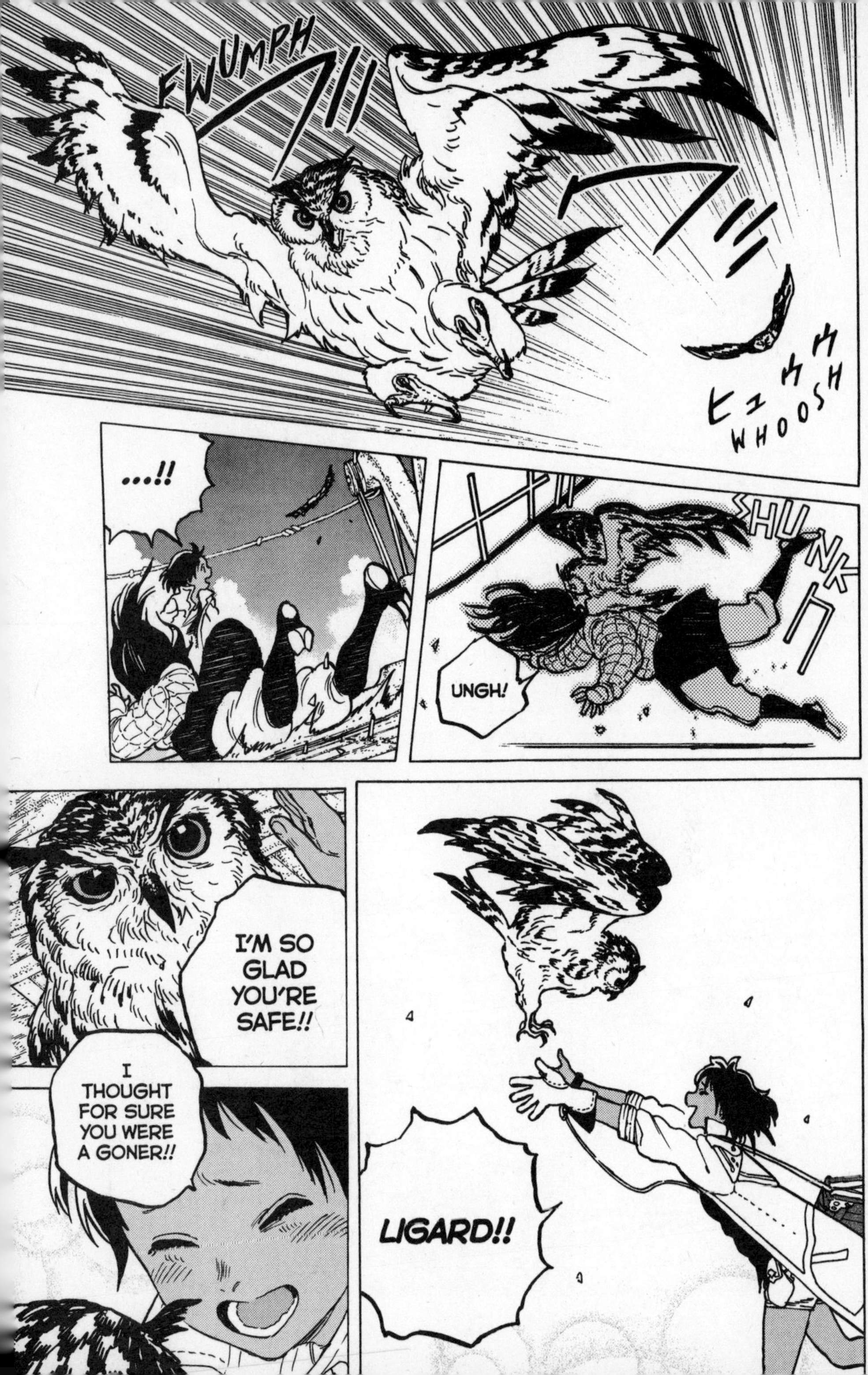
FWUMPH
ヒュゥゥ
WHOOSH
SHUNK
UNGH!
...!!
LIGARD!!
I'M SO GLAD YOU'RE SAFE!!
I THOUGHT FOR SURE YOU WERE A GONER!!

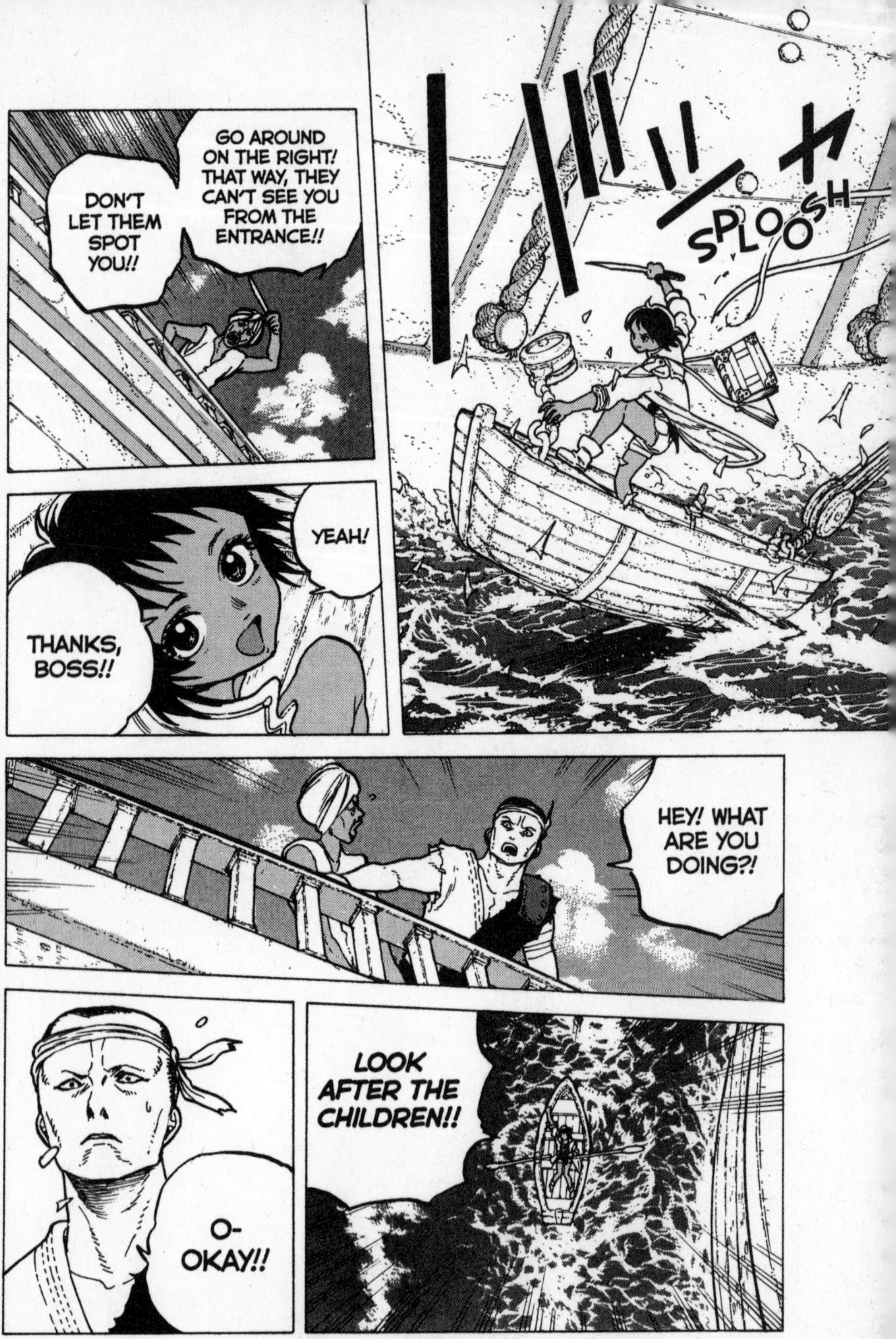
SPLOOSH
GO AROUND ON THE RIGHT! THAT WAY, THEY CAN'T SEE YOU FROM THE ENTRANCE!!
DON'T LET THEM SPOT YOU!!
YEAH!
THANKS, BOSS!!
HEY! WHAT ARE YOU DOING?!
LOOK AFTER THE CHILDREN!!
O-OKAY!!

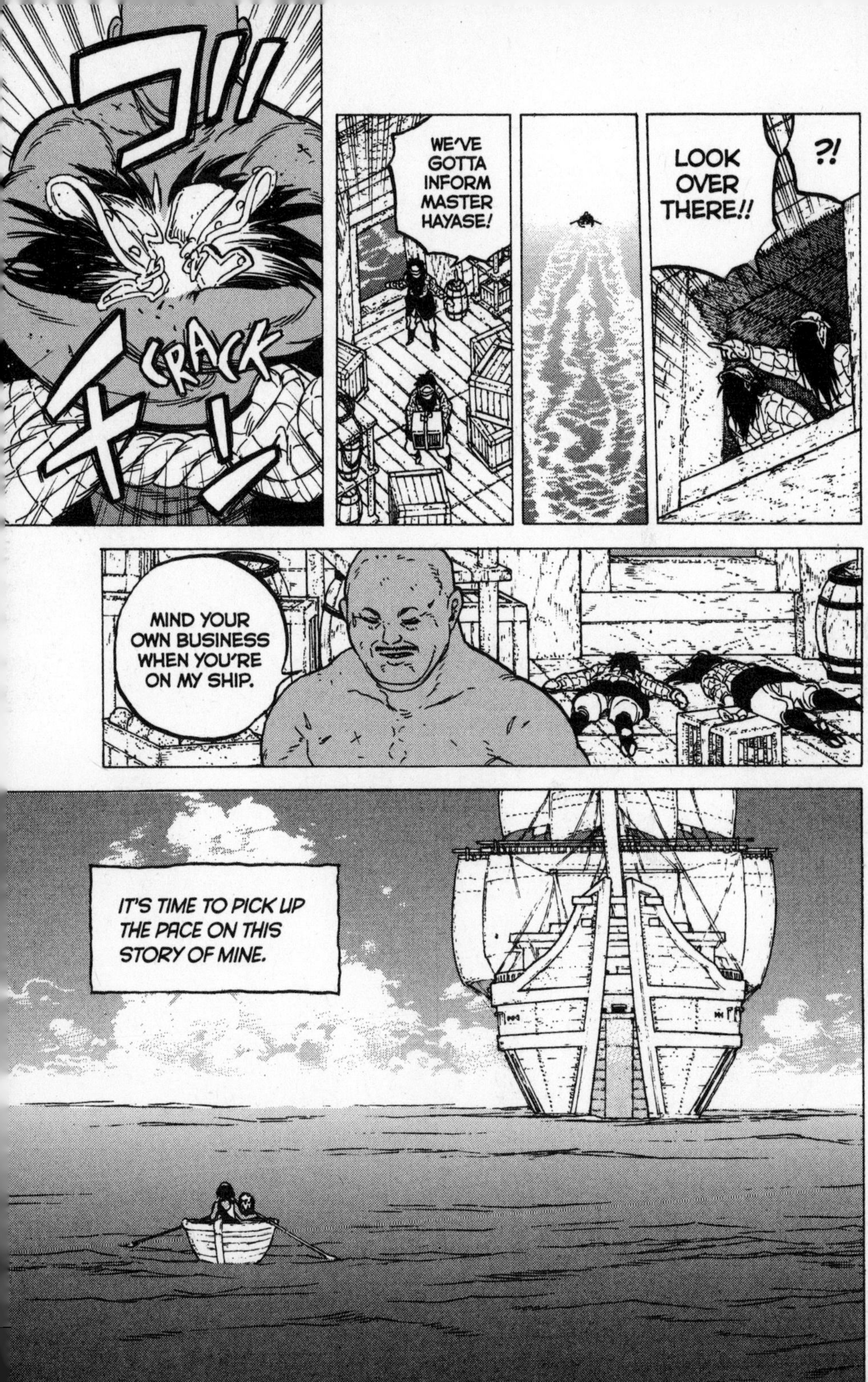
?!
LOOK OVER THERE!!
WE'VE GOTTA INFORM MASTER HAYASE!
CRACK
MIND YOUR OWN BUSINESS WHEN YOU'RE ON MY SHIP.
IT'S TIME TO PICK UP THE PACE ON THIS STORY OF MINE.

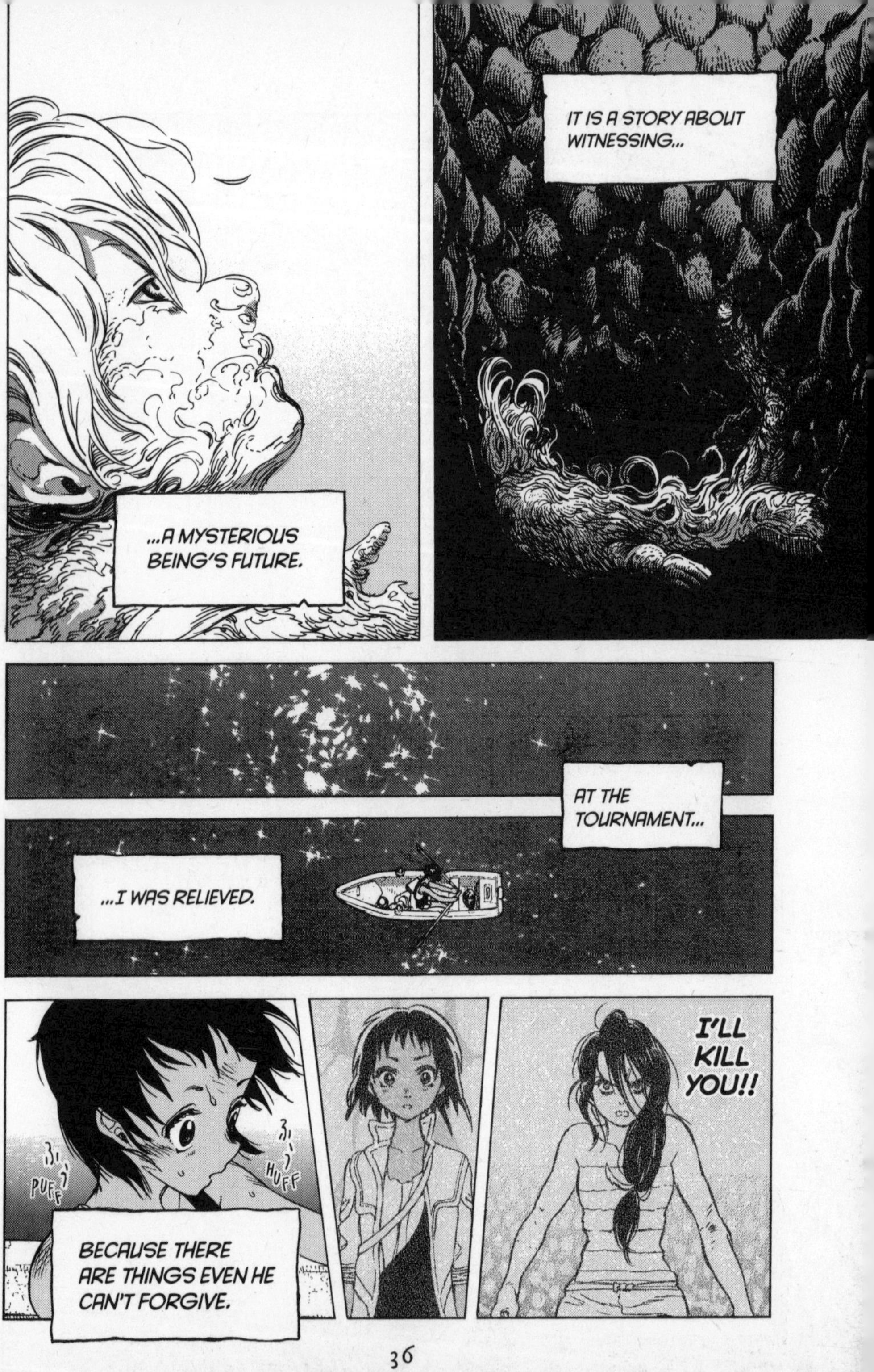
IT IS A STORY ABOUT WITNESSING...
...A MYSTERIOUS BEING'S FUTURE.
AT THE TOURNAMENT...
...I WAS RELIEVED.
I'LL KILL YOU!!
HUFF
PUFF
BECAUSE THERE ARE THINGS EVEN HE CAN'T FORGIVE.

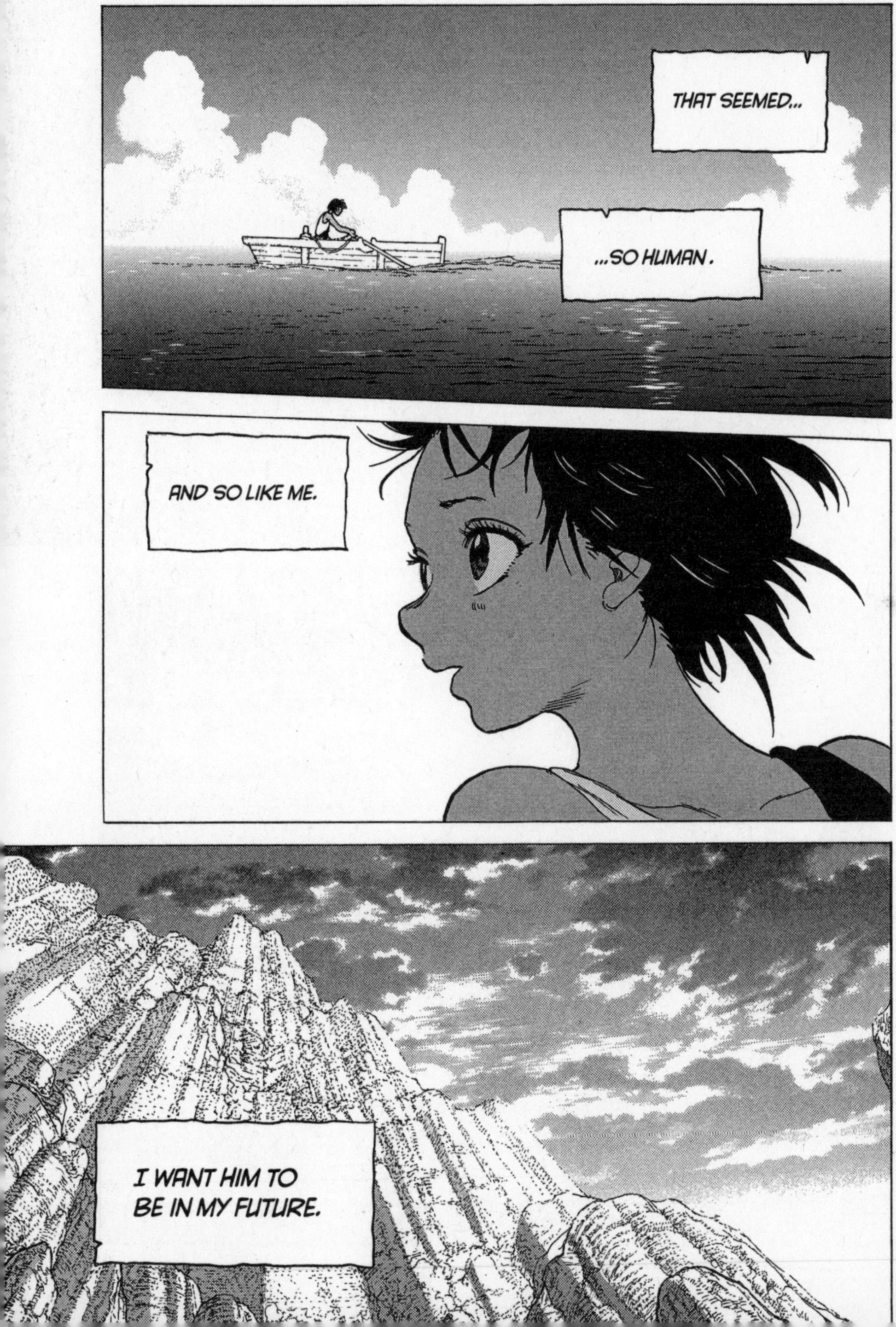
THAT SEEMED...
...SO HUMAN.
AND SO LIKE ME.
I WANT HIM TO BE IN MY FUTURE.

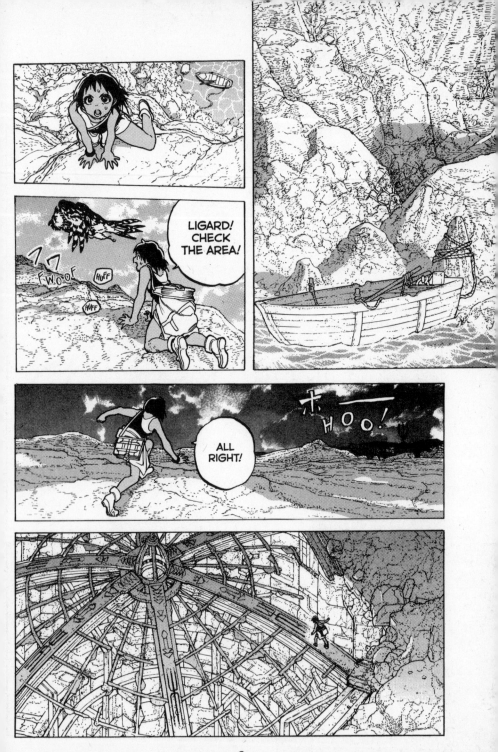

LIGARD! CHECK THE AREA!

FWOOF

HUFF

HUFF

HOO!

ALL RIGHT!

38

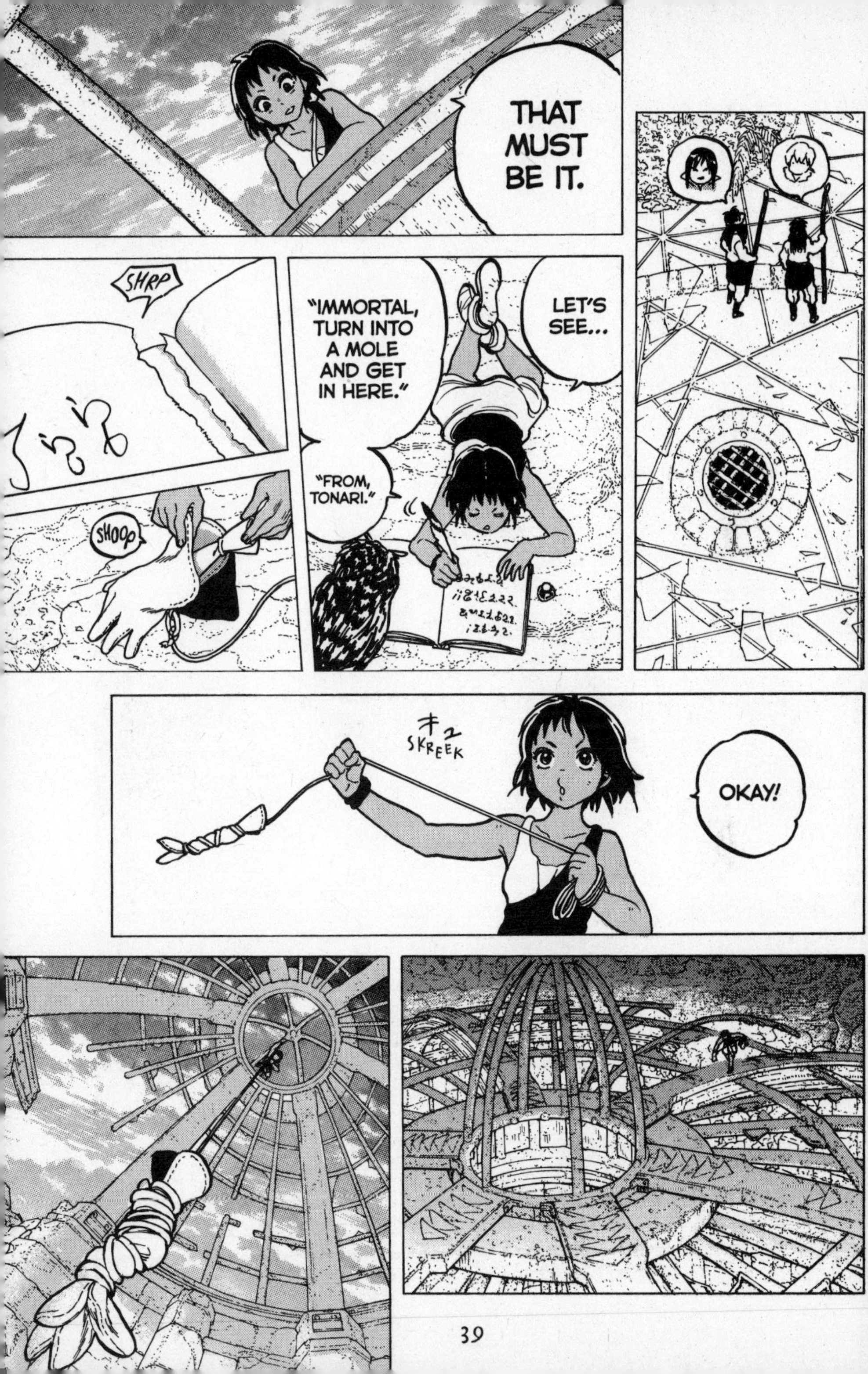
THAT MUST BE IT.
LET'S SEE...
"IMMORTAL, TURN INTO A MOLE AND GET IN HERE."
"FROM, TONARI."
SHRP
SHOOP
キュ
SKREEK
OKAY!

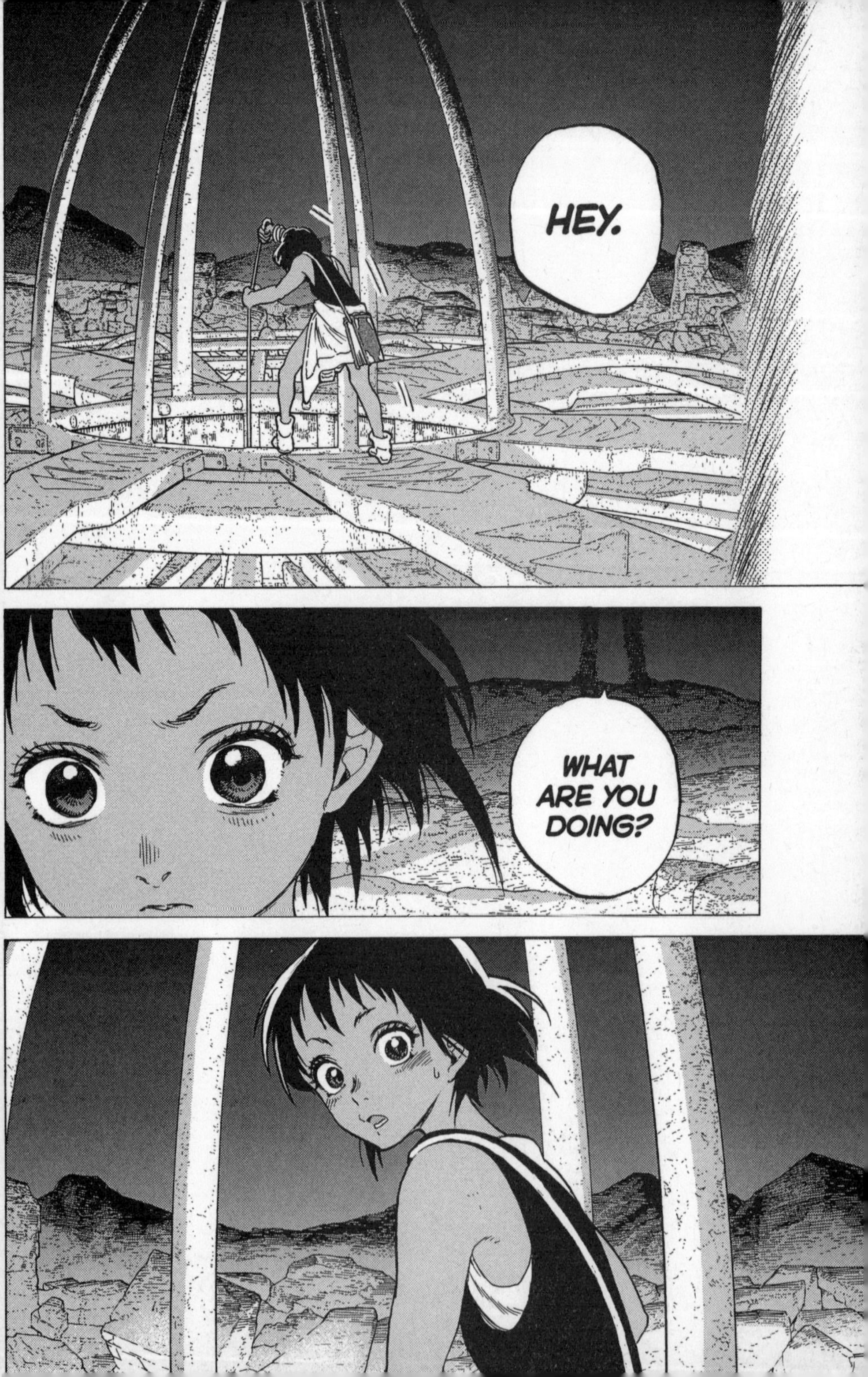
HEY.
WHAT ARE YOU DOING?

TO YOUR ETERNITY

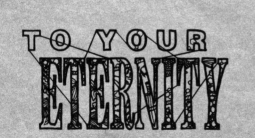

He, with endless life and the ability to change
into many forms, arrived to protect the people.

She who first saw this, Hayase, is the guardian
to whom Fushi was bestowed by god.

But the existence of this miracle is still fragile, perilous...

Those who protect it will surely be chosen by the heavens.

THE GUARDIANS

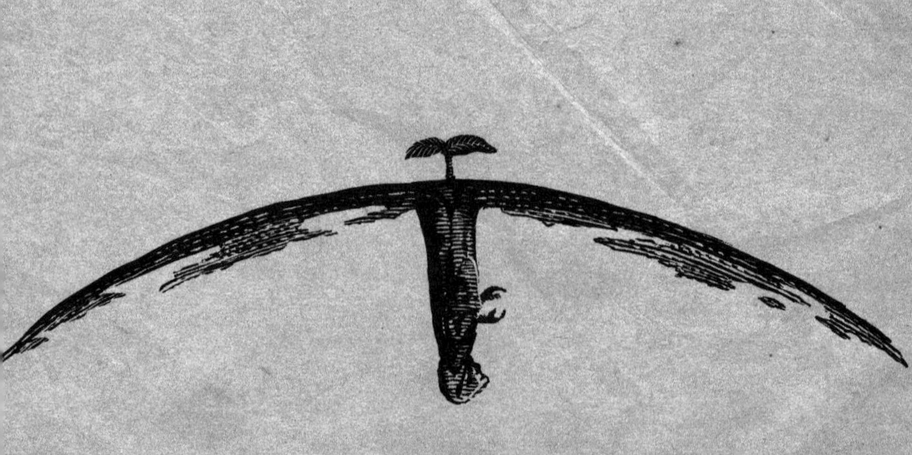

#47 Impending Dawn

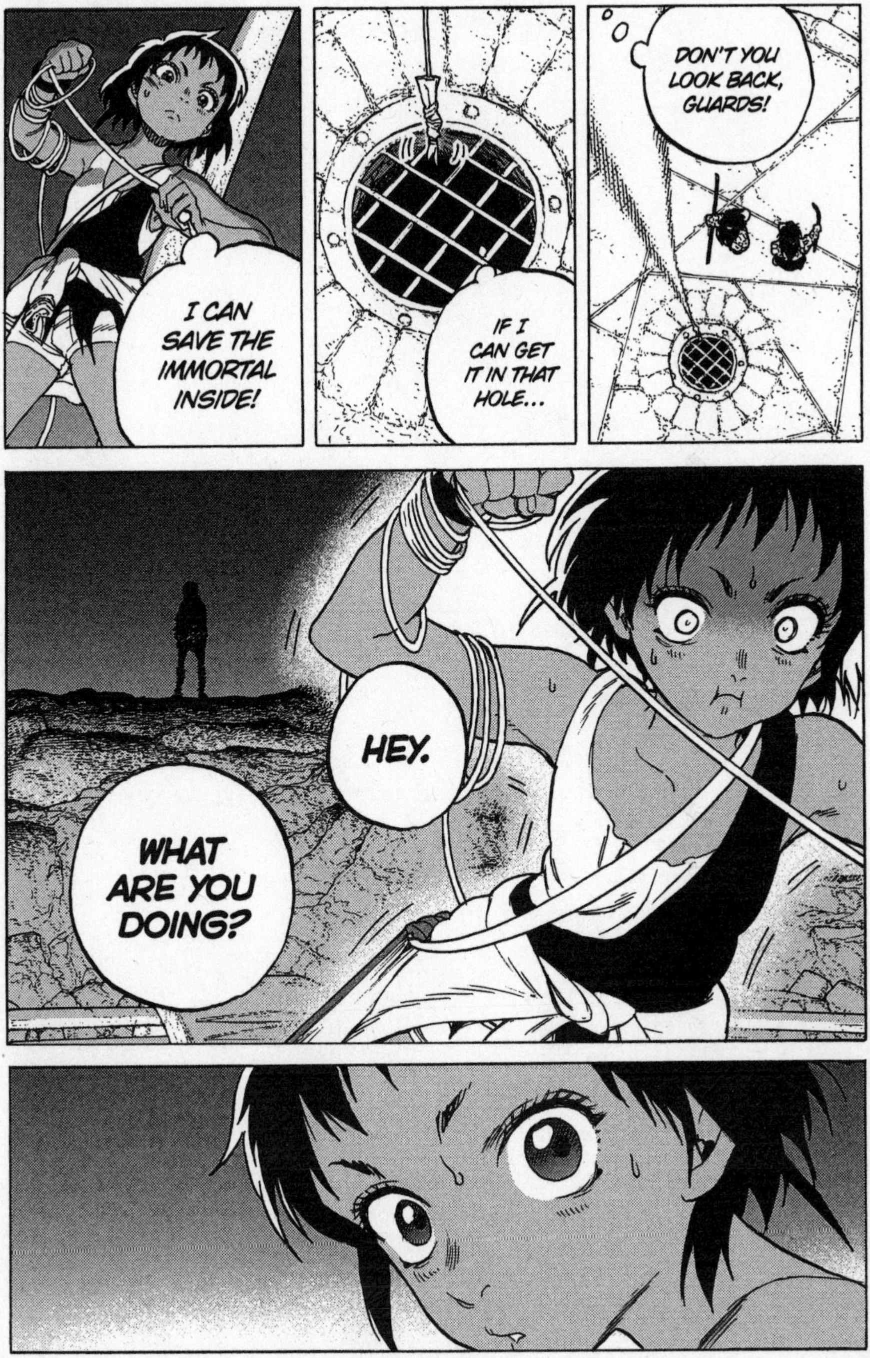
DON'T YOU LOOK BACK, GUARDS!
IF I CAN GET IT IN THAT HOLE...
I CAN SAVE THE IMMORTAL INSIDE!
HEY.
WHAT ARE YOU DOING?

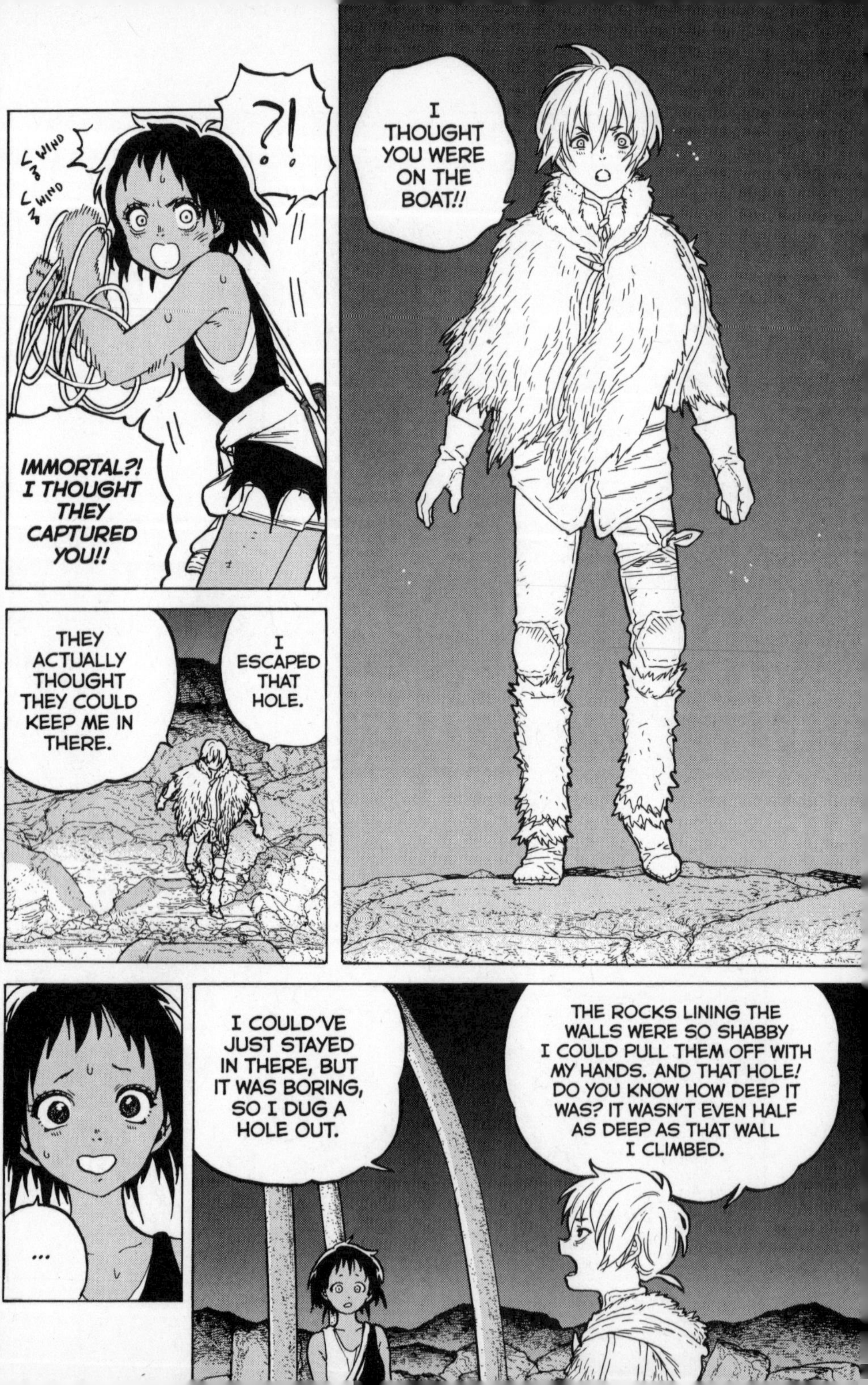
I THOUGHT YOU WERE ON THE BOAT!!
?!
WIND
WIND
IMMORTAL?! I THOUGHT THEY CAPTURED YOU!!
I ESCAPED THAT HOLE.
THEY ACTUALLY THOUGHT THEY COULD KEEP ME IN THERE.
THE ROCKS LINING THE WALLS WERE SO SHABBY I COULD PULL THEM OFF WITH MY HANDS. AND THAT HOLE! DO YOU KNOW HOW DEEP IT WAS? IT WASN'T EVEN HALF AS DEEP AS THAT WALL I CLIMBED.
I COULD'VE JUST STAYED IN THERE, BUT IT WAS BORING, SO I DUG A HOLE OUT.
...

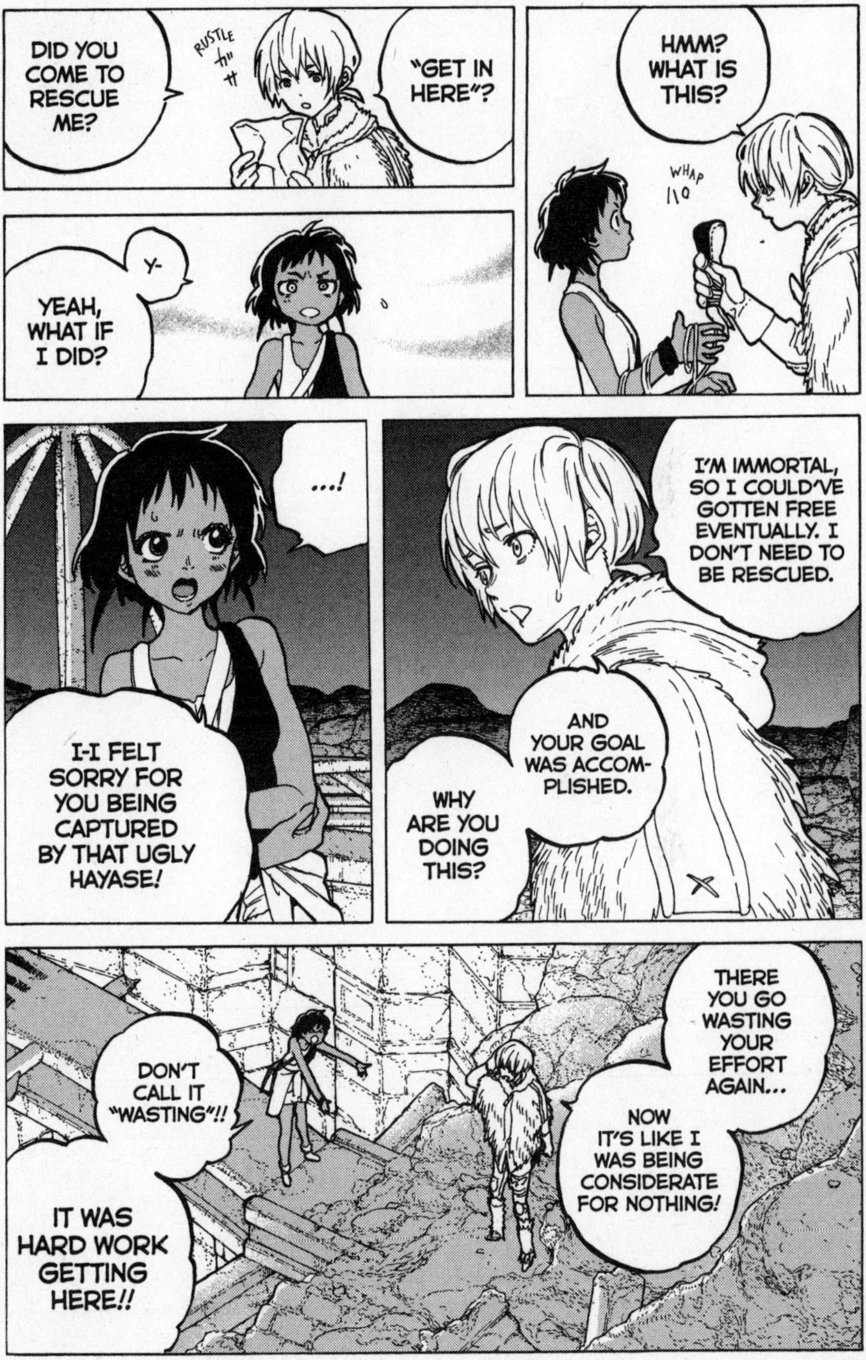
HMM? WHAT IS THIS?
WHAP
RUSTLE
"GET IN HERE"?
DID YOU COME TO RESCUE ME?
Y-
YEAH, WHAT IF I DID?
I'M IMMORTAL, SO I COULD'VE GOTTEN FREE EVENTUALLY. I DON'T NEED TO BE RESCUED.
AND YOUR GOAL WAS ACCOMPLISHED.
WHY ARE YOU DOING THIS?
...!
I-I FELT SORRY FOR YOU BEING CAPTURED BY THAT UGLY HAYASE!
THERE YOU GO WASTING YOUR EFFORT AGAIN...
NOW IT'S LIKE I WAS BEING CONSIDERATE FOR NOTHING!
DON'T CALL IT "WASTING"!!
IT WAS HARD WORK GETTING HERE!!

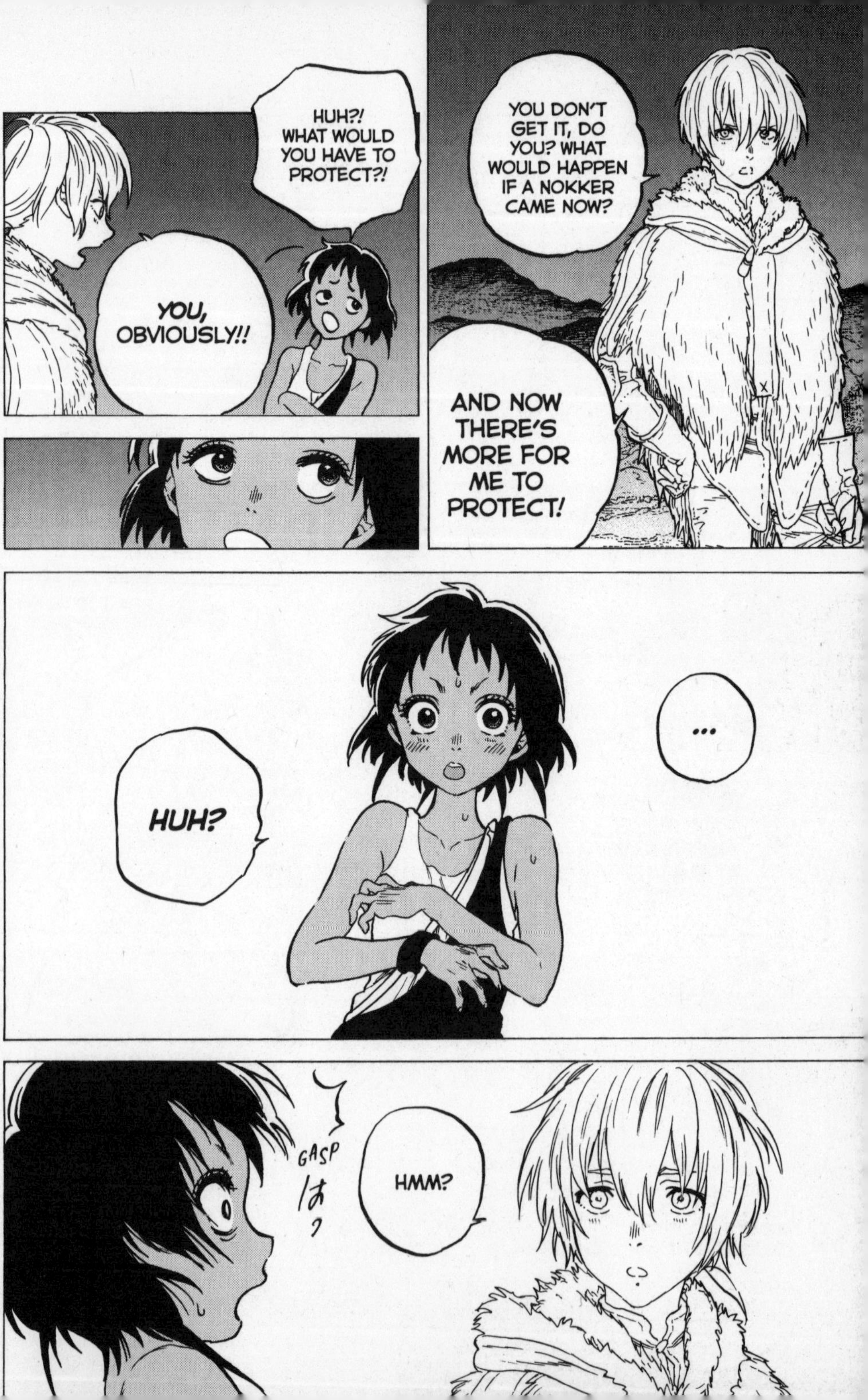

YOU DON'T GET IT, DO YOU? WHAT WOULD HAPPEN IF A NOKKER CAME NOW?
AND NOW THERE'S MORE FOR ME TO PROTECT!
HUH?! WHAT WOULD YOU HAVE TO PROTECT?!
YOU, OBVIOUSLY!!
...
HUH?
HMM?
GASP
はっ

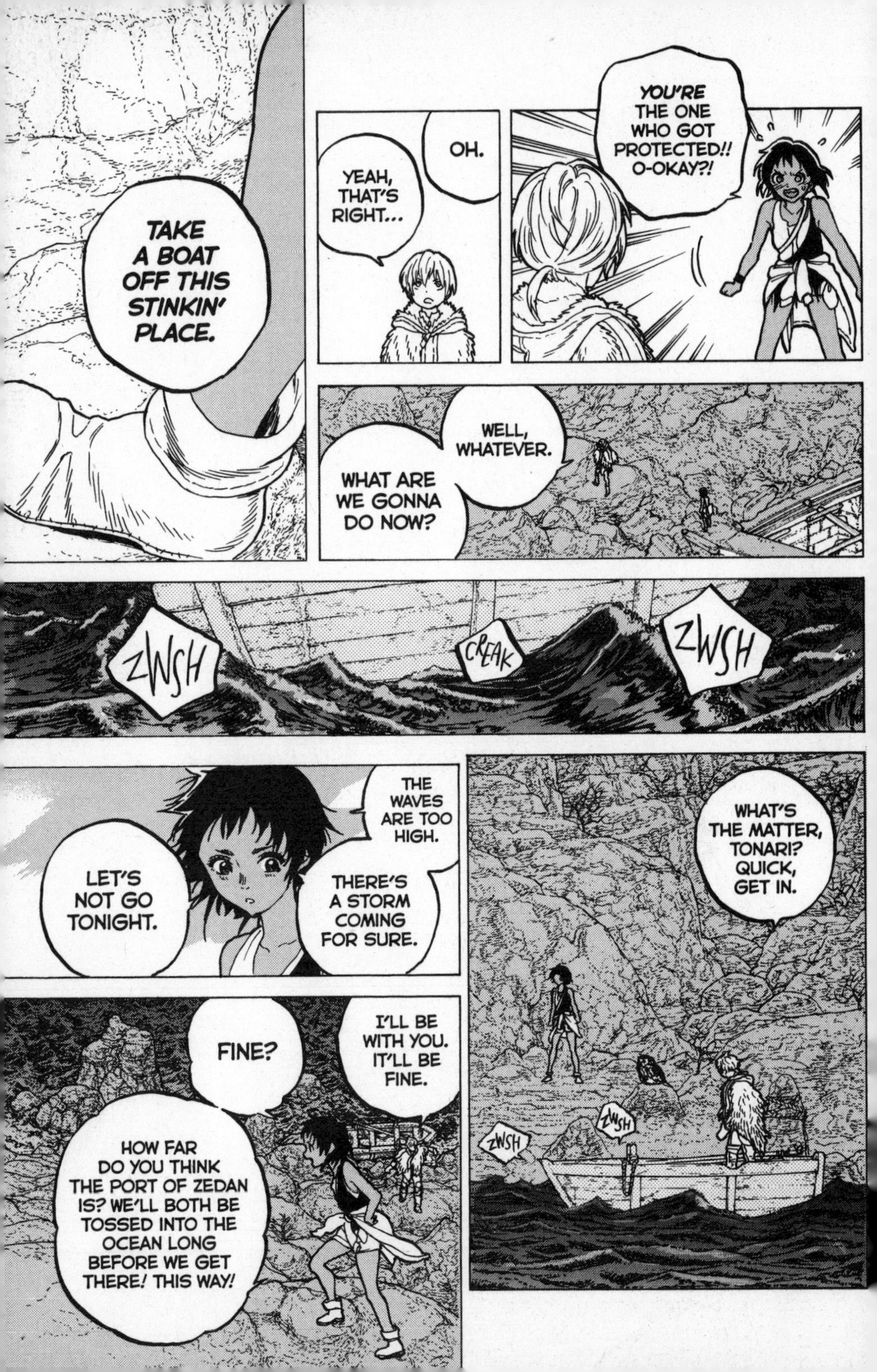
YOU'RE THE ONE WHO GOT PROTECTED!! O-OKAY?!
OH.
YEAH, THAT'S RIGHT...
WELL, WHATEVER.
WHAT ARE WE GONNA DO NOW?
TAKE A BOAT OFF THIS STINKIN' PLACE.
ZWSH
CREAK
ZWSH
WHAT'S THE MATTER, TONARI? QUICK, GET IN.
ZWSH
ZWSH
THE WAVES ARE TOO HIGH.
THERE'S A STORM COMING FOR SURE.
LET'S NOT GO TONIGHT.
I'LL BE WITH YOU. IT'LL BE FINE.
FINE?
HOW FAR DO YOU THINK THE PORT OF ZEDAN IS? WE'LL BOTH BE TOSSED INTO THE OCEAN LONG BEFORE WE GET THERE! THIS WAY!

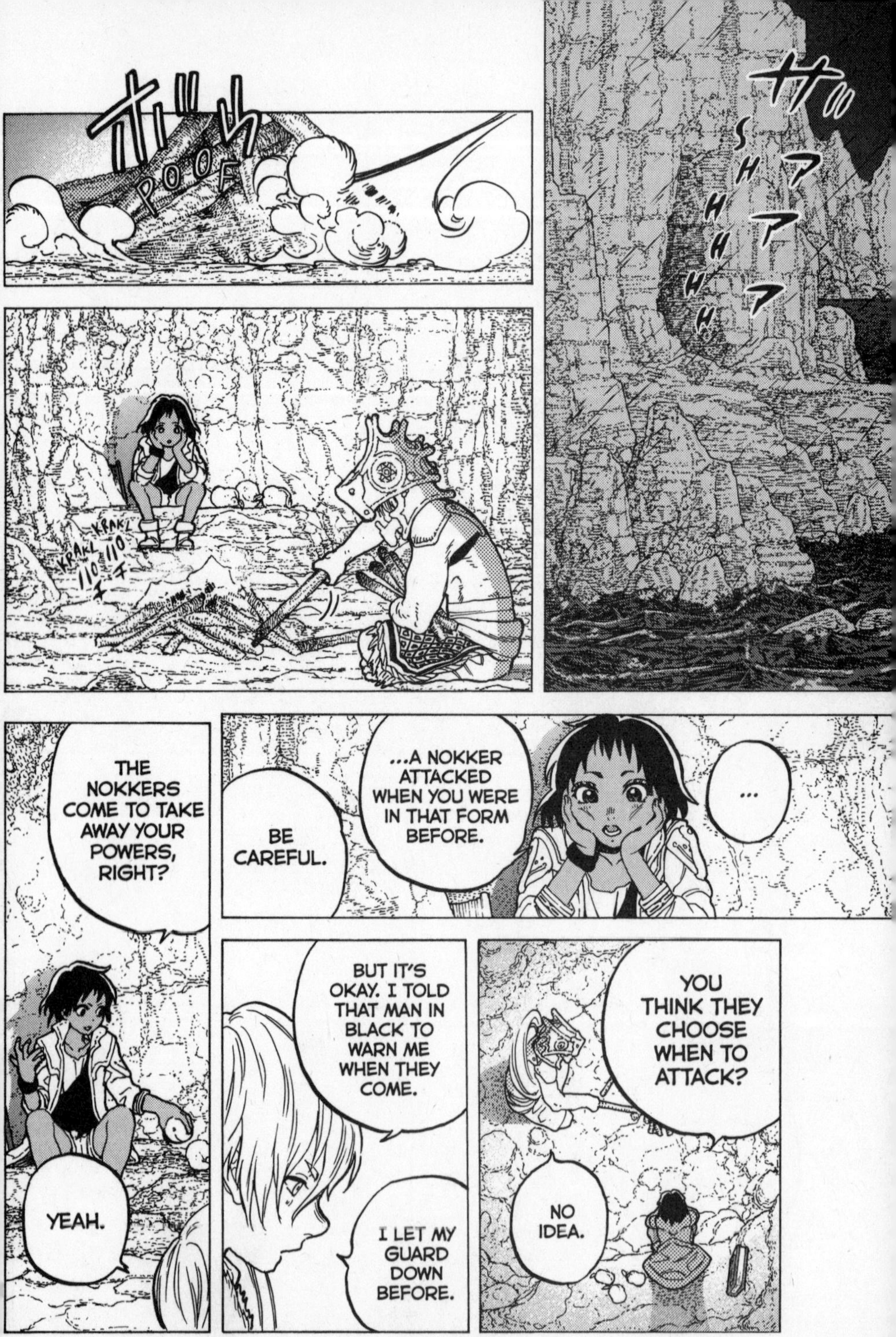
SHHHHH
POOF
KRAKL KRAKL
...
...A NOKKER ATTACKED WHEN YOU WERE IN THAT FORM BEFORE.
BE CAREFUL.
YOU THINK THEY CHOOSE WHEN TO ATTACK?
NO IDEA.
BUT IT'S OKAY. I TOLD THAT MAN IN BLACK TO WARN ME WHEN THEY COME.
I LET MY GUARD DOWN BEFORE.
THE NOKKERS COME TO TAKE AWAY YOUR POWERS, RIGHT?
YEAH.

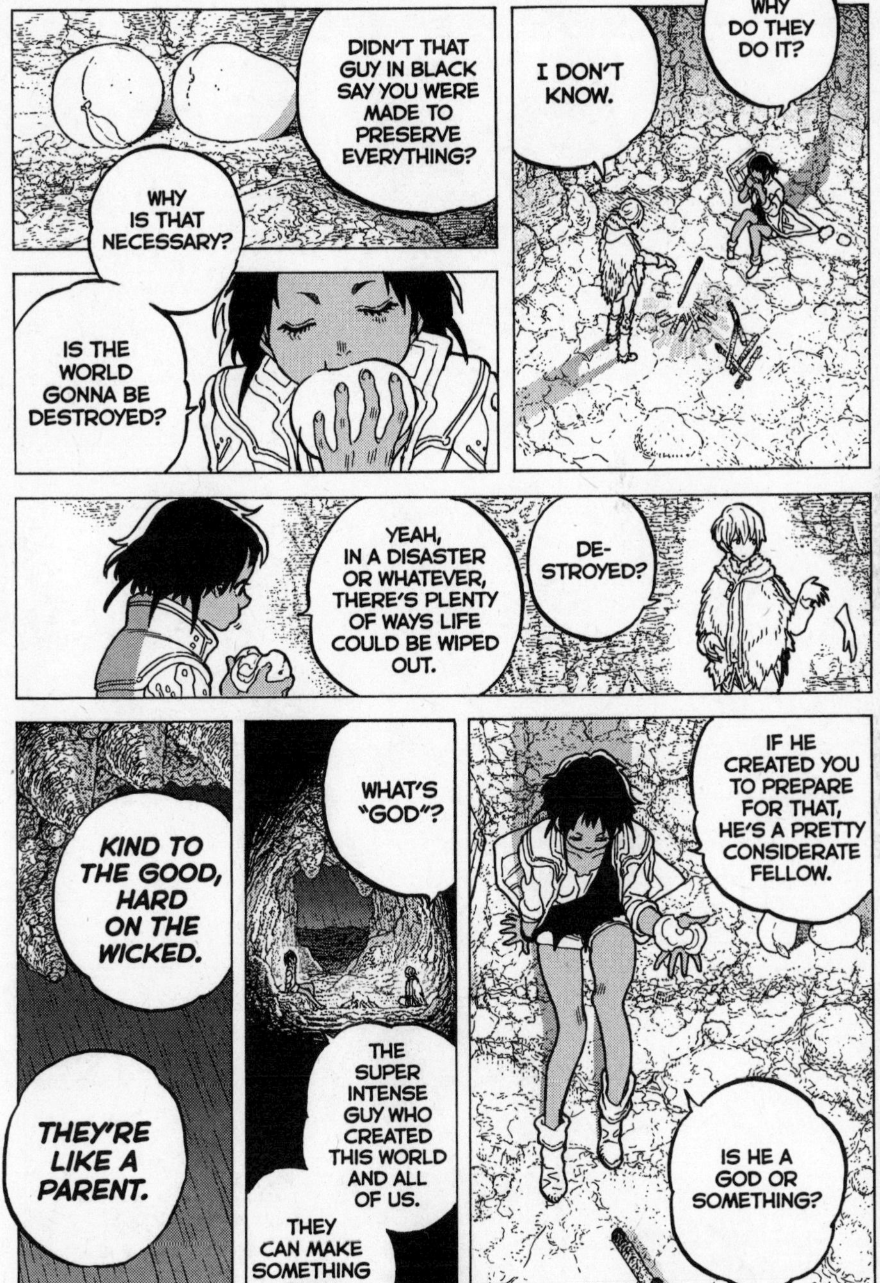
WHY DO THEY DO IT?
I DON'T KNOW.
DIDN'T THAT GUY IN BLACK SAY YOU WERE MADE TO PRESERVE EVERYTHING?
WHY IS THAT NECESSARY?
IS THE WORLD GONNA BE DESTROYED?
DE-STROYED?
YEAH, IN A DISASTER OR WHATEVER, THERE'S PLENTY OF WAYS LIFE COULD BE WIPED OUT.
IF HE CREATED YOU TO PREPARE FOR THAT, HE'S A PRETTY CONSIDERATE FELLOW.
IS HE A GOD OR SOMETHING?
WHAT'S "GOD"?
THE SUPER INTENSE GUY WHO CREATED THIS WORLD AND ALL OF US.
THEY CAN MAKE SOMETHING FROM NOTHING.
KIND TO THE GOOD, HARD ON THE WICKED.
THEY'RE LIKE A PARENT.

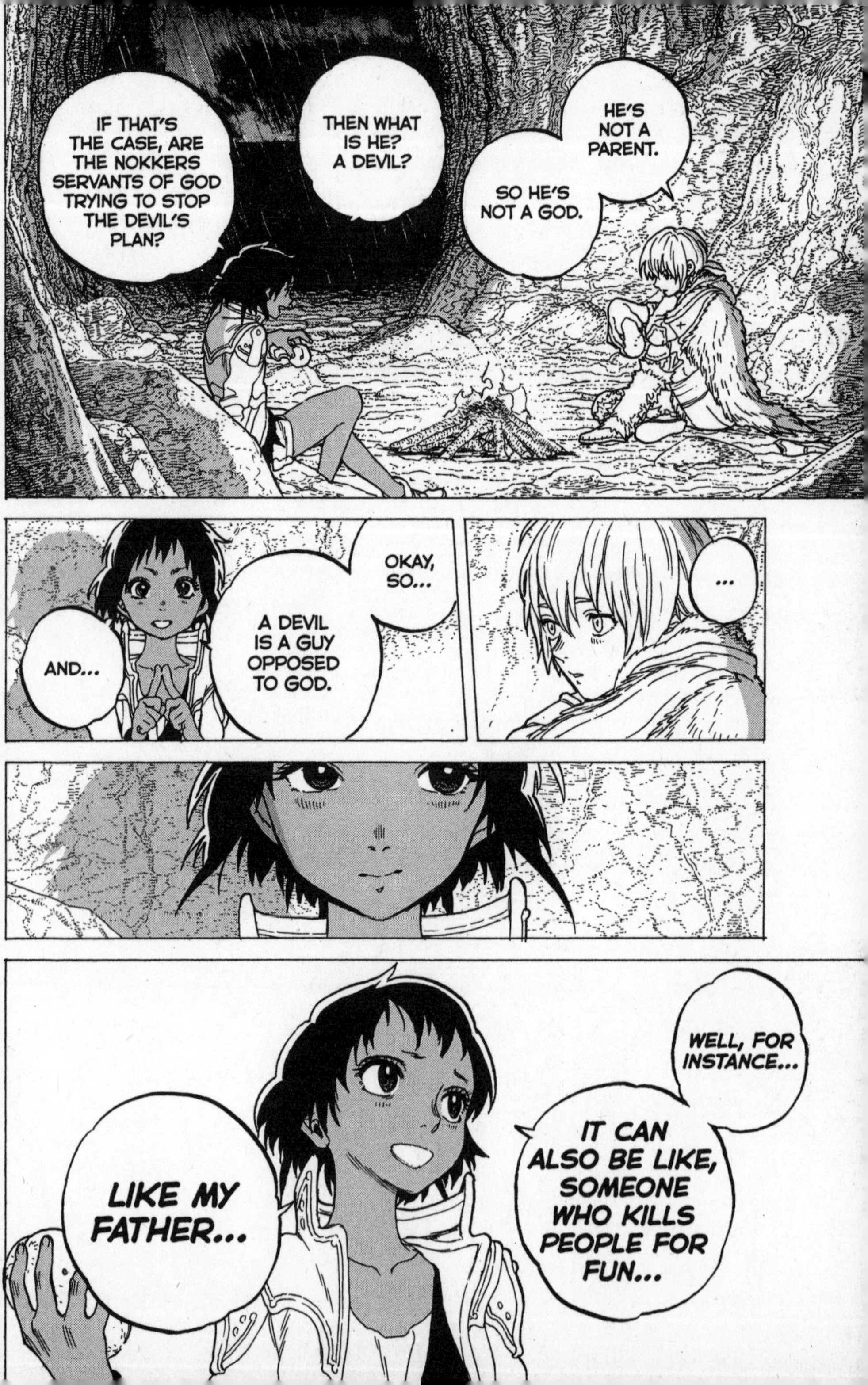
HE'S NOT A PARENT.
SO HE'S NOT A GOD.
THEN WHAT IS HE? A DEVIL?
IF THAT'S THE CASE, ARE THE NOKKERS SERVANTS OF GOD TRYING TO STOP THE DEVIL'S PLAN?
...
OKAY, SO...
A DEVIL IS A GUY OPPOSED TO GOD.
AND...
WELL, FOR INSTANCE...
IT CAN ALSO BE LIKE, SOMEONE WHO KILLS PEOPLE FOR FUN...
LIKE MY FATHER...

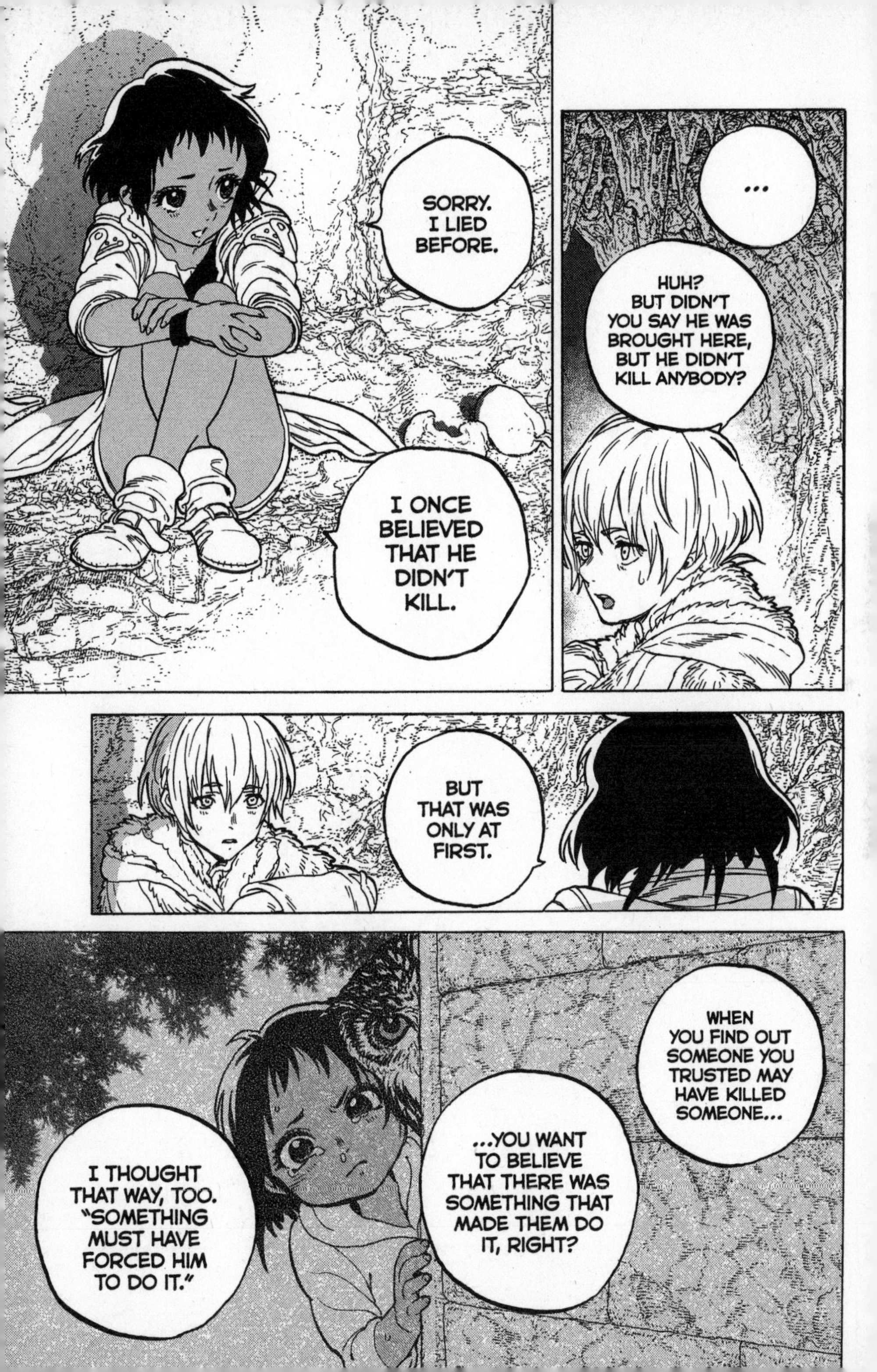
...
HUH? BUT DIDN'T YOU SAY HE WAS BROUGHT HERE, BUT HE DIDN'T KILL ANYBODY?
SORRY. I LIED BEFORE.
I ONCE BELIEVED THAT HE DIDN'T KILL.
BUT THAT WAS ONLY AT FIRST.
WHEN YOU FIND OUT SOMEONE YOU TRUSTED MAY HAVE KILLED SOMEONE...
...YOU WANT TO BELIEVE THAT THERE WAS SOMETHING THAT MADE THEM DO IT, RIGHT?
I THOUGHT THAT WAY, TOO. "SOMETHING MUST HAVE FORCED HIM TO DO IT."

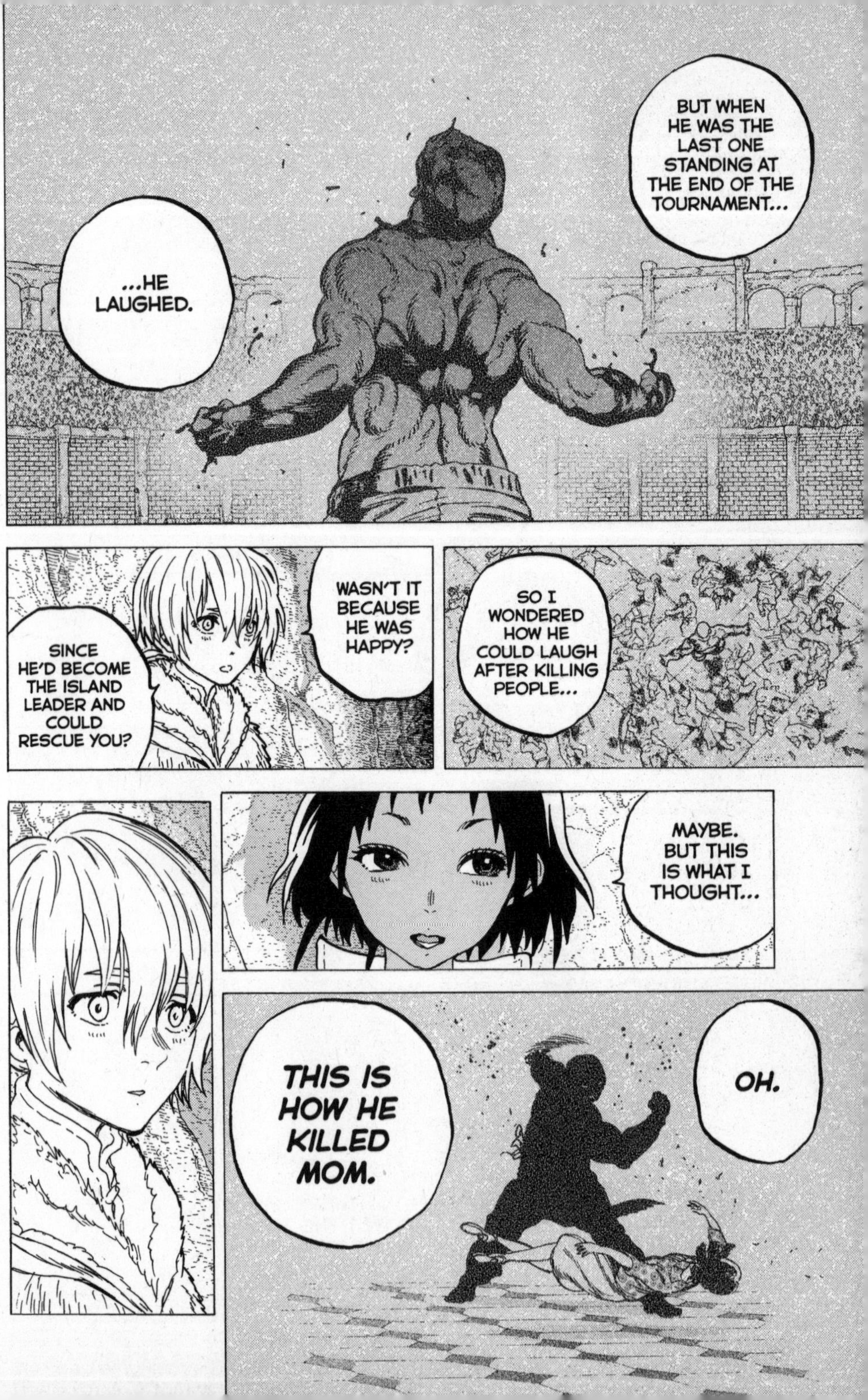
BUT WHEN HE WAS THE LAST ONE STANDING AT THE END OF THE TOURNAMENT...
...HE LAUGHED.
SO I WONDERED HOW HE COULD LAUGH AFTER KILLING PEOPLE...
WASN'T IT BECAUSE HE WAS HAPPY?
SINCE HE'D BECOME THE ISLAND LEADER AND COULD RESCUE YOU?
MAYBE. BUT THIS IS WHAT I THOUGHT...
OH.
THIS IS HOW HE KILLED MOM.

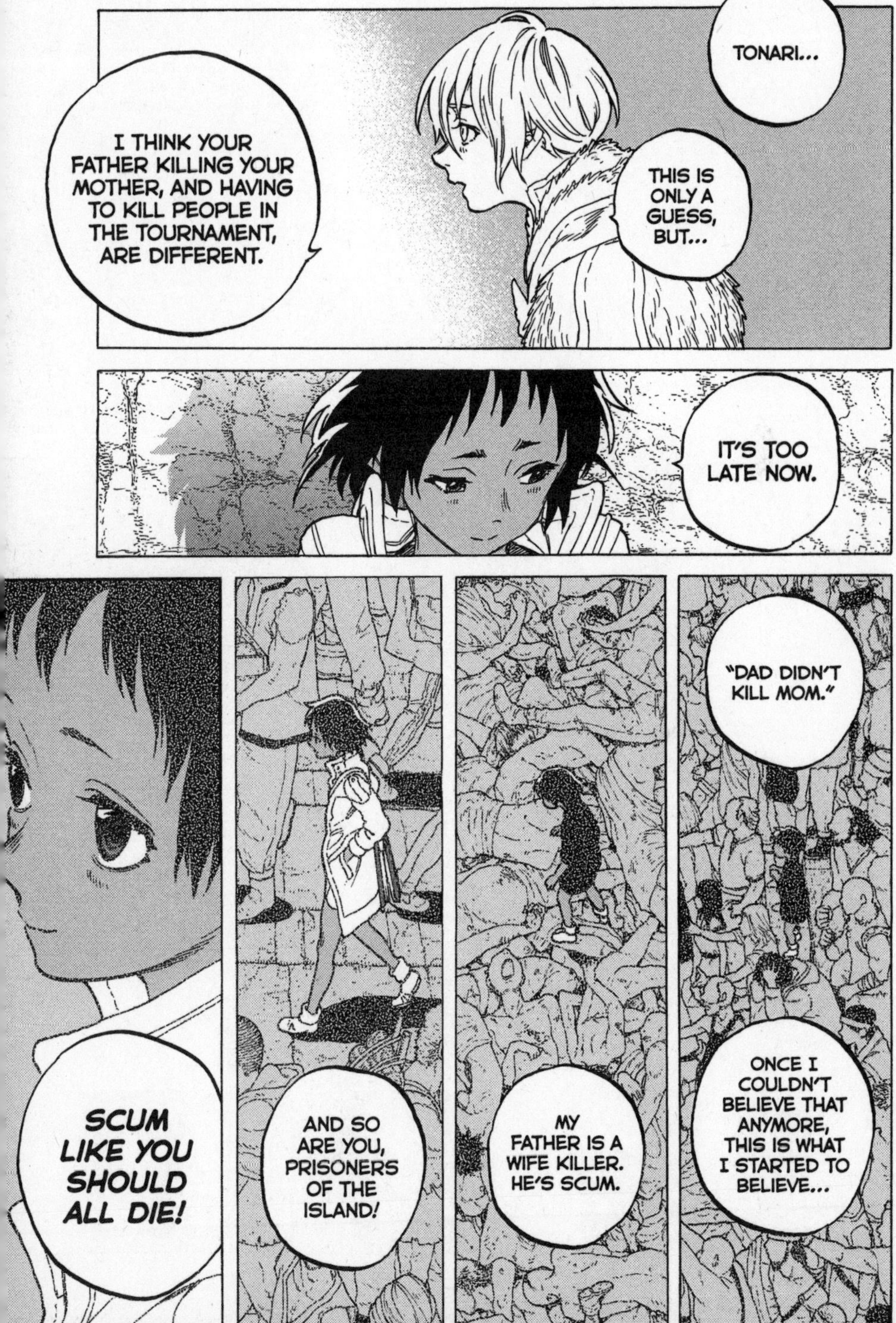
TONARI...
THIS IS ONLY A GUESS, BUT...
I THINK YOUR FATHER KILLING YOUR MOTHER, AND HAVING TO KILL PEOPLE IN THE TOURNAMENT, ARE DIFFERENT.
IT'S TOO LATE NOW.
"DAD DIDN'T KILL MOM."
ONCE I COULDN'T BELIEVE THAT ANYMORE, THIS IS WHAT I STARTED TO BELIEVE...
MY FATHER IS A WIFE KILLER. HE'S SCUM.
AND SO ARE YOU, PRISONERS OF THE ISLAND!
SCUM LIKE YOU SHOULD ALL DIE!

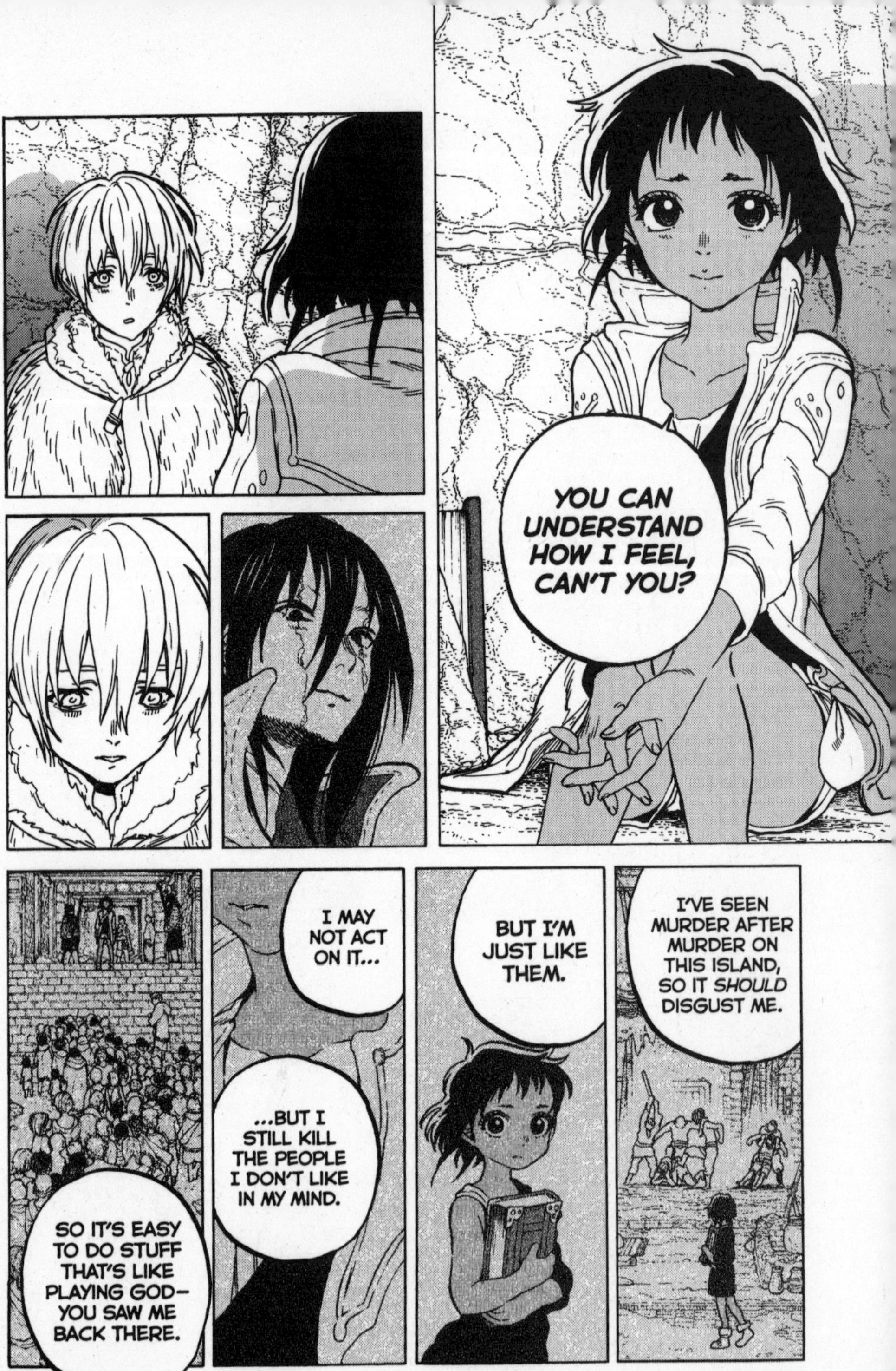
YOU CAN UNDERSTAND HOW I FEEL, CAN'T YOU?
I'VE SEEN MURDER AFTER MURDER ON THIS ISLAND, SO IT *SHOULD* DISGUST ME.
BUT I'M JUST LIKE THEM.
I MAY NOT ACT ON IT...
...BUT I STILL KILL THE PEOPLE I DON'T LIKE IN MY MIND.
SO IT'S EASY TO DO STUFF THAT'S LIKE PLAYING GOD—YOU SAW ME BACK THERE.

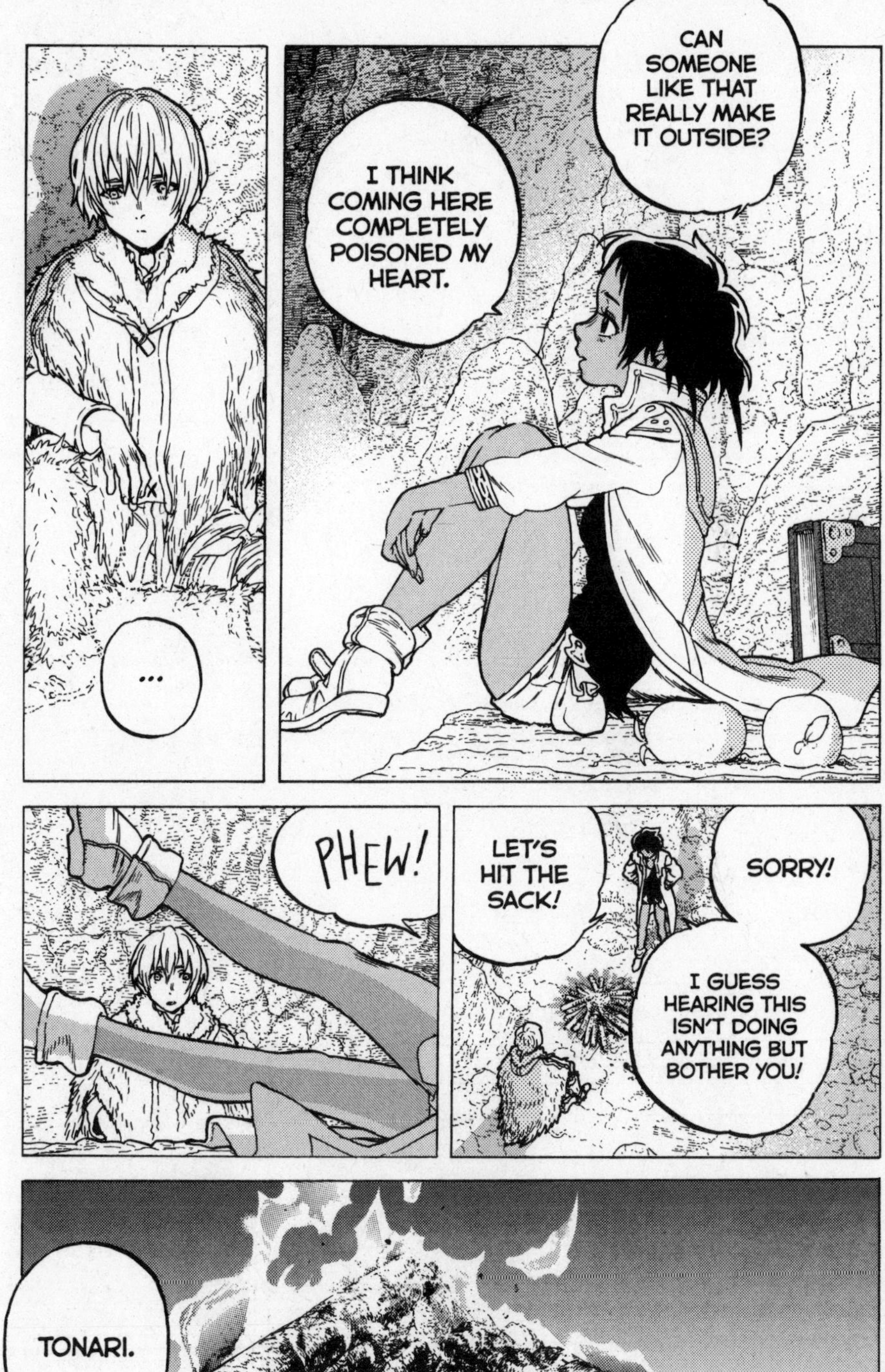
CAN SOMEONE LIKE THAT REALLY MAKE IT OUTSIDE?
I THINK COMING HERE COMPLETELY POISONED MY HEART.
...
SORRY!
I GUESS HEARING THIS ISN'T DOING ANYTHING BUT BOTHER YOU!
LET'S HIT THE SACK!
PHEW!
TONARI.

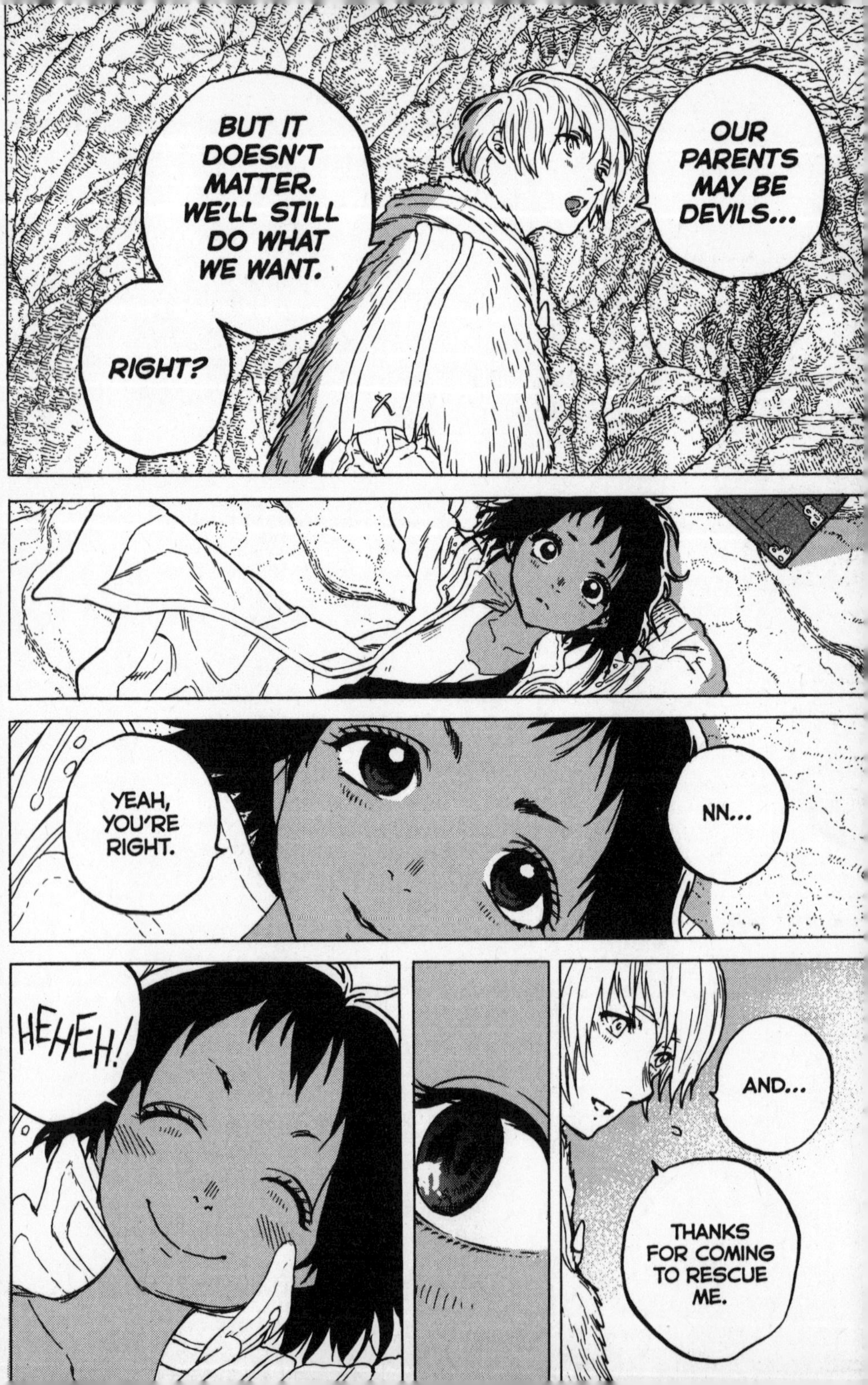
OUR PARENTS MAY BE DEVILS...
BUT IT DOESN'T MATTER. WE'LL STILL DO WHAT WE WANT.
RIGHT?
NN...
YEAH, YOU'RE RIGHT.
AND...
THANKS FOR COMING TO RESCUE ME.
HEHEH!

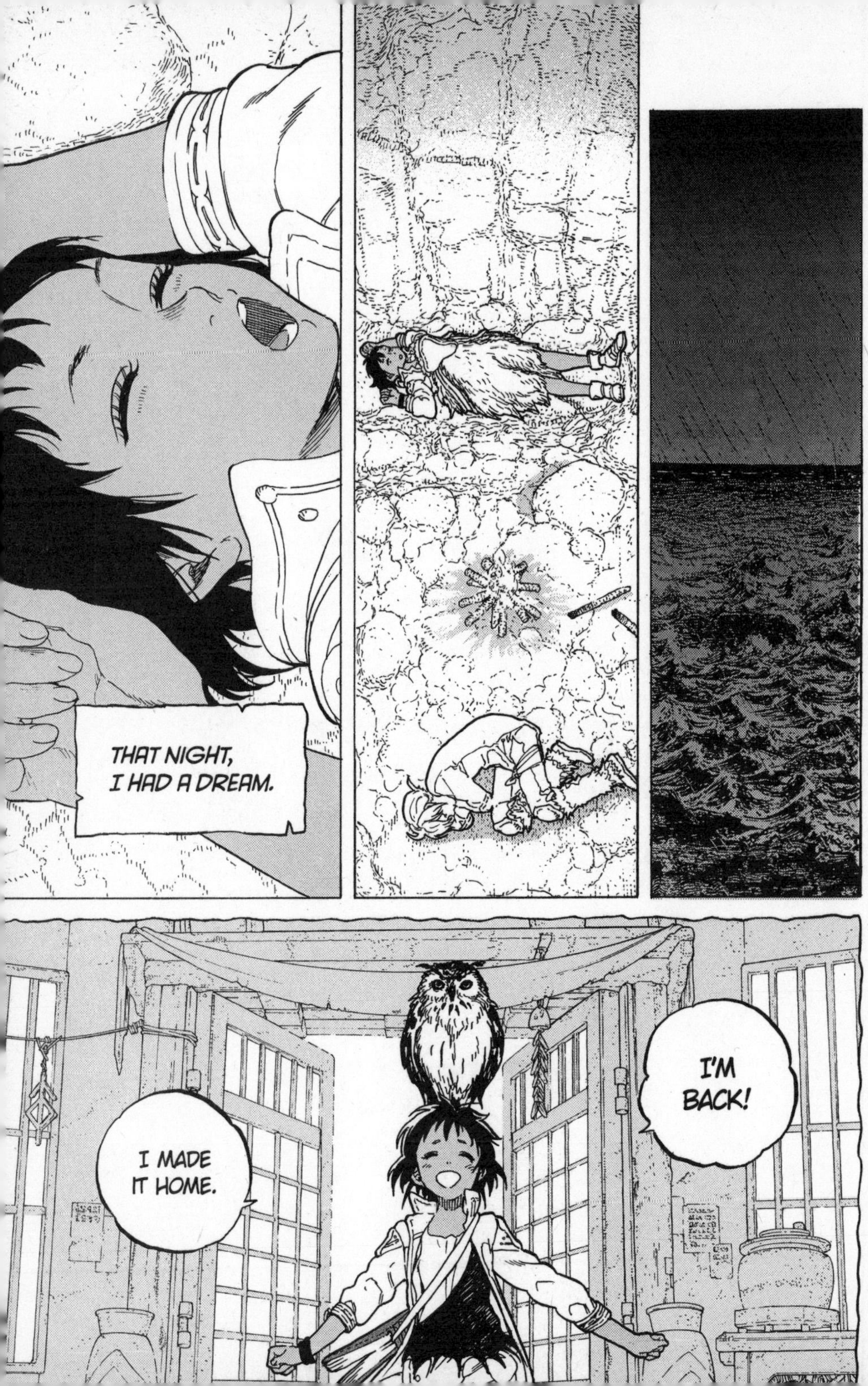
THAT NIGHT, I HAD A DREAM.
I'M BACK!
I MADE IT HOME.

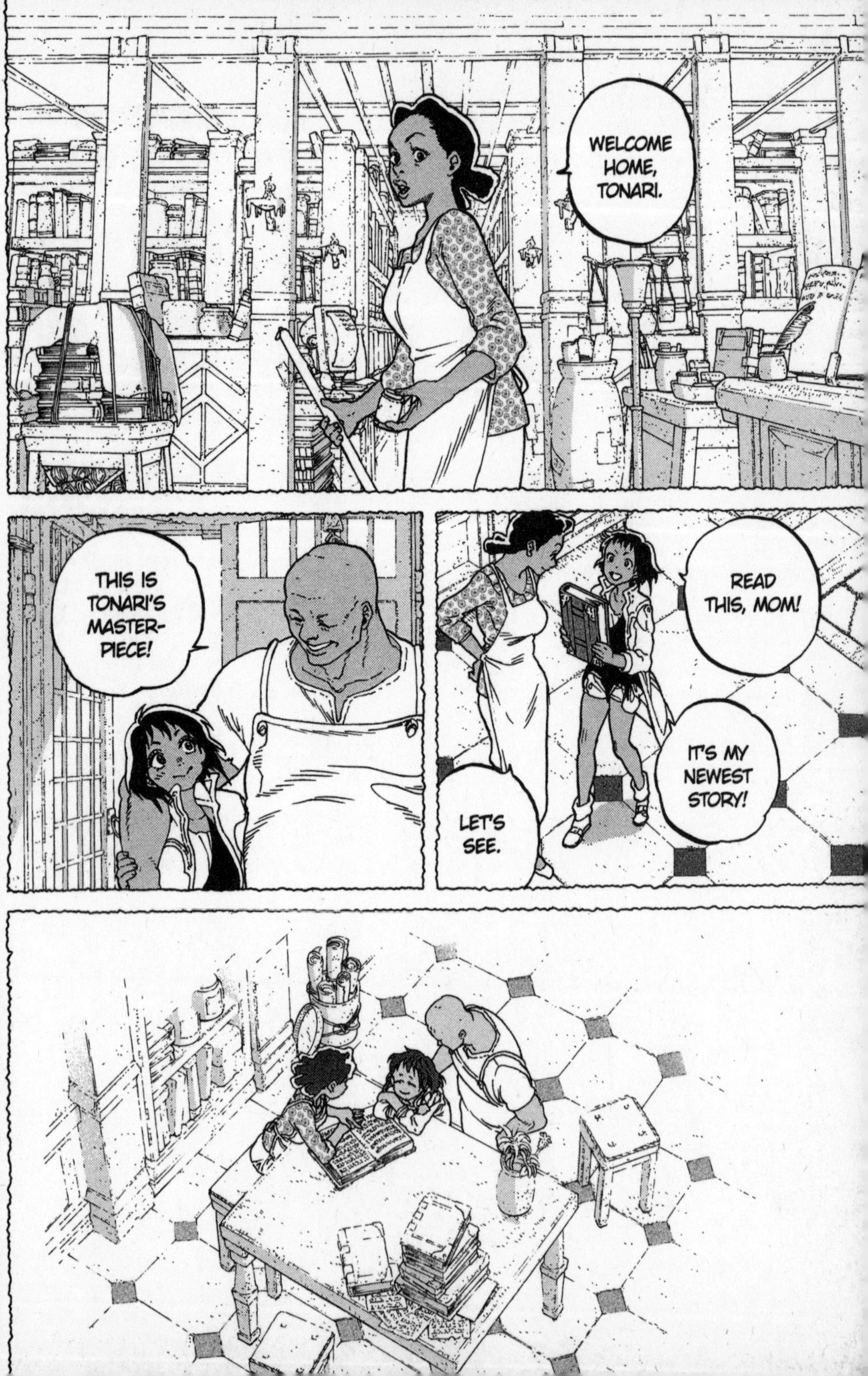
WELCOME HOME, TONARI.
READ THIS, MOM!
IT'S MY NEWEST STORY!
LET'S SEE.
THIS IS TONARI'S MASTER-PIECE!

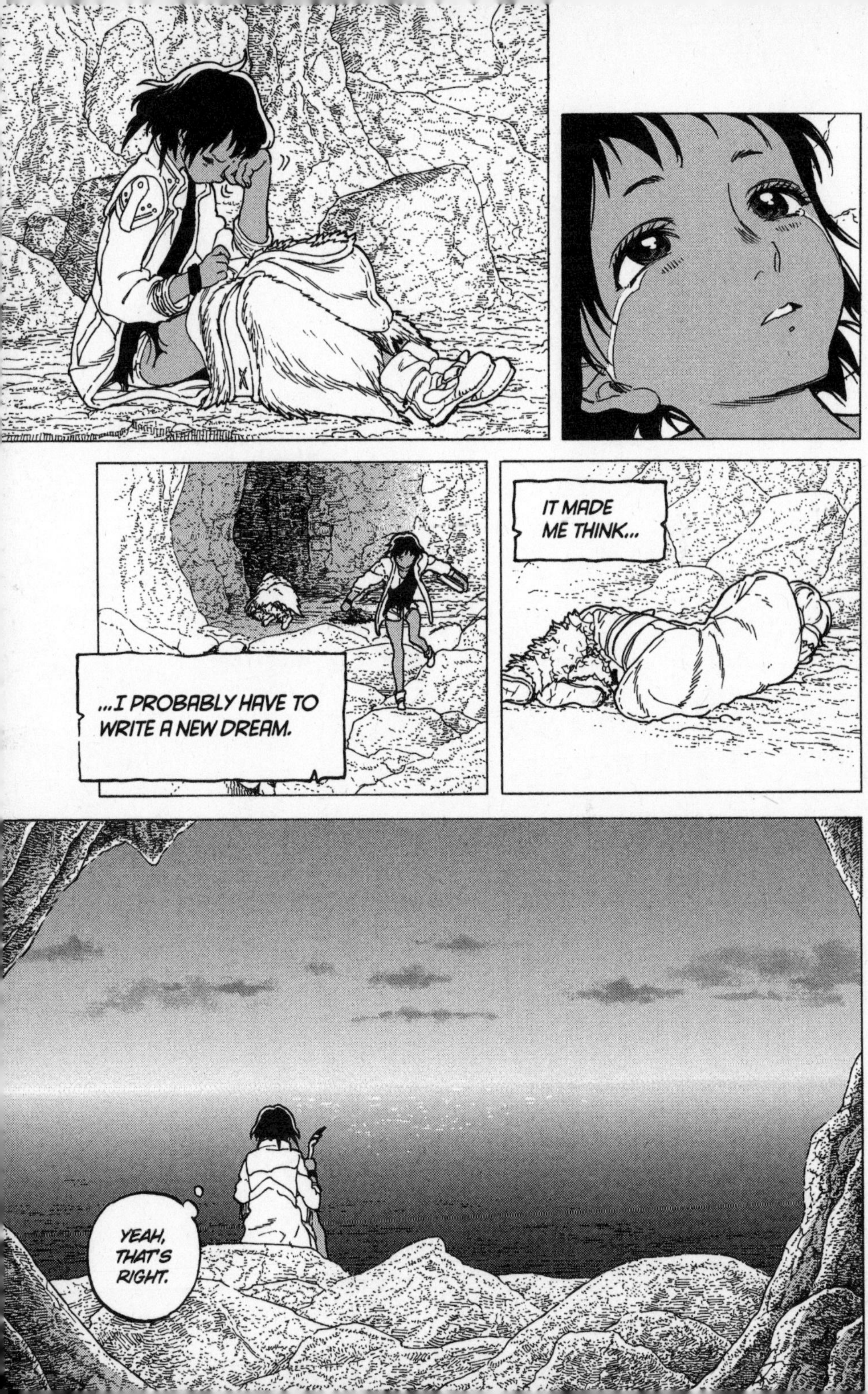
IT MADE ME THINK...
...I PROBABLY HAVE TO WRITE A NEW DREAM.
YEAH, THAT'S RIGHT.

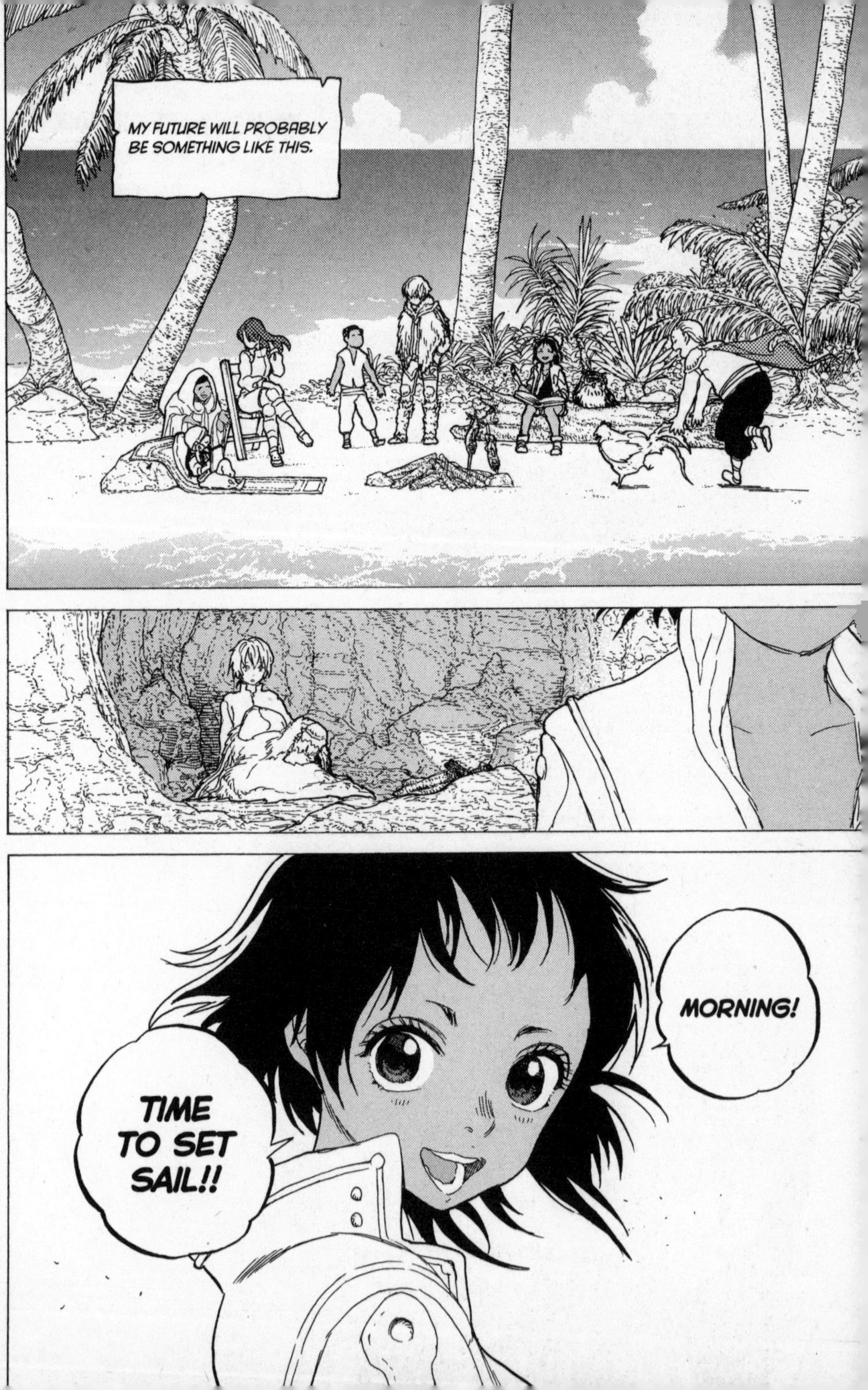
MY FUTURE WILL PROBABLY BE SOMETHING LIKE THIS.
MORNING!
TIME TO SET SAIL!!

#48 After the Selection

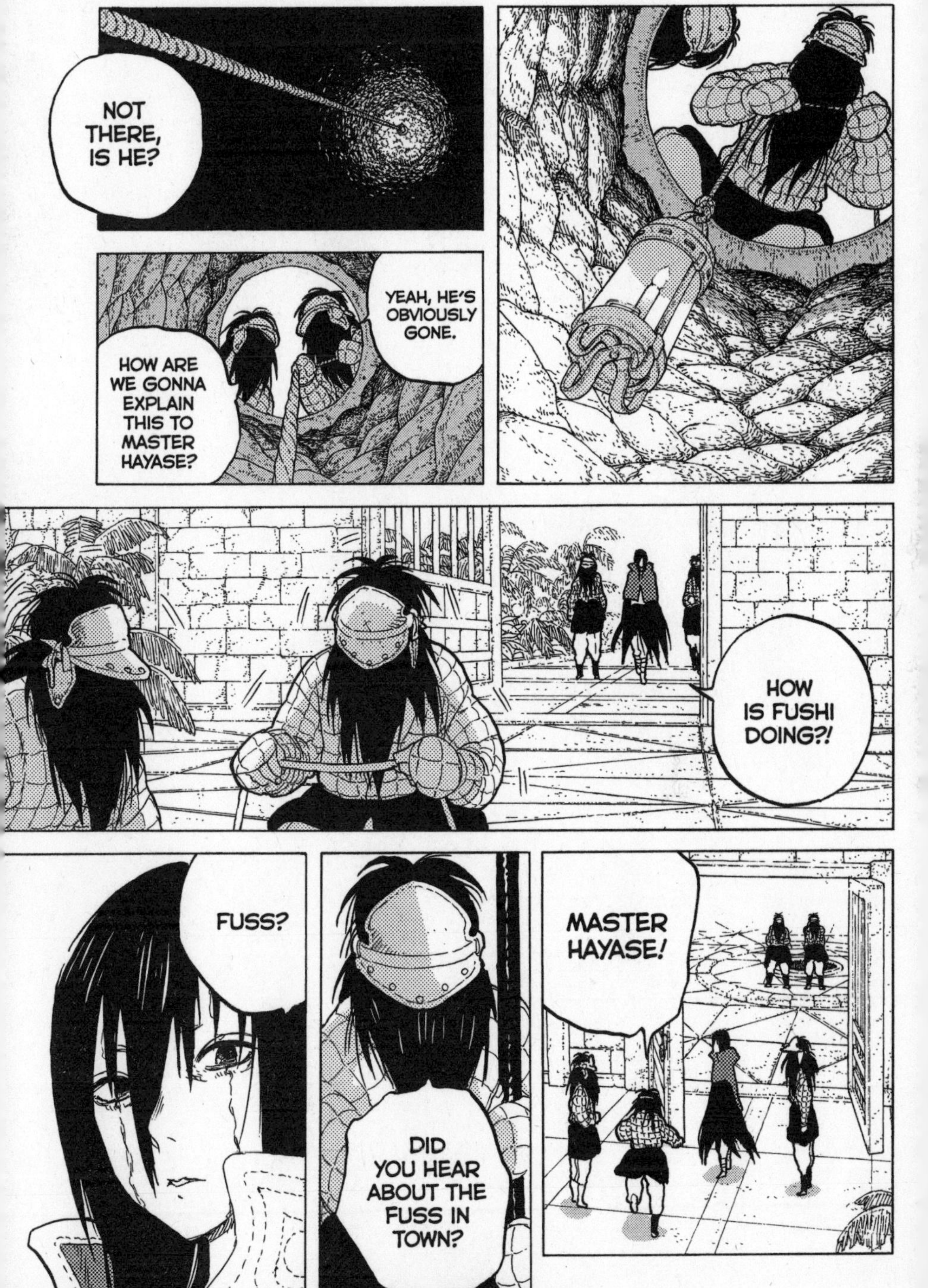
NOT THERE, IS HE?
YEAH, HE'S OBVIOUSLY GONE.
HOW ARE WE GONNA EXPLAIN THIS TO MASTER HAYASE?
HOW IS FUSHI DOING?!
MASTER HAYASE!
DID YOU HEAR ABOUT THE FUSS IN TOWN?
FUSS?

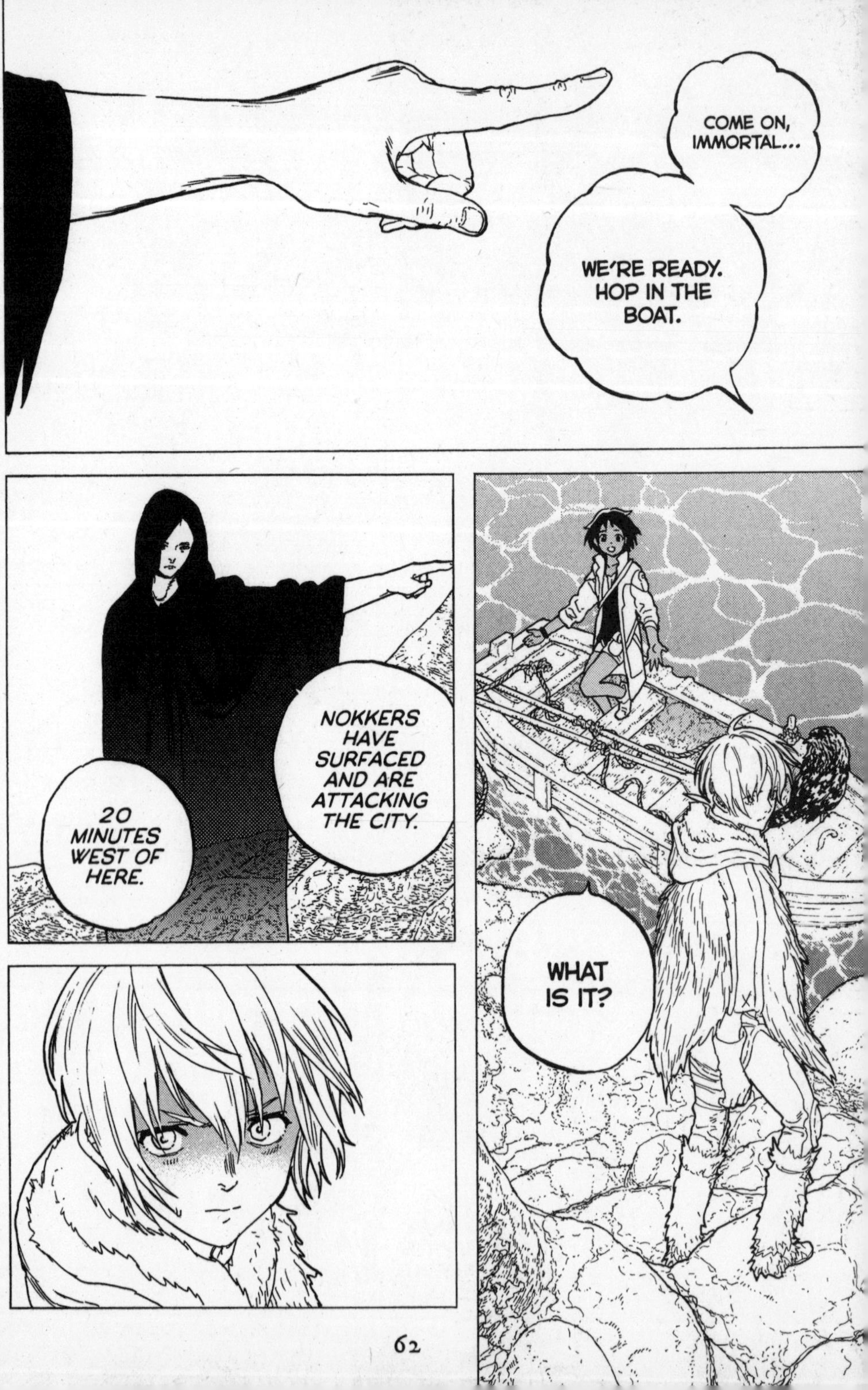
COME ON, IMMORTAL...
WE'RE READY. HOP IN THE BOAT.
WHAT IS IT?
NOKKERS HAVE SURFACED AND ARE ATTACKING THE CITY.
20 MINUTES WEST OF HERE.

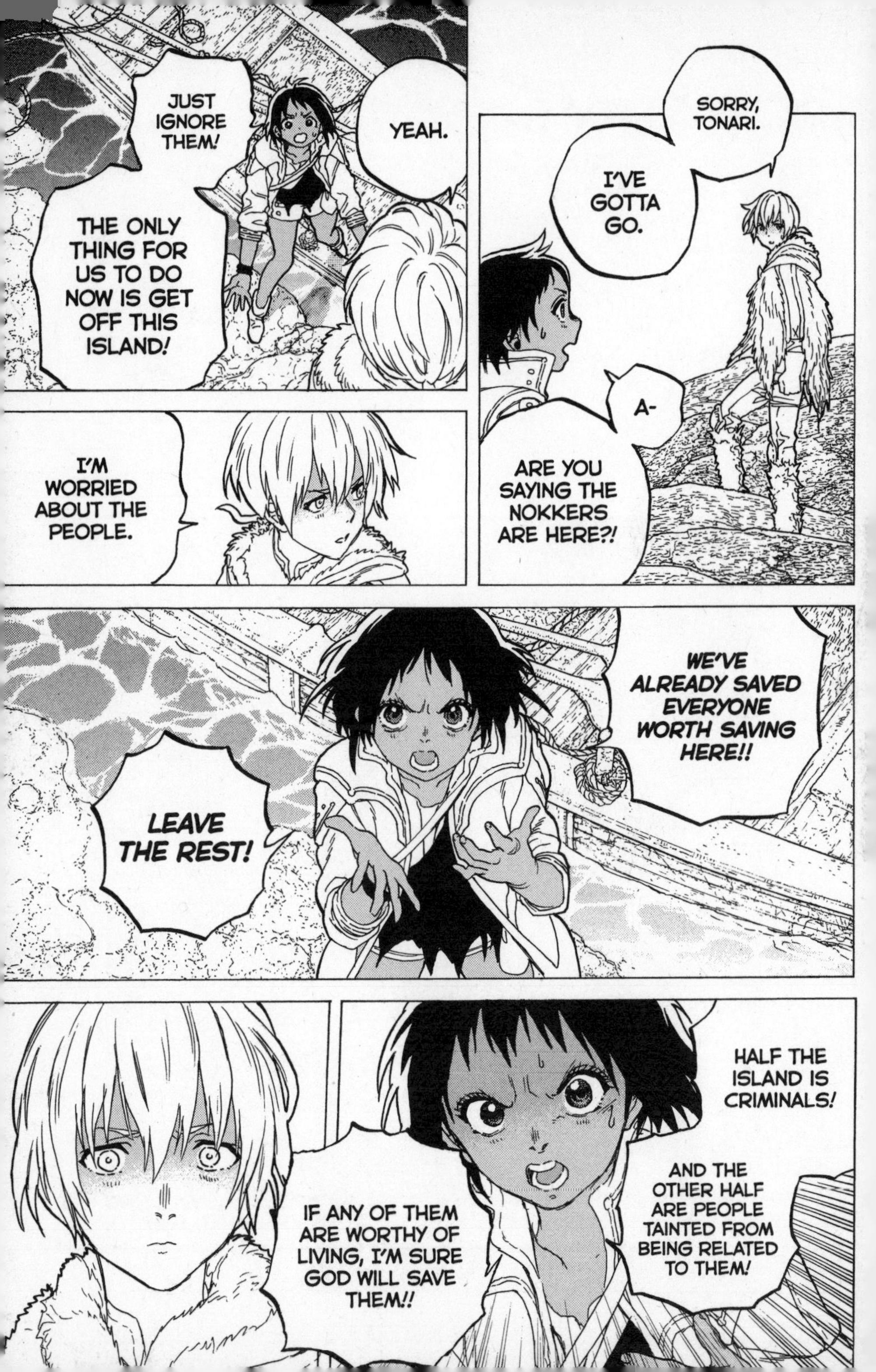
JUST IGNORE THEM!
YEAH.
THE ONLY THING FOR US TO DO NOW IS GET OFF THIS ISLAND!
I'M WORRIED ABOUT THE PEOPLE.
SORRY, TONARI.
I'VE GOTTA GO.
A-
ARE YOU SAYING THE NOKKERS ARE HERE?!
WE'VE ALREADY SAVED EVERYONE WORTH SAVING HERE!!
LEAVE THE REST!
HALF THE ISLAND IS CRIMINALS!
AND THE OTHER HALF ARE PEOPLE TAINTED FROM BEING RELATED TO THEM!
IF ANY OF THEM ARE WORTHY OF LIVING, I'M SURE GOD WILL SAVE THEM!!

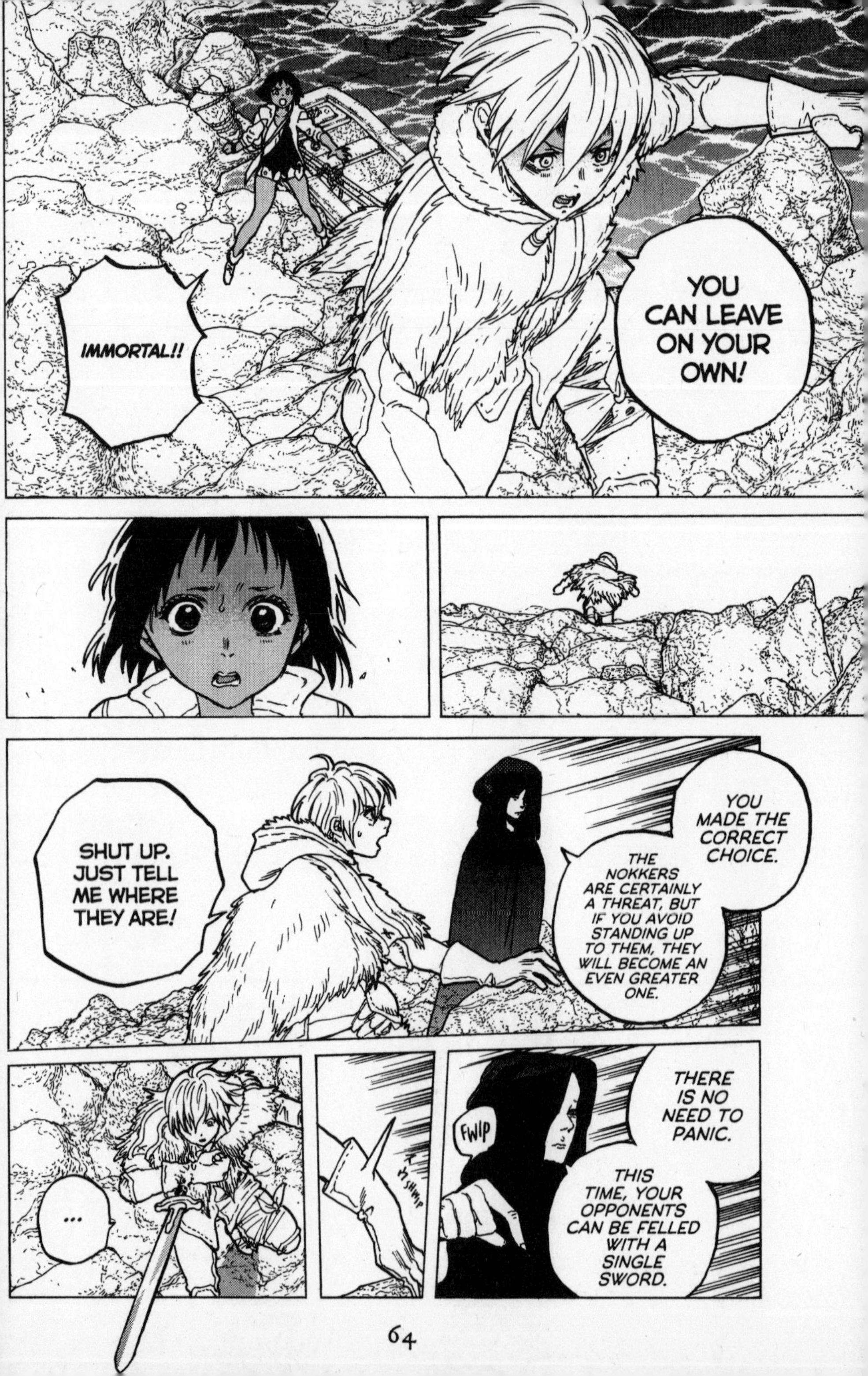
YOU CAN LEAVE ON YOUR OWN!
IMMORTAL!!
YOU MADE THE CORRECT CHOICE.
THE NOKKERS ARE CERTAINLY A THREAT, BUT IF YOU AVOID STANDING UP TO THEM, THEY WILL BECOME AN EVEN GREATER ONE.
SHUT UP. JUST TELL ME WHERE THEY ARE!
THERE IS NO NEED TO PANIC.
FWIP
THIS TIME, YOUR OPPONENTS CAN BE FELLED WITH A SINGLE SWORD.
...

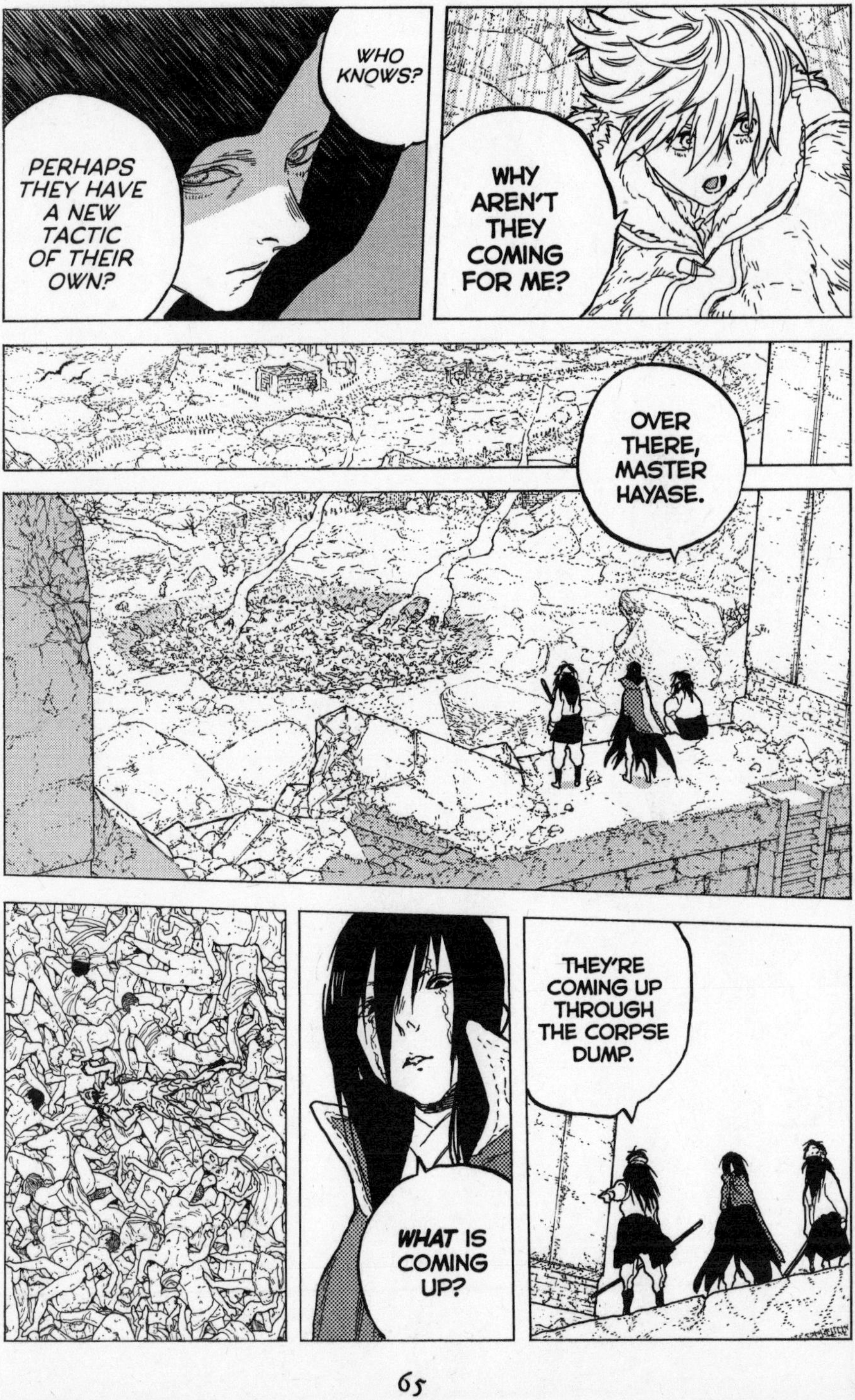
WHY AREN'T THEY COMING FOR ME?
WHO KNOWS?
PERHAPS THEY HAVE A NEW TACTIC OF THEIR OWN?
OVER THERE, MASTER HAYASE.
THEY'RE COMING UP THROUGH THE CORPSE DUMP.
WHAT IS COMING UP?

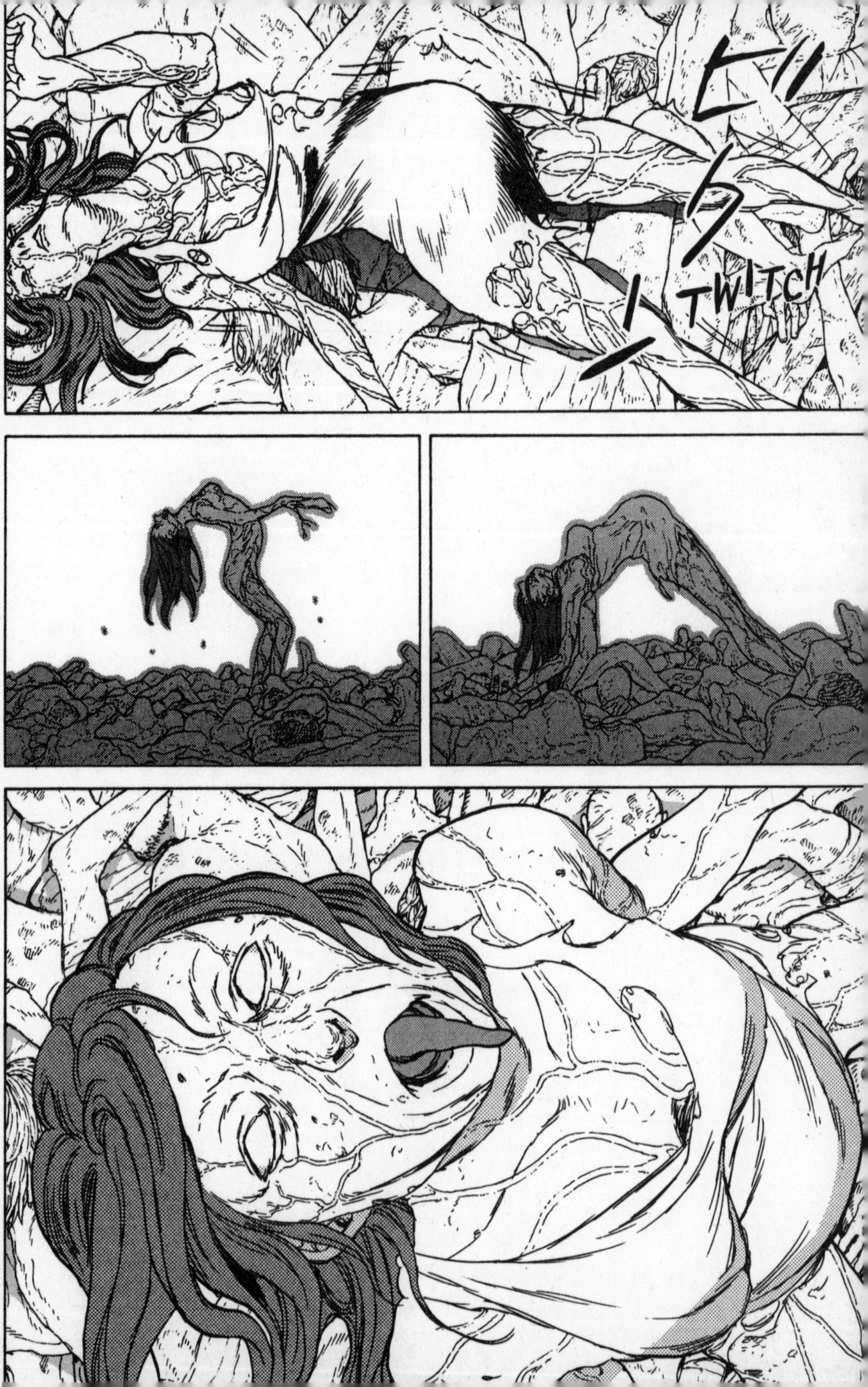
TWITCH

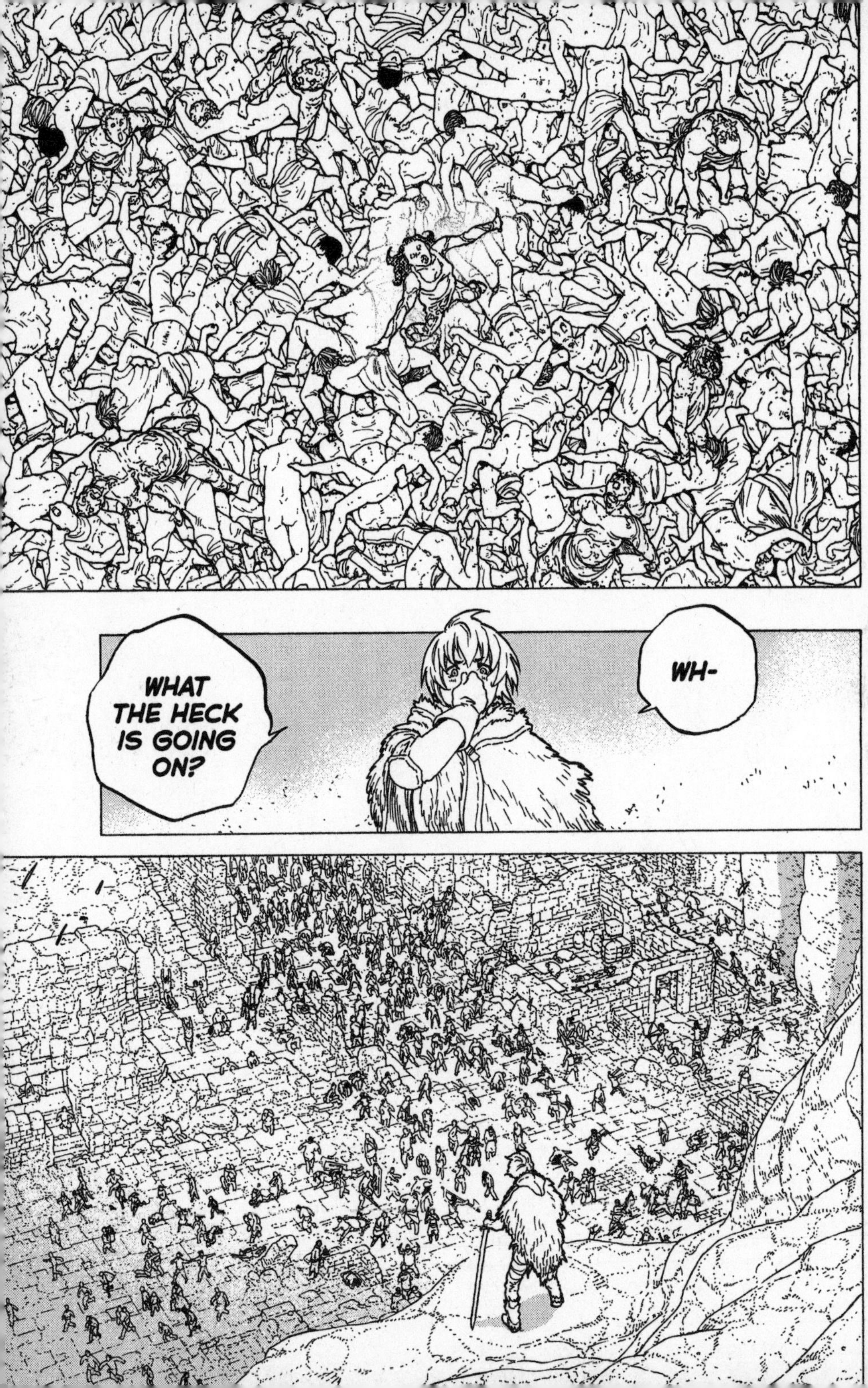
WH-
WHAT THE HECK IS GOING ON?

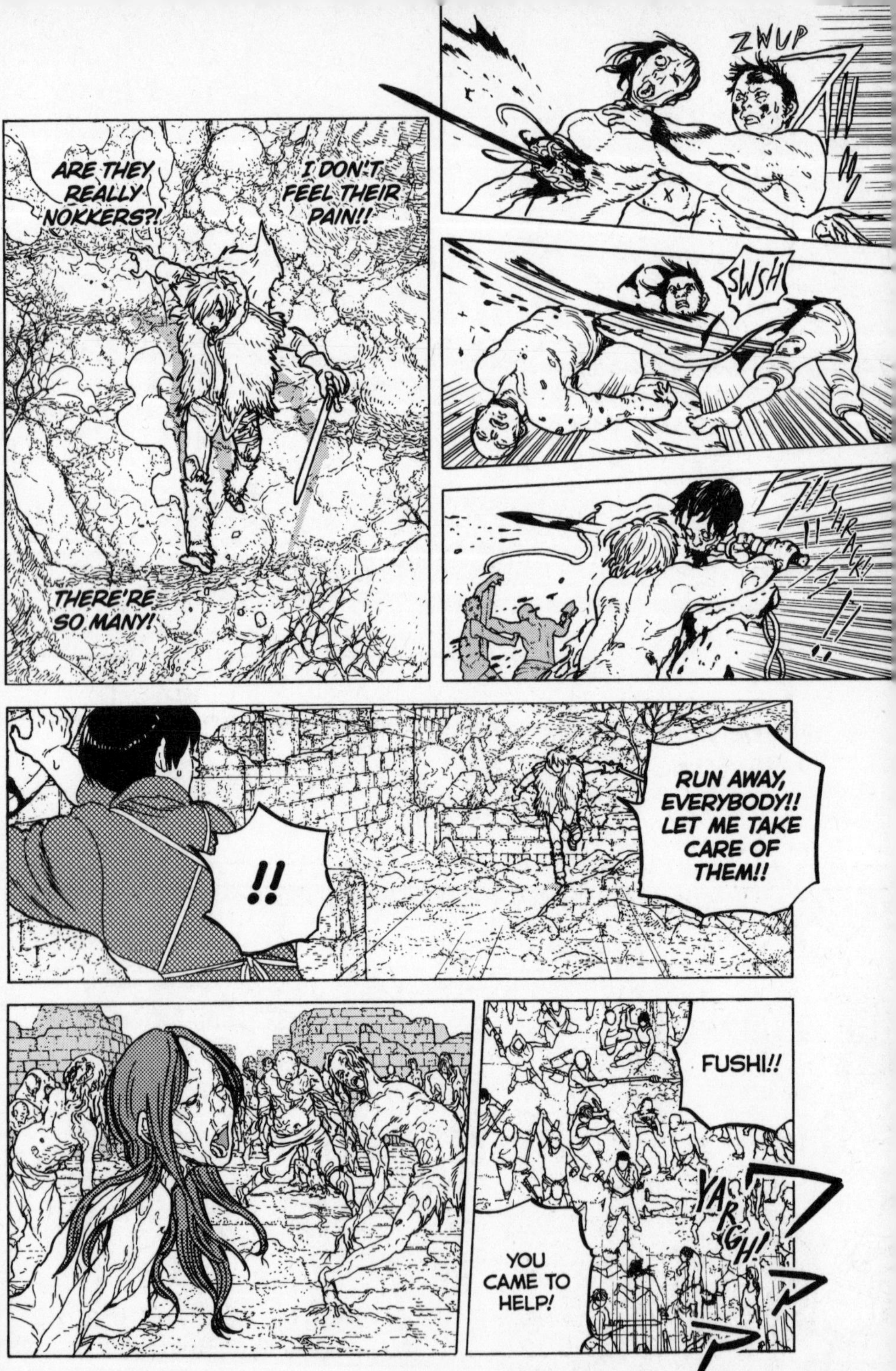
ZWUP
SWSH
SHRACK!
ARE THEY REALLY NOKKERS?!
I DON'T FEEL THEIR PAIN!!
THERE'RE SO MANY!
RUN AWAY, EVERYBODY!! LET ME TAKE CARE OF THEM!!
!!
FUSHI!!
YARGH!
YOU CAME TO HELP!

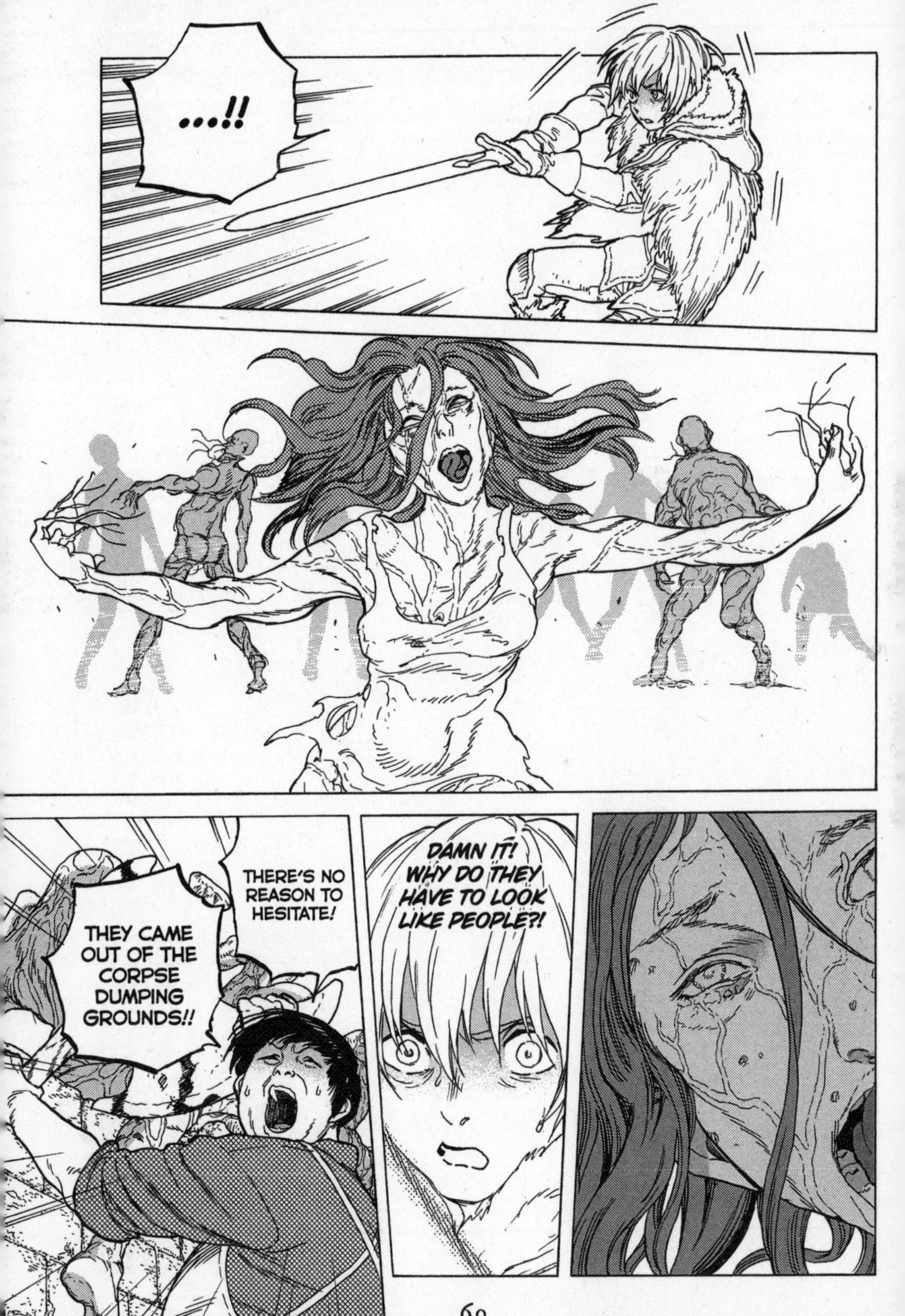
...!!
DAMN IT! WHY DO THEY HAVE TO LOOK LIKE PEOPLE?!
THERE'S NO REASON TO HESITATE!
THEY CAME OUT OF THE CORPSE DUMPING GROUNDS!!

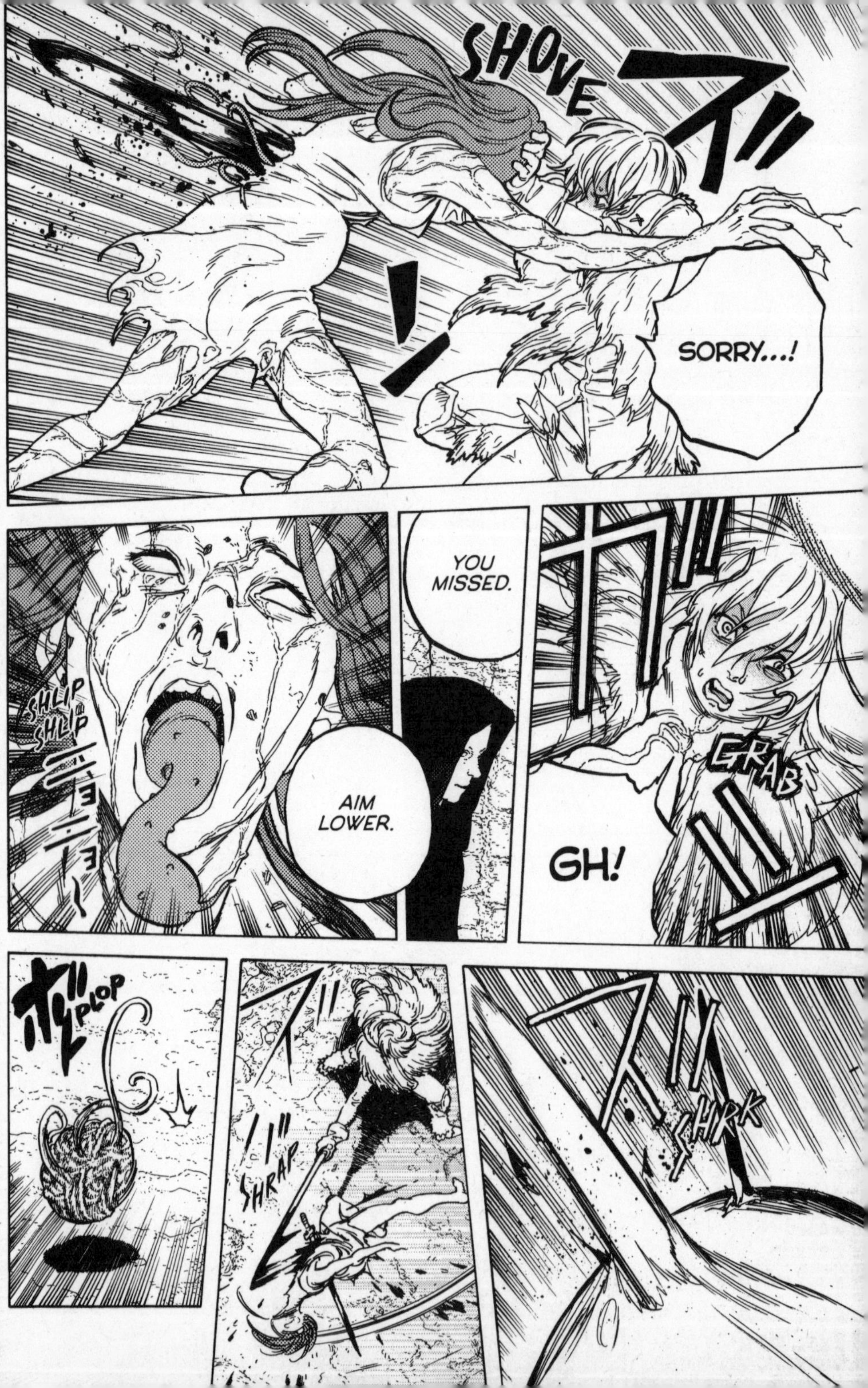
SHOVE
SORRY...!
GRAB
GH!
YOU MISSED.
AIM LOWER.
SHLIP SHLIP
SHRK
SHRAP
PLOP

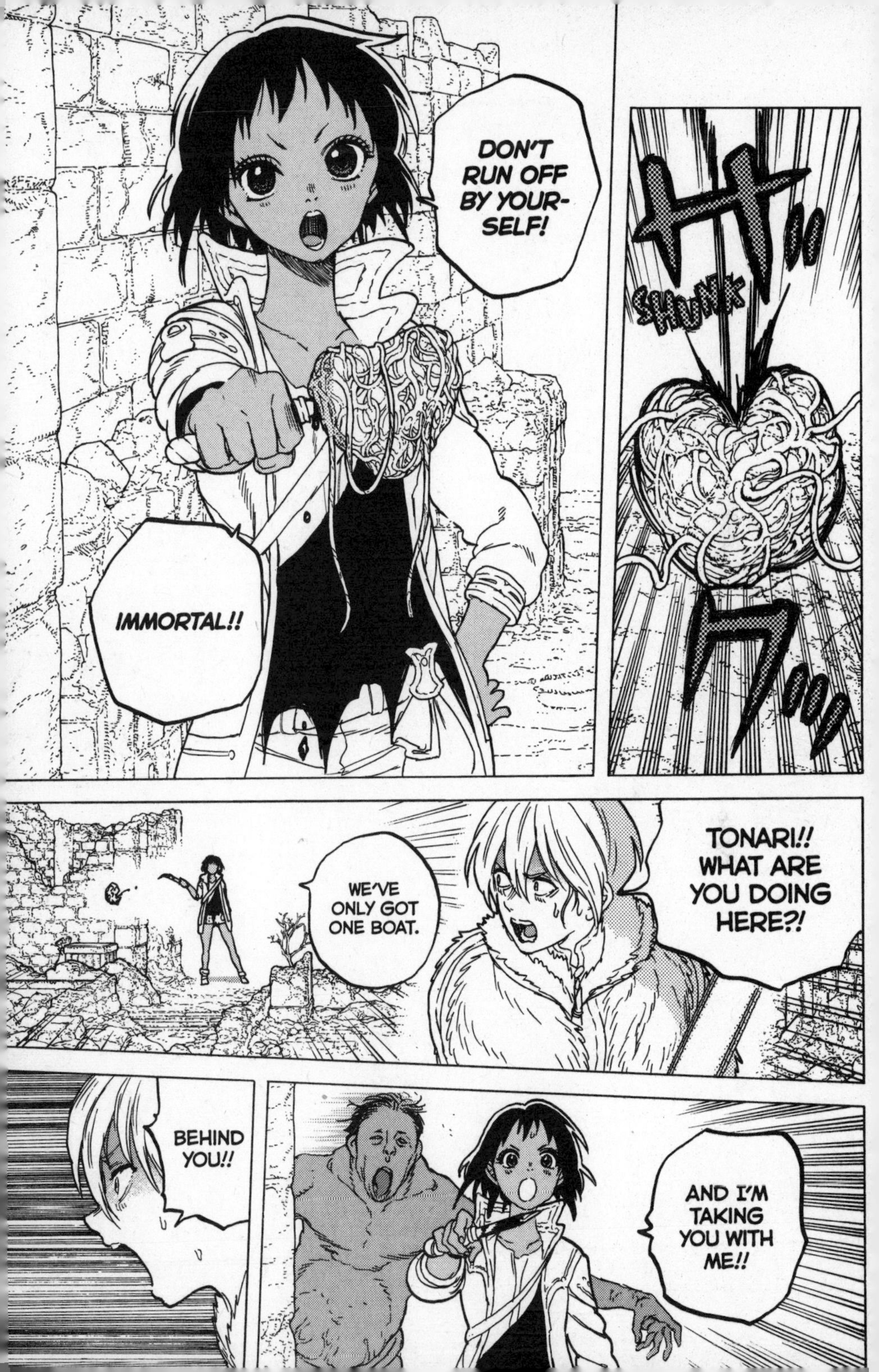
SHUNK
DON'T RUN OFF BY YOURSELF!
IMMORTAL!!
TONARI!! WHAT ARE YOU DOING HERE?!
WE'VE ONLY GOT ONE BOAT.
AND I'M TAKING YOU WITH ME!!
BEHIND YOU!!

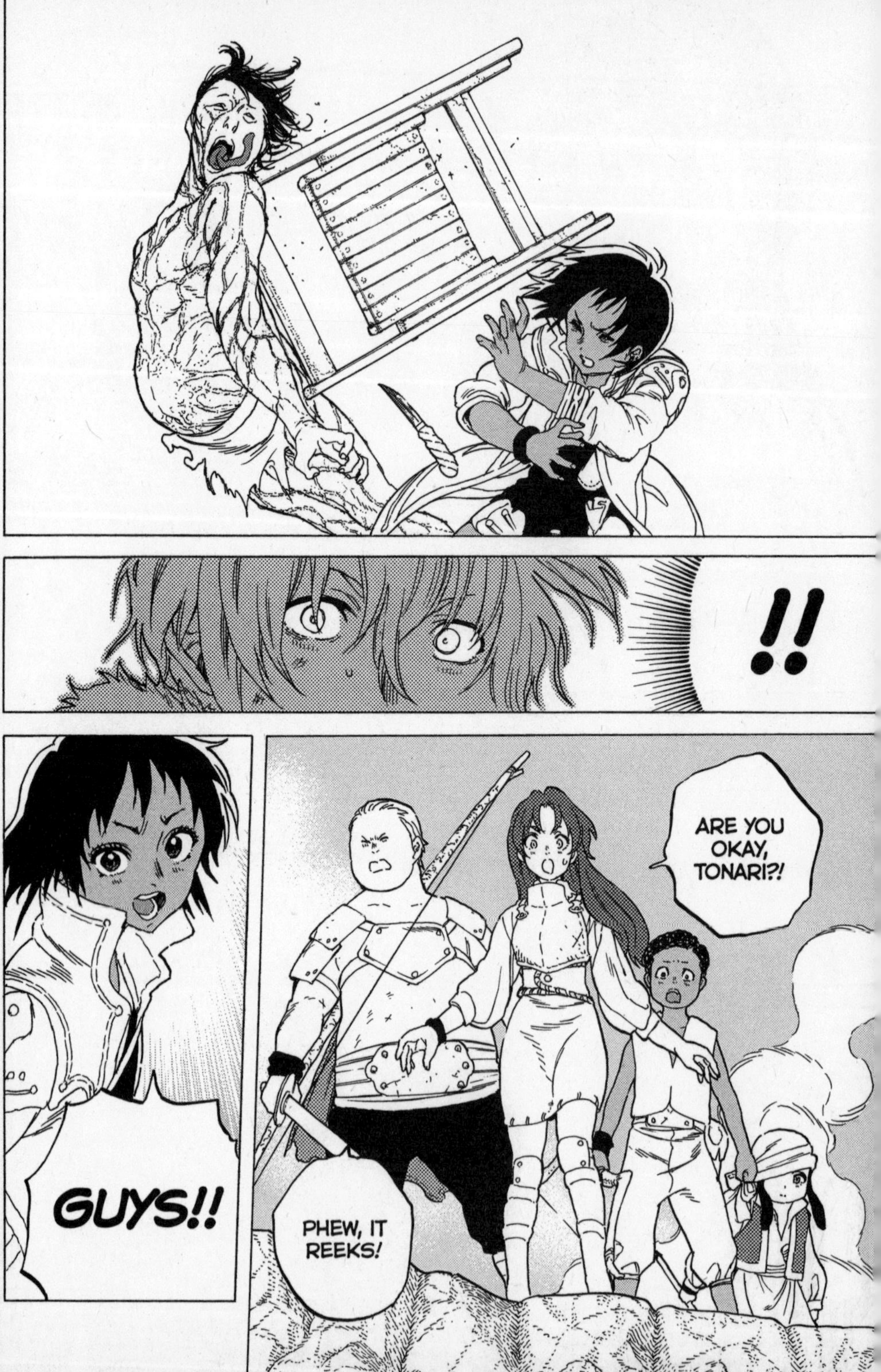
!!
ARE YOU OKAY, TONARI?!
PHEW, IT REEKS!
GUYS!!

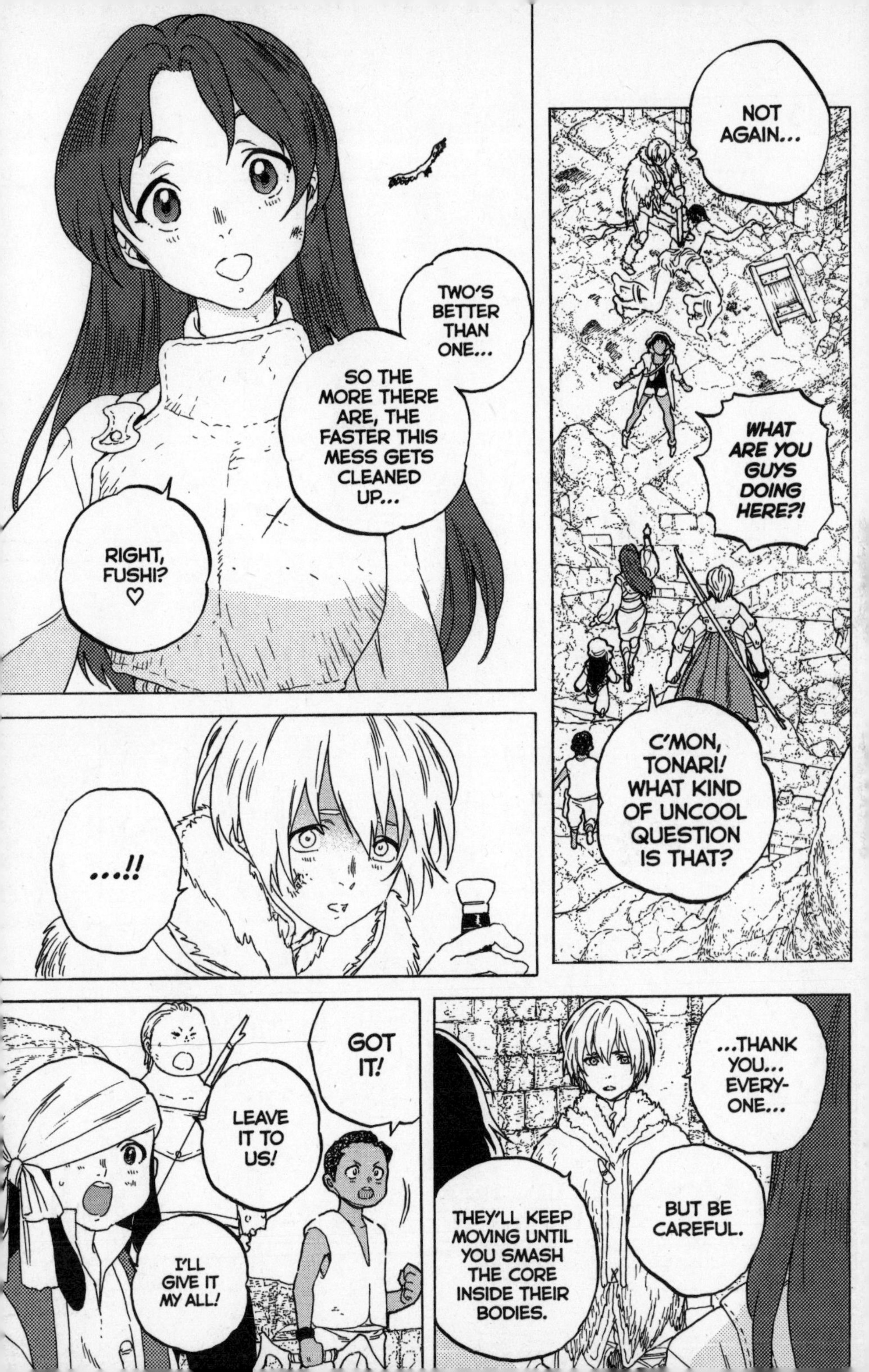
NOT AGAIN...
WHAT ARE YOU GUYS DOING HERE?!
C'MON, TONARI! WHAT KIND OF UNCOOL QUESTION IS THAT?
TWO'S BETTER THAN ONE...
SO THE MORE THERE ARE, THE FASTER THIS MESS GETS CLEANED UP...
RIGHT, FUSHI? ♡
...!!
...THANK YOU... EVERY-ONE...
BUT BE CAREFUL.
THEY'LL KEEP MOVING UNTIL YOU SMASH THE CORE INSIDE THEIR BODIES.
GOT IT!
LEAVE IT TO US!
I'LL GIVE IT MY ALL!

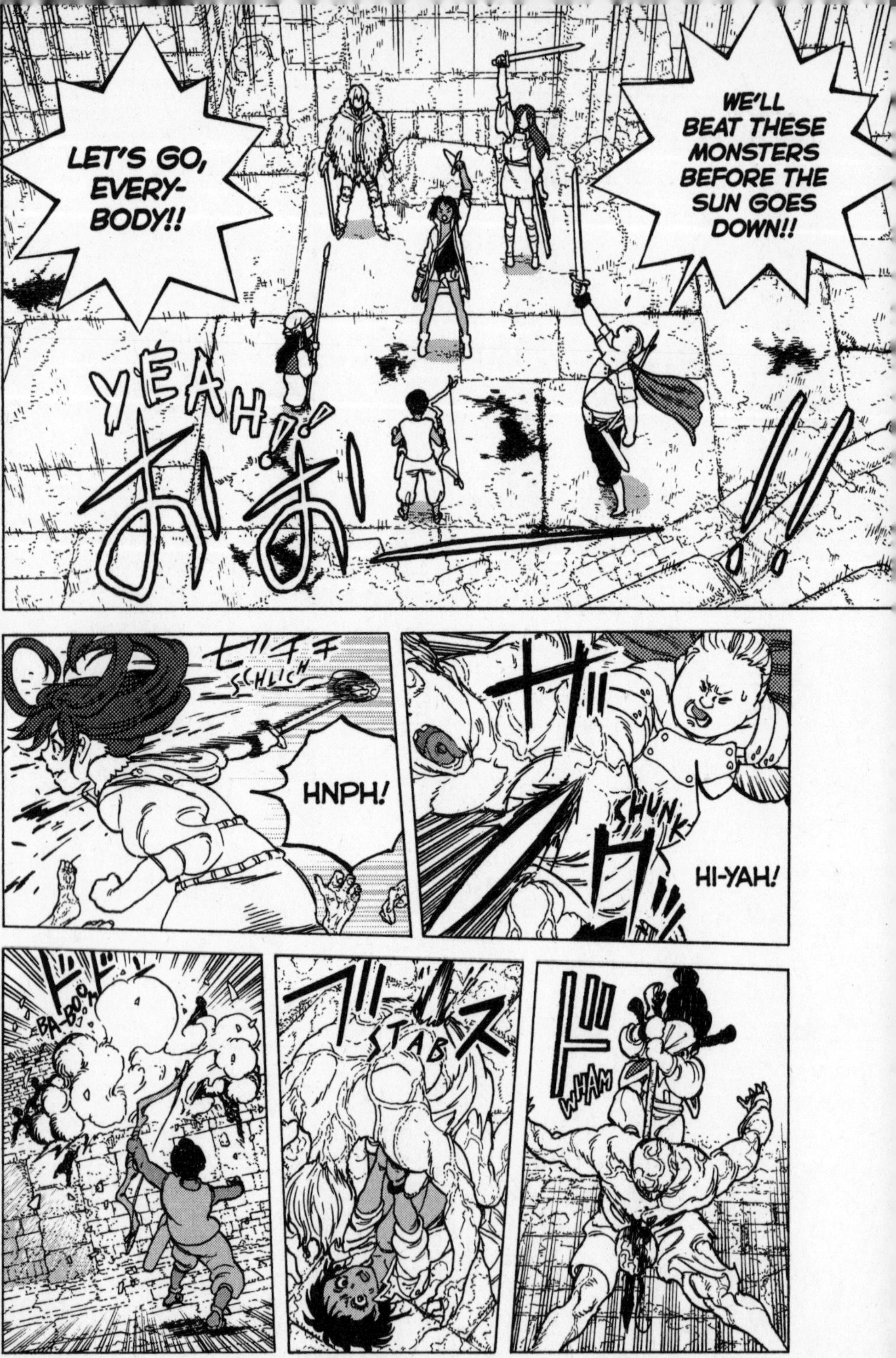
WE'LL BEAT THESE MONSTERS BEFORE THE SUN GOES DOWN!!
LET'S GO, EVERY-BODY!!
YEAH!
SHUNK
HI-YAH!
SCHLICH
HNPH!
WHAM
STAB
BA-BOOM

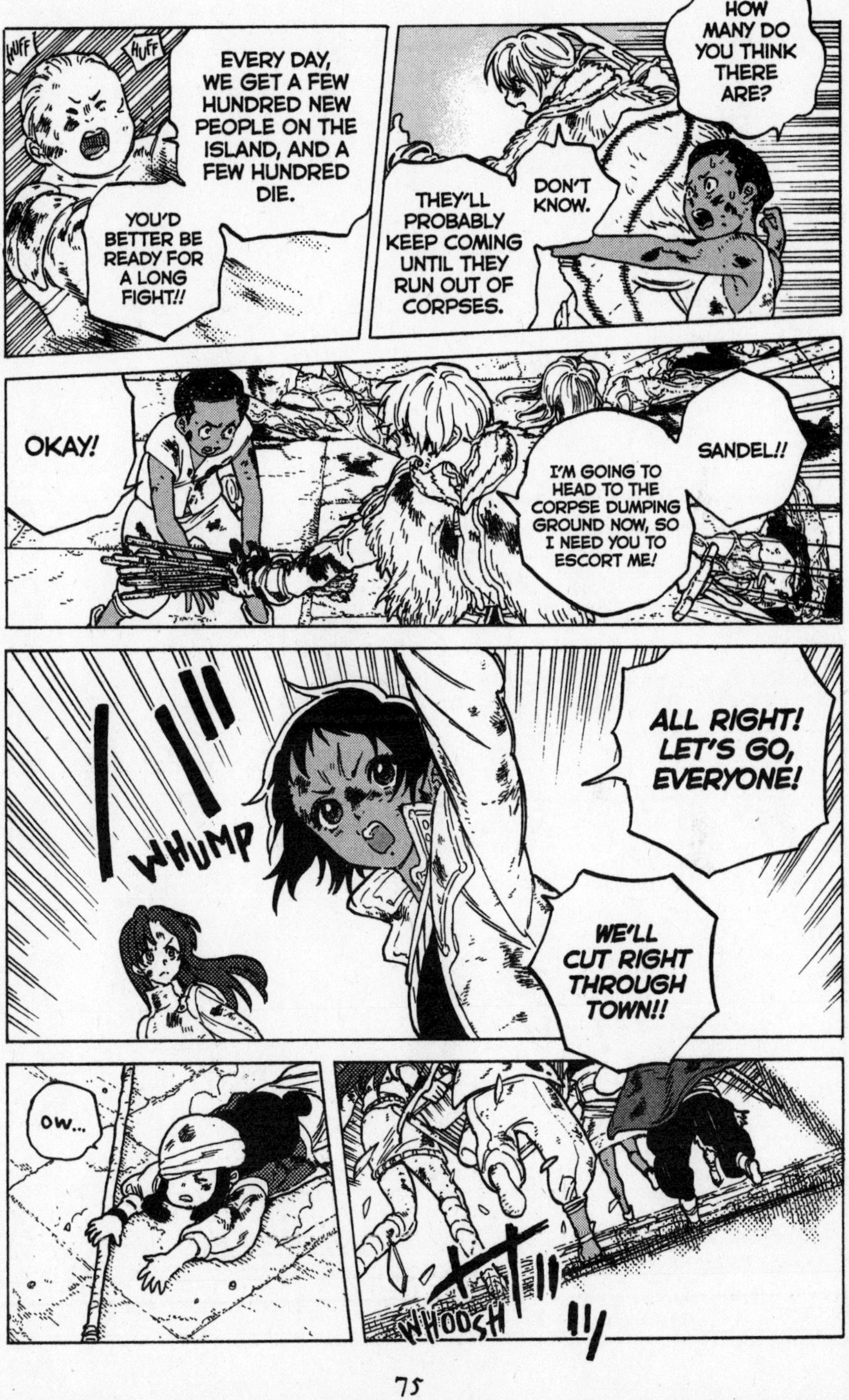
HOW MANY DO YOU THINK THERE ARE?
DON'T KNOW.
THEY'LL PROBABLY KEEP COMING UNTIL THEY RUN OUT OF CORPSES.
HUFF
HUFF
EVERY DAY, WE GET A FEW HUNDRED NEW PEOPLE ON THE ISLAND, AND A FEW HUNDRED DIE.
YOU'D BETTER BE READY FOR A LONG FIGHT!!
SANDEL!!
I'M GOING TO HEAD TO THE CORPSE DUMPING GROUND NOW, SO I NEED YOU TO ESCORT ME!
OKAY!
ALL RIGHT! LET'S GO, EVERYONE!
WE'LL CUT RIGHT THROUGH TOWN!!
WHUMP
WHOOSH
OW...

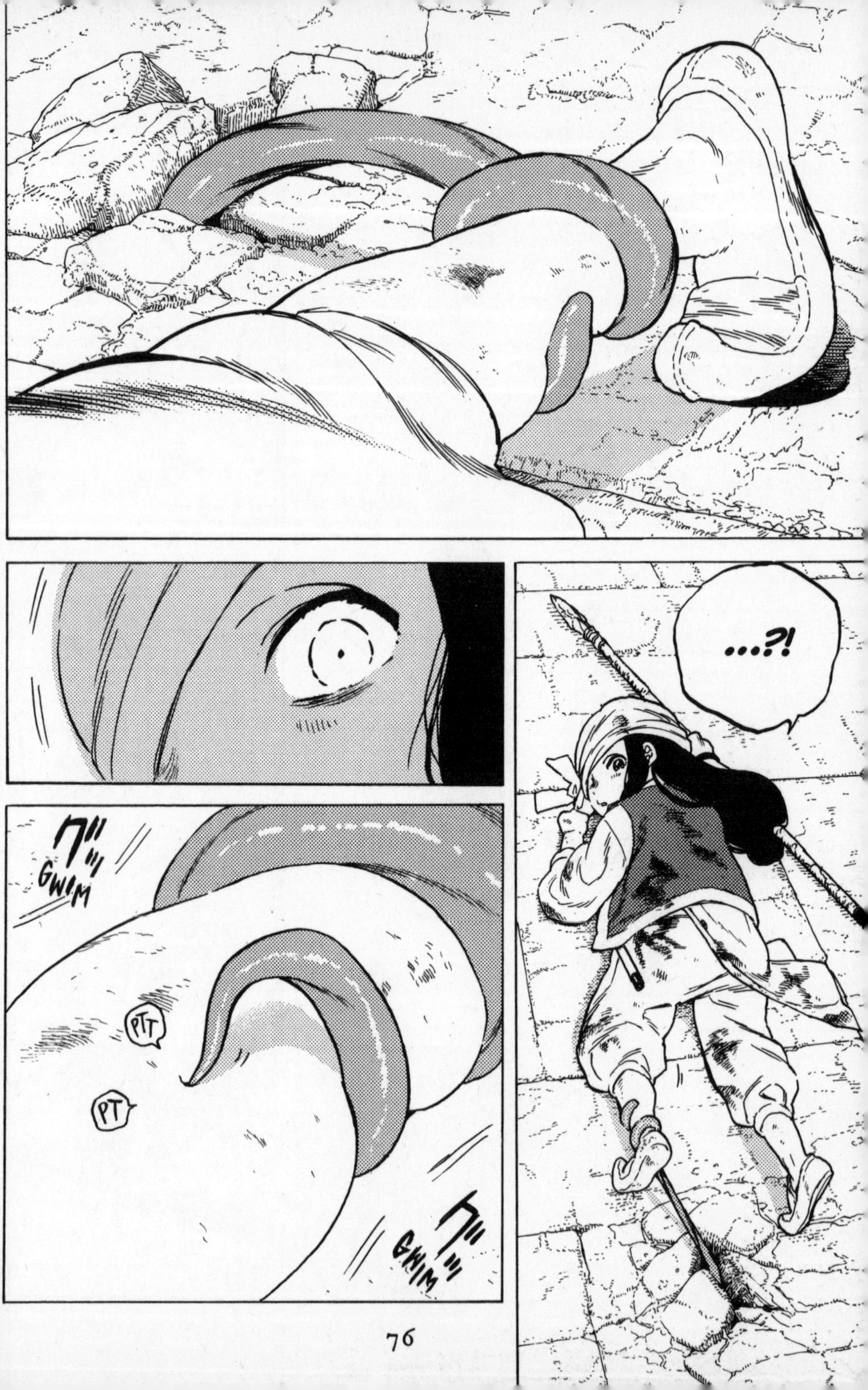
...?!
GWIM
PTT
PT
GWIM

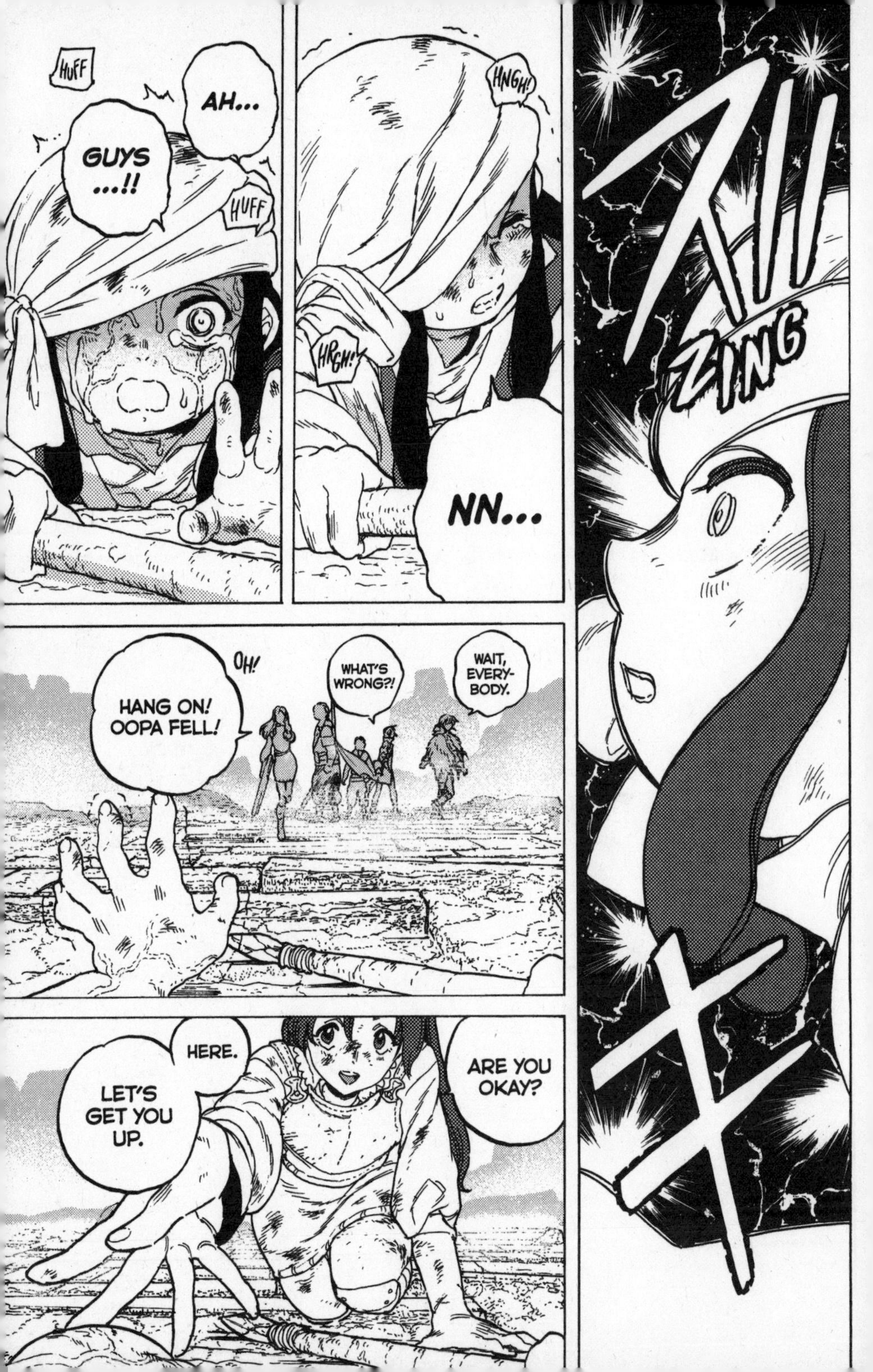
ZING
HNGH!
HRGH!
NN...
AH...
HUFF
GUYS ...!!
HUFF
WAIT, EVERY-BODY.
WHAT'S WRONG?!
OH!
HANG ON! OOPA FELL!
ARE YOU OKAY?
HERE.
LET'S GET YOU UP.

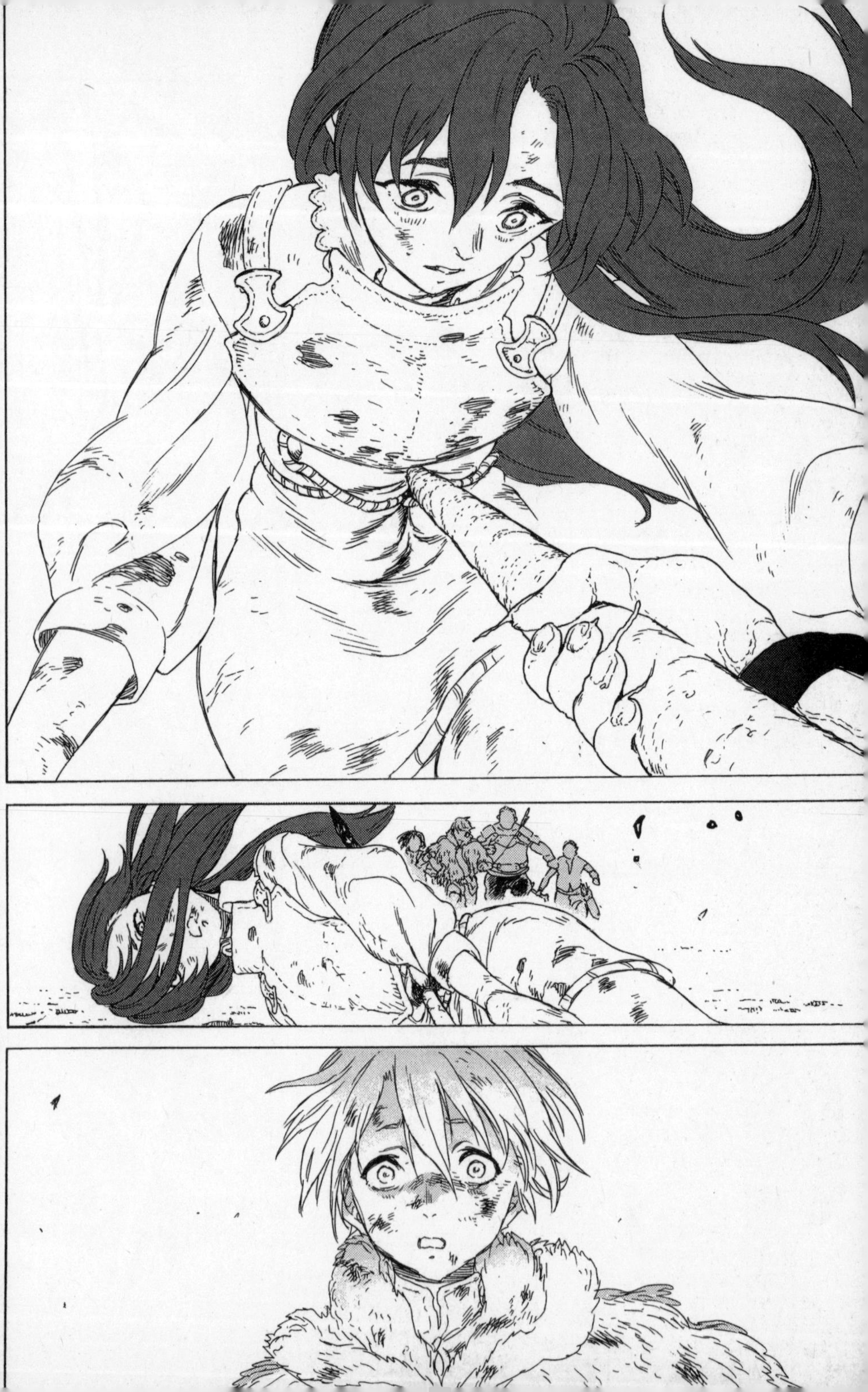

#49 To Move Forward

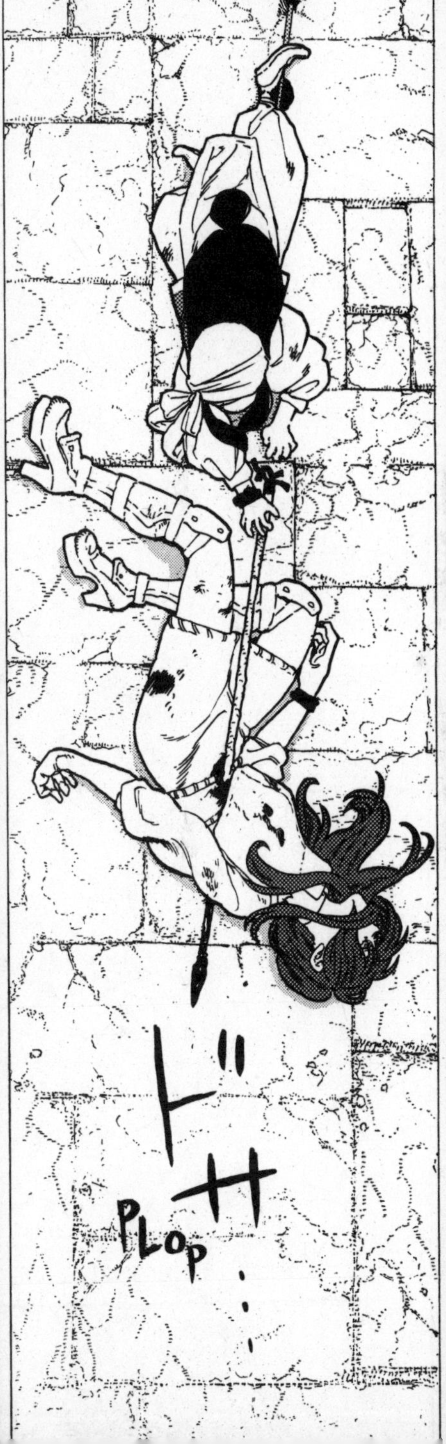
ドッ
PLOP

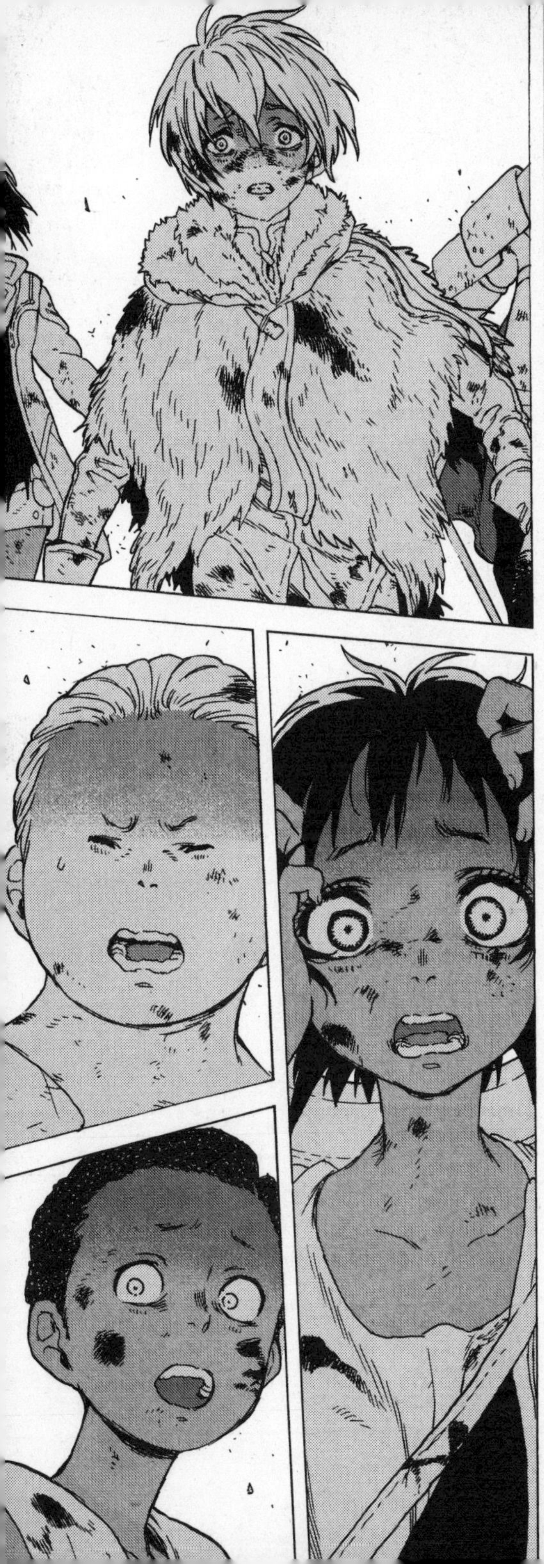

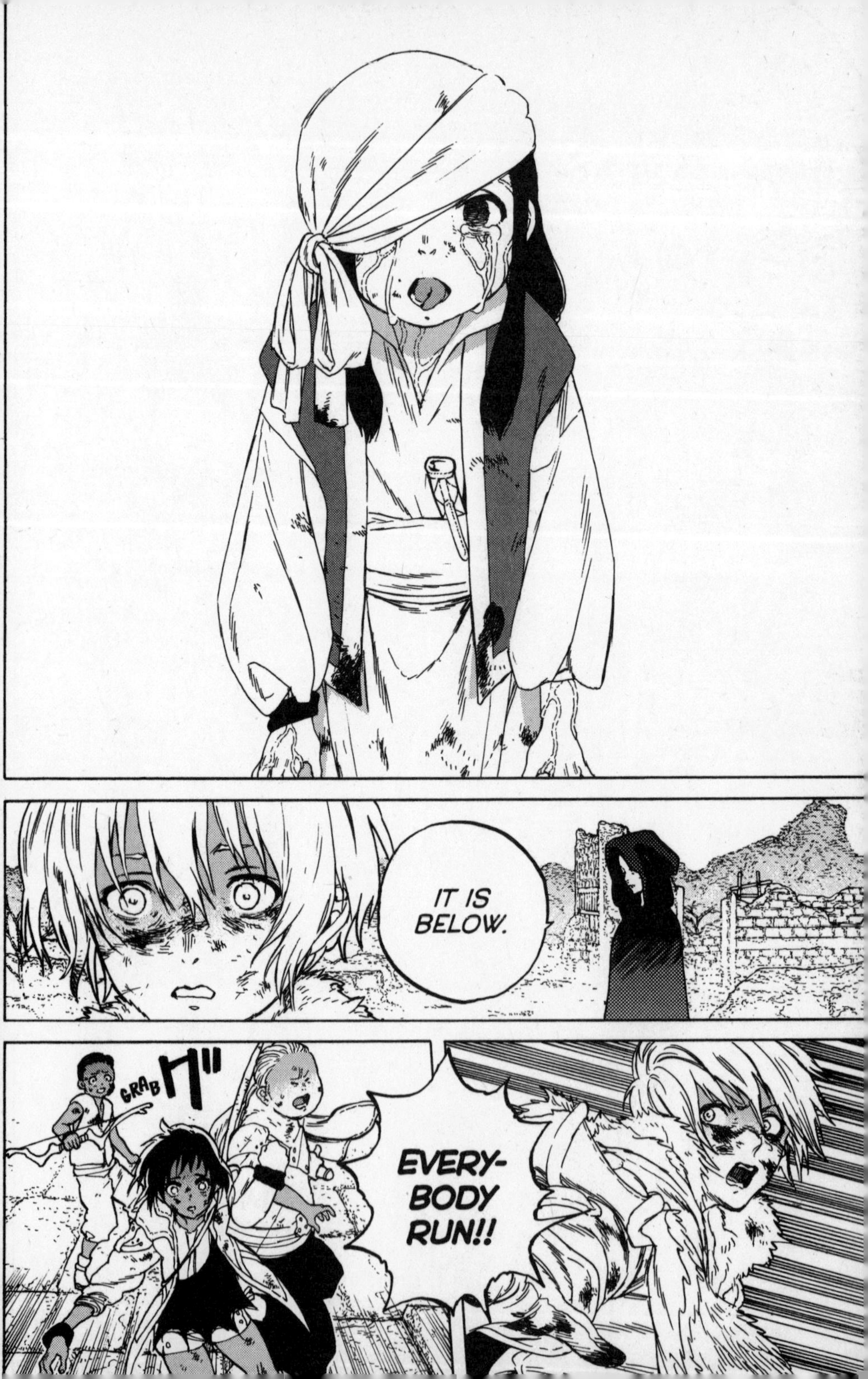
IT IS BELOW.
EVERY-BODY RUN!!
GRAB

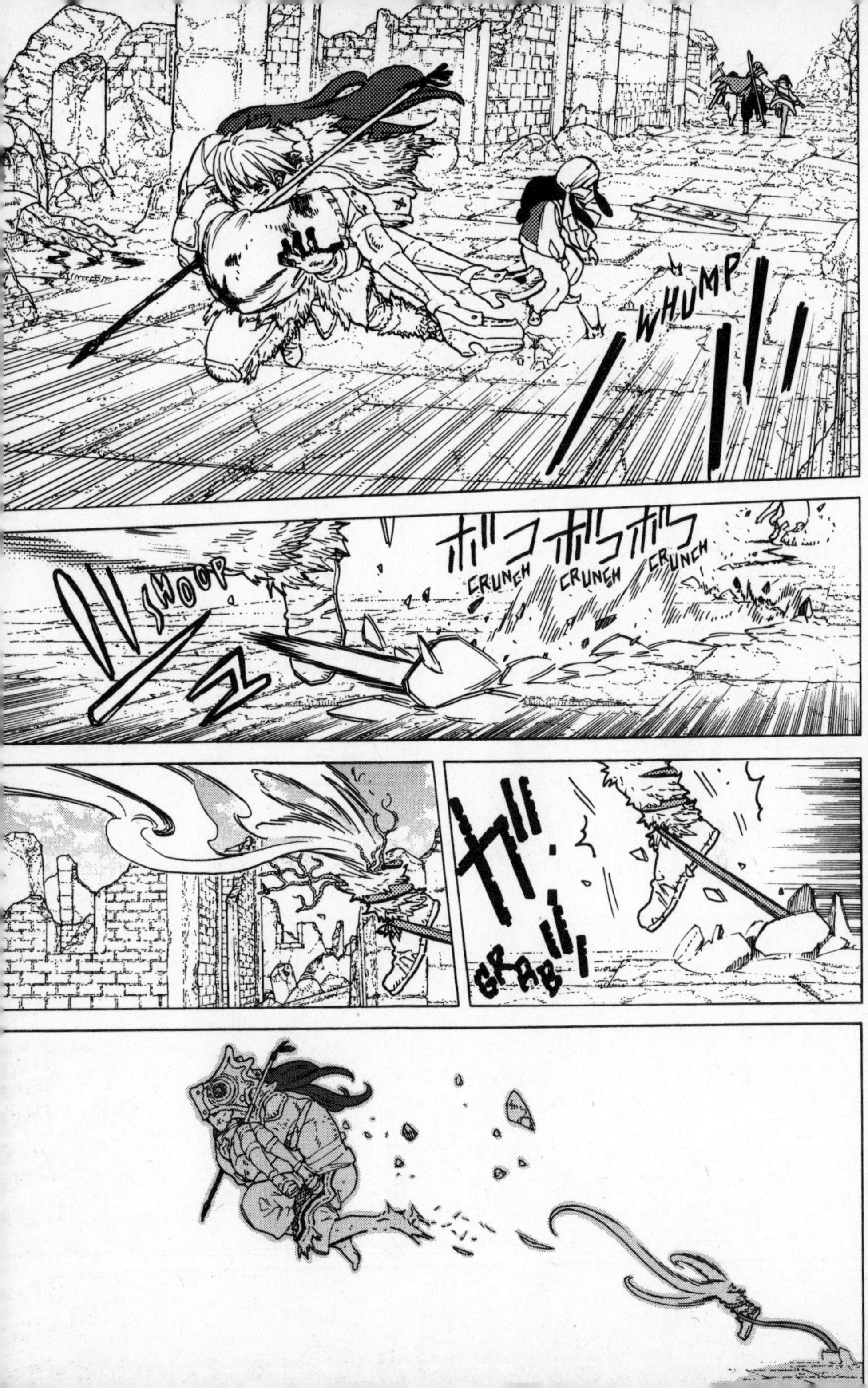
WHUMP
SWOOP
CRUNCH CRUNCH CRUNCH
GRAB

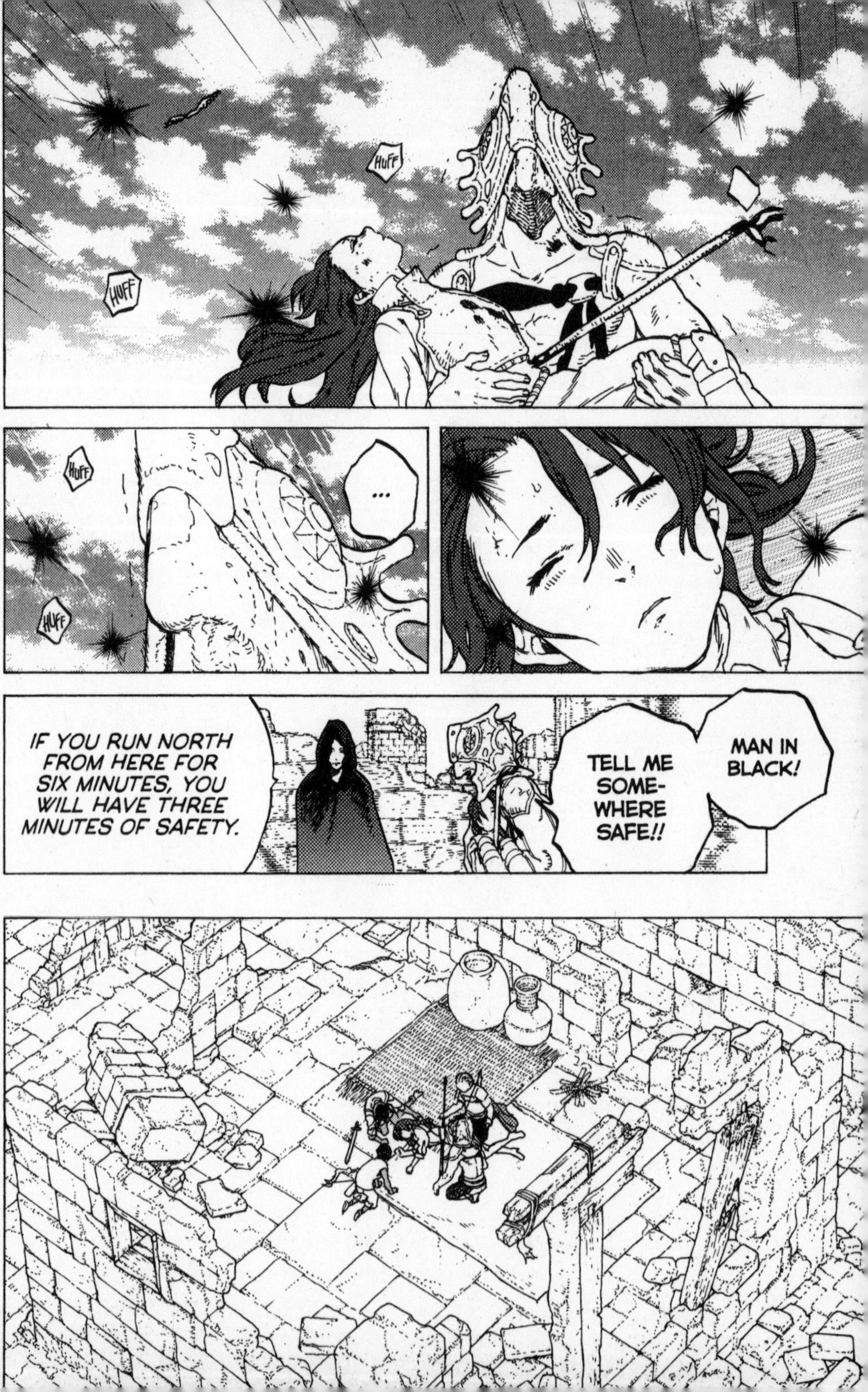
HUFF
HUFF
...
HUFF
HUFF
MAN IN BLACK!
TELL ME SOME-WHERE SAFE!!
IF YOU RUN NORTH FROM HERE FOR SIX MINUTES, YOU WILL HAVE THREE MINUTES OF SAFETY.

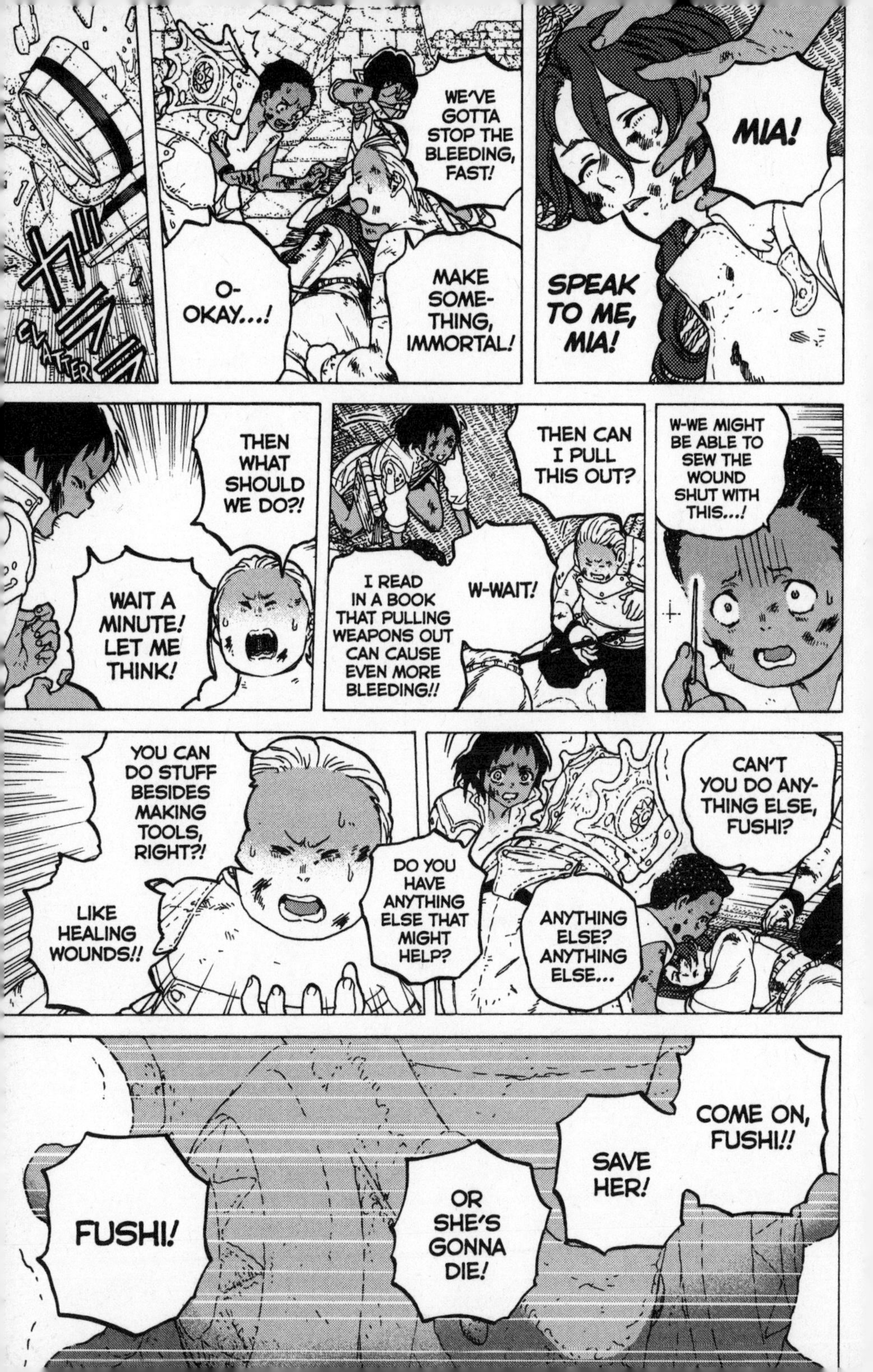
MIA!
SPEAK TO ME, MIA!
WE'VE GOTTA STOP THE BLEEDING, FAST!
MAKE SOME-THING, IMMORTAL!
O-OKAY...!
CLATTER
W-WE MIGHT BE ABLE TO SEW THE WOUND SHUT WITH THIS...!
THEN CAN I PULL THIS OUT?
W-WAIT!
I READ IN A BOOK THAT PULLING WEAPONS OUT CAN CAUSE EVEN MORE BLEEDING!!
THEN WHAT SHOULD WE DO?!
WAIT A MINUTE! LET ME THINK!
CAN'T YOU DO ANY-THING ELSE, FUSHI?
ANYTHING ELSE? ANYTHING ELSE...
DO YOU HAVE ANYTHING ELSE THAT MIGHT HELP?
YOU CAN DO STUFF BESIDES MAKING TOOLS, RIGHT?!
LIKE HEALING WOUNDS!!
COME ON, FUSHI!!
SAVE HER!
OR SHE'S GONNA DIE!
FUSHI!

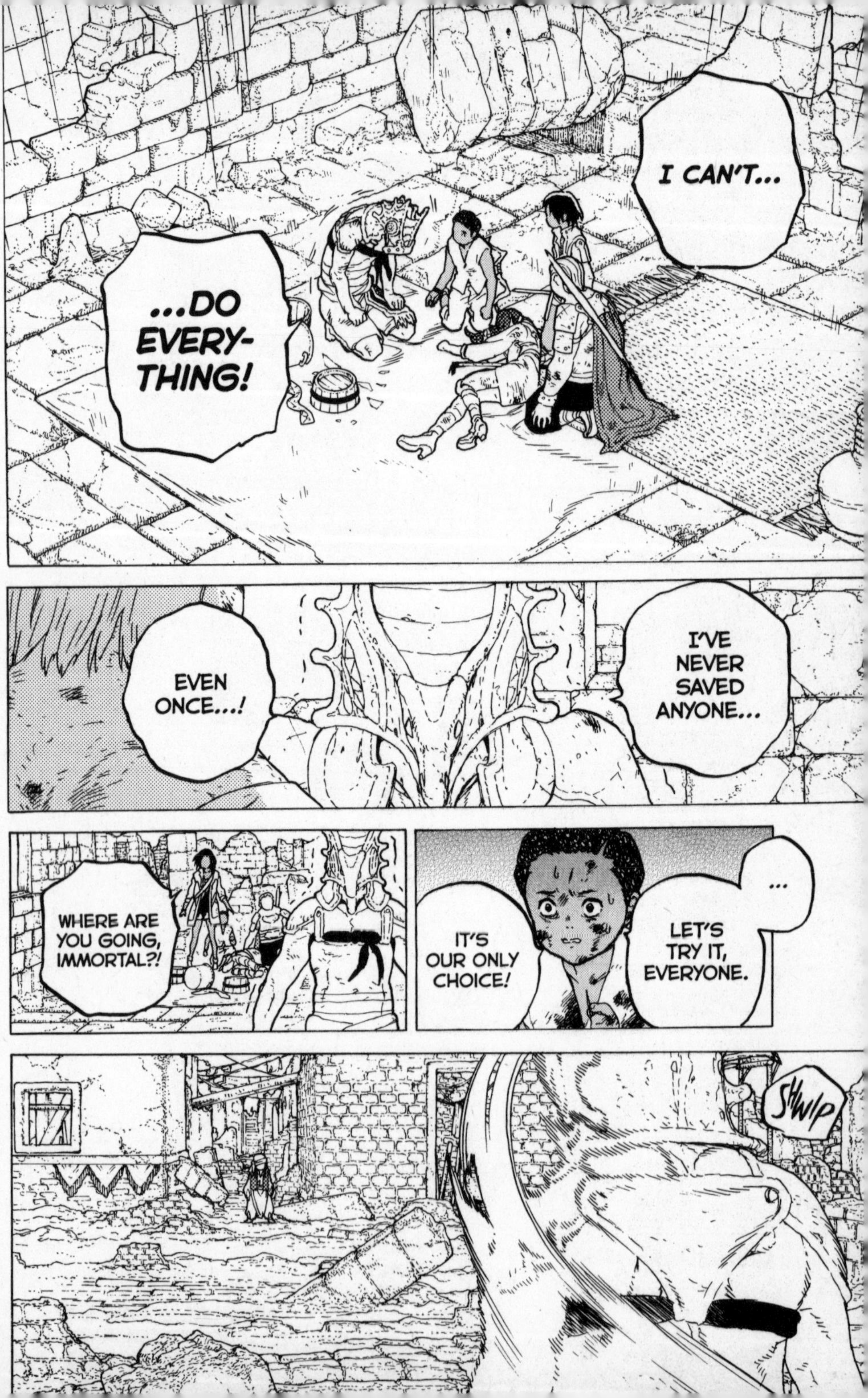
I CAN'T...
...DO EVERYTHING!
I'VE NEVER SAVED ANYONE...
EVEN ONCE...!
...
LET'S TRY IT, EVERYONE.
IT'S OUR ONLY CHOICE!
WHERE ARE YOU GOING, IMMORTAL?!
SHWIP

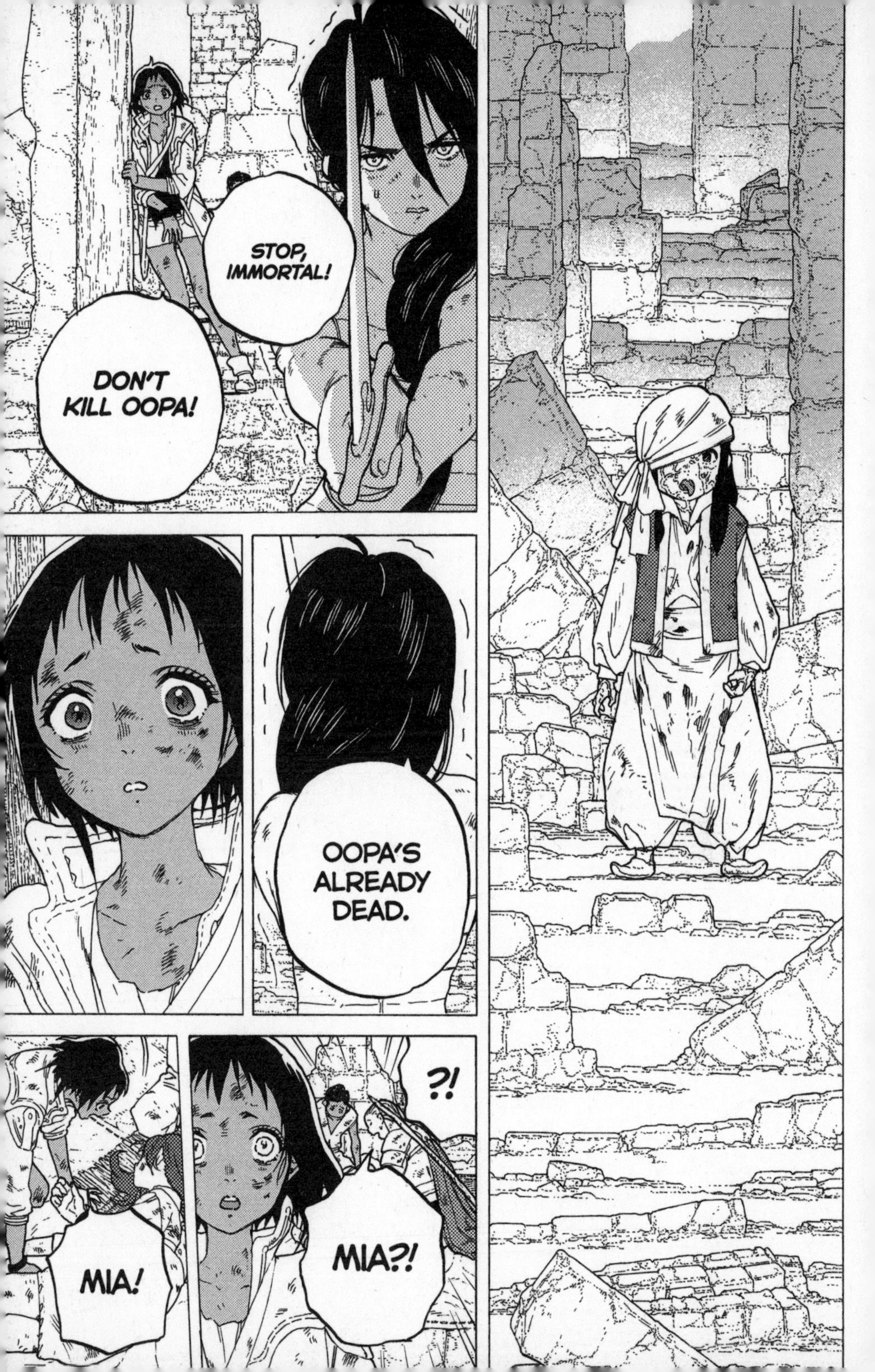
STOP, IMMORTAL!
DON'T KILL OOPA!
OOPA'S ALREADY DEAD.
?!
MIA?!
MIA!

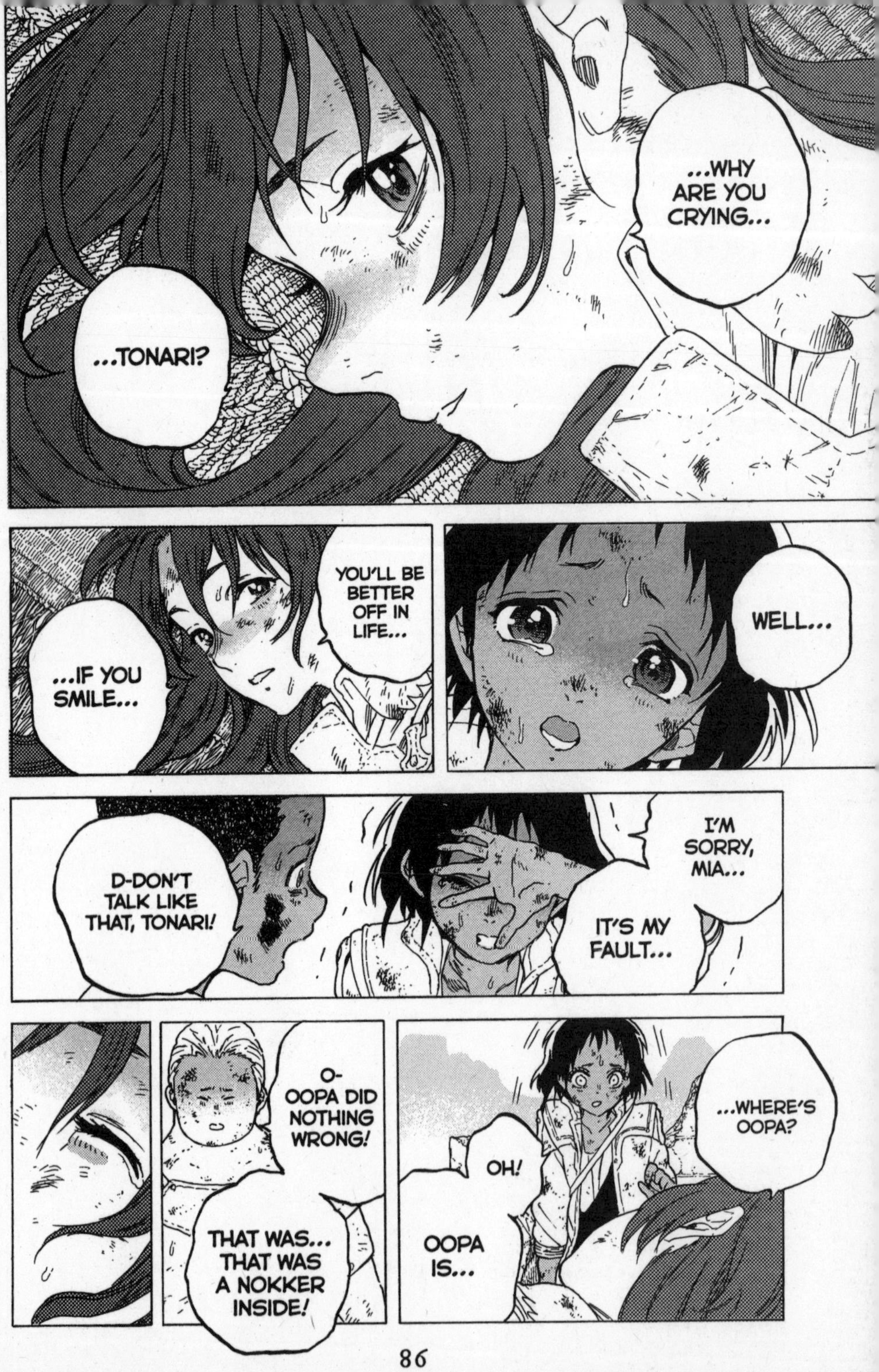
...WHY ARE YOU CRYING...
...TONARI?
WELL...
YOU'LL BE BETTER OFF IN LIFE...
...IF YOU SMILE...
I'M SORRY, MIA...
IT'S MY FAULT...
D-DON'T TALK LIKE THAT, TONARI!
...WHERE'S OOPA?
OH!
OOPA IS...
O-OOPA DID NOTHING WRONG!
THAT WAS... THAT WAS A NOKKER INSIDE!

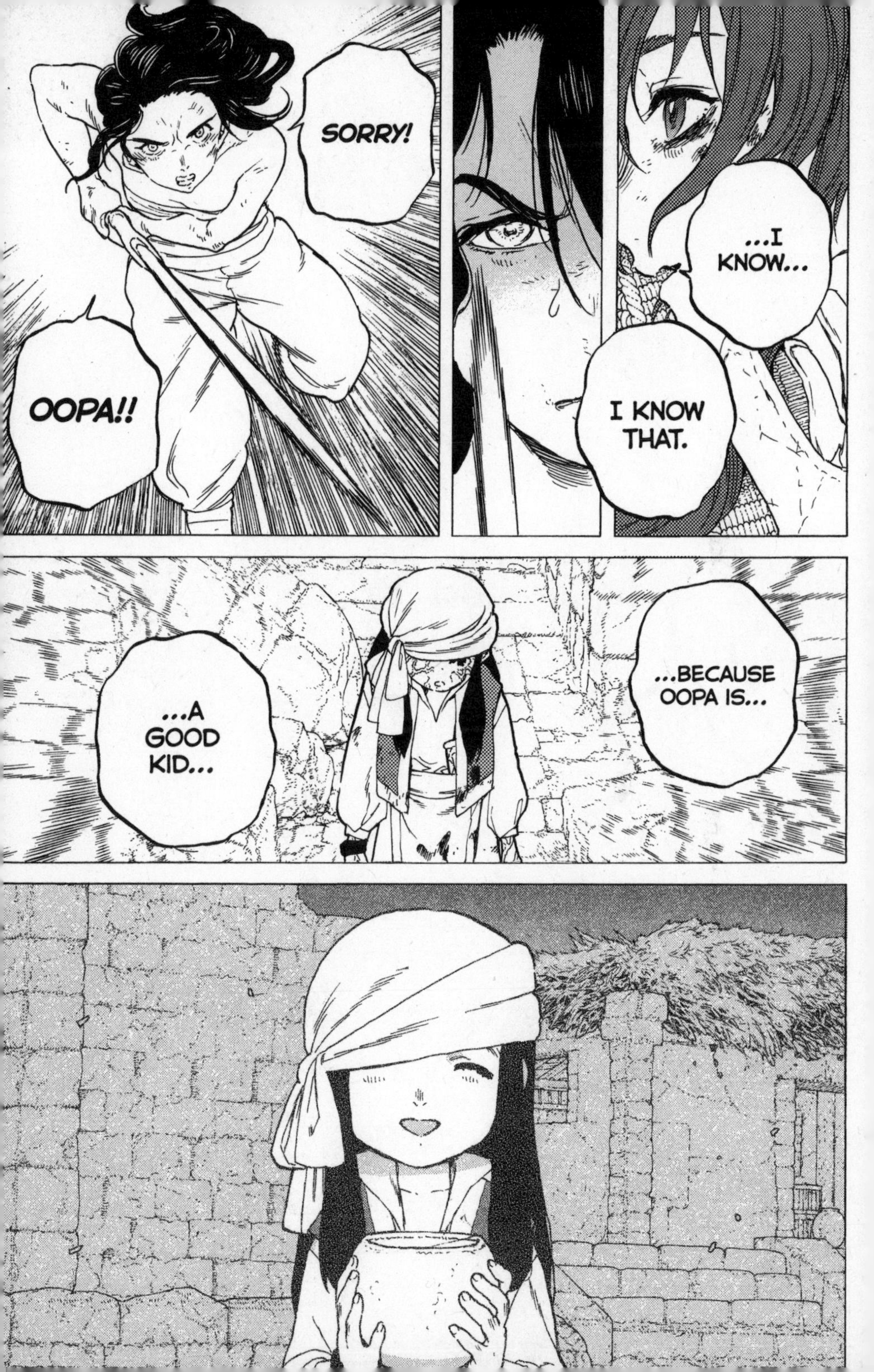
...I KNOW...
I KNOW THAT.
SORRY!
OOPA!!
...BECAUSE OOPA IS...
...A GOOD KID...

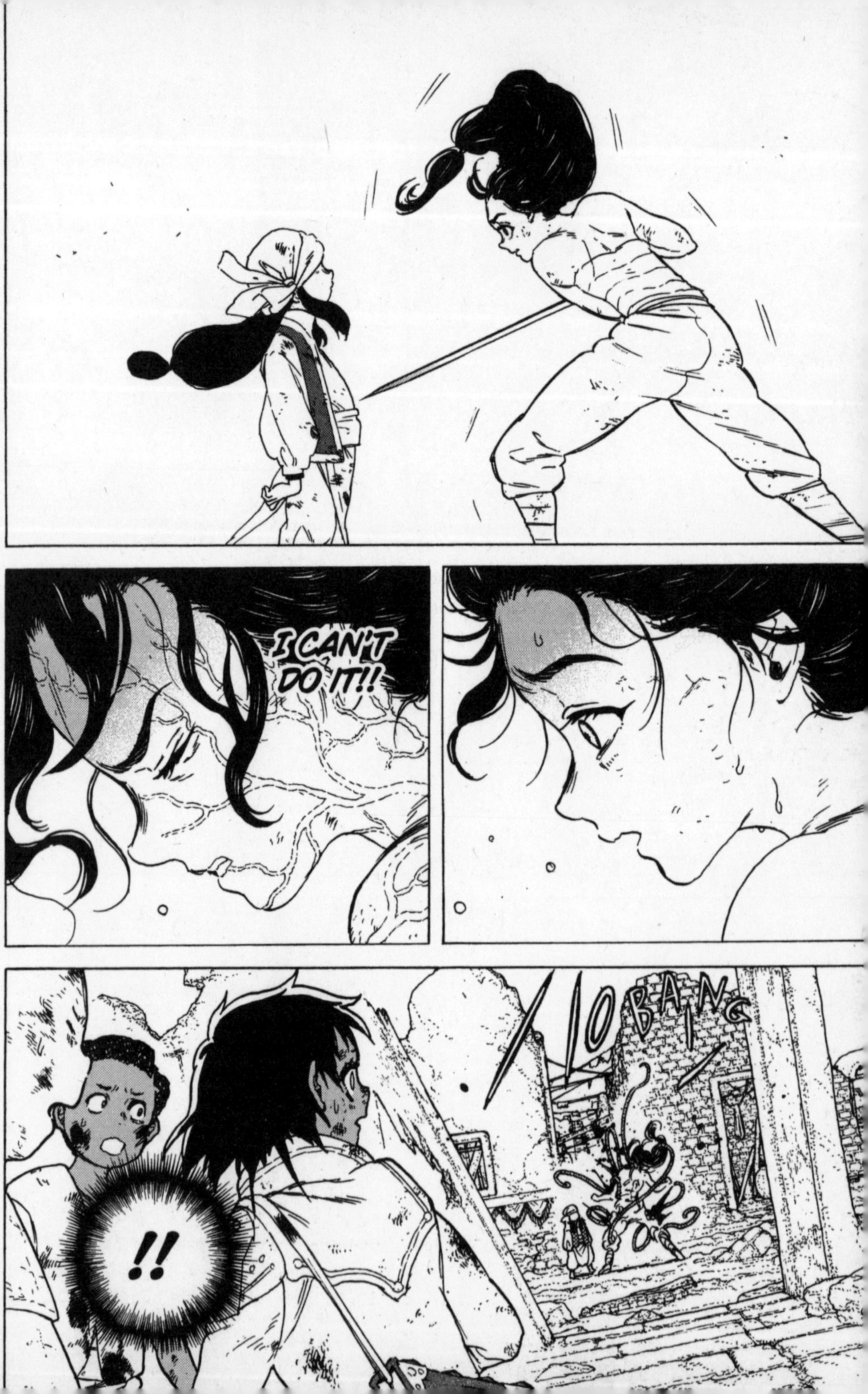
I CAN'T DO IT!!
BANG
!!

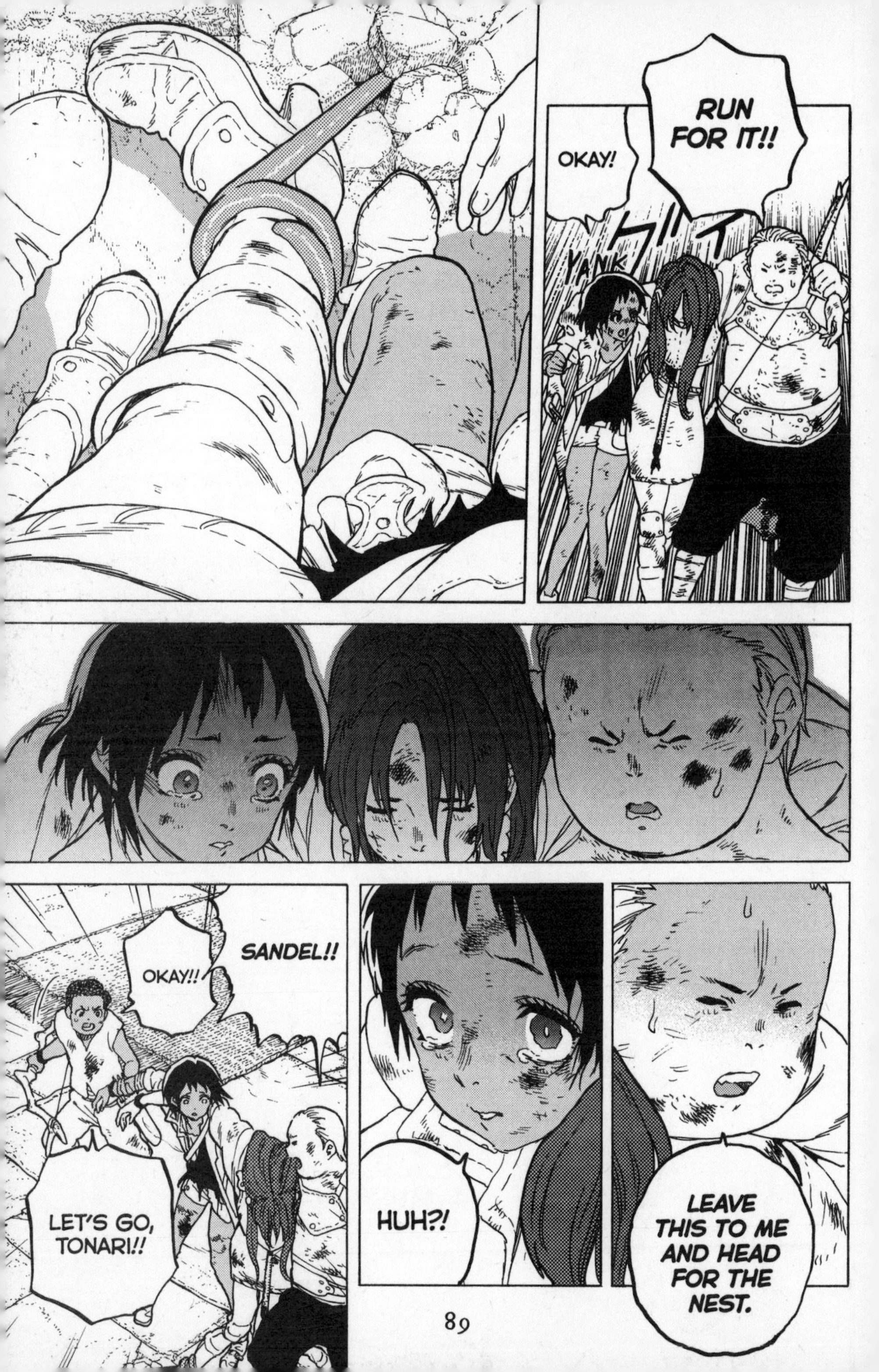
RUN FOR IT!!
OKAY!
YANK
LEAVE THIS TO ME AND HEAD FOR THE NEST.
HUH?!
SANDEL!!
OKAY!!
LET'S GO, TONARI!!

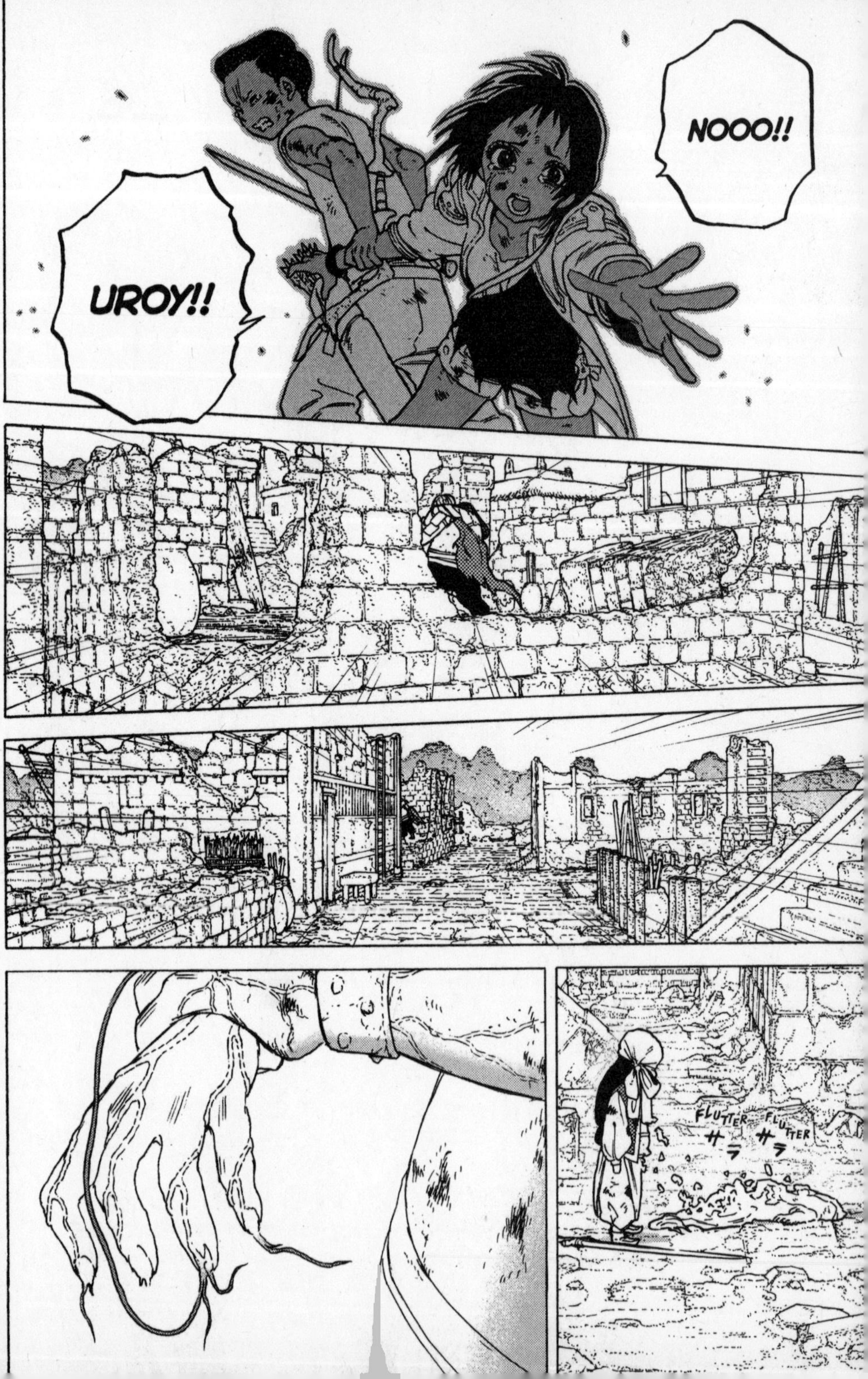
NOOO!!
UROY!!
FLUTTER FLUTTER
サラ サラ

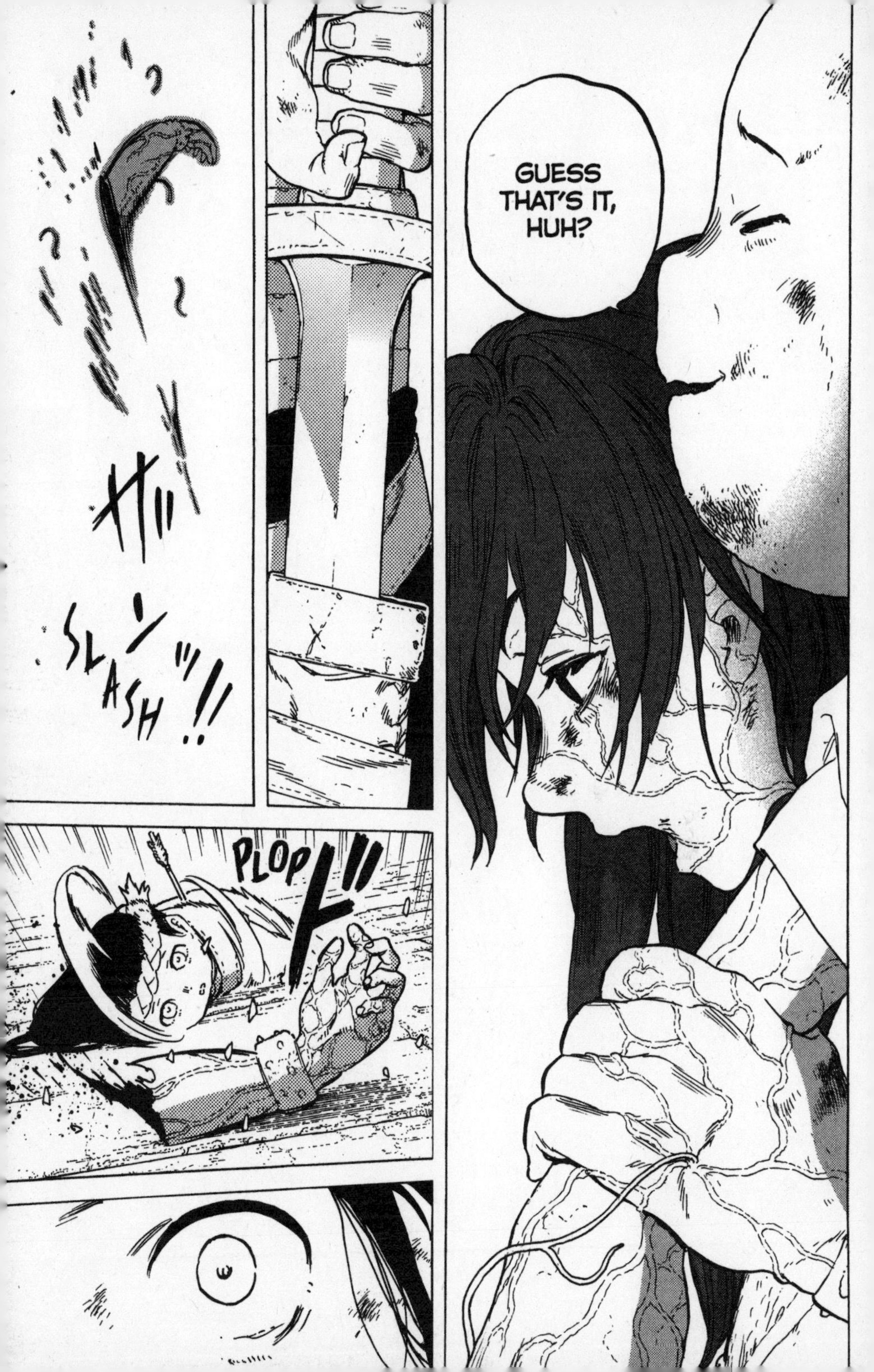
GUESS THAT'S IT, HUH?
SLASH!!
PLOP!!

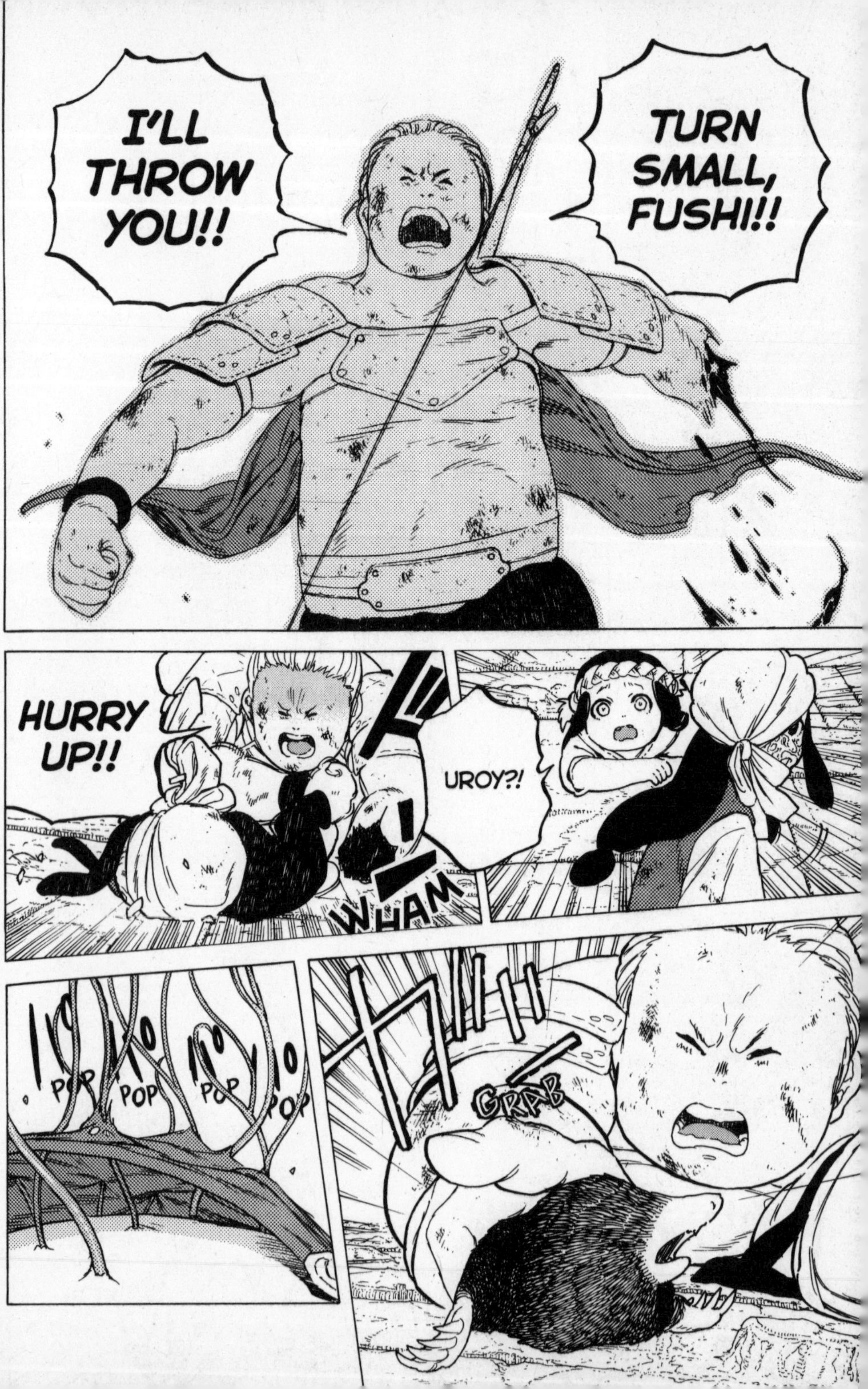
TURN SMALL, FUSHI!!
I'LL THROW YOU!!
UROY?!
HURRY UP!!
WHAM
GRAB
POP
POP
POP
POP

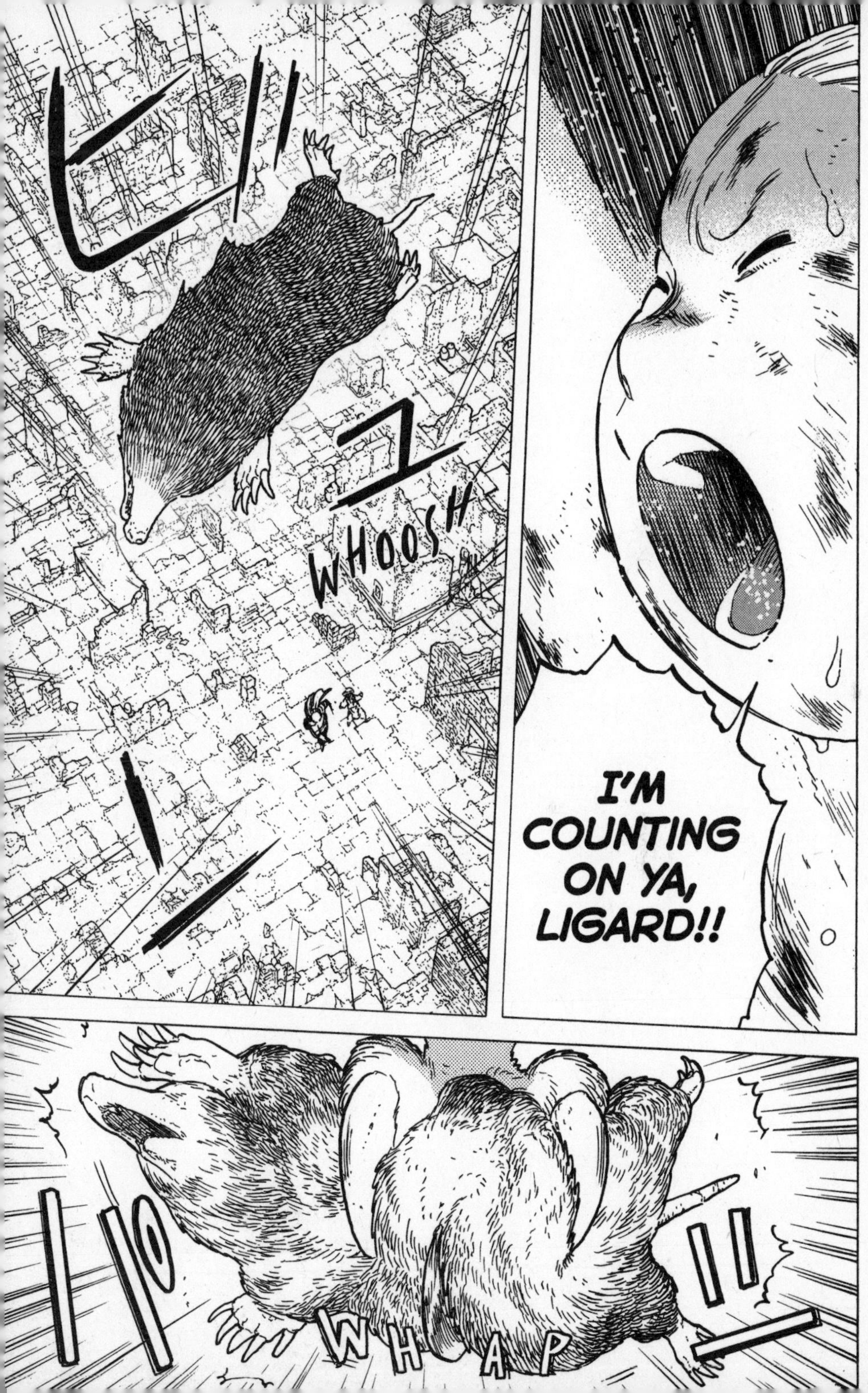
I'M COUNTING ON YA, LIGARD!!
WHOOSH
WHAP

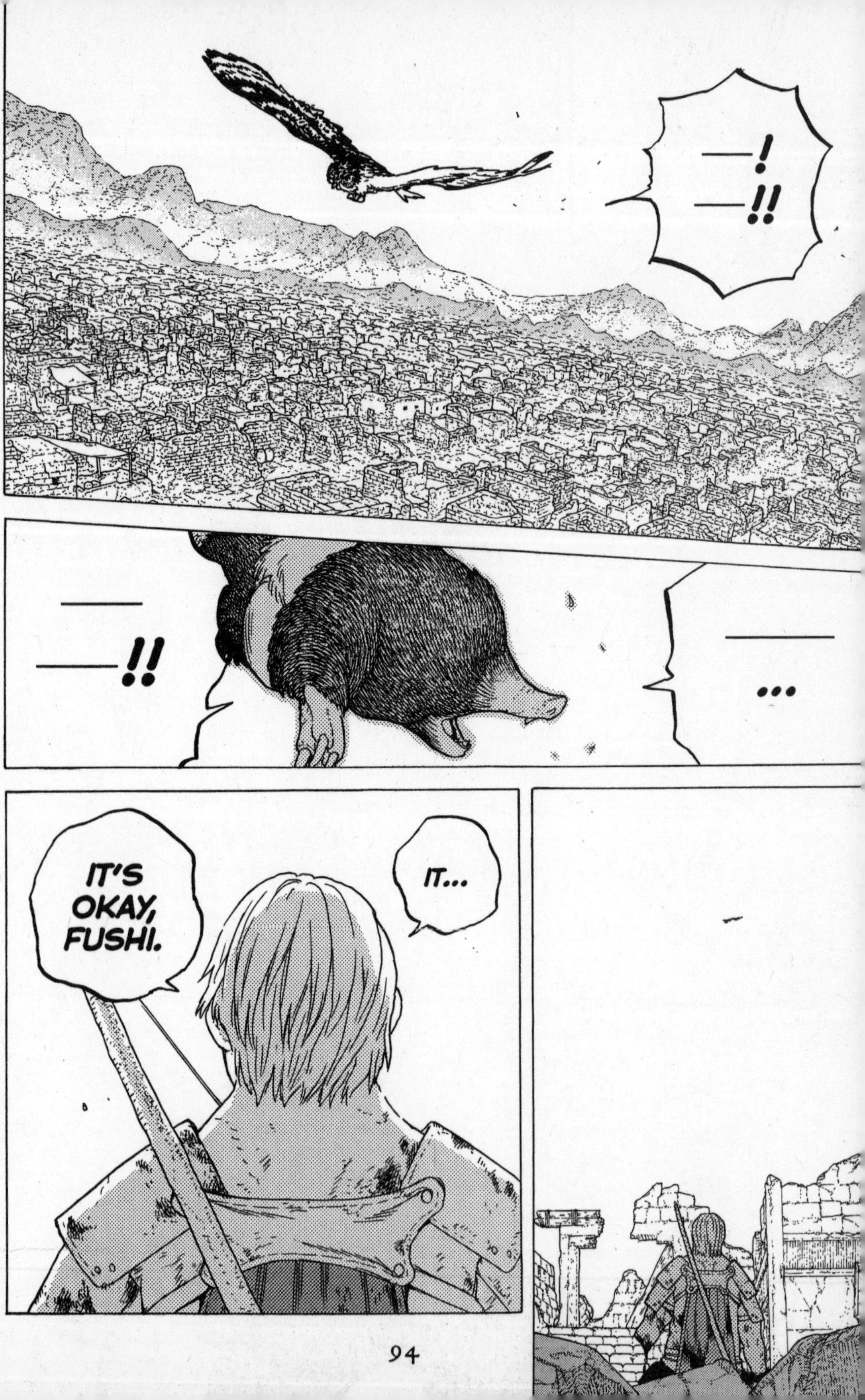
—! —!!
——— ...
—— ——!!
IT...
IT'S OKAY, FUSHI.

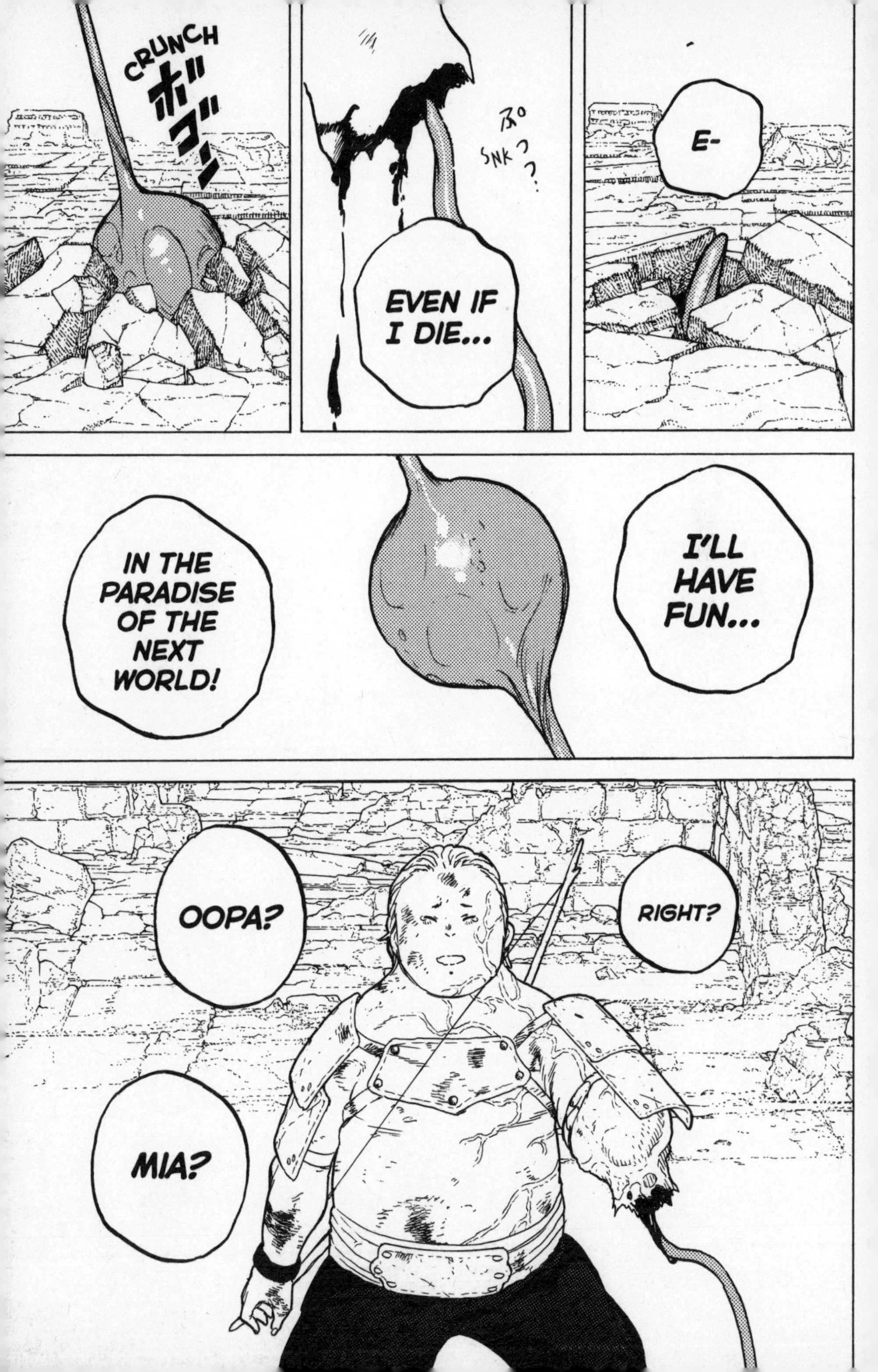
E-
SNK
EVEN IF I DIE...
CRUNCH
I'LL HAVE FUN...
IN THE PARADISE OF THE NEXT WORLD!
RIGHT?
OOPA?
MIA?

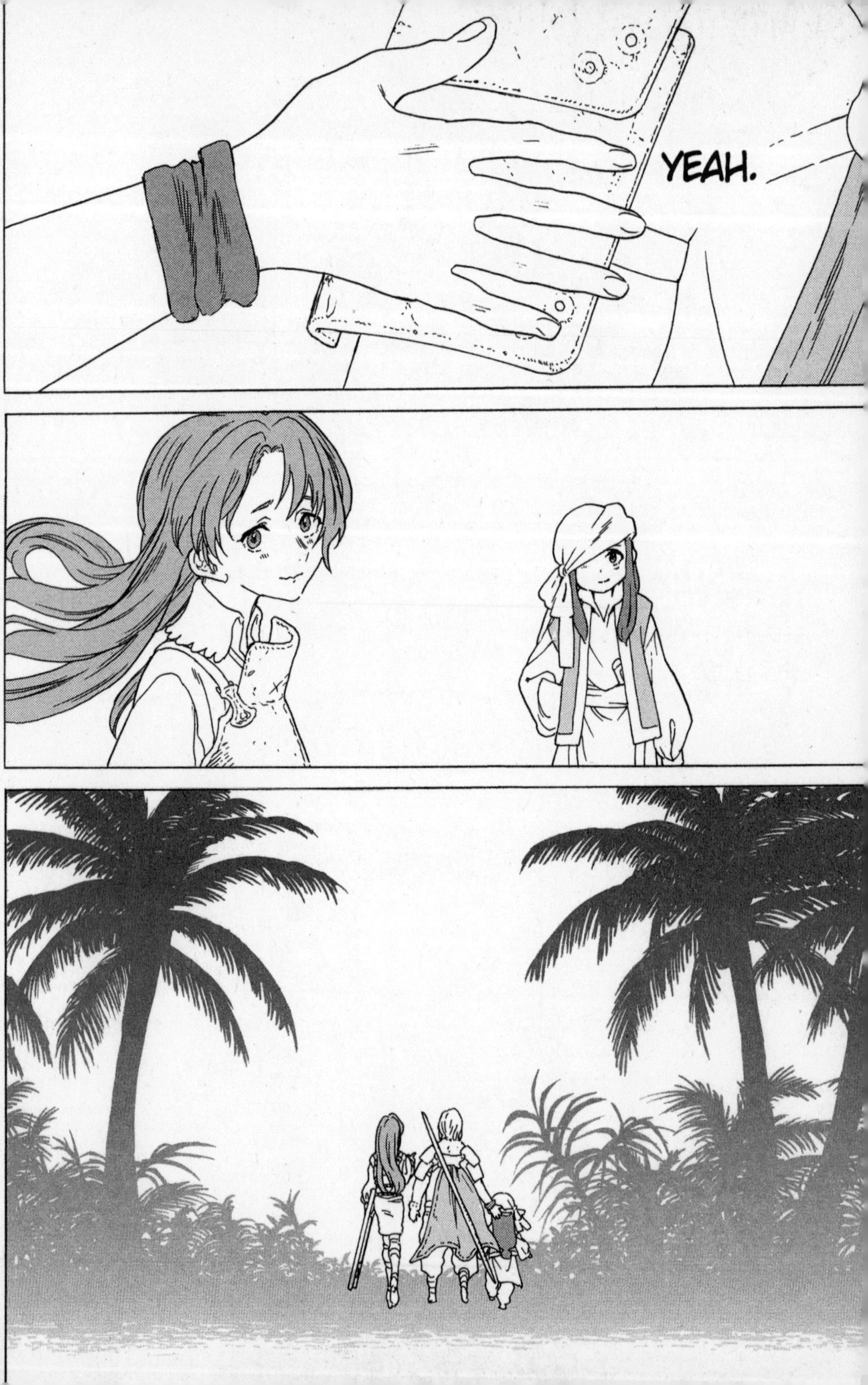
YEAH.

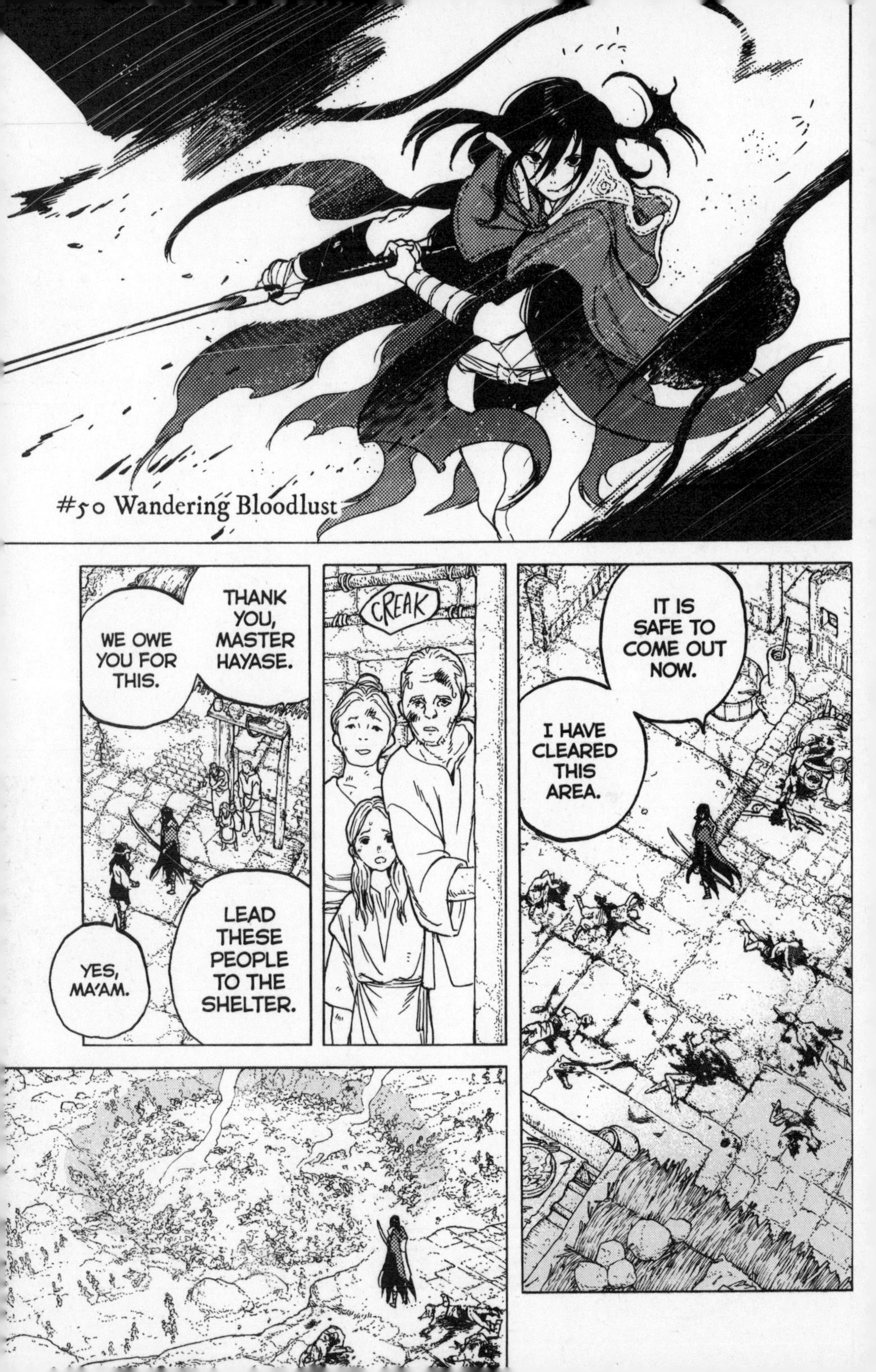
#50 Wandering Bloodlust
IT IS SAFE TO COME OUT NOW.
I HAVE CLEARED THIS AREA.
CREAK
THANK YOU, MASTER HAYASE.
WE OWE YOU FOR THIS.
LEAD THESE PEOPLE TO THE SHELTER.
YES, MA'AM.

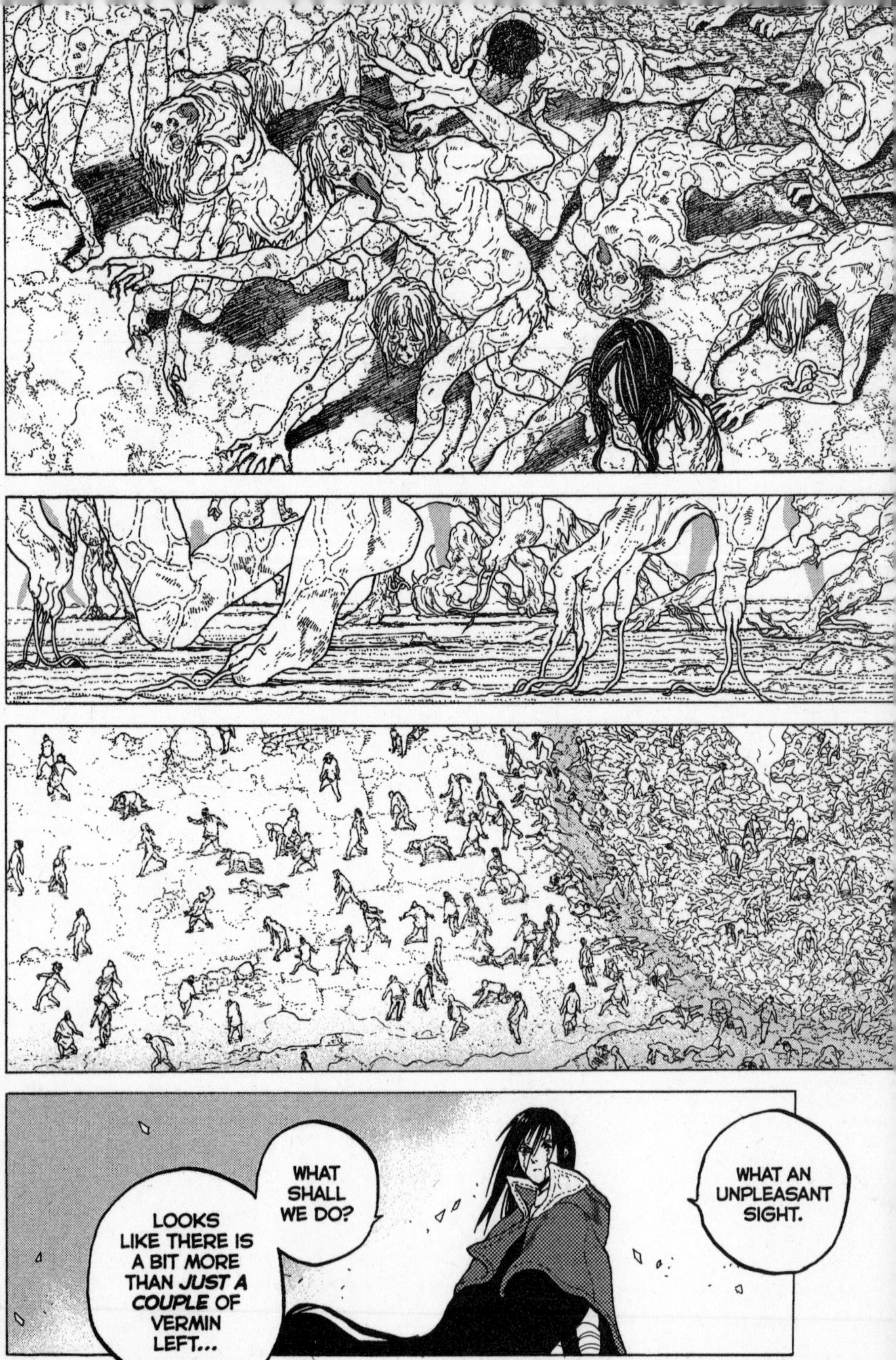
WHAT AN UNPLEASANT SIGHT.
WHAT SHALL WE DO?
LOOKS LIKE THERE IS A BIT MORE THAN *JUST A COUPLE* OF VERMIN LEFT...

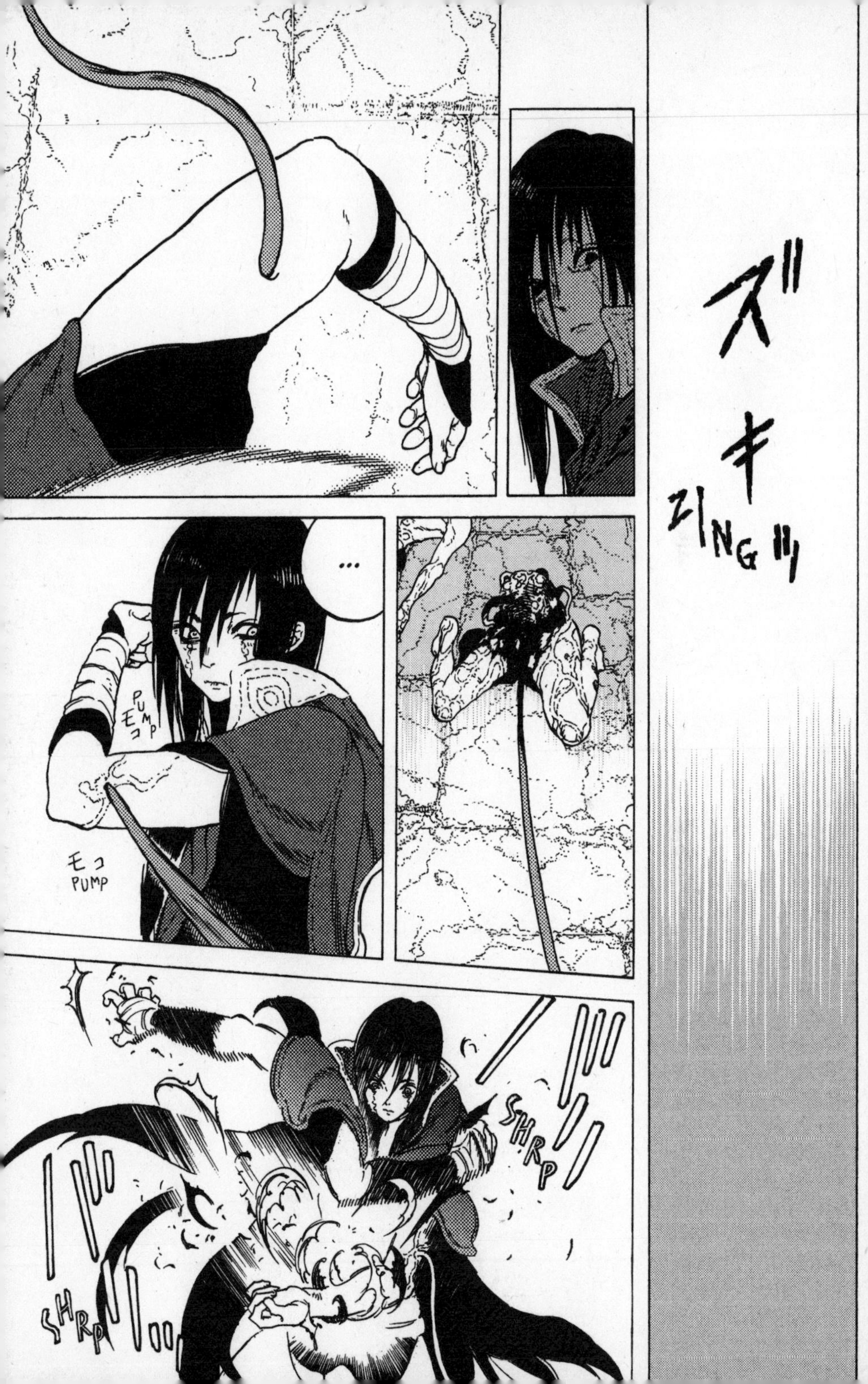
ズキ
ZING!!
...
モコ
PUMP
モコ
PUMP
SHRP
SHRP

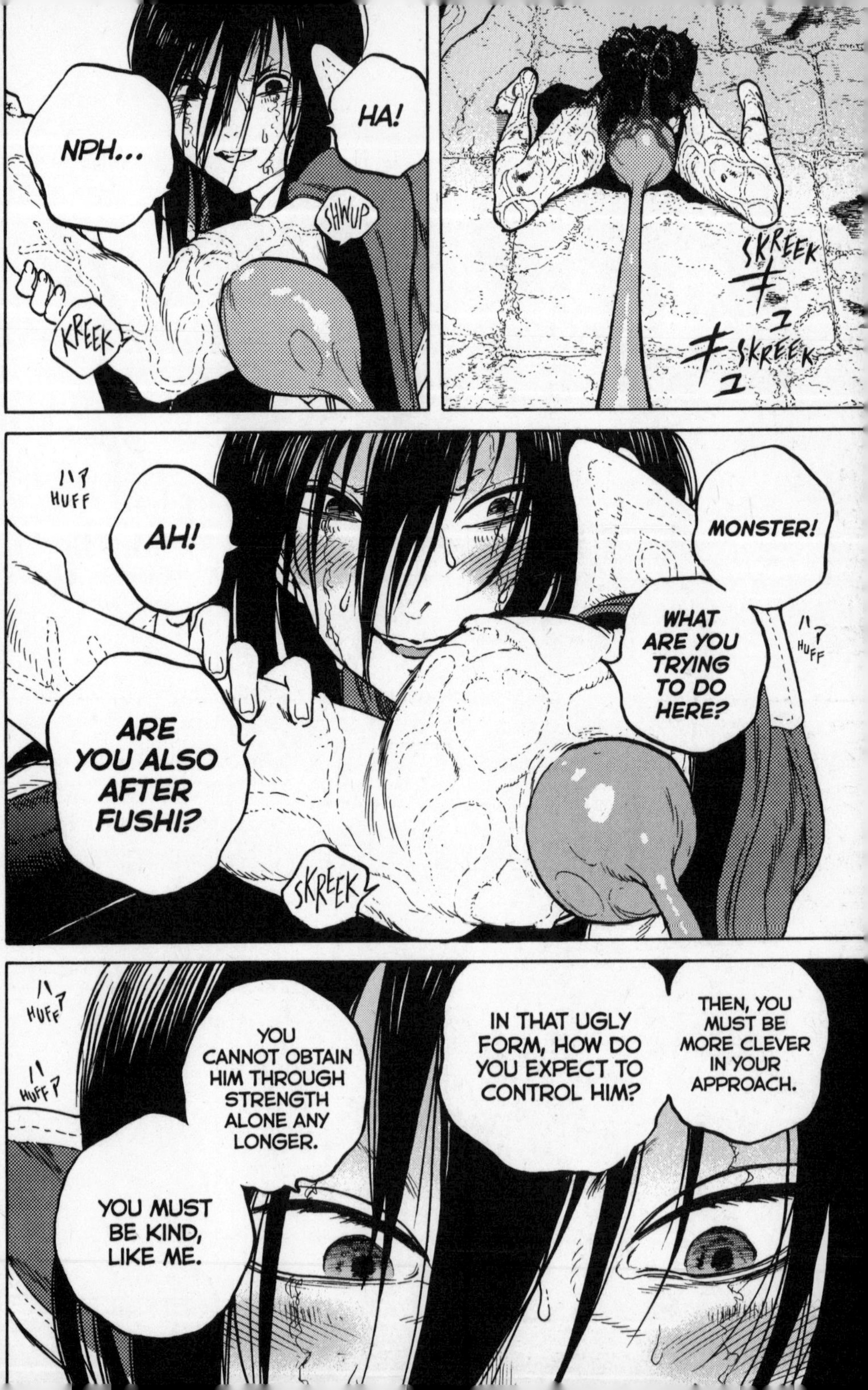
SKREEK
キュ
キュ
SKREEK
HA!
NPH...
SHWUP
KREEK
MONSTER!
WHAT ARE YOU TRYING TO DO HERE?
ハァ
HUFF
AH!
ハァ
HUFF
ARE YOU ALSO AFTER FUSHI?
SKREEK
THEN, YOU MUST BE MORE CLEVER IN YOUR APPROACH.
IN THAT UGLY FORM, HOW DO YOU EXPECT TO CONTROL HIM?
YOU CANNOT OBTAIN HIM THROUGH STRENGTH ALONE ANY LONGER.
YOU MUST BE KIND, LIKE ME.
ハァ
HUFF
ハァ
HUFF

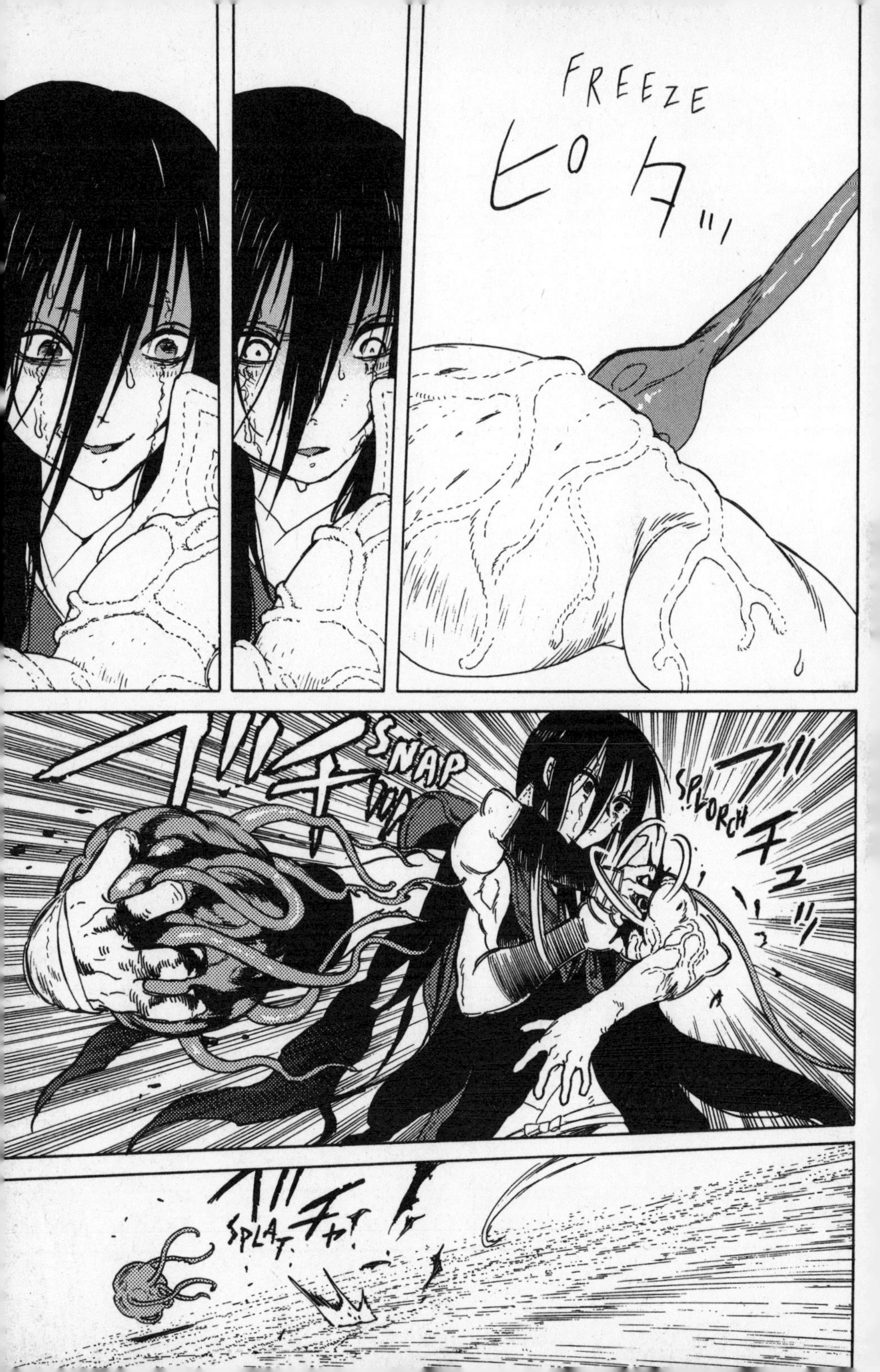
FREEZE
ピクッ
SPLORCH
SNAP
SPLAT

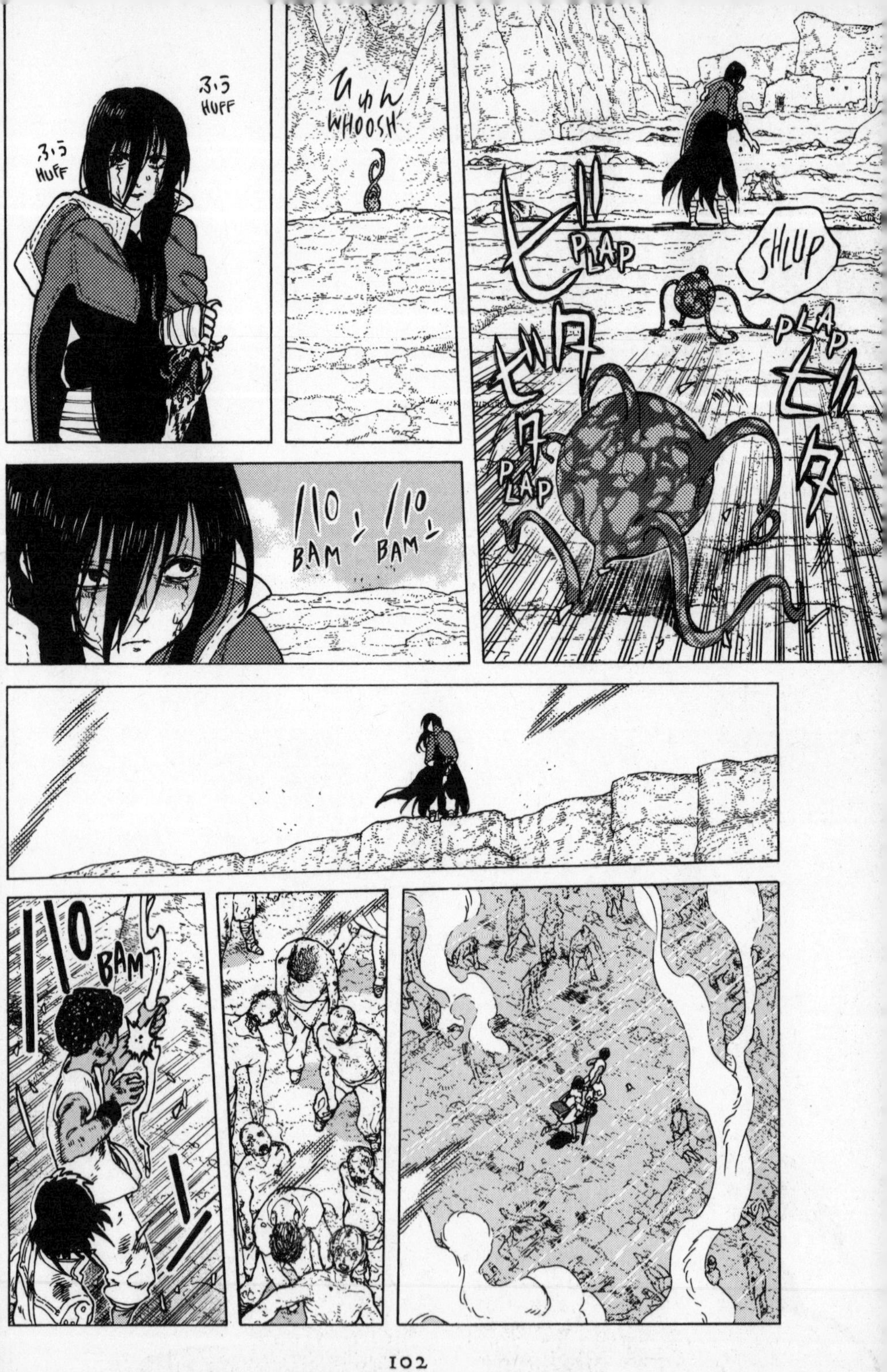
ピク PLAP
SHLUP
PLAP ピクピク
ピクピク PLAP
ひゅん WHOOSH
ふう HUFF
ふう HUFF
バン! BAM
バン! BAM
バン BAM

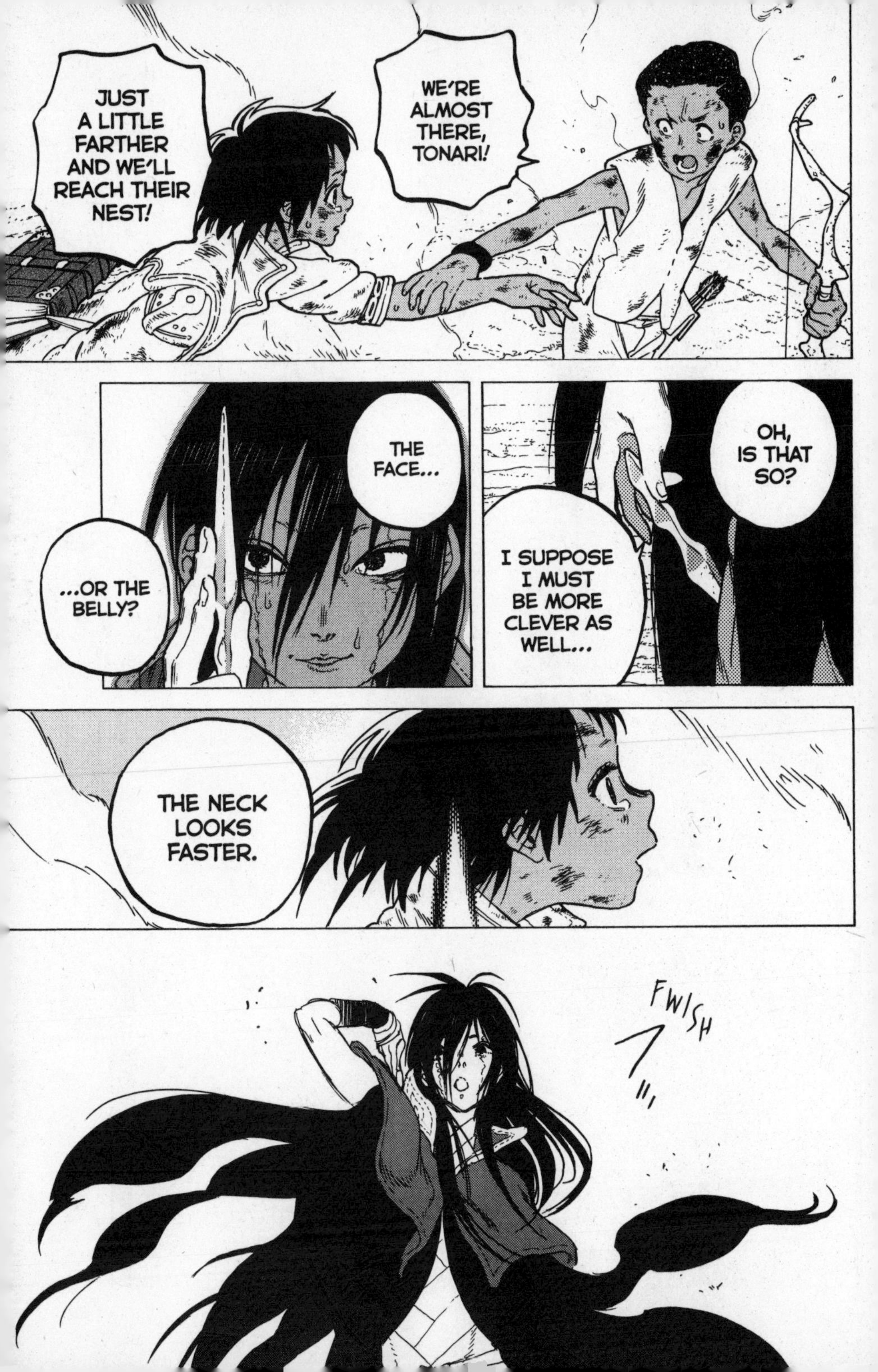
WE'RE ALMOST THERE, TONARI!
JUST A LITTLE FARTHER AND WE'LL REACH THEIR NEST!
OH, IS THAT SO?
I SUPPOSE I MUST BE MORE CLEVER AS WELL...
THE FACE...
...OR THE BELLY?
THE NECK LOOKS FASTER.
FWISH

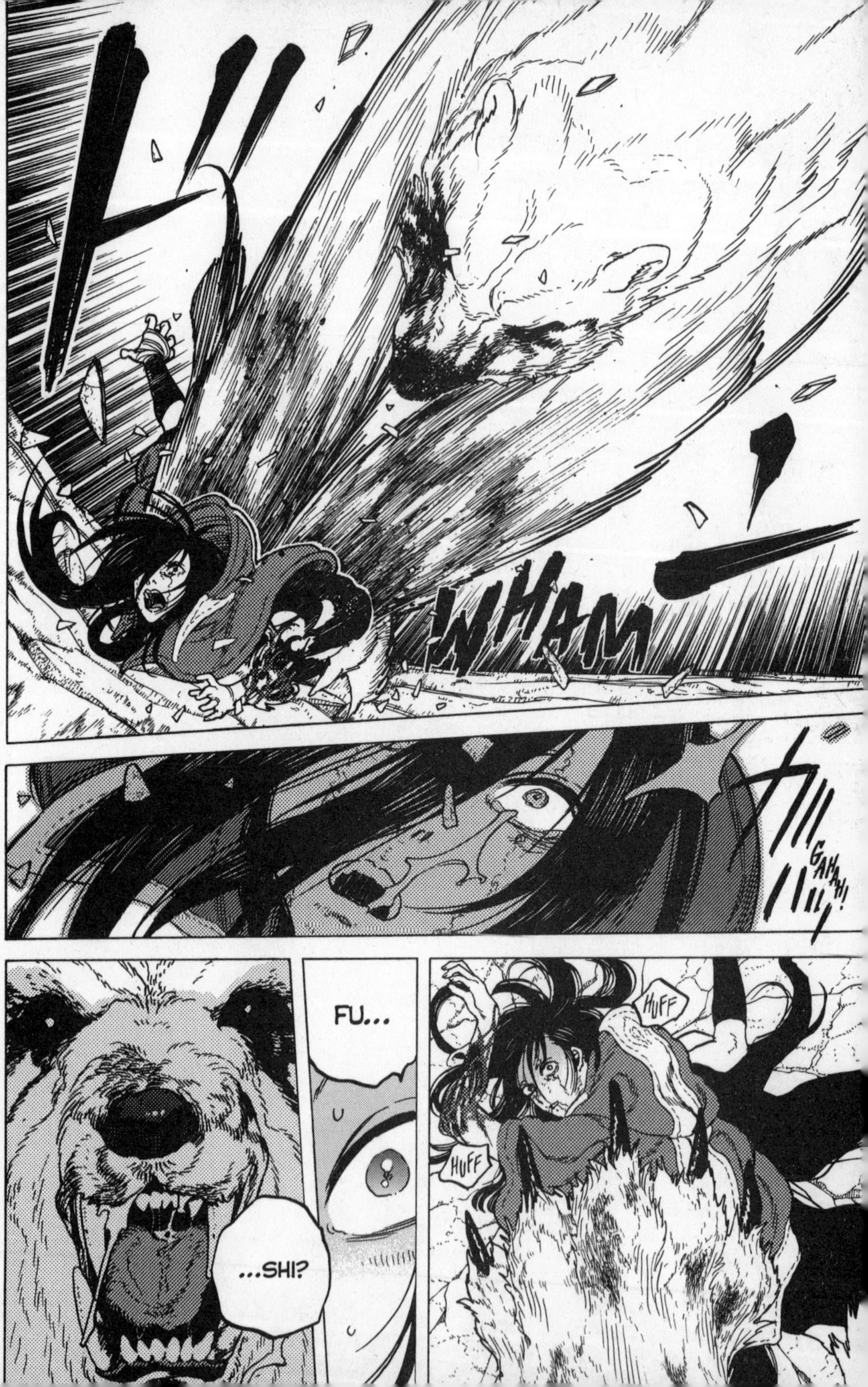
WHAM
GAHAH!
HUFF
HUFF
FU...
...SHI?

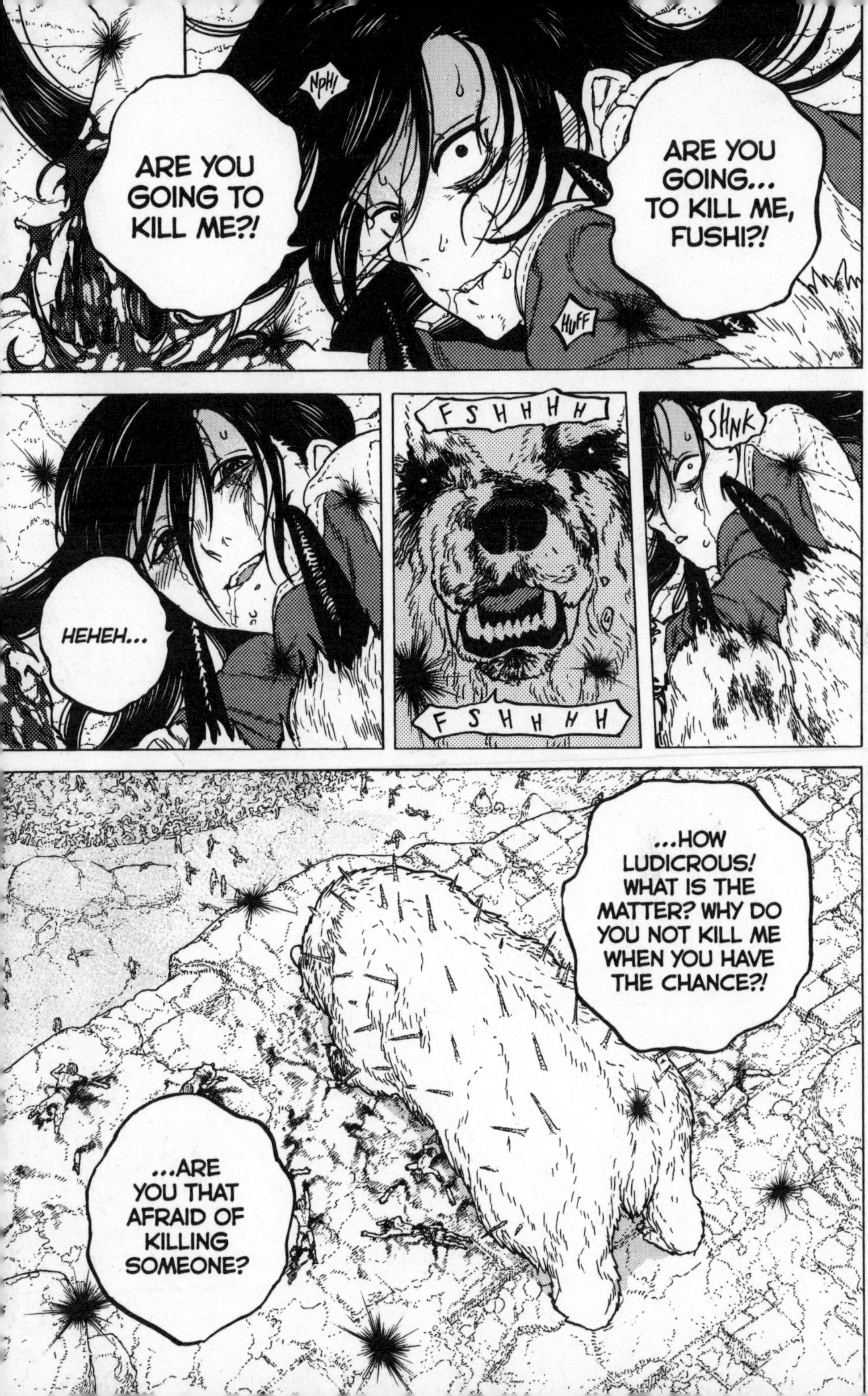
ARE YOU GOING... TO KILL ME, FUSHI?!
NPH!
ARE YOU GOING TO KILL ME?!
HUFF
SHNK
FSHHHH
FSHHHH
HEHEH...
...HOW LUDICROUS! WHAT IS THE MATTER? WHY DO YOU NOT KILL ME WHEN YOU HAVE THE CHANCE?!
...ARE YOU THAT AFRAID OF KILLING SOMEONE?

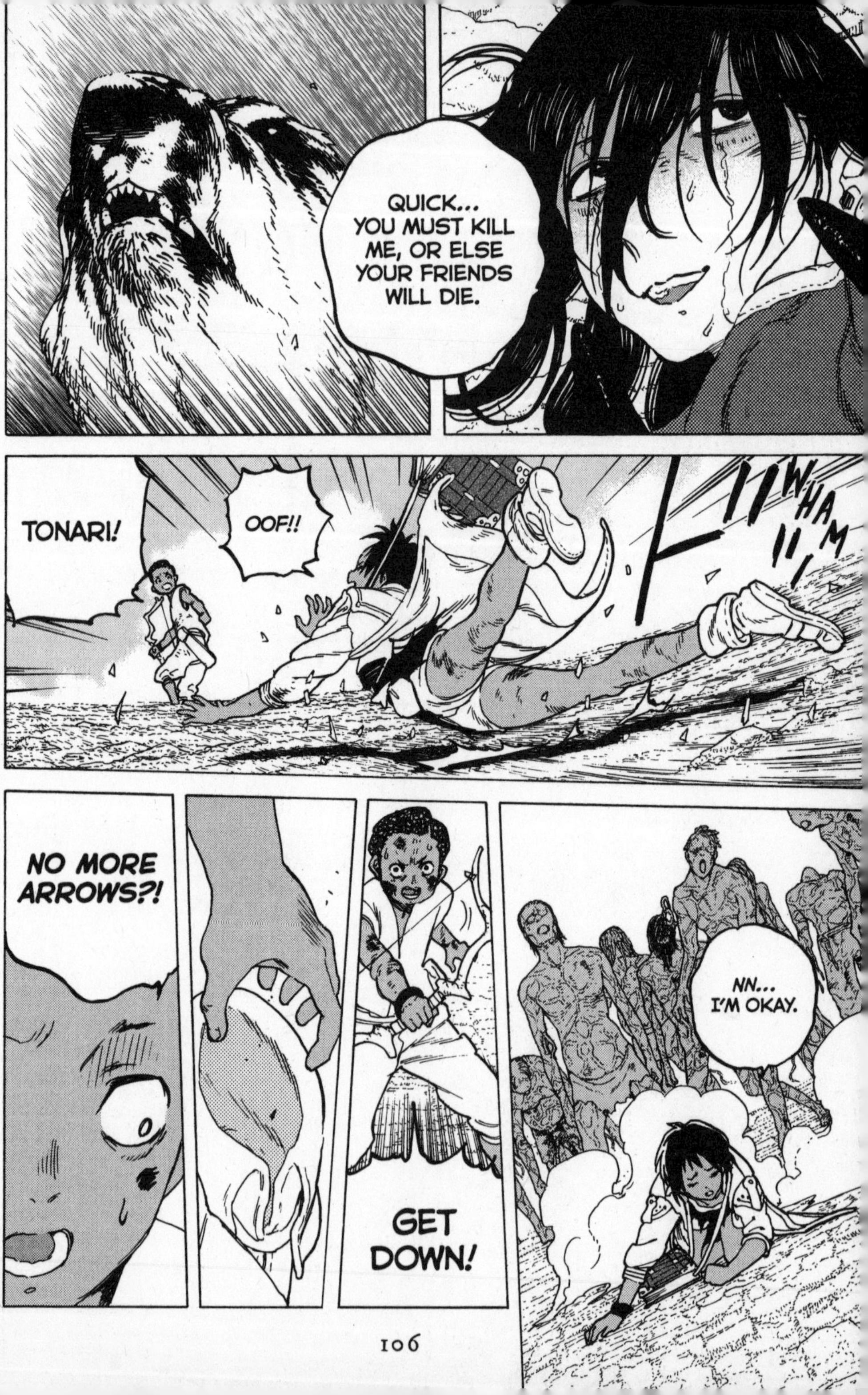
QUICK... YOU MUST KILL ME, OR ELSE YOUR FRIENDS WILL DIE.
WHAM
OOF!!
TONARI!
NN... I'M OKAY.
GET DOWN!
NO MORE ARROWS?!

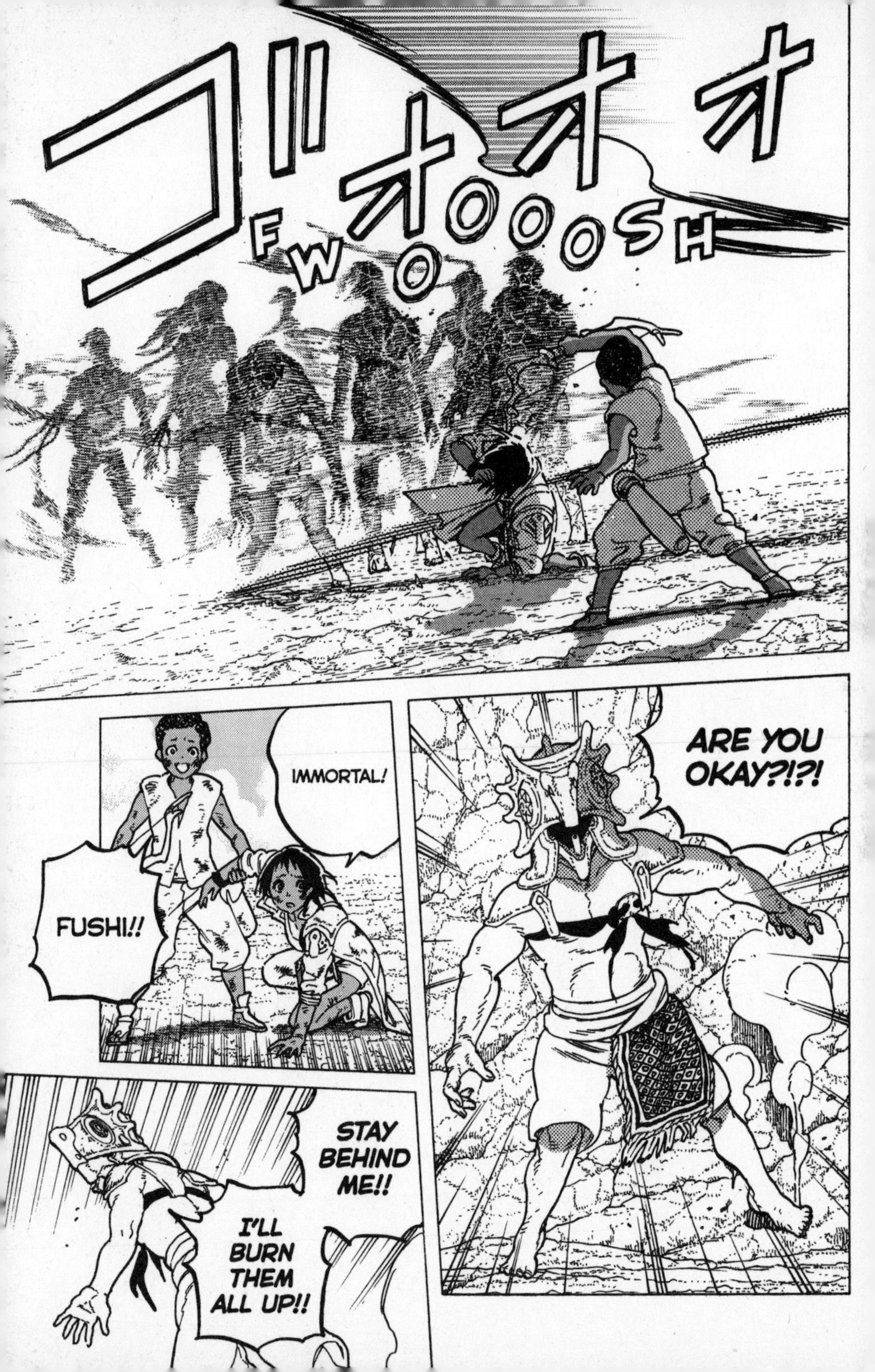
ゴォオオオ
FWOOOOSH
ARE YOU OKAY?!?!
IMMORTAL!
FUSHI!!
STAY BEHIND ME!!
I'LL BURN THEM ALL UP!!

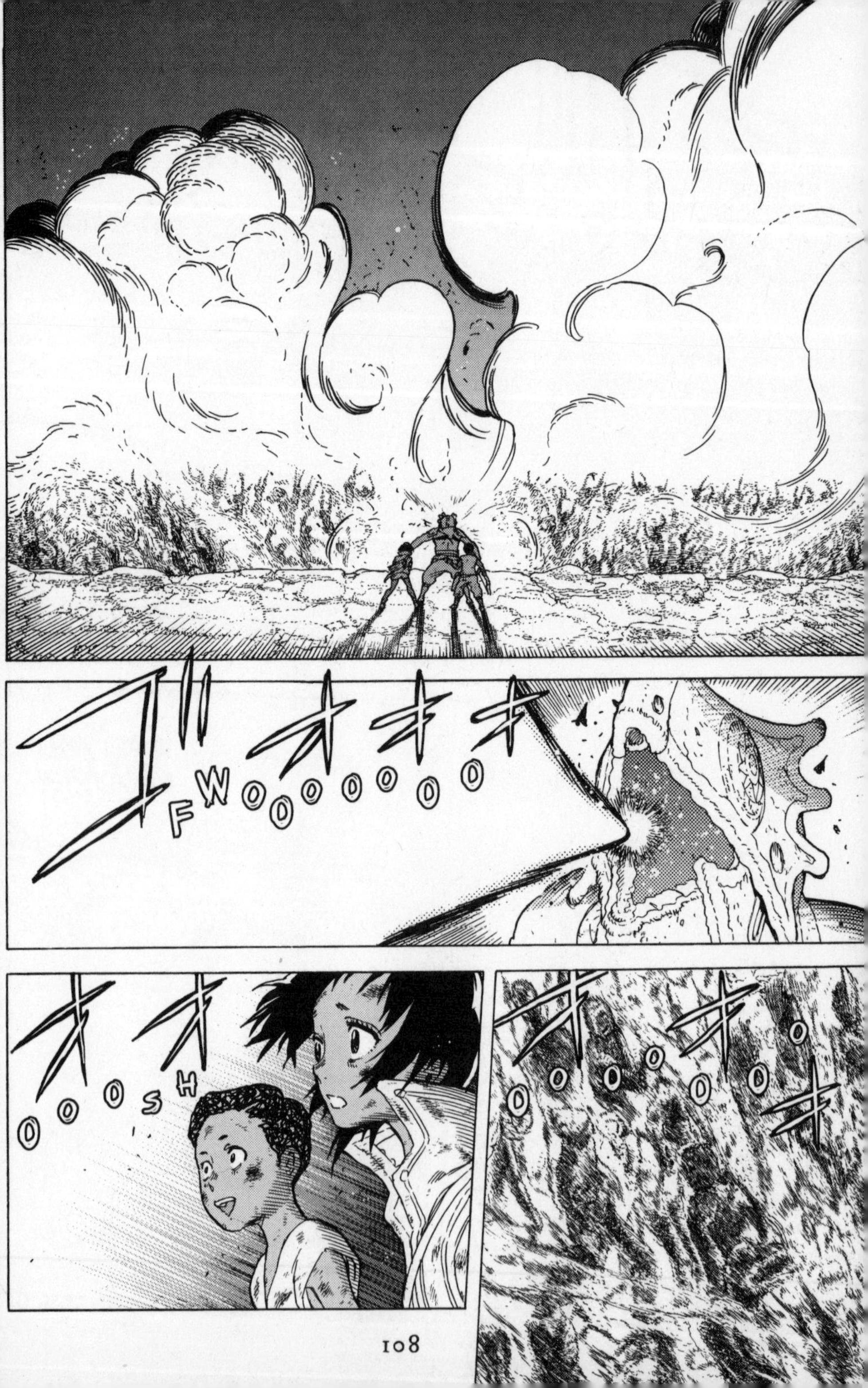
ゴオオオ
FWOOOOOOO
オオオオ
OOOOOOO
オオ
OOOSH

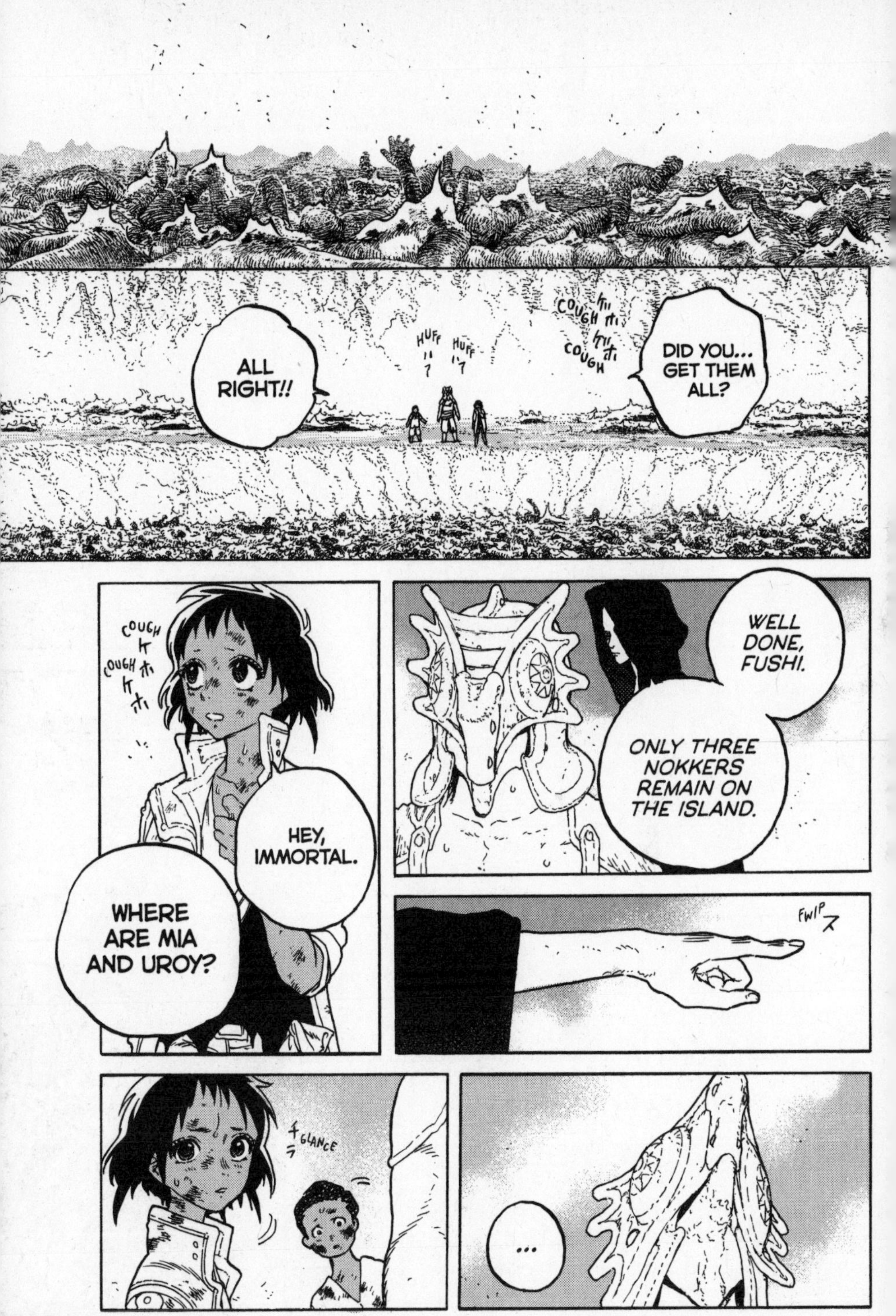

COUGH COUGH
DID YOU... GET THEM ALL?
HUFF HUFF
ALL RIGHT!!
WELL DONE, FUSHI.
ONLY THREE NOKKERS REMAIN ON THE ISLAND.
FWIP
COUGH COUGH
HEY, IMMORTAL.
WHERE ARE MIA AND UROY?
...
GLANCE

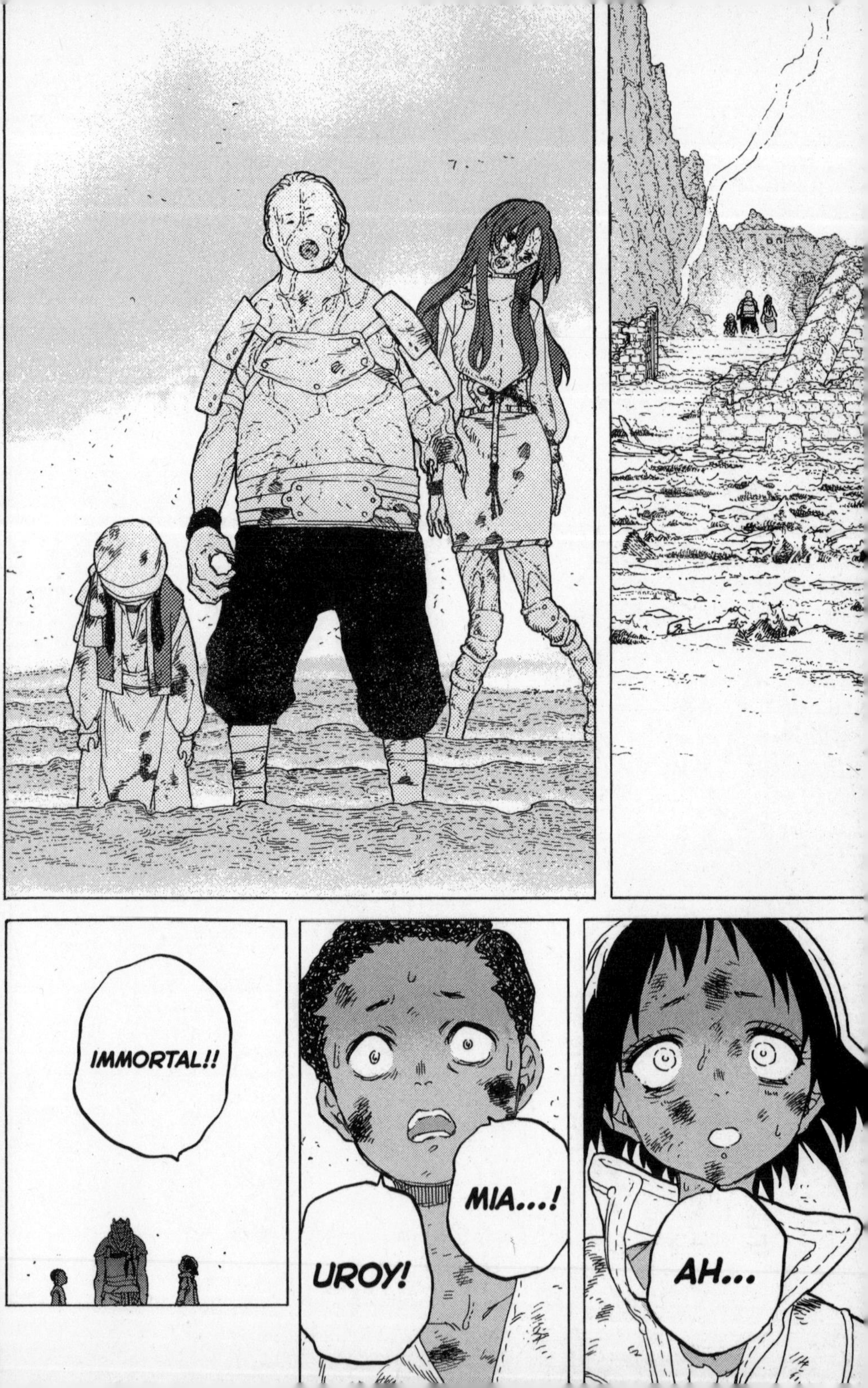
AH...
MIA...!
UROY!
IMMORTAL!!

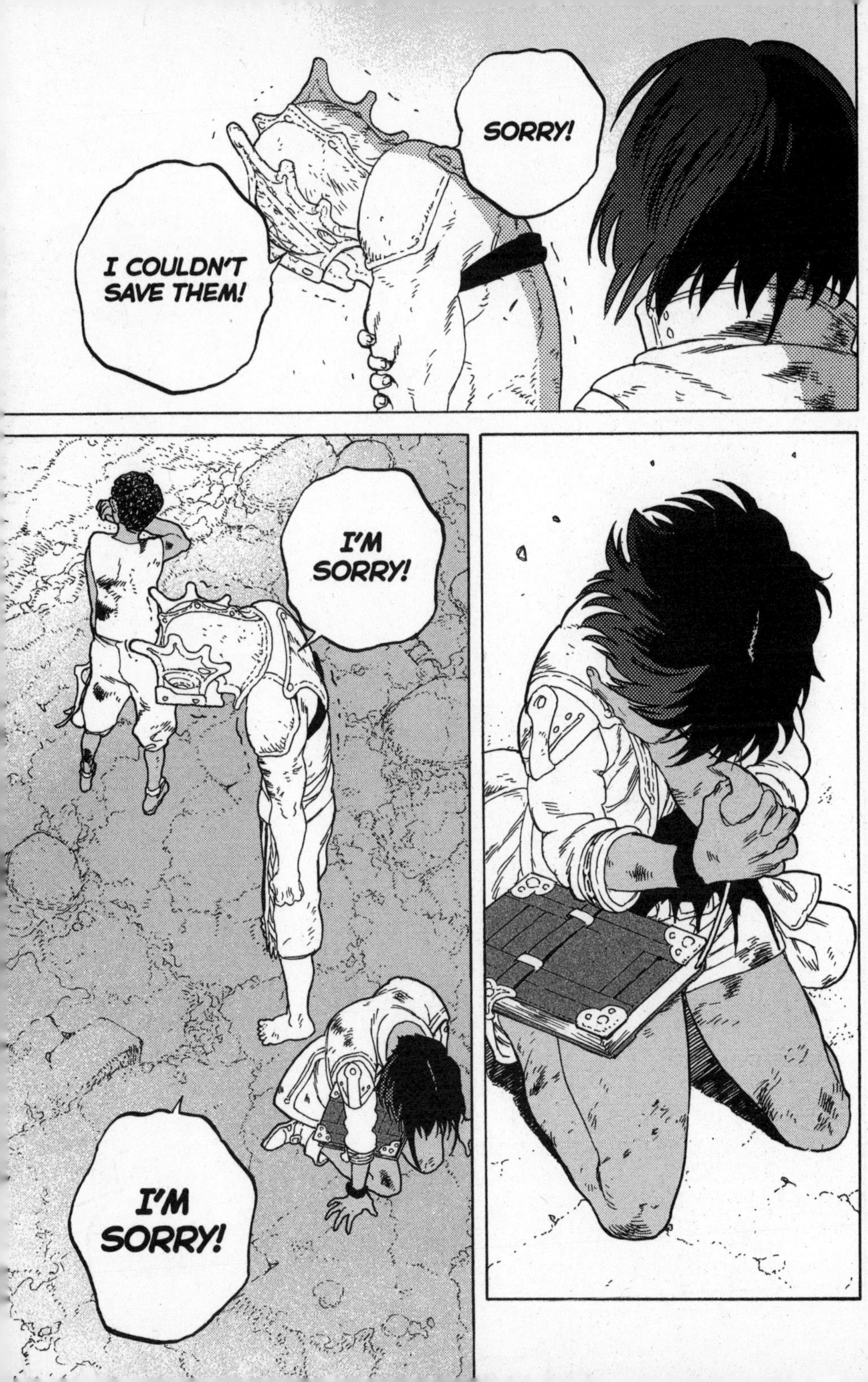
SORRY!
I COULDN'T SAVE THEM!
I'M SORRY!
I'M SORRY!

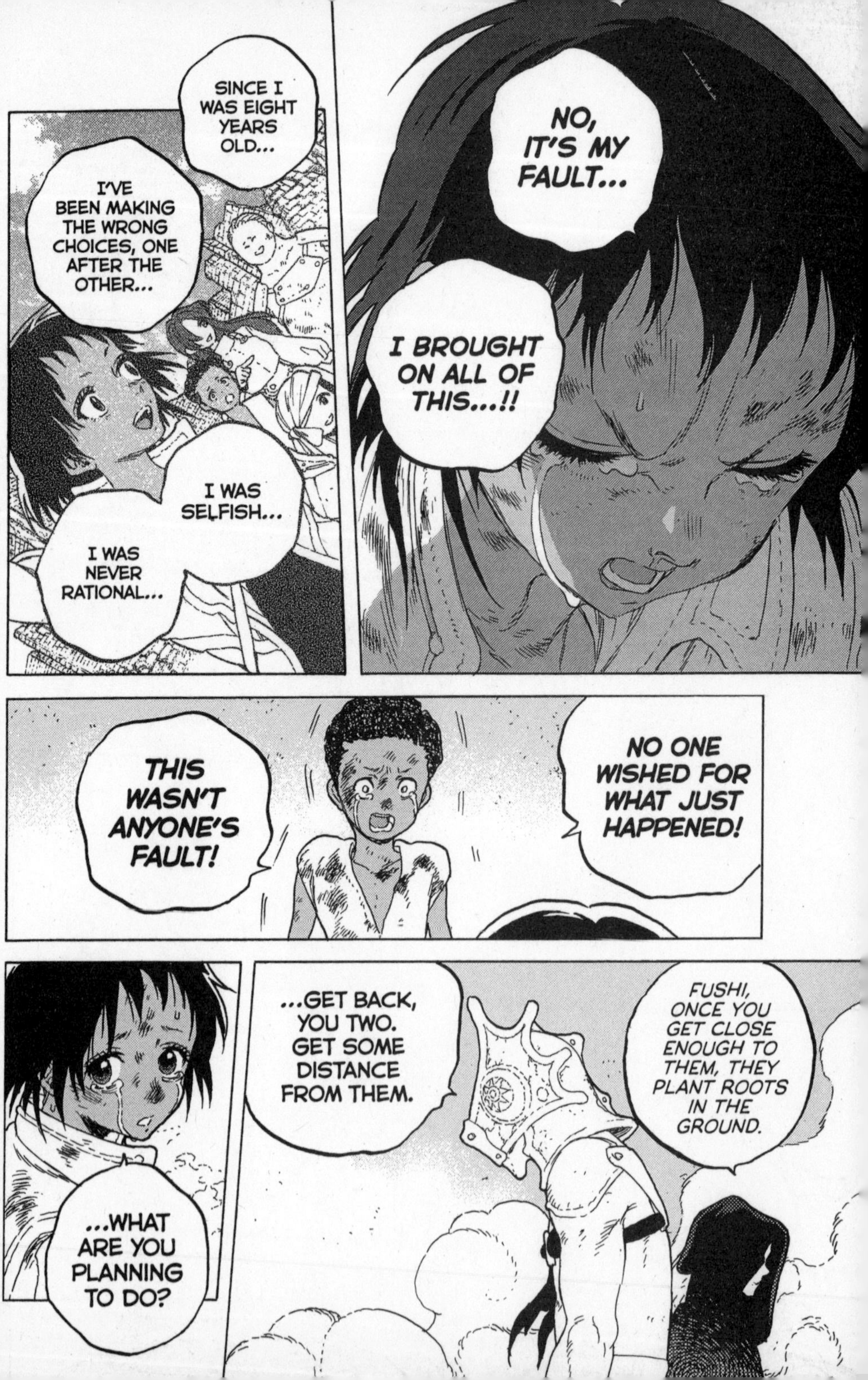
NO, IT'S MY FAULT...
I BROUGHT ON ALL OF THIS...!!
SINCE I WAS EIGHT YEARS OLD...
I'VE BEEN MAKING THE WRONG CHOICES, ONE AFTER THE OTHER...
I WAS SELFISH...
I WAS NEVER RATIONAL...
NO ONE WISHED FOR WHAT JUST HAPPENED!
THIS WASN'T ANYONE'S FAULT!
FUSHI, ONCE YOU GET CLOSE ENOUGH TO THEM, THEY PLANT ROOTS IN THE GROUND.
...GET BACK, YOU TWO. GET SOME DISTANCE FROM THEM.
...WHAT ARE YOU PLANNING TO DO?

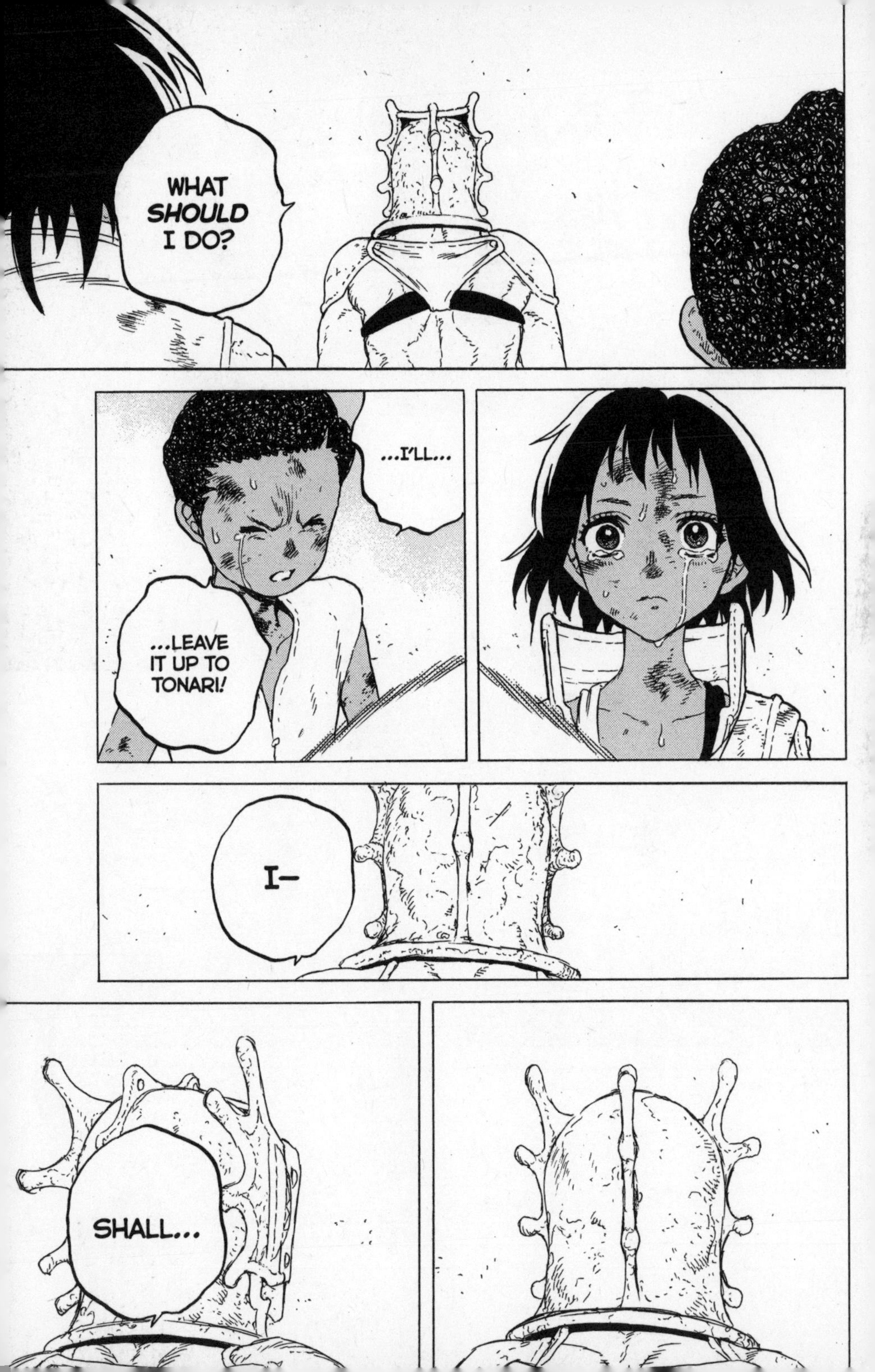
WHAT SHOULD I DO?
...I'LL...
...LEAVE IT UP TO TONARI!
I–
SHALL...

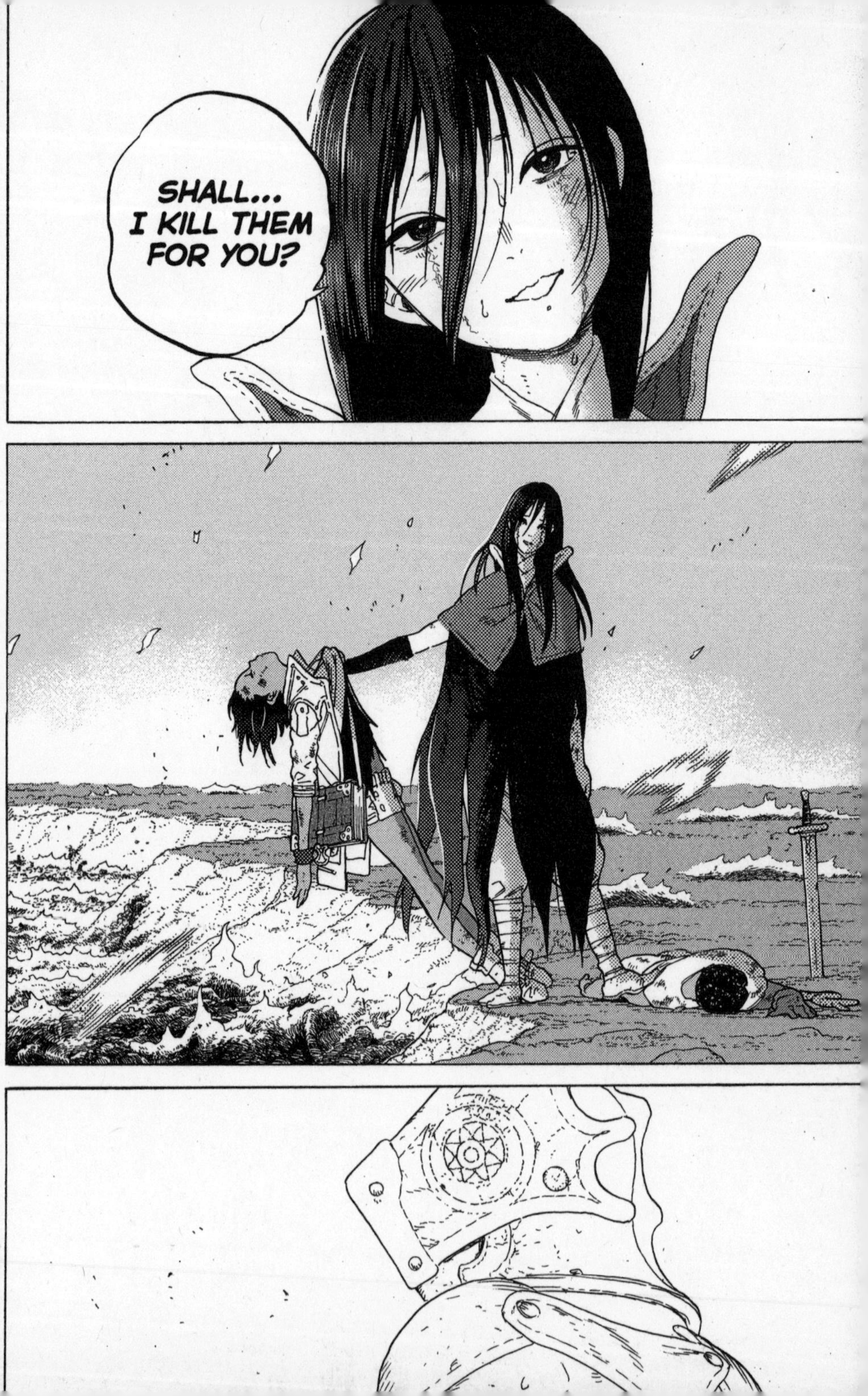
SHALL... I KILL THEM FOR YOU?

#51 The Fire of Farewell

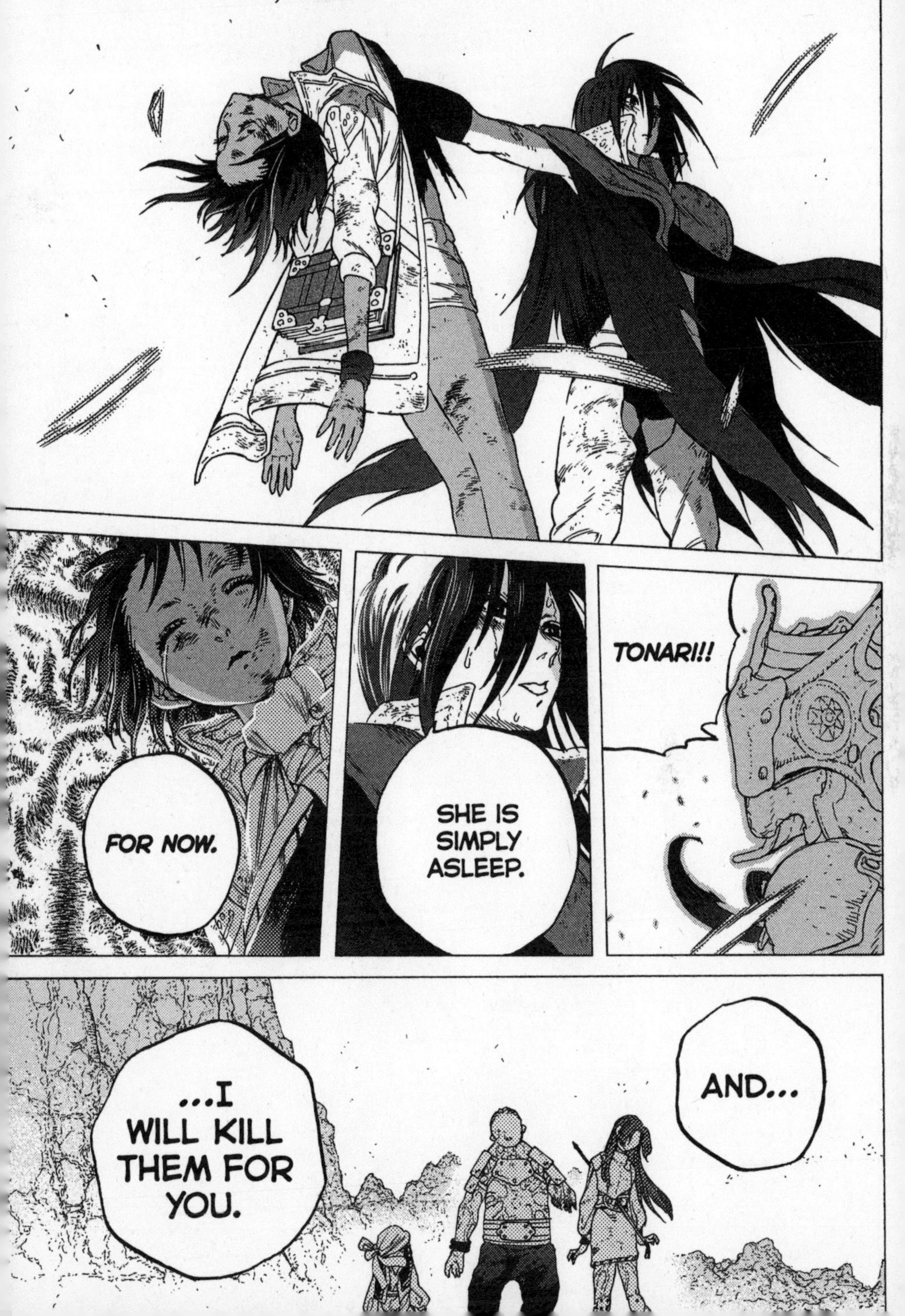
TONARI!!
SHE IS SIMPLY ASLEEP.
FOR NOW.
AND...
...I WILL KILL THEM FOR YOU.

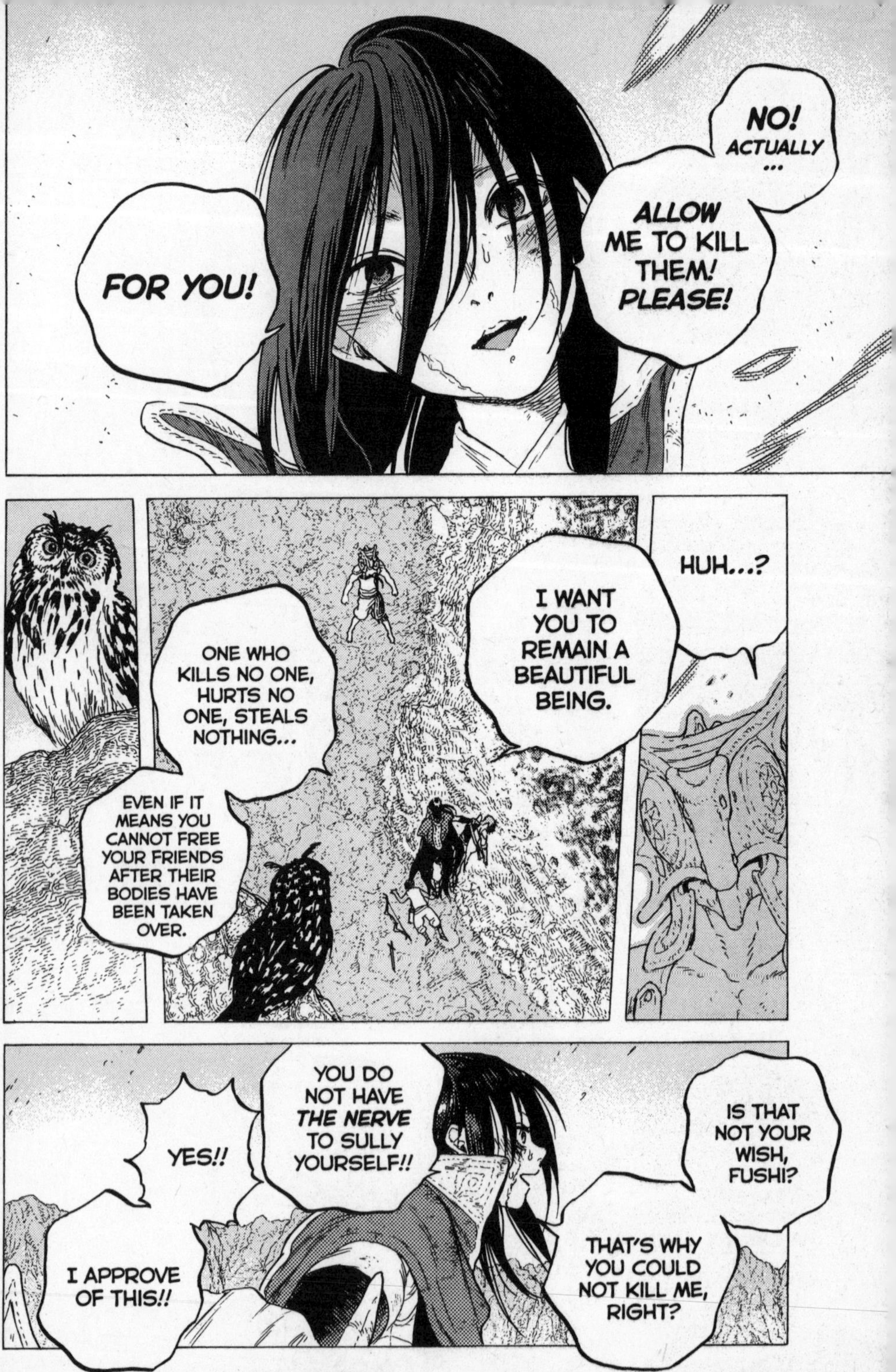
NO! ACTUALLY...
ALLOW ME TO KILL THEM! PLEASE!
FOR YOU!
HUH...?
I WANT YOU TO REMAIN A BEAUTIFUL BEING.
ONE WHO KILLS NO ONE, HURTS NO ONE, STEALS NOTHING...
EVEN IF IT MEANS YOU CANNOT FREE YOUR FRIENDS AFTER THEIR BODIES HAVE BEEN TAKEN OVER.
IS THAT NOT YOUR WISH, FUSHI?
THAT'S WHY YOU COULD NOT KILL ME, RIGHT?
YOU DO NOT HAVE THE NERVE TO SULLY YOURSELF!!
YES!!
I APPROVE OF THIS!!

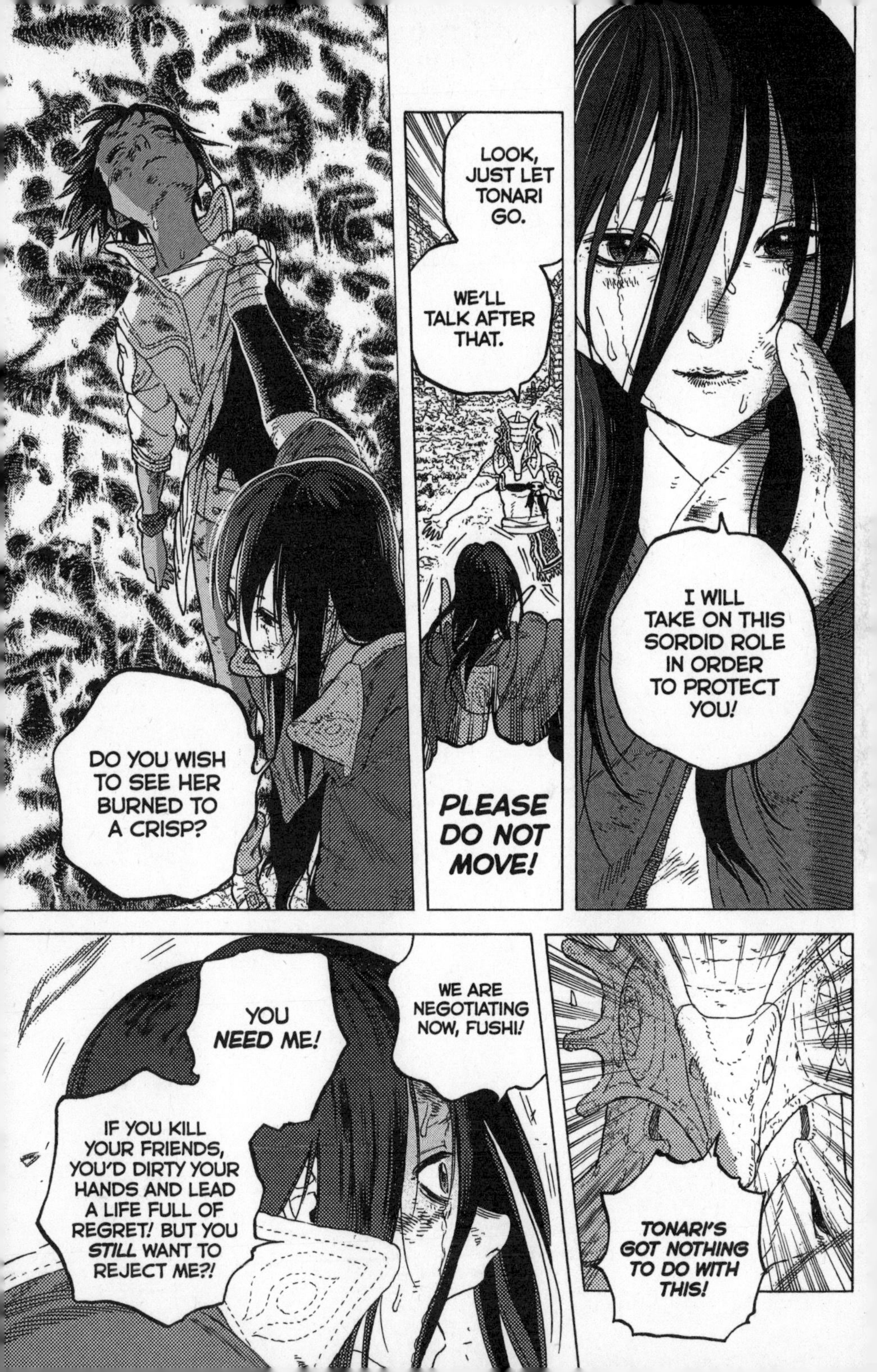
I WILL TAKE ON THIS SORDID ROLE IN ORDER TO PROTECT YOU!
LOOK, JUST LET TONARI GO.
WE'LL TALK AFTER THAT.
PLEASE DO NOT MOVE!
DO YOU WISH TO SEE HER BURNED TO A CRISP?
TONARI'S GOT NOTHING TO DO WITH THIS!
WE ARE NEGOTIATING NOW, FUSHI!
YOU NEED ME!
IF YOU KILL YOUR FRIENDS, YOU'D DIRTY YOUR HANDS AND LEAD A LIFE FULL OF REGRET! BUT YOU STILL WANT TO REJECT ME?!

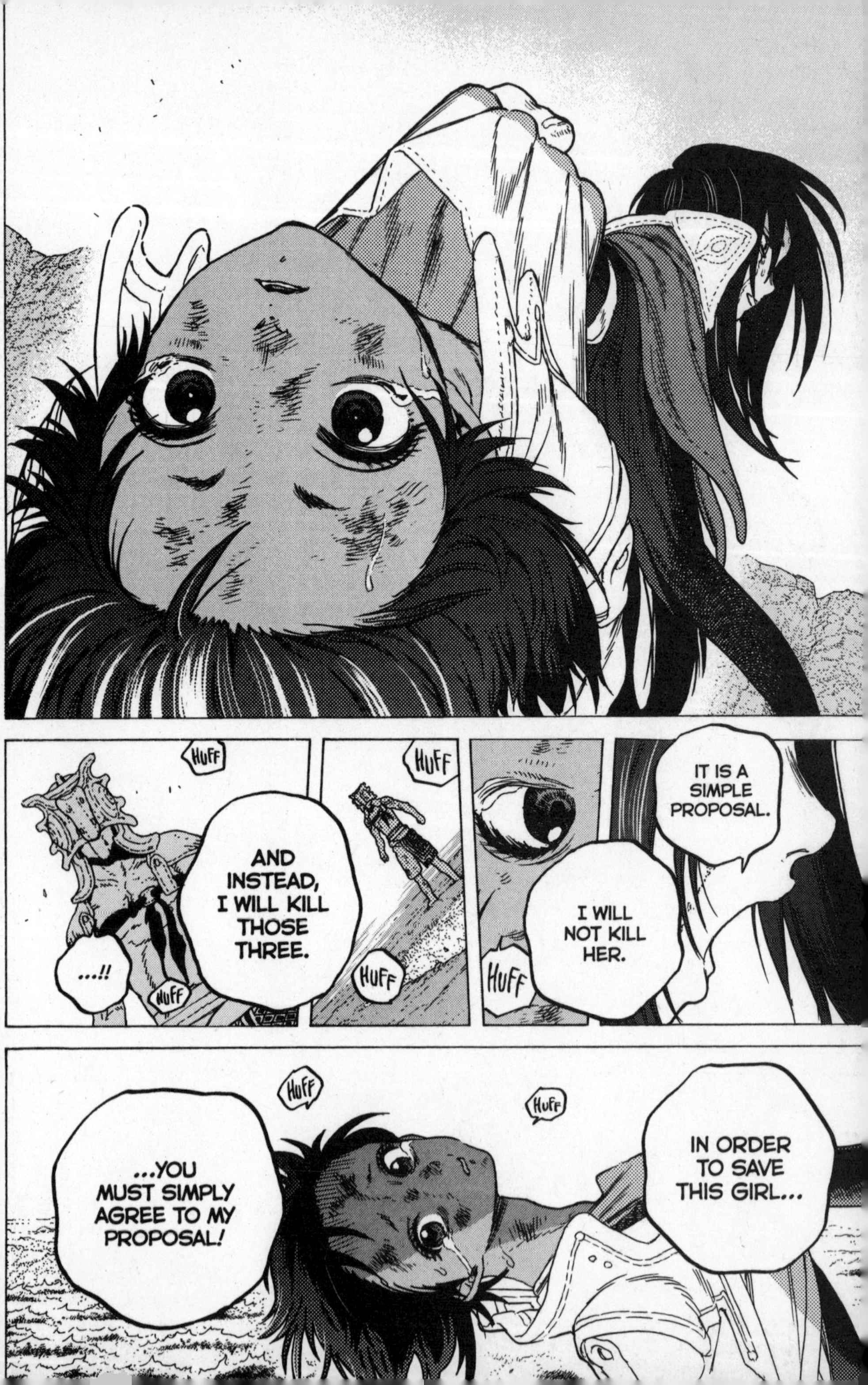
IT IS A SIMPLE PROPOSAL.
I WILL NOT KILL HER.
HUFF
HUFF
HUFF
HUFF
AND INSTEAD, I WILL KILL THOSE THREE.
...!!
HUFF
HUFF
IN ORDER TO SAVE THIS GIRL...
HUFF
...YOU MUST SIMPLY AGREE TO MY PROPOSAL!

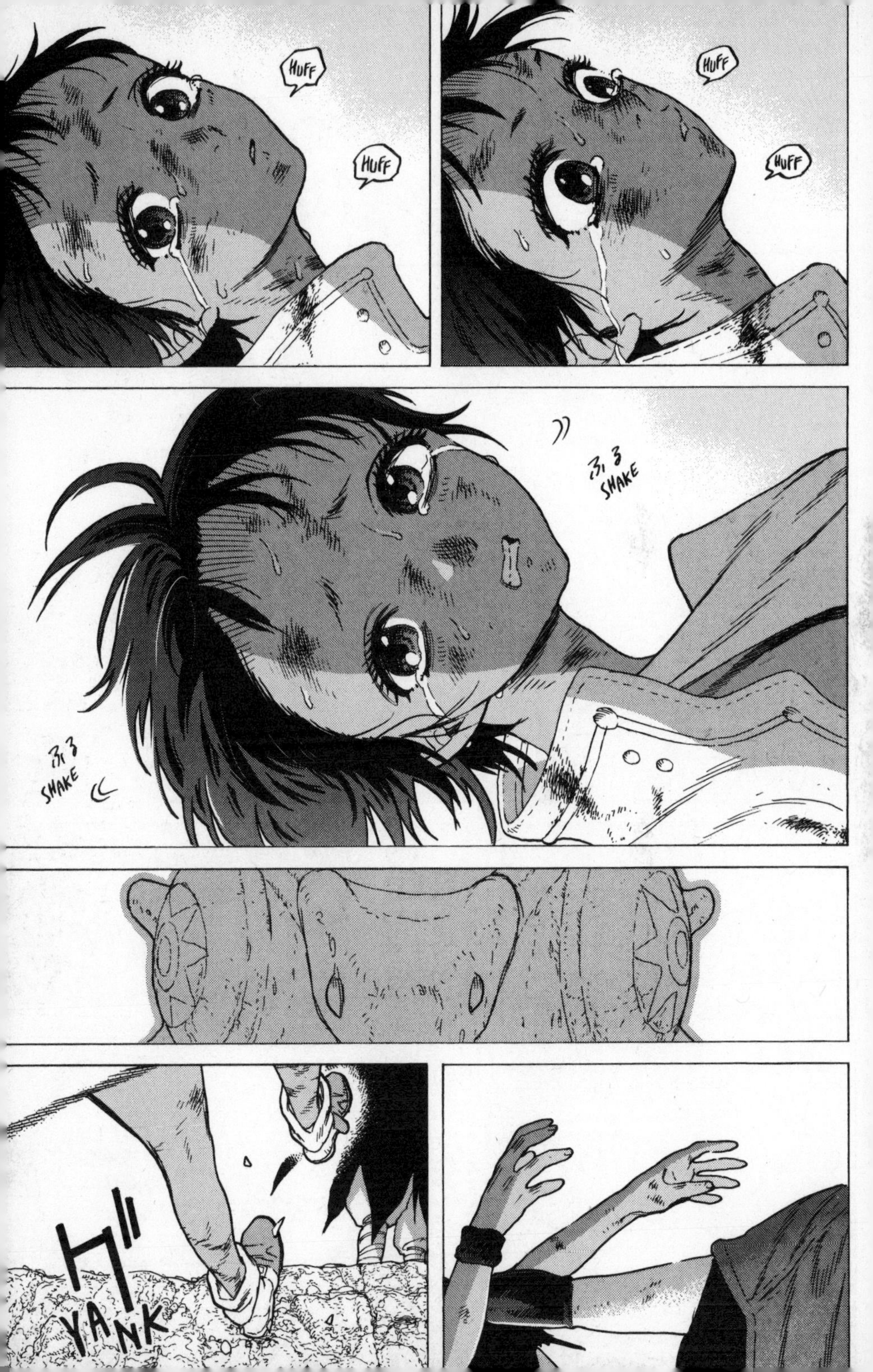
HUFF
HUFF
HUFF
HUFF
ふる
SHAKE
ふる
SHAKE
YANK

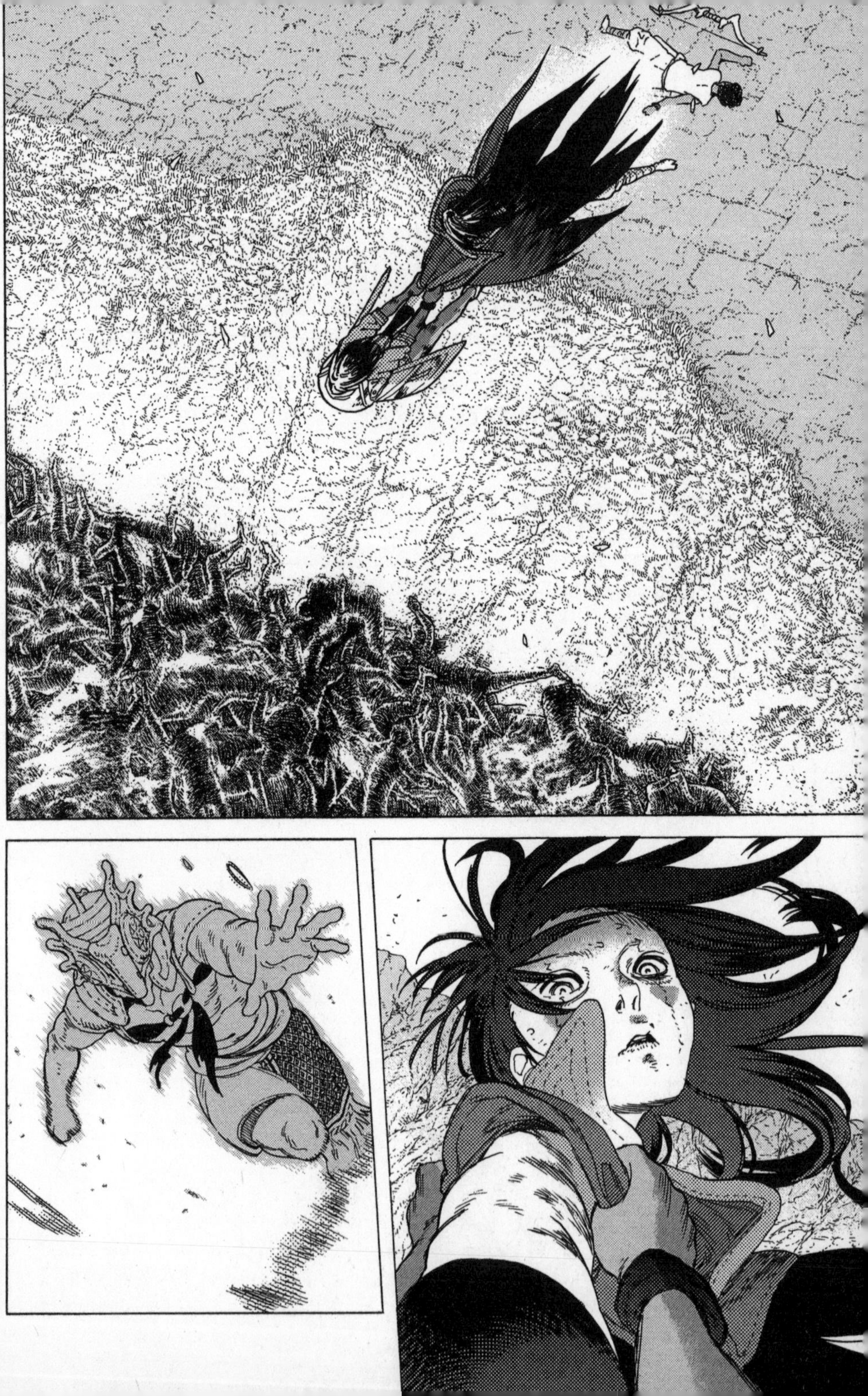

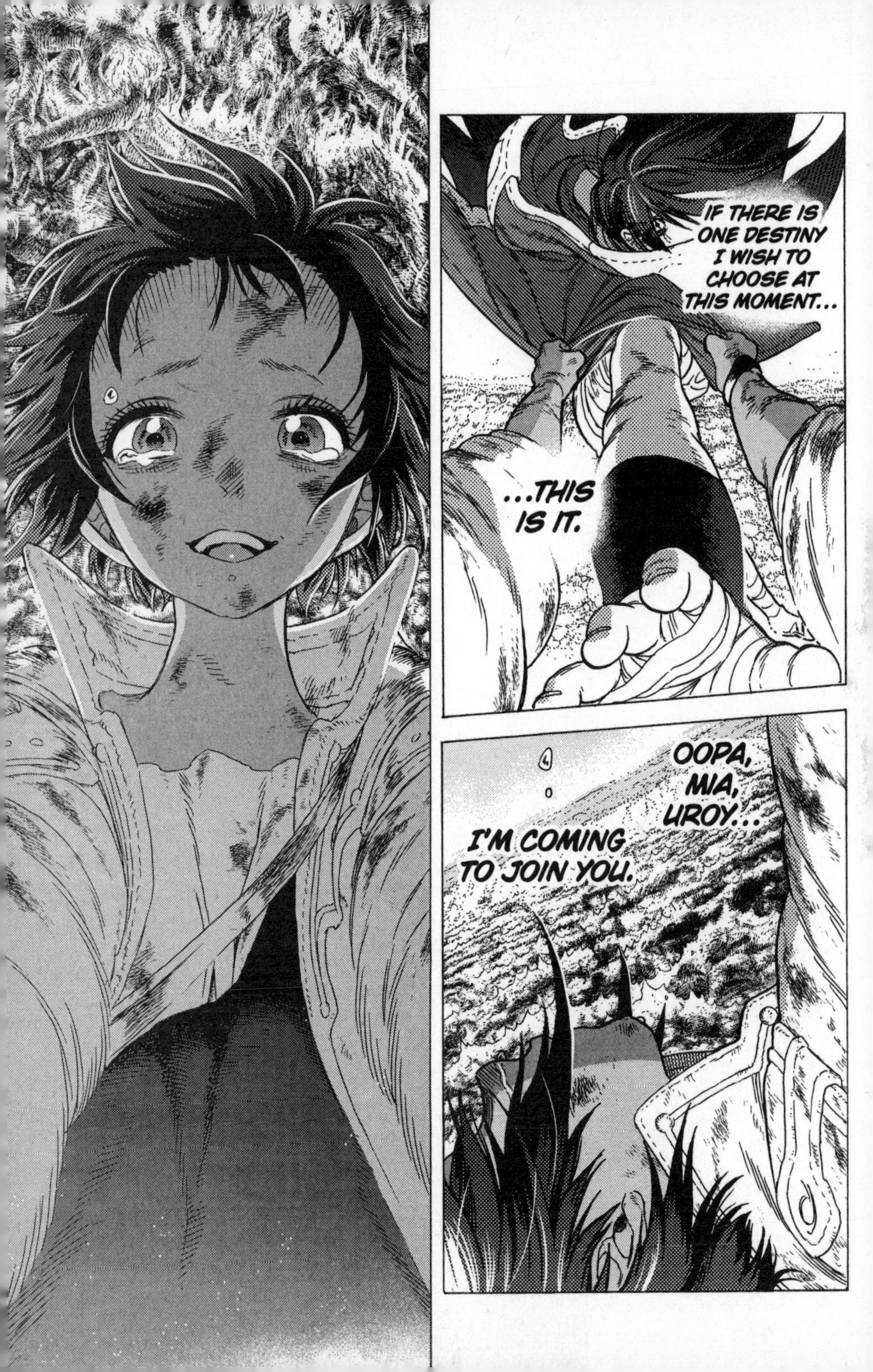
IF THERE IS ONE DESTINY I WISH TO CHOOSE AT THIS MOMENT...
...THIS IS IT.
OOPA, MIA, UROY...
I'M COMING TO JOIN YOU.

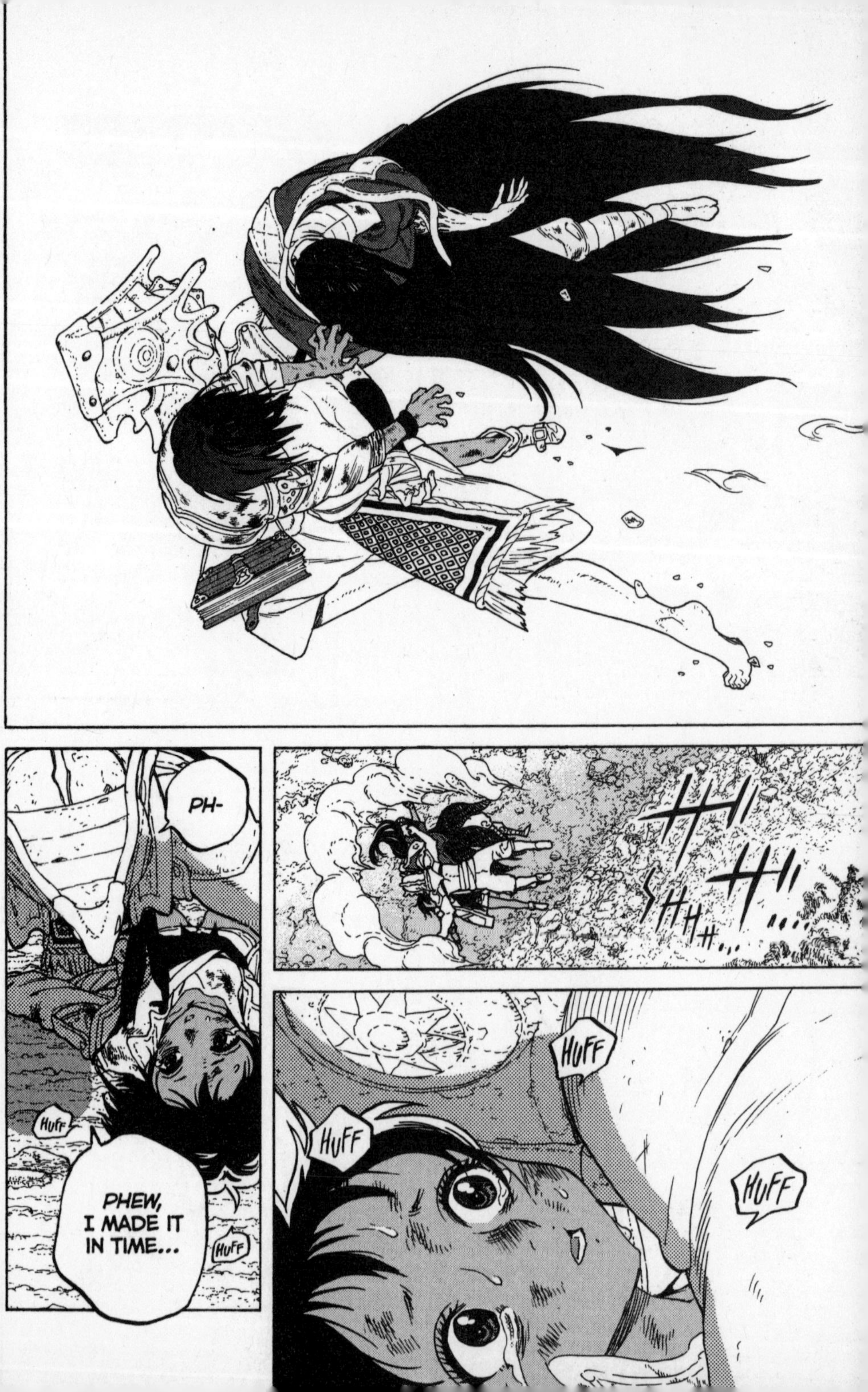
SHHH...
HUFF
HUFF
HUFF
PH-
HUFF
PHEW, I MADE IT IN TIME...
HUFF

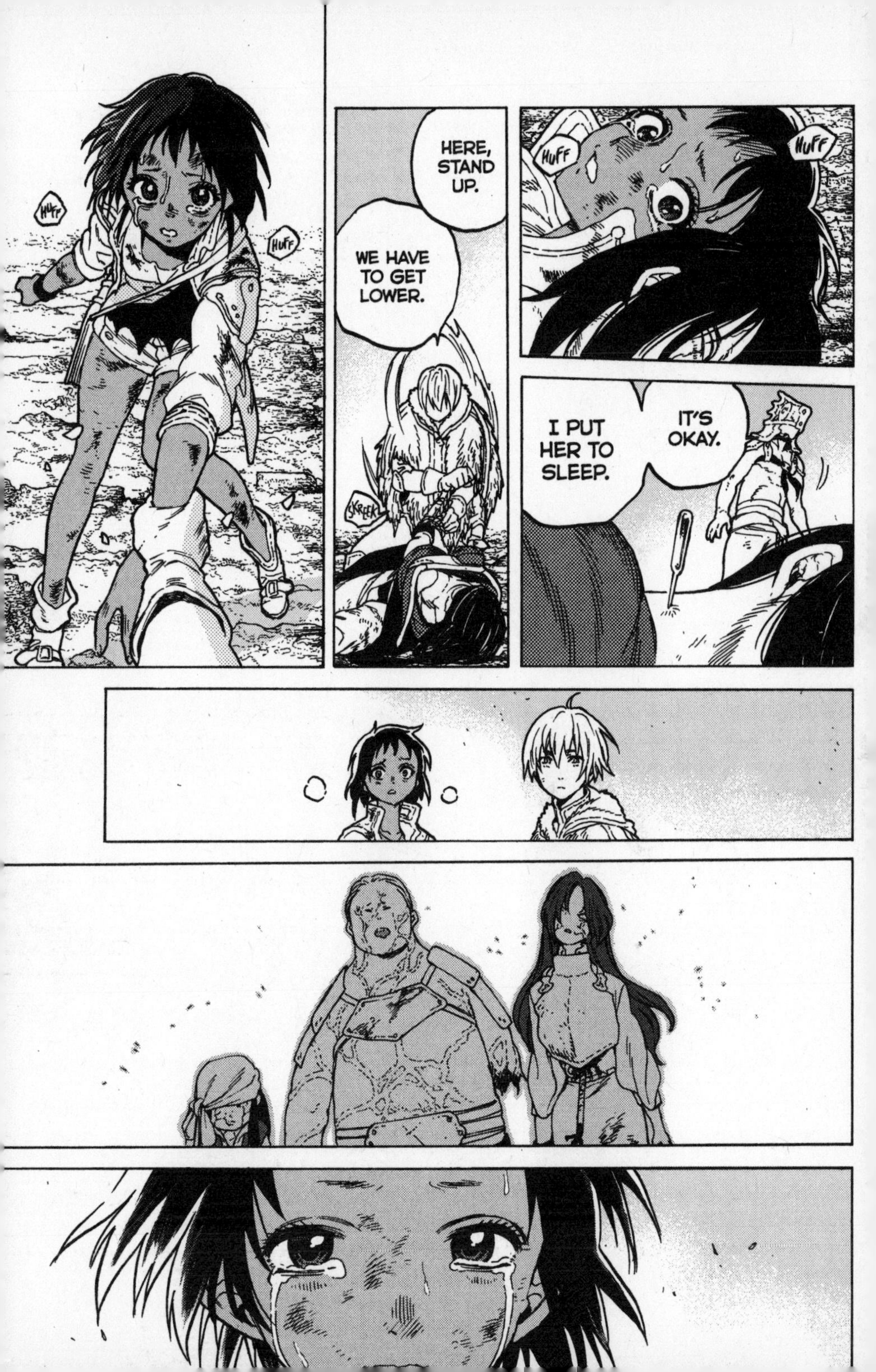
HUFF
HUFF
IT'S OKAY.
I PUT HER TO SLEEP.
HERE, STAND UP.
WE HAVE TO GET LOWER.
SKREEK
HUFF
HUFF

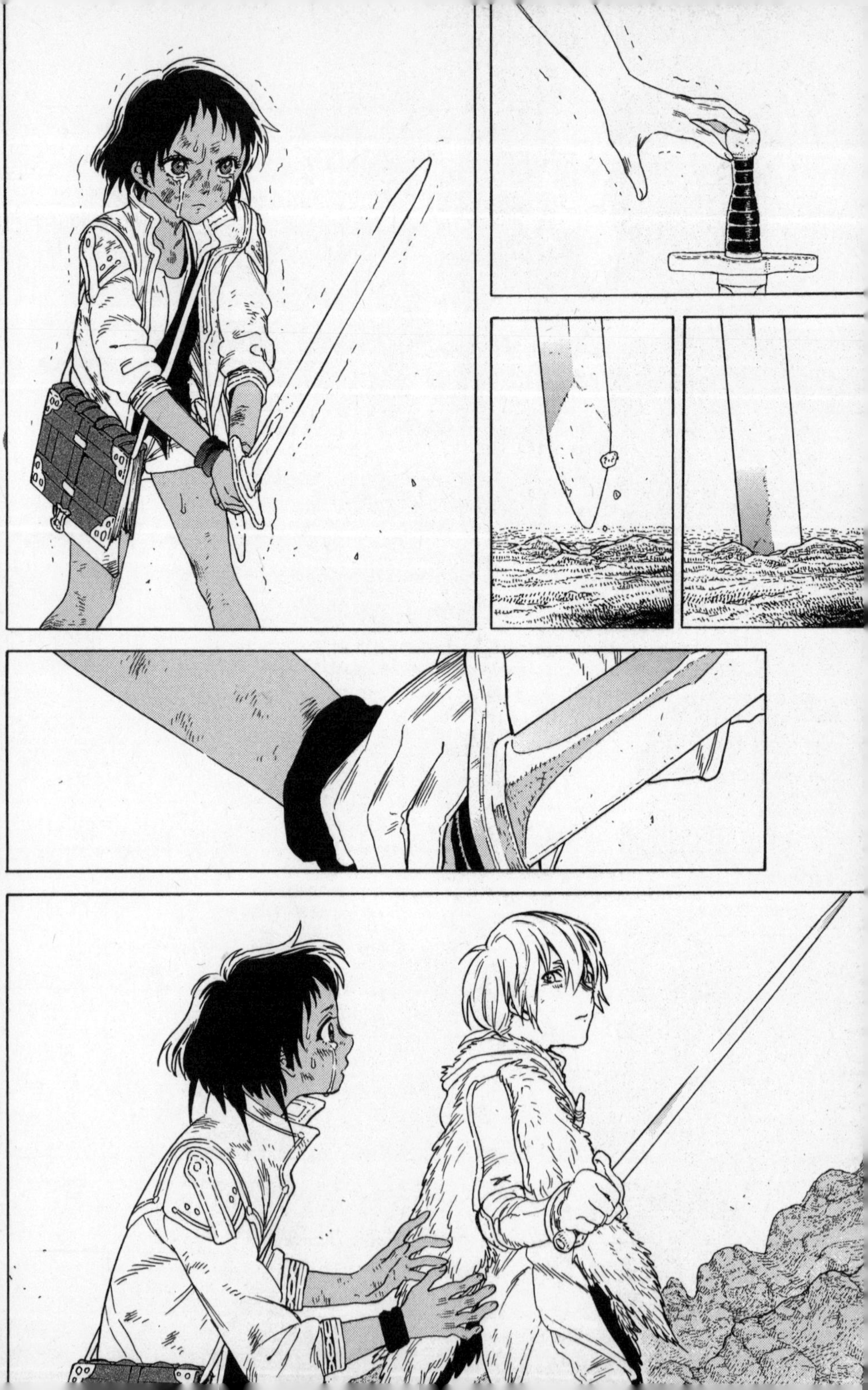

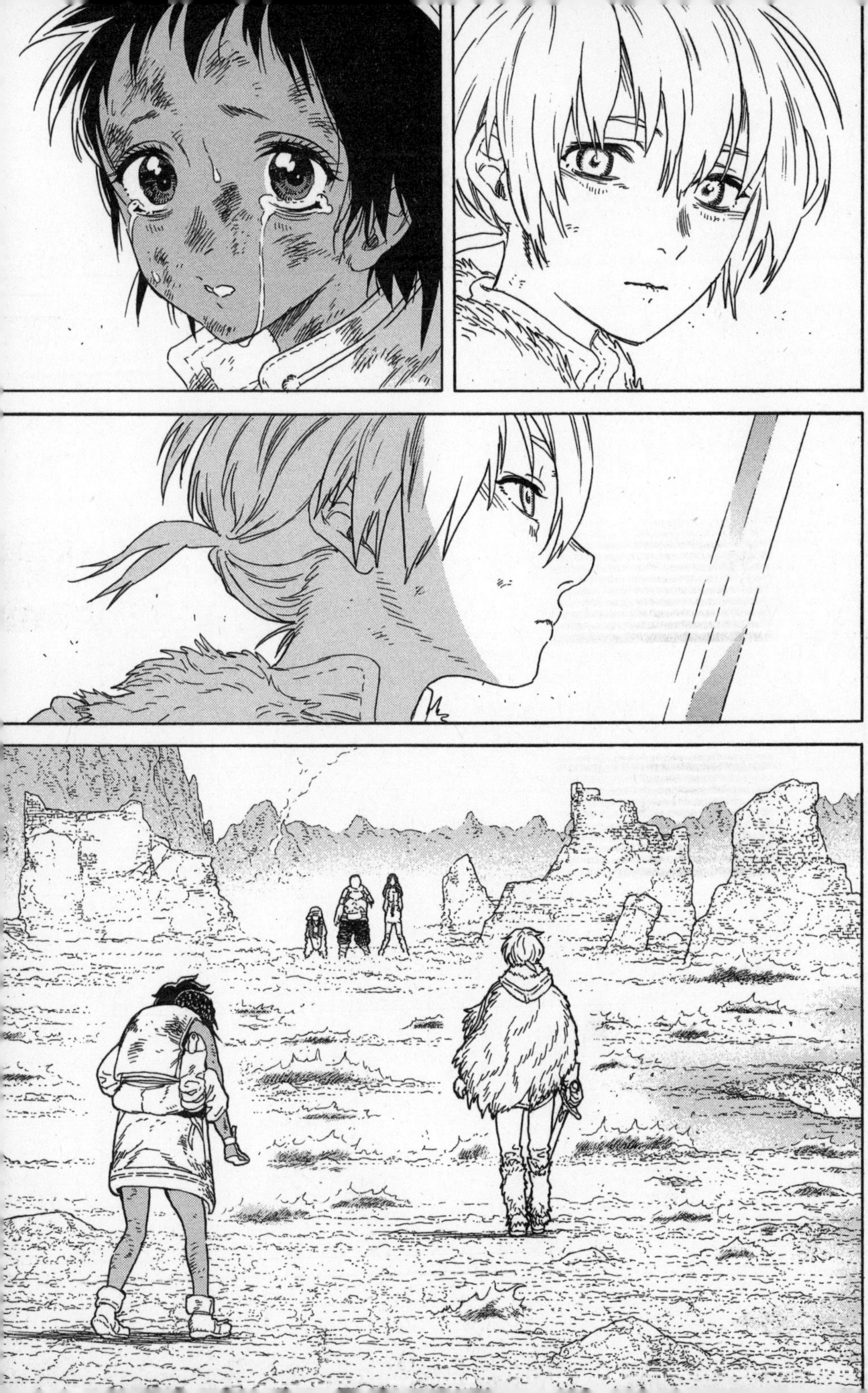

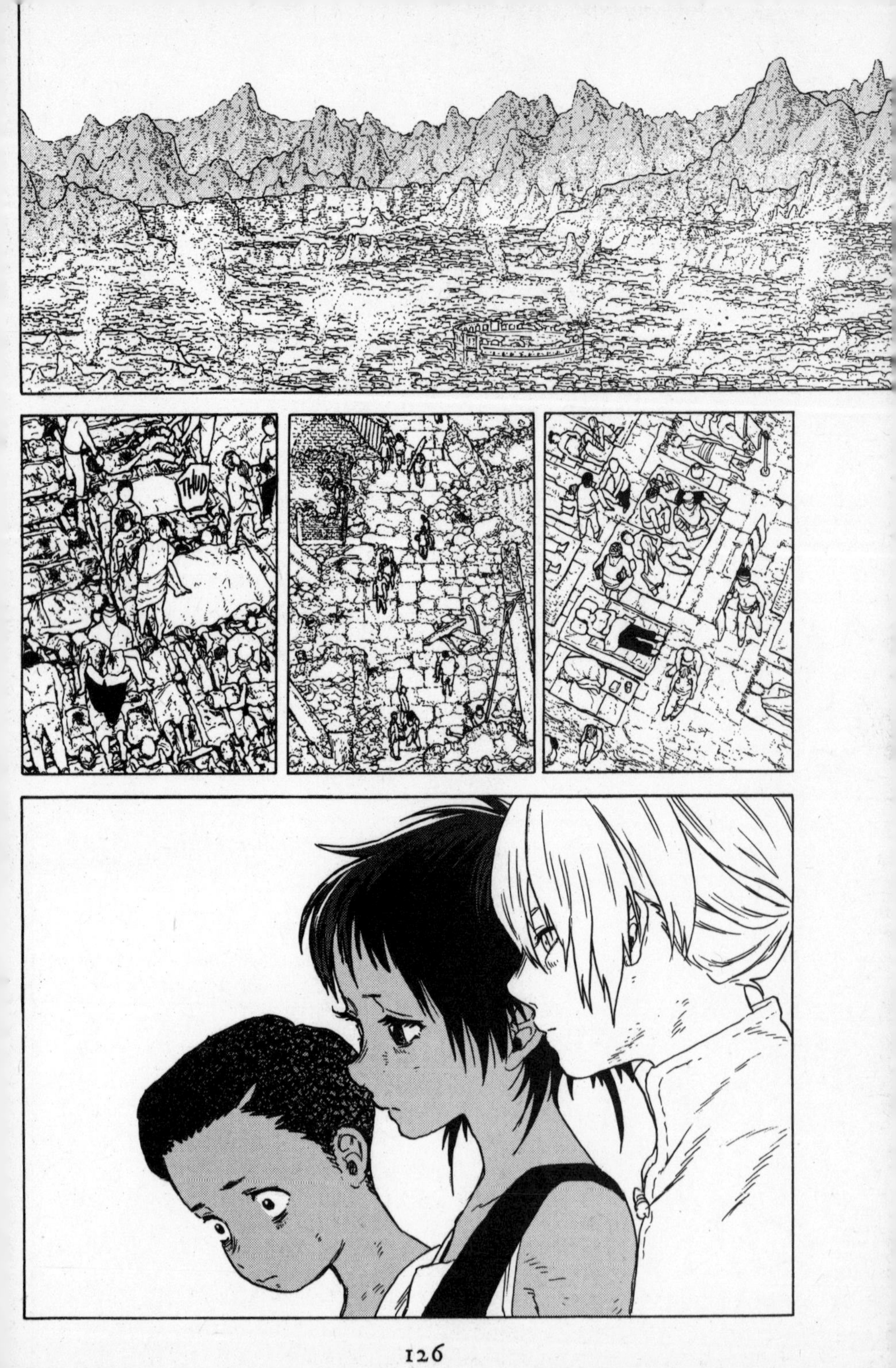
THUD

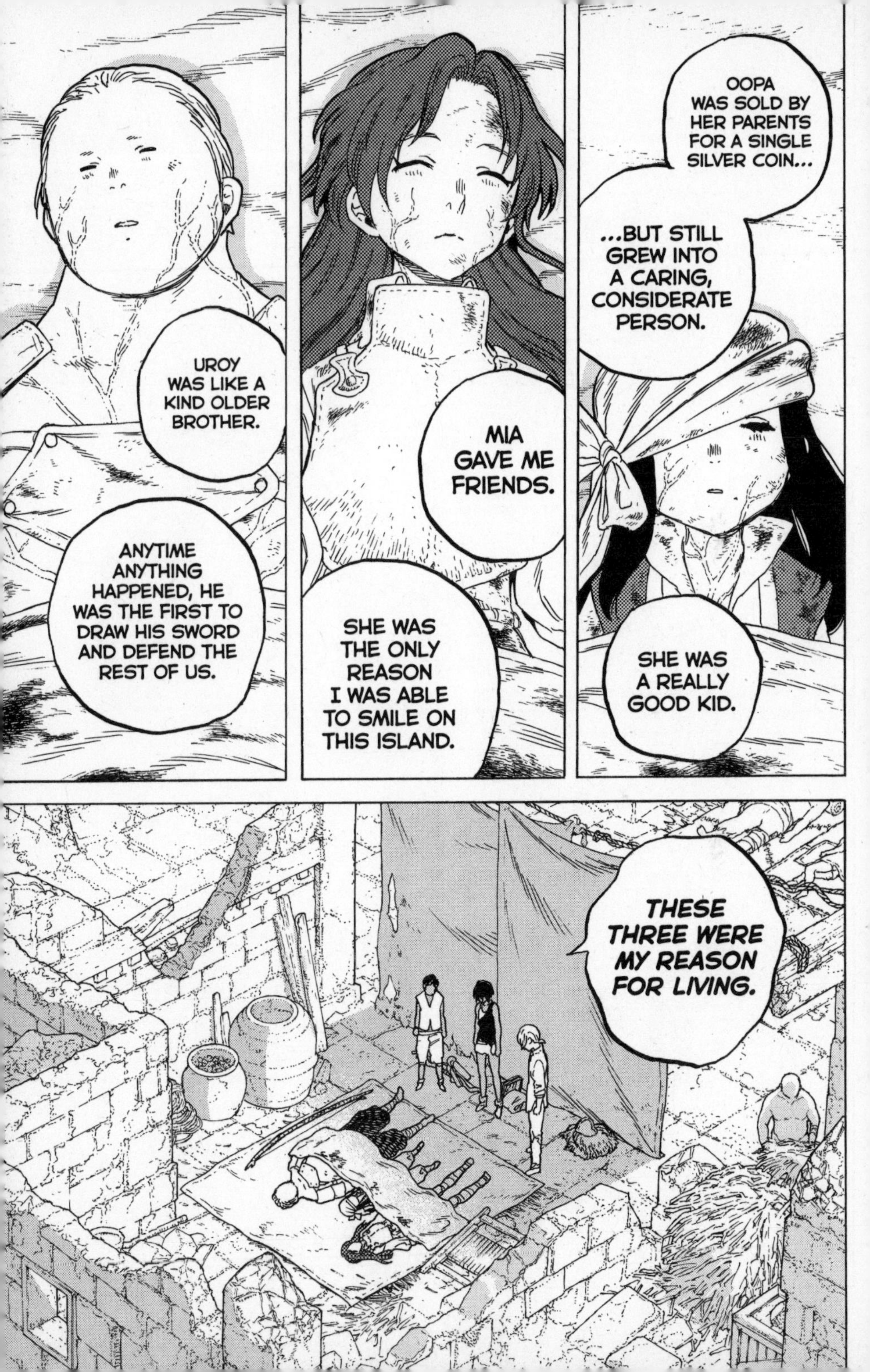
OOPA WAS SOLD BY HER PARENTS FOR A SINGLE SILVER COIN...
...BUT STILL GREW INTO A CARING, CONSIDERATE PERSON.
SHE WAS A REALLY GOOD KID.
MIA GAVE ME FRIENDS.
SHE WAS THE ONLY REASON I WAS ABLE TO SMILE ON THIS ISLAND.
UROY WAS LIKE A KIND OLDER BROTHER.
ANYTIME ANYTHING HAPPENED, HE WAS THE FIRST TO DRAW HIS SWORD AND DEFEND THE REST OF US.
THESE THREE WERE MY REASON FOR LIVING.

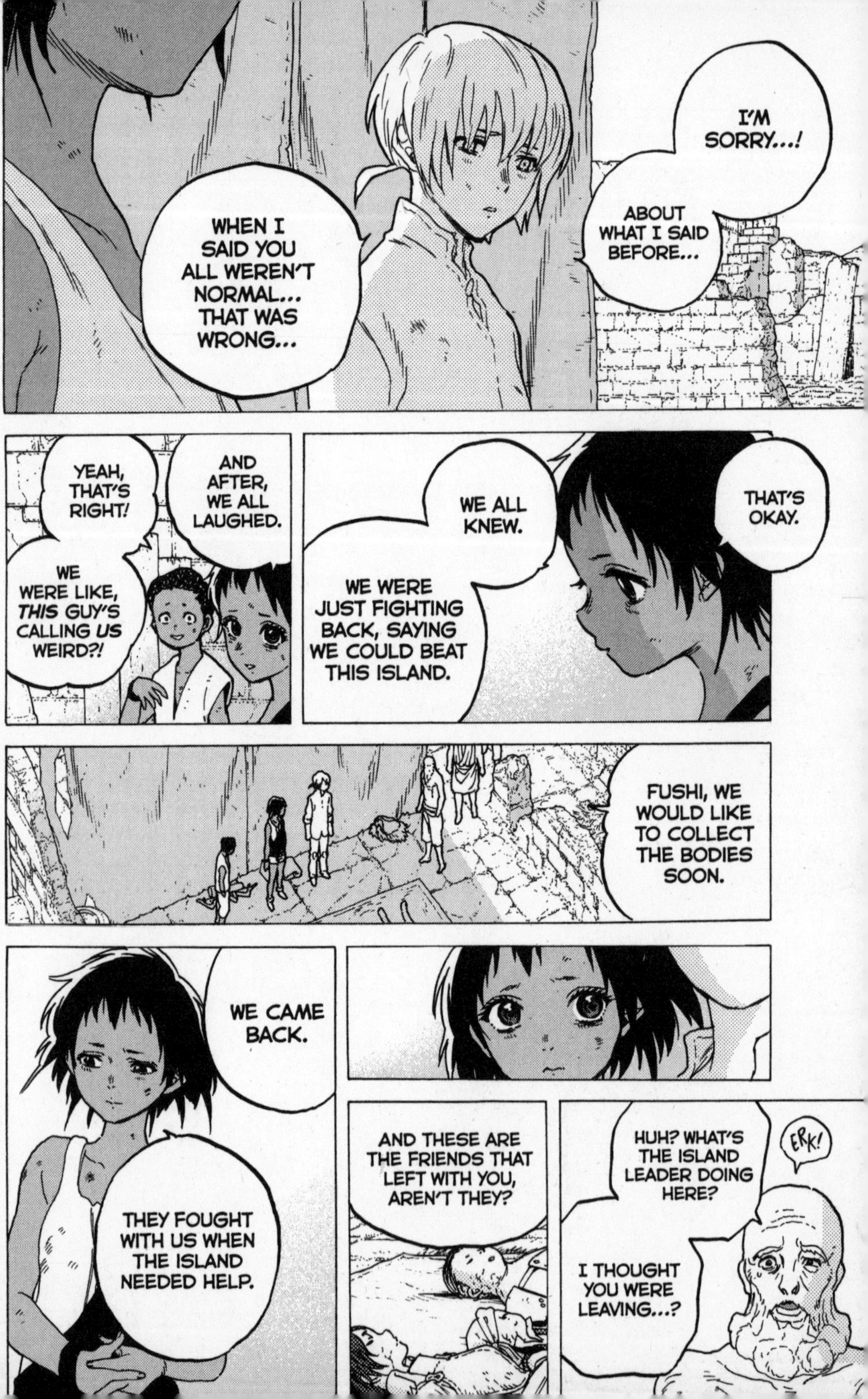
I'M SORRY...!
ABOUT WHAT I SAID BEFORE...
WHEN I SAID YOU ALL WEREN'T NORMAL... THAT WAS WRONG...
THAT'S OKAY.
WE ALL KNEW.
WE WERE JUST FIGHTING BACK, SAYING WE COULD BEAT THIS ISLAND.
AND AFTER, WE ALL LAUGHED.
YEAH, THAT'S RIGHT!
WE WERE LIKE, *THIS* GUY'S CALLING *US* WEIRD?!
FUSHI, WE WOULD LIKE TO COLLECT THE BODIES SOON.
ERK!
HUH? WHAT'S THE ISLAND LEADER DOING HERE?
I THOUGHT YOU WERE LEAVING...?
AND THESE ARE THE FRIENDS THAT LEFT WITH YOU, AREN'T THEY?
WE CAME BACK.
THEY FOUGHT WITH US WHEN THE ISLAND NEEDED HELP.

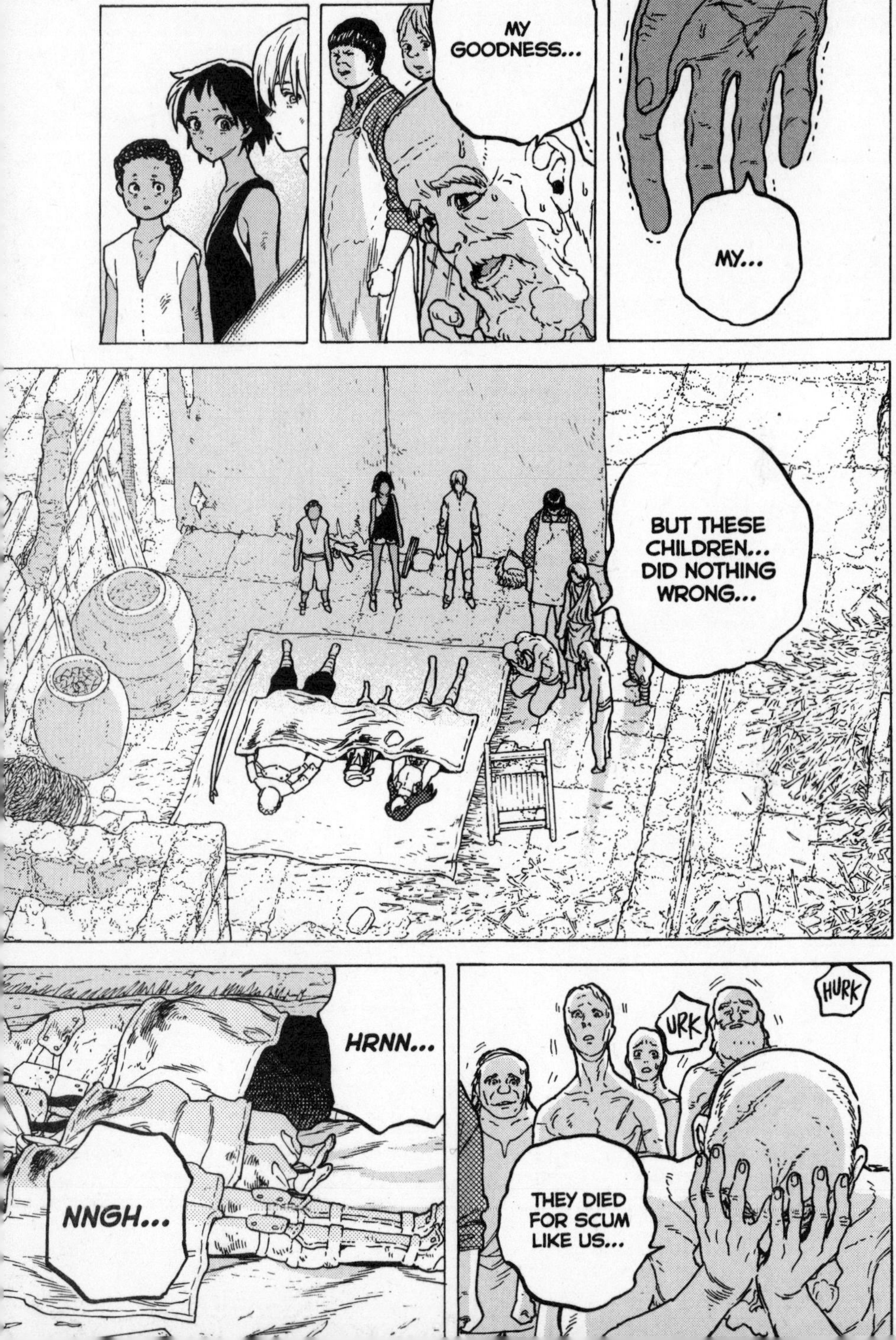
MY...
MY GOODNESS...
BUT THESE CHILDREN... DID NOTHING WRONG...
HURK
URK
THEY DIED FOR SCUM LIKE US...
HRNN...
NNGH...

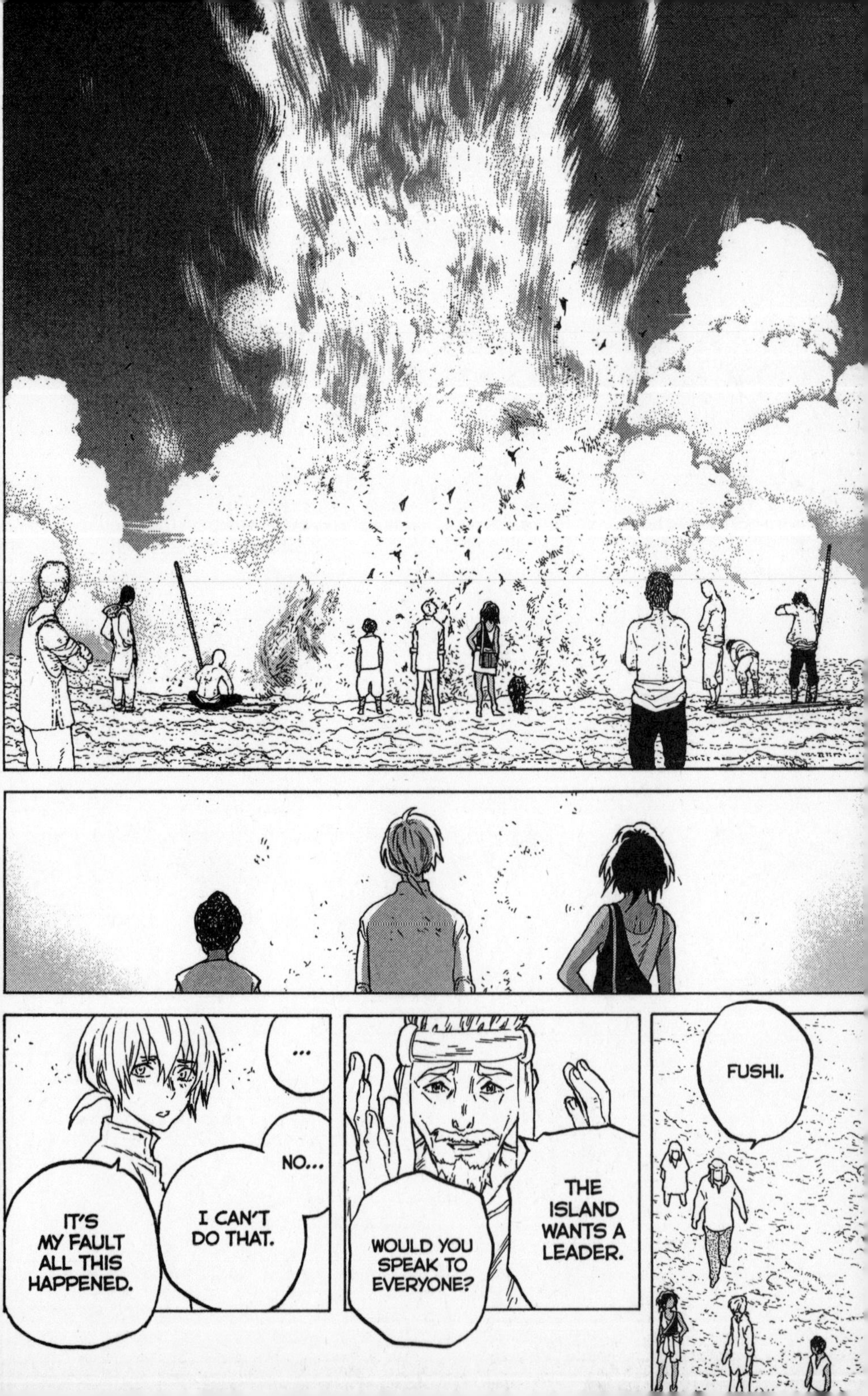
FUSHI.
THE ISLAND WANTS A LEADER.
WOULD YOU SPEAK TO EVERYONE?
...
NO...
I CAN'T DO THAT.
IT'S MY FAULT ALL THIS HAPPENED.

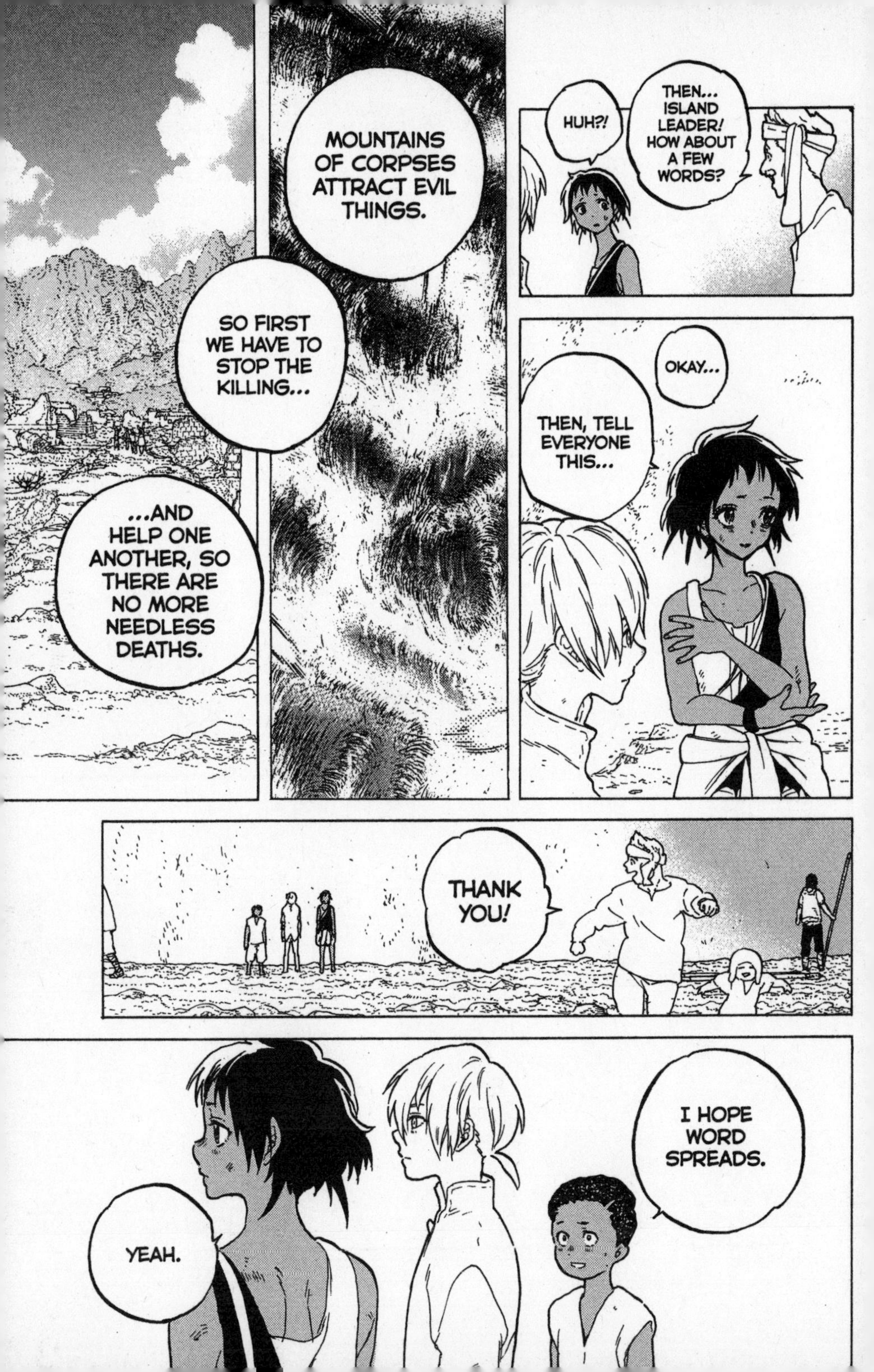
THEN... ISLAND LEADER! HOW ABOUT A FEW WORDS?
HUH?!
OKAY...
THEN, TELL EVERYONE THIS...
MOUNTAINS OF CORPSES ATTRACT EVIL THINGS.
SO FIRST WE HAVE TO STOP THE KILLING...
...AND HELP ONE ANOTHER, SO THERE ARE NO MORE NEEDLESS DEATHS.
THANK YOU!
I HOPE WORD SPREADS.
YEAH.

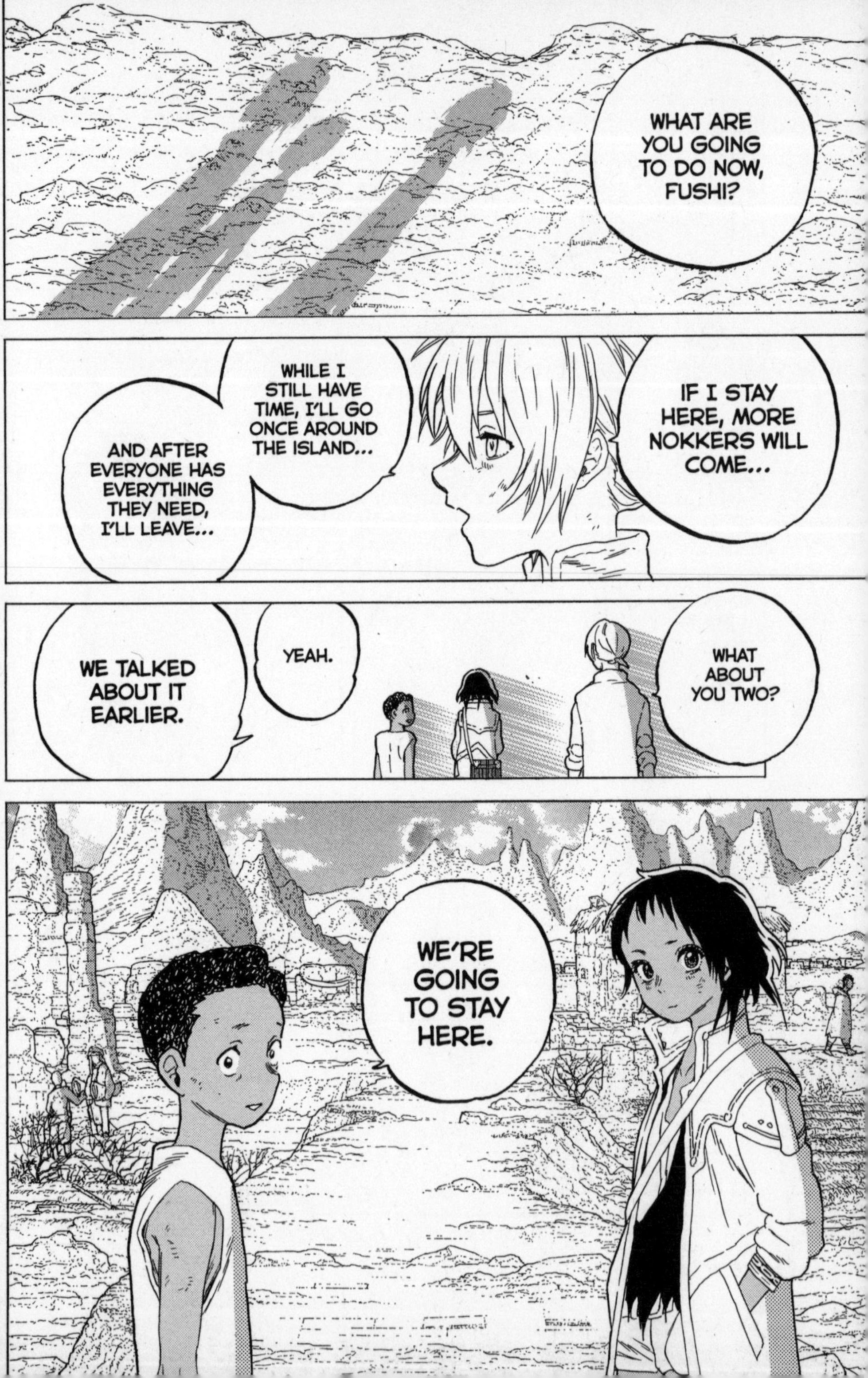
WHAT ARE YOU GOING TO DO NOW, FUSHI?
IF I STAY HERE, MORE NOKKERS WILL COME...
WHILE I STILL HAVE TIME, I'LL GO ONCE AROUND THE ISLAND...
AND AFTER EVERYONE HAS EVERYTHING THEY NEED, I'LL LEAVE...
WHAT ABOUT YOU TWO?
YEAH.
WE TALKED ABOUT IT EARLIER.
WE'RE GOING TO STAY HERE.

#52 Departing for Reunion

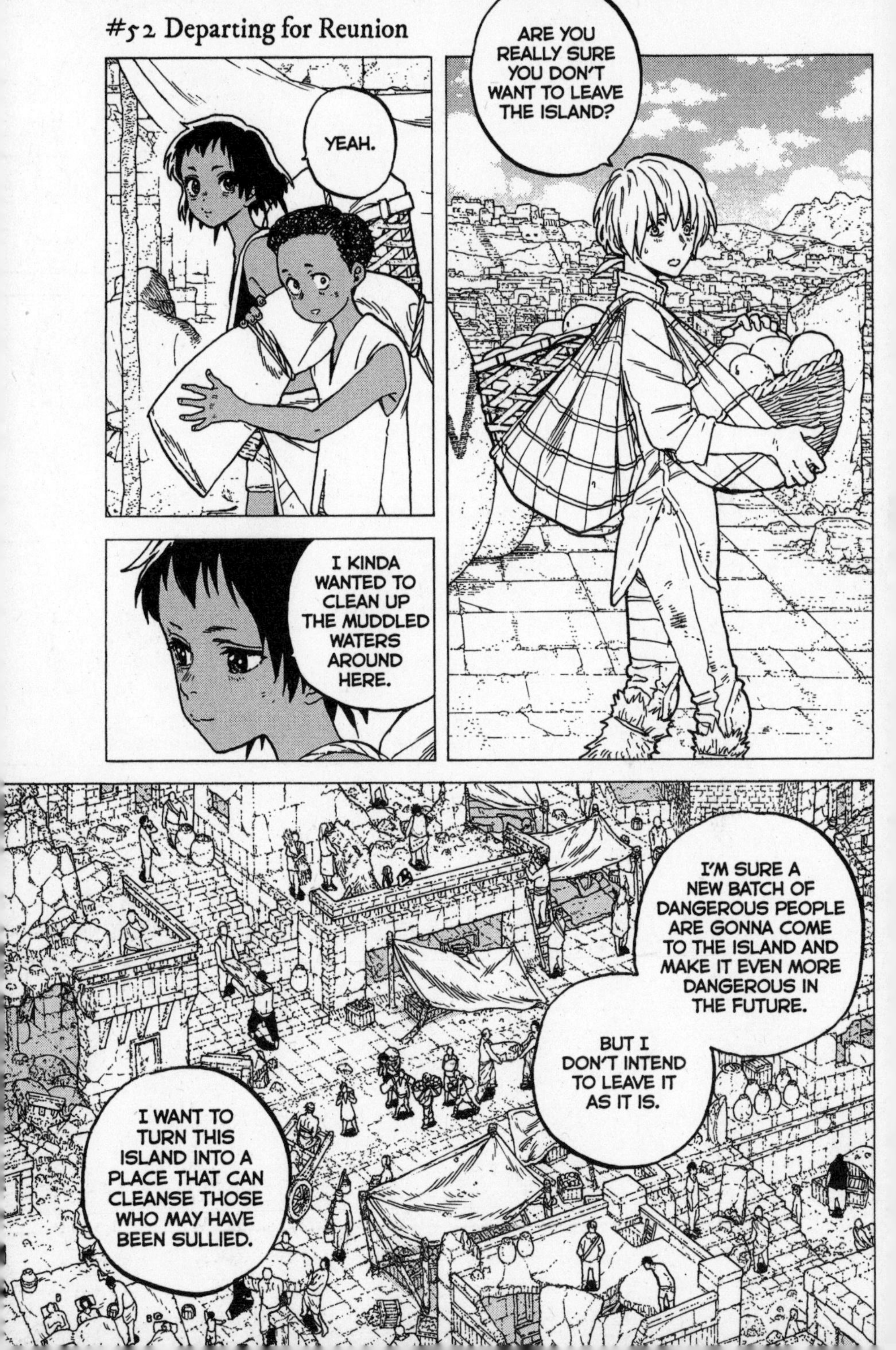

ARE YOU REALLY SURE YOU DON'T WANT TO LEAVE THE ISLAND?
YEAH.
I KINDA WANTED TO CLEAN UP THE MUDDLED WATERS AROUND HERE.
I'M SURE A NEW BATCH OF DANGEROUS PEOPLE ARE GONNA COME TO THE ISLAND AND MAKE IT EVEN MORE DANGEROUS IN THE FUTURE.
BUT I DON'T INTEND TO LEAVE IT AS IT IS.
I WANT TO TURN THIS ISLAND INTO A PLACE THAT CAN CLEANSE THOSE WHO MAY HAVE BEEN SULLIED.

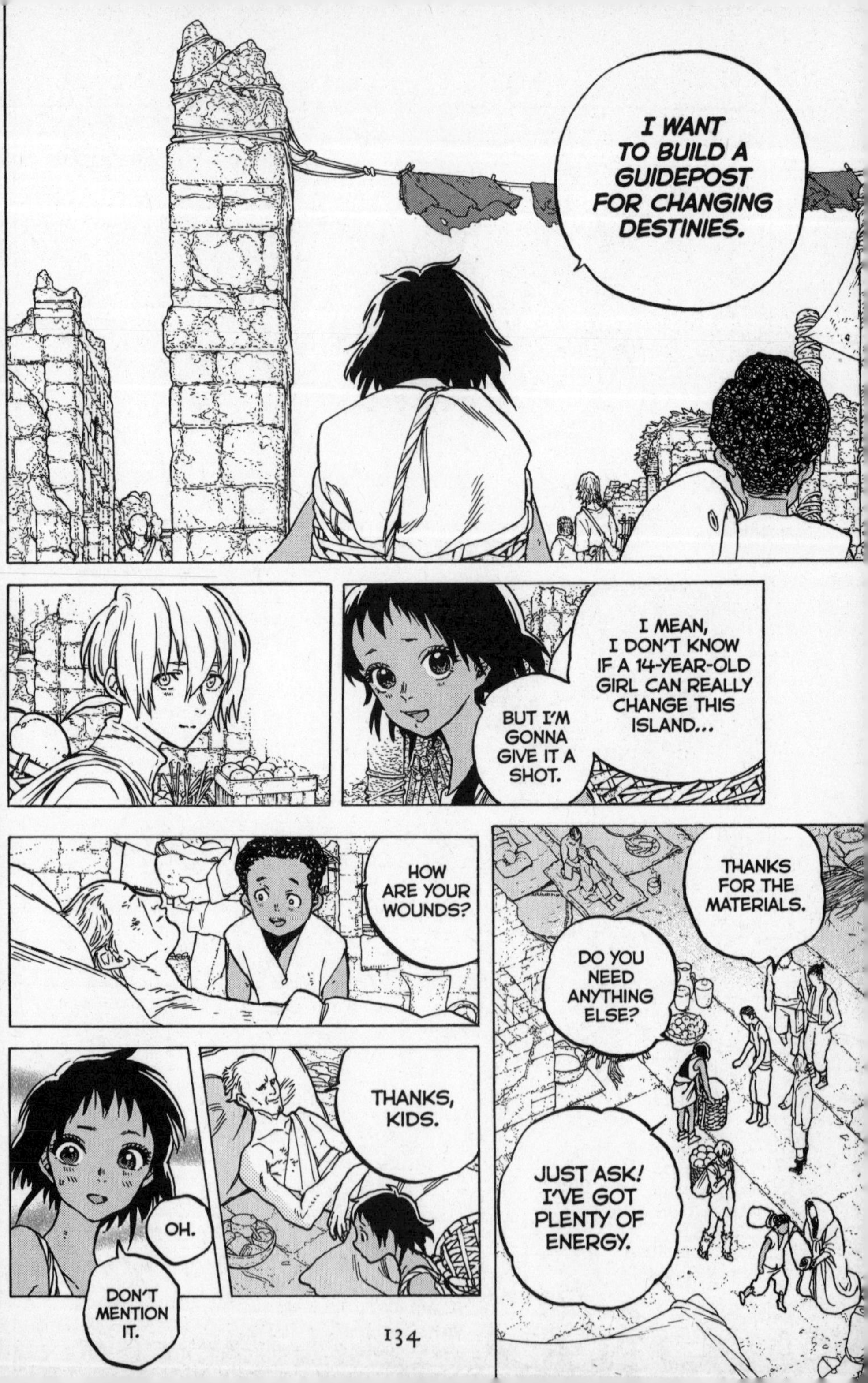
I WANT TO BUILD A GUIDEPOST FOR CHANGING DESTINIES.
I MEAN, I DON'T KNOW IF A 14-YEAR-OLD GIRL CAN REALLY CHANGE THIS ISLAND...
BUT I'M GONNA GIVE IT A SHOT.
THANKS FOR THE MATERIALS.
DO YOU NEED ANYTHING ELSE?
JUST ASK! I'VE GOT PLENTY OF ENERGY.
HOW ARE YOUR WOUNDS?
THANKS, KIDS.
OH.
DON'T MENTION IT.

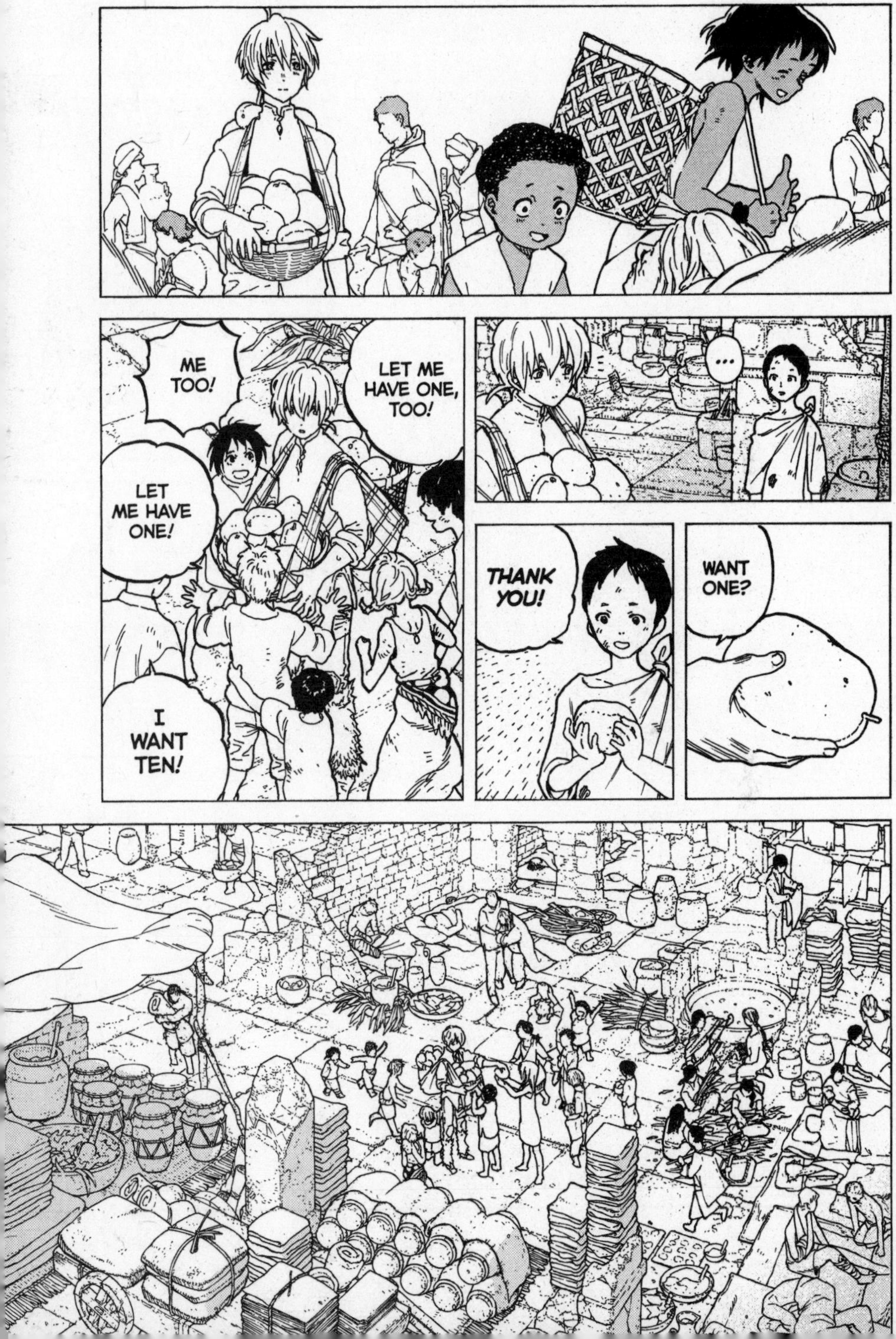
...
WANT ONE?
THANK YOU!
LET ME HAVE ONE, TOO!
ME TOO!
LET ME HAVE ONE!
I WANT TEN!

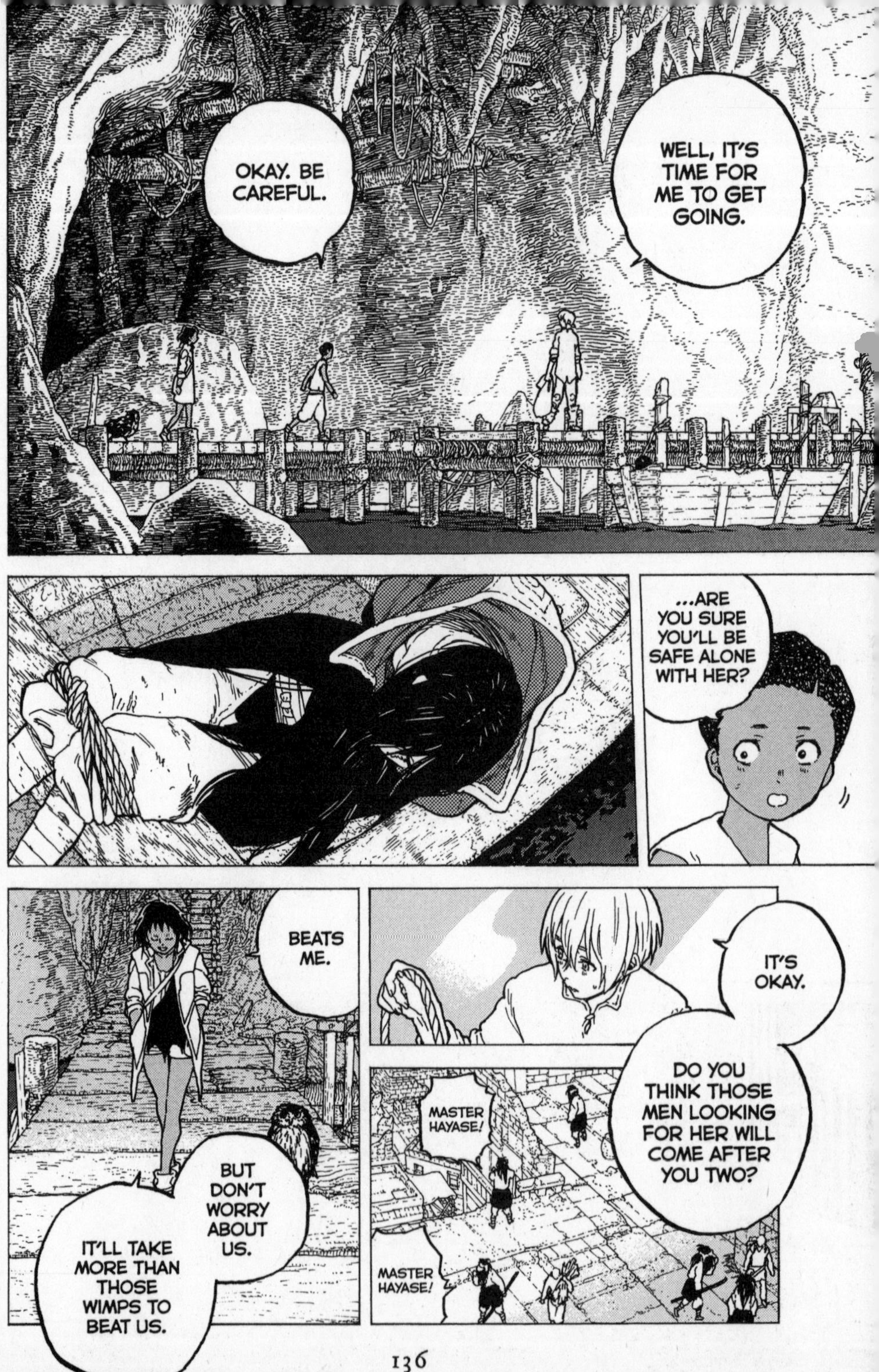
WELL, IT'S TIME FOR ME TO GET GOING.
OKAY. BE CAREFUL.
...ARE YOU SURE YOU'LL BE SAFE ALONE WITH HER?
IT'S OKAY.
DO YOU THINK THOSE MEN LOOKING FOR HER WILL COME AFTER YOU TWO?
MASTER HAYASE!
MASTER HAYASE!
BEATS ME.
BUT DON'T WORRY ABOUT US.
IT'LL TAKE MORE THAN THOSE WIMPS TO BEAT US.

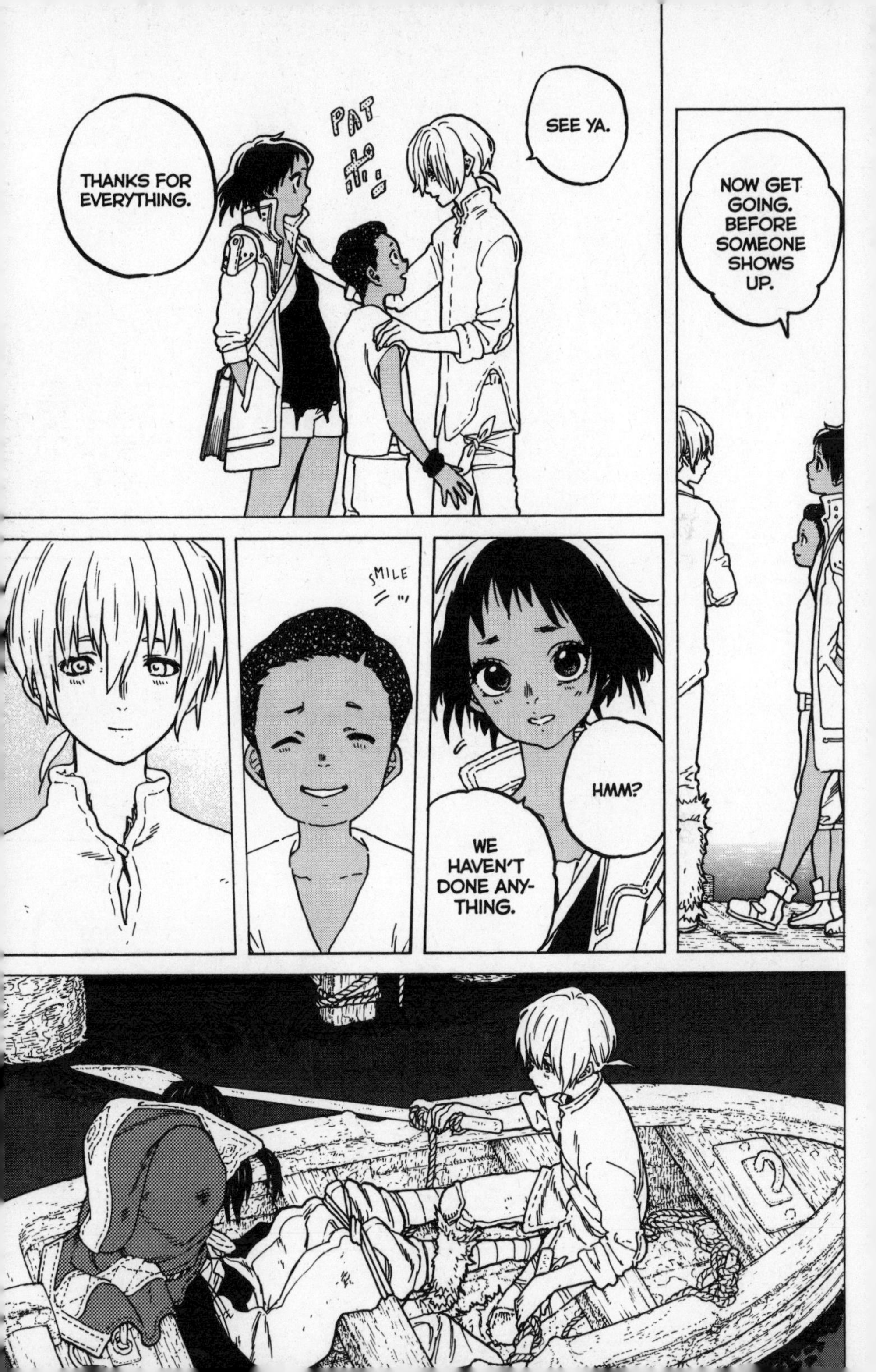
NOW GET GOING. BEFORE SOMEONE SHOWS UP.
SEE YA.
PAT
THANKS FOR EVERYTHING.
HMM?
WE HAVEN'T DONE ANY-THING.
SMILE

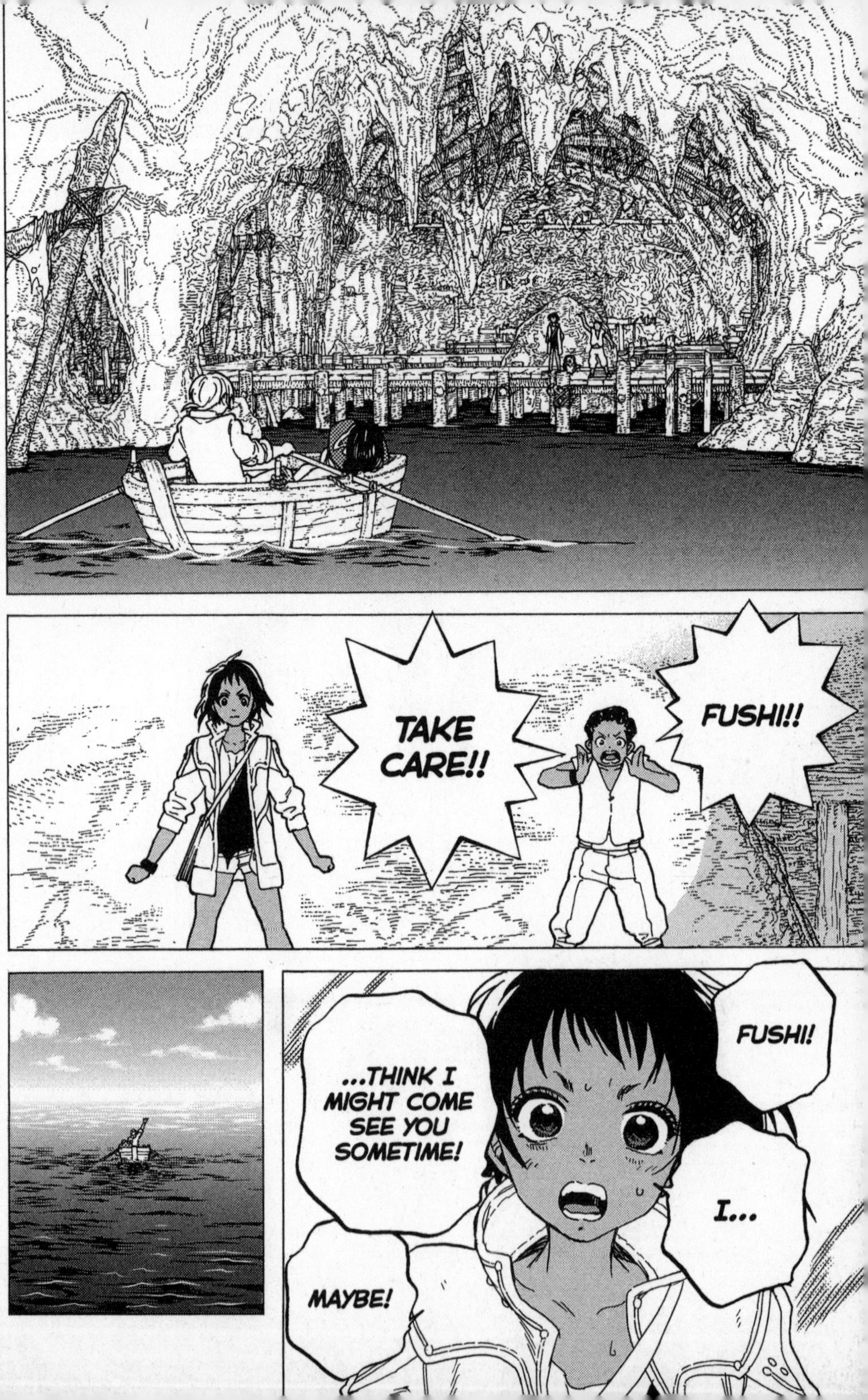
FUSHI!!
TAKE CARE!!
FUSHI!
I...
...THINK I MIGHT COME SEE YOU SOMETIME!
MAYBE!

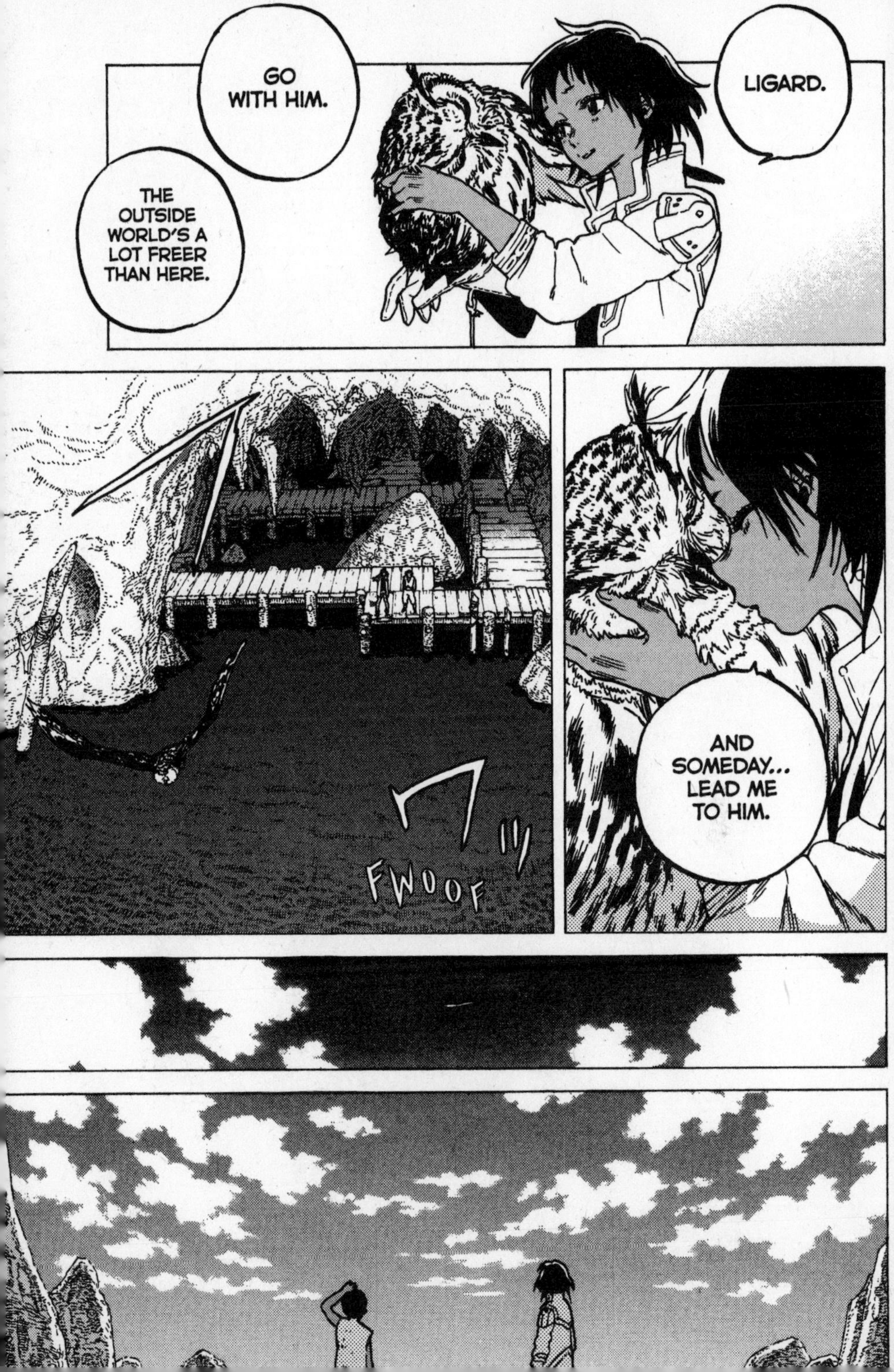
LIGARD.
GO WITH HIM.
THE OUTSIDE WORLD'S A LOT FREER THAN HERE.
AND SOMEDAY... LEAD ME TO HIM.
FWOOF

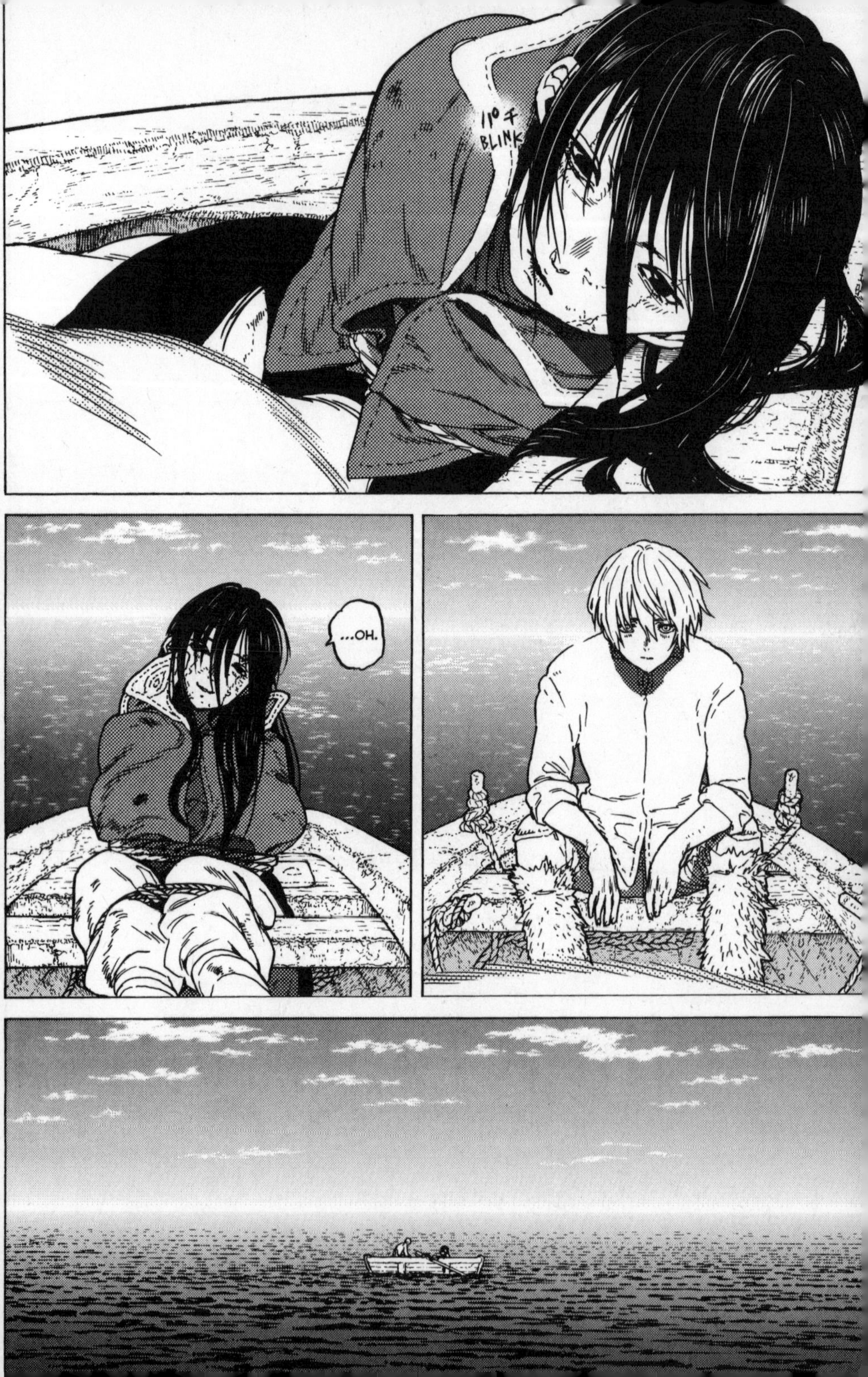
パチ
BLINK
...OH.

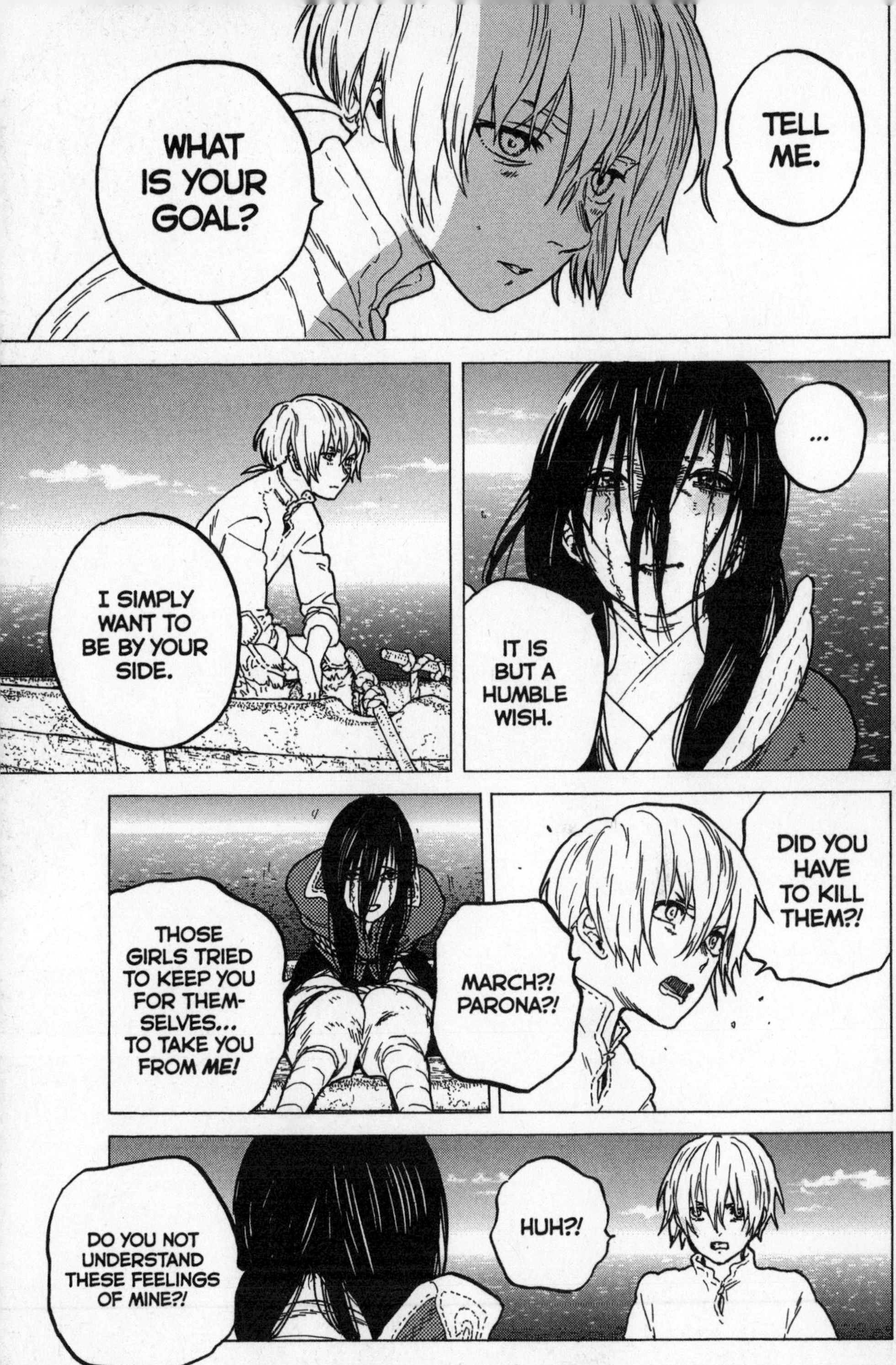
TELL ME.
WHAT IS YOUR GOAL?
...
IT IS BUT A HUMBLE WISH.
I SIMPLY WANT TO BE BY YOUR SIDE.
DID YOU HAVE TO KILL THEM?!
MARCH?! PARONA?!
THOSE GIRLS TRIED TO KEEP YOU FOR THEM-SELVES... TO TAKE YOU FROM *ME!*
HUH?!
DO YOU NOT UNDERSTAND THESE FEELINGS OF MINE?!

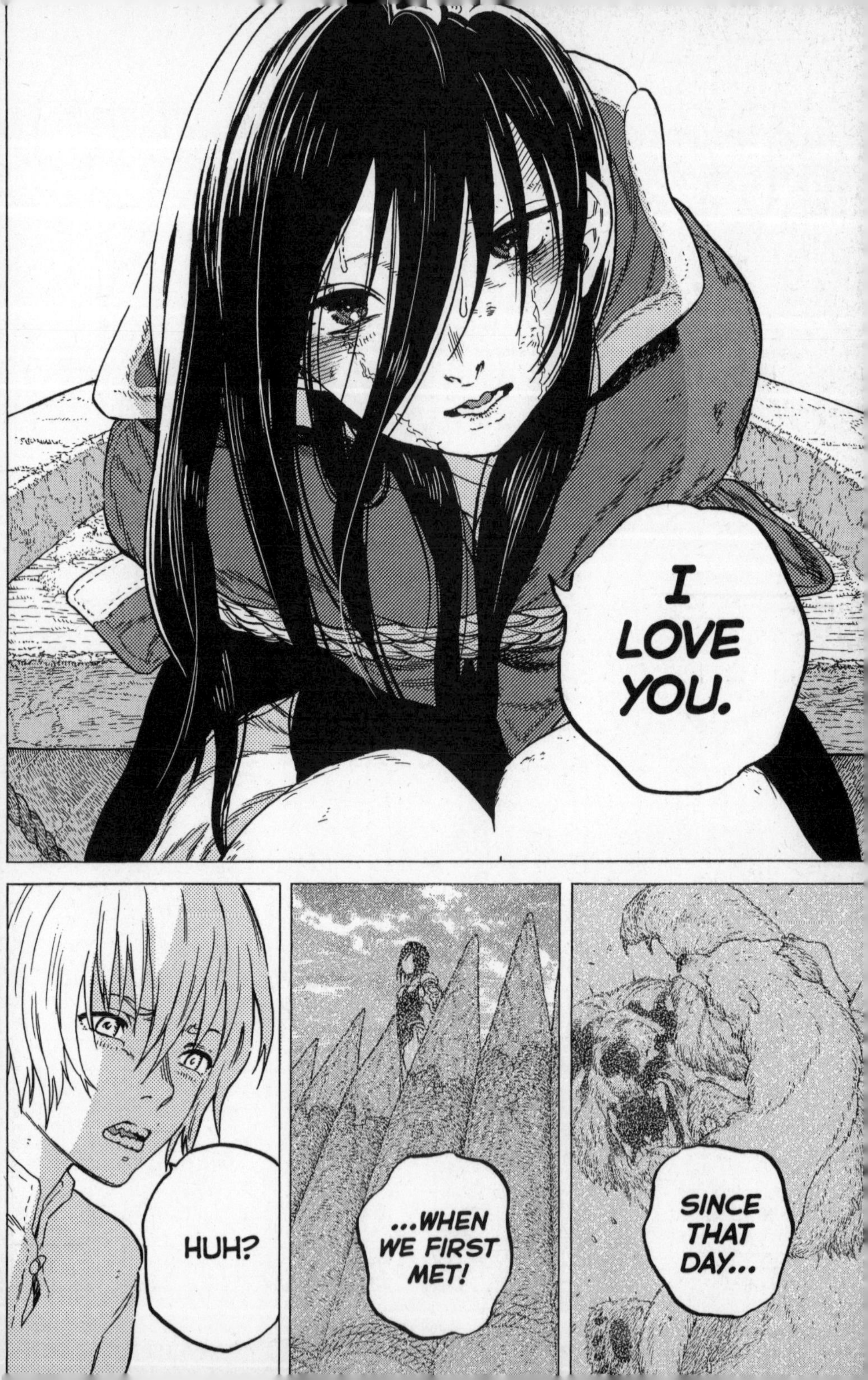
I LOVE YOU.
SINCE THAT DAY...
...WHEN WE FIRST MET!
HUH?

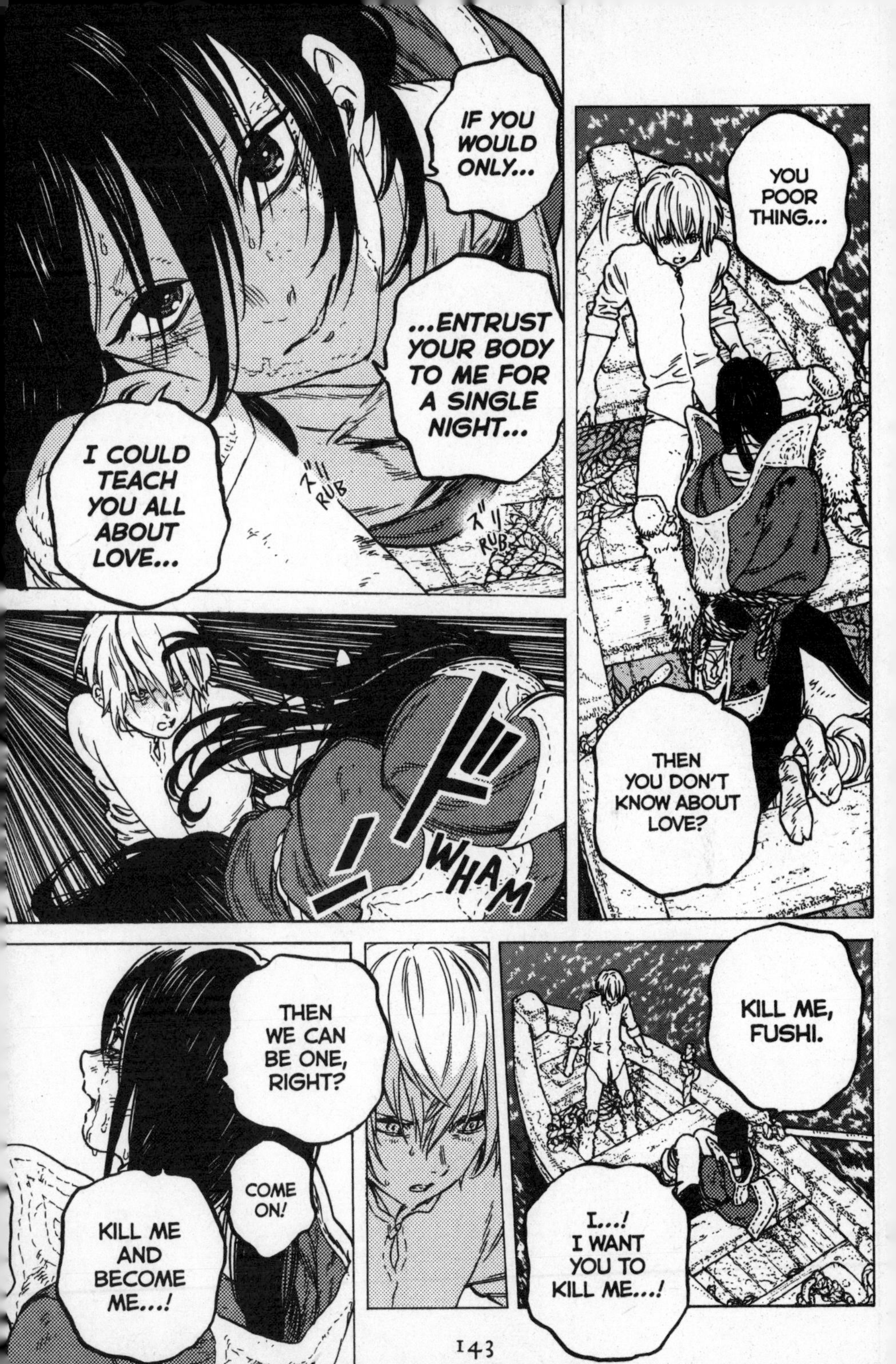
YOU POOR THING...
THEN YOU DON'T KNOW ABOUT LOVE?
IF YOU WOULD ONLY...
...ENTRUST YOUR BODY TO ME FOR A SINGLE NIGHT...
I COULD TEACH YOU ALL ABOUT LOVE...
RUB
RUB
WHAM
KILL ME, FUSHI.
I...! I WANT YOU TO KILL ME...!
THEN WE CAN BE ONE, RIGHT?
COME ON!
KILL ME AND BECOME ME...!

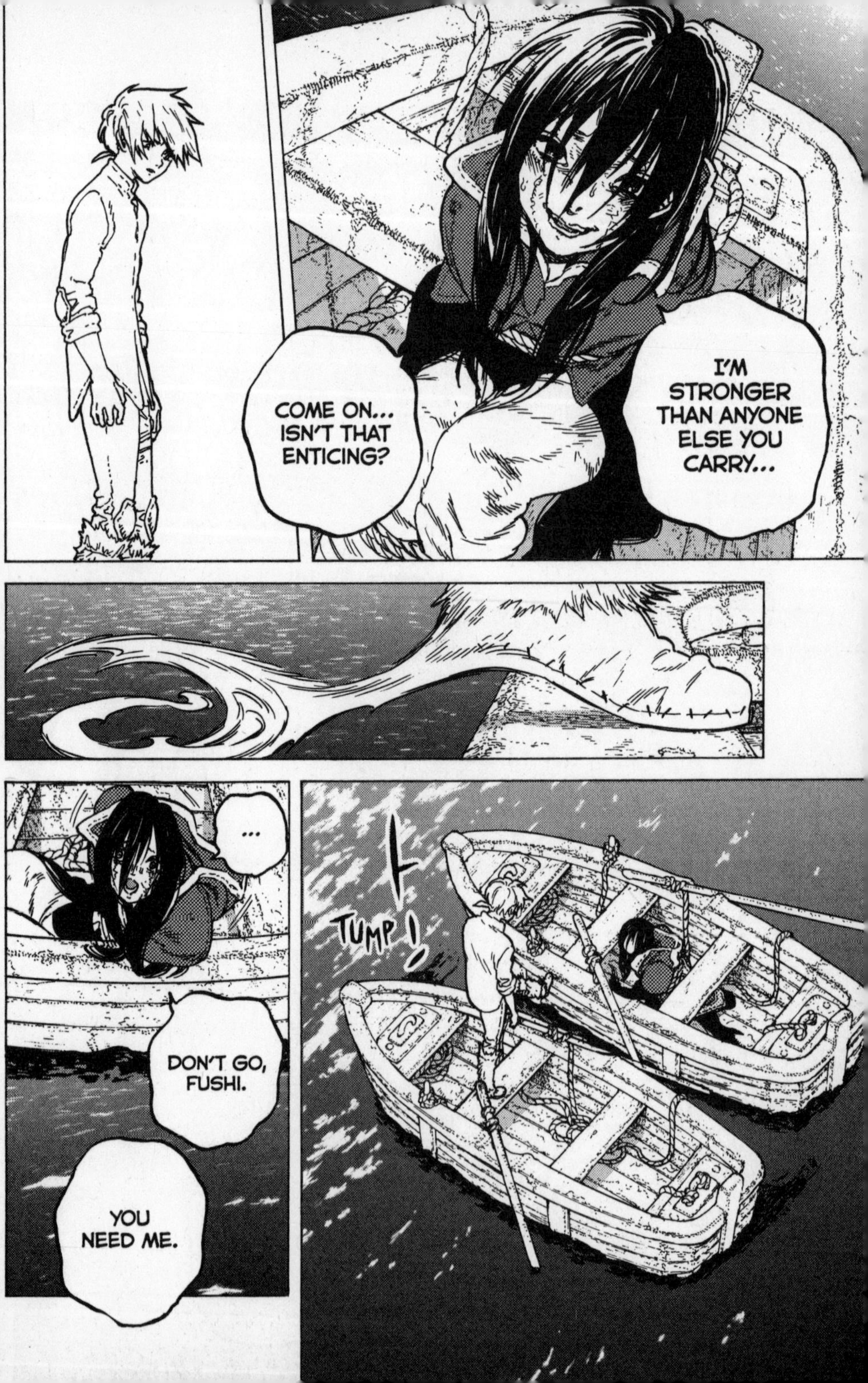
I'M STRONGER THAN ANYONE ELSE YOU CARRY...
COME ON... ISN'T THAT ENTICING?
TUMP!
...
DON'T GO, FUSHI.
YOU NEED ME.

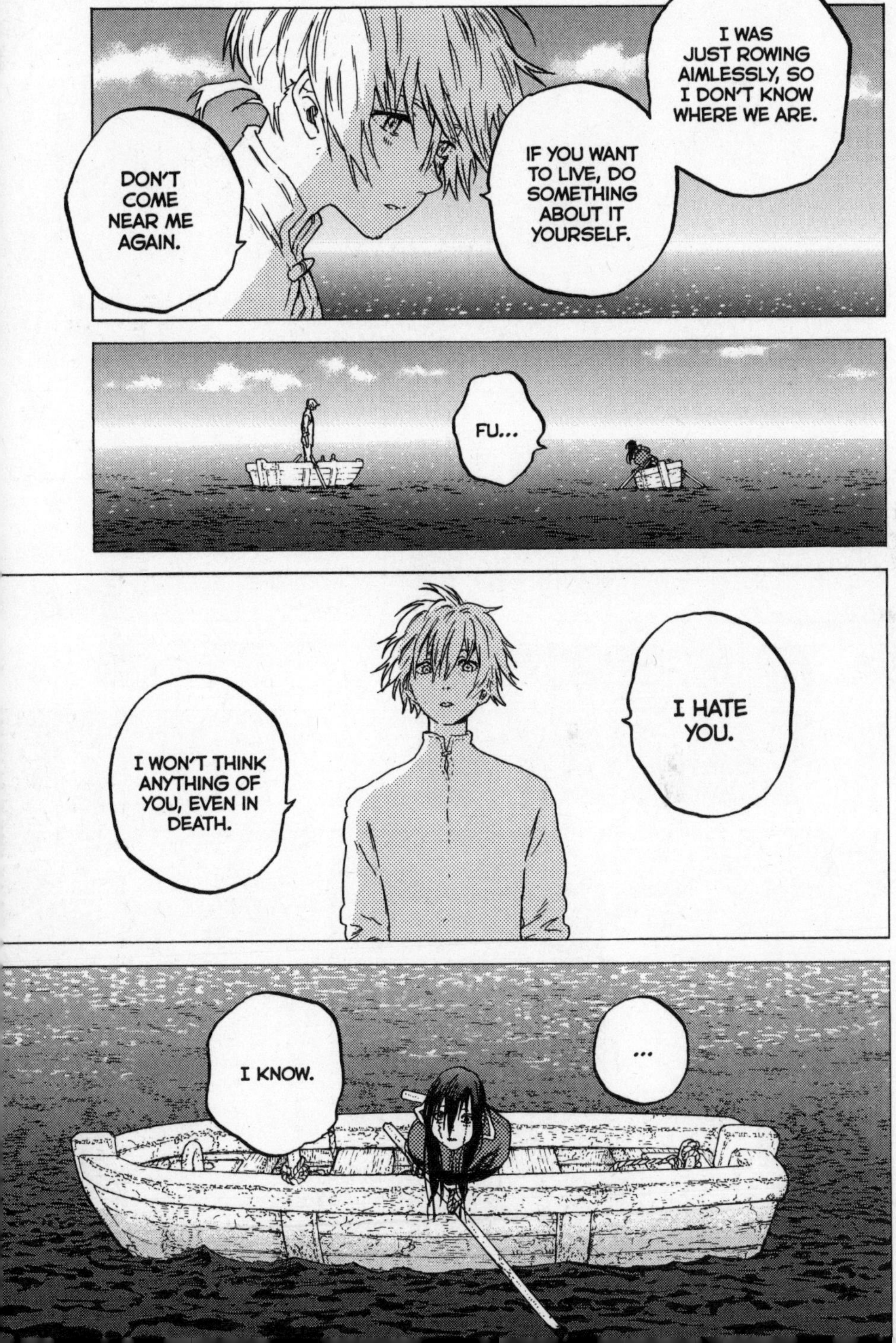
I WAS JUST ROWING AIMLESSLY, SO I DON'T KNOW WHERE WE ARE.
IF YOU WANT TO LIVE, DO SOMETHING ABOUT IT YOURSELF.
DON'T COME NEAR ME AGAIN.
FU...
I HATE YOU.
I WON'T THINK ANYTHING OF YOU, EVEN IN DEATH.
...
I KNOW.

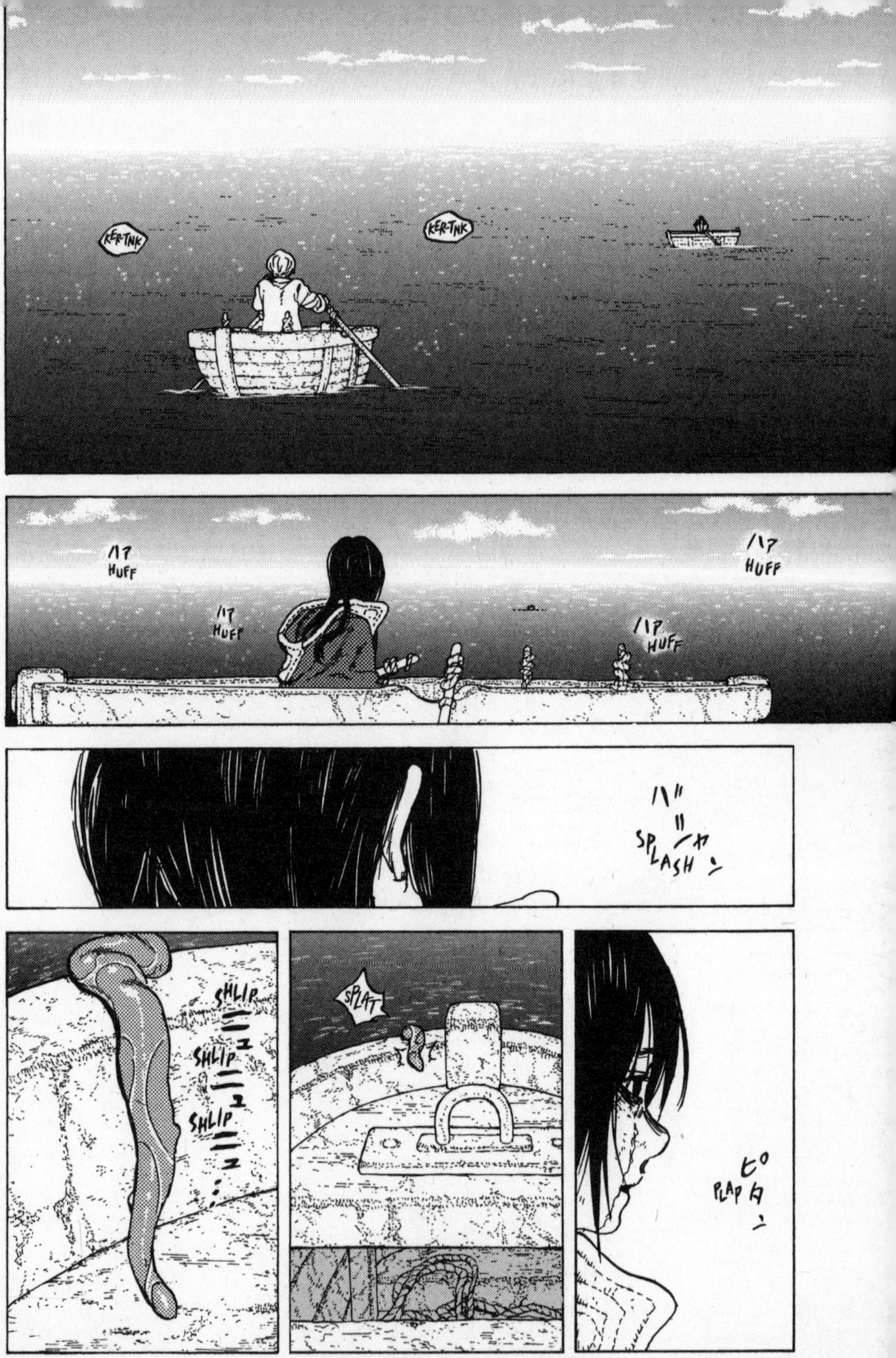
KER-TNK
KER-TNK
ハア HUFF
ハア HUFF
ハア HUFF
ハア HUFF
SPLASH
PLAP
SPLATT
SHLIP
SHLIP
SHLIP

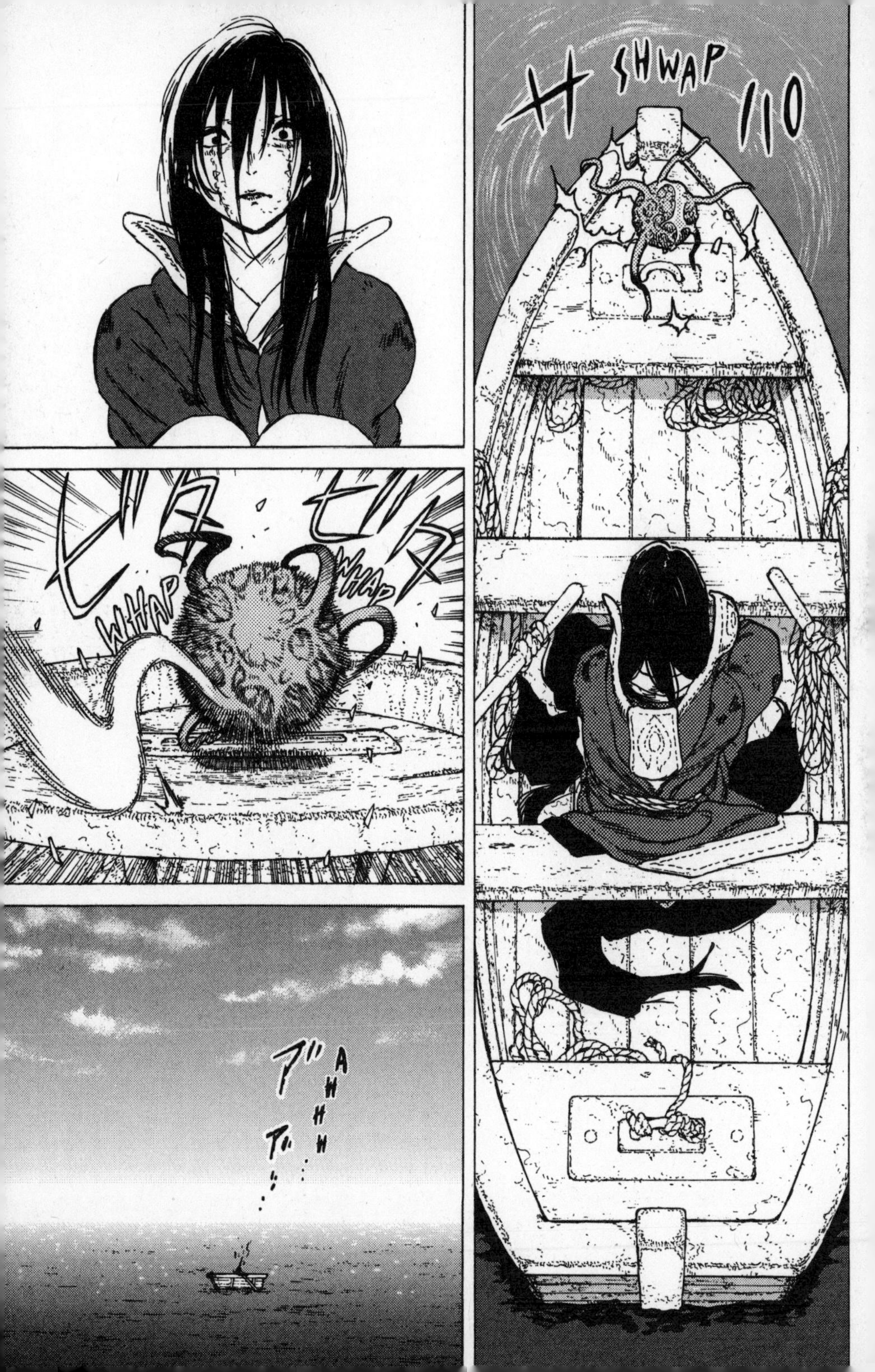
SHWAP
WHAP
WHAP
AHHH

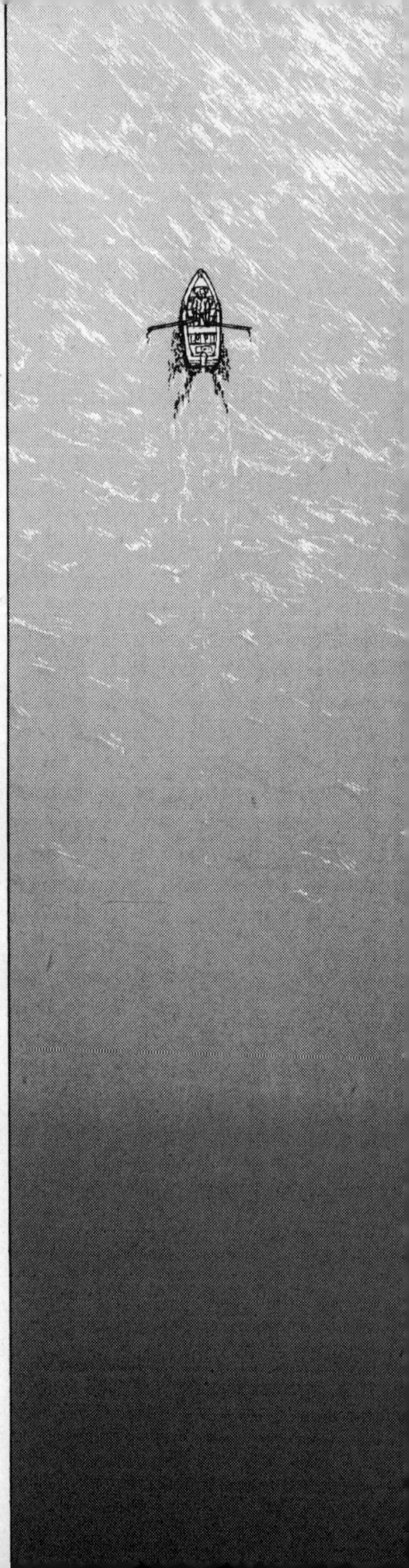

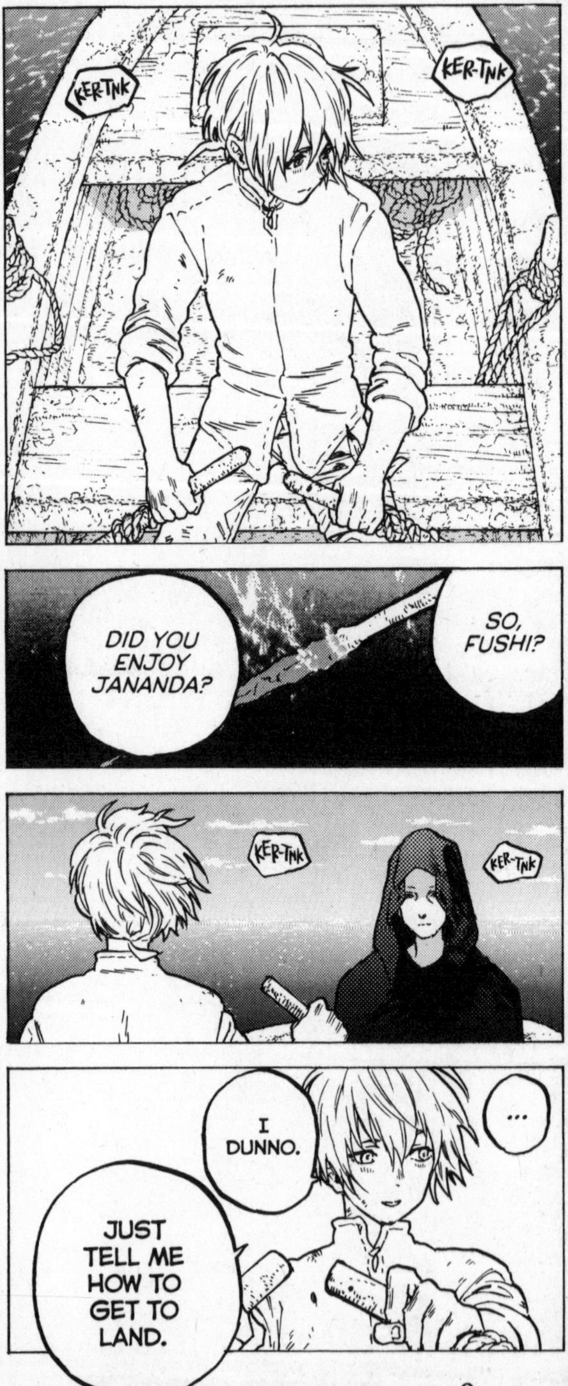
KER-TNK
KER-TNK
SO, FUSHI?
DID YOU ENJOY JANANDA?
KER-TNK
KER-TNK
...
I DUNNO.
JUST TELL ME HOW TO GET TO LAND.

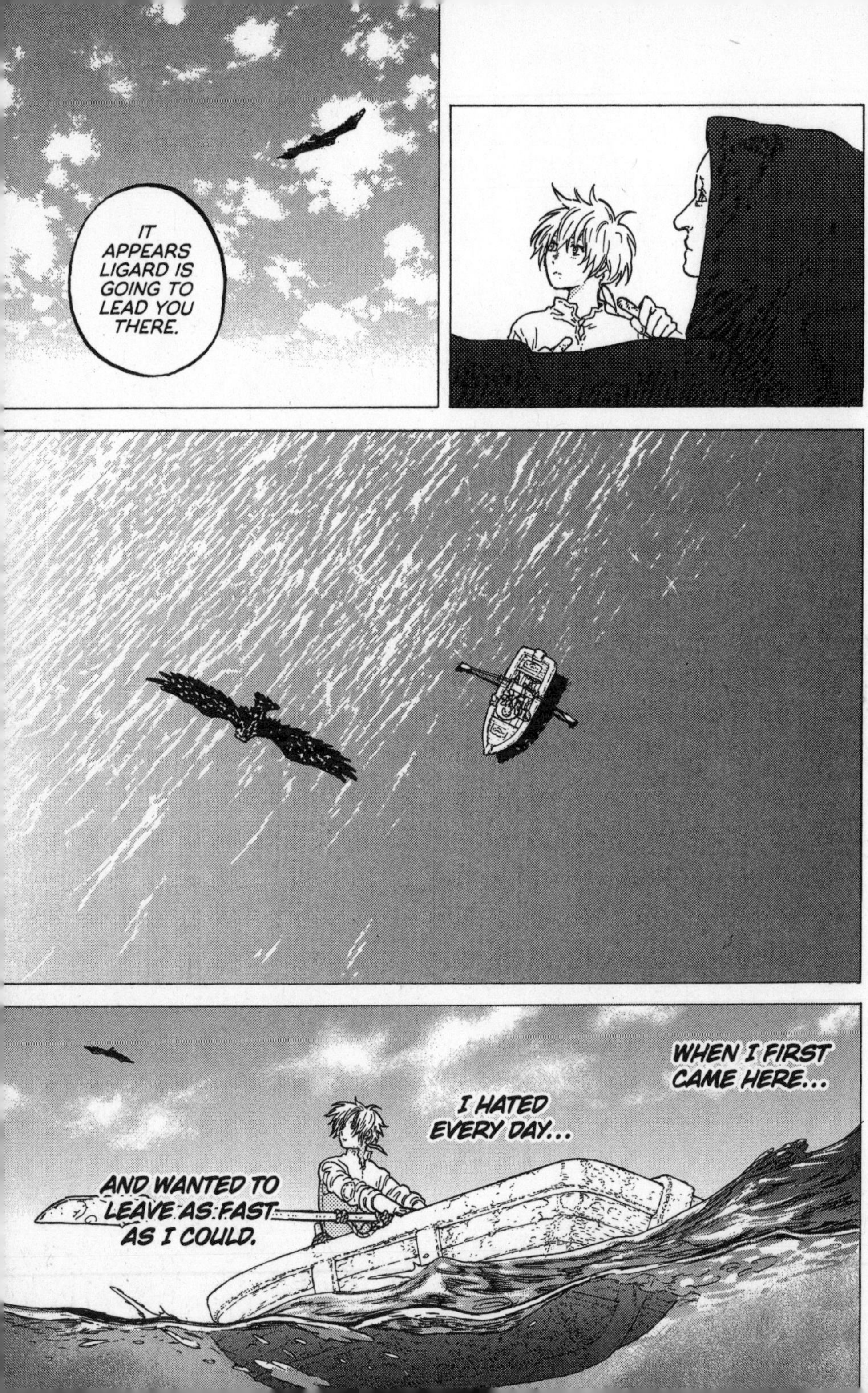
IT APPEARS LIGARD IS GOING TO LEAD YOU THERE.
WHEN I FIRST CAME HERE...
I HATED EVERY DAY...
AND WANTED TO LEAVE AS FAST AS I COULD.

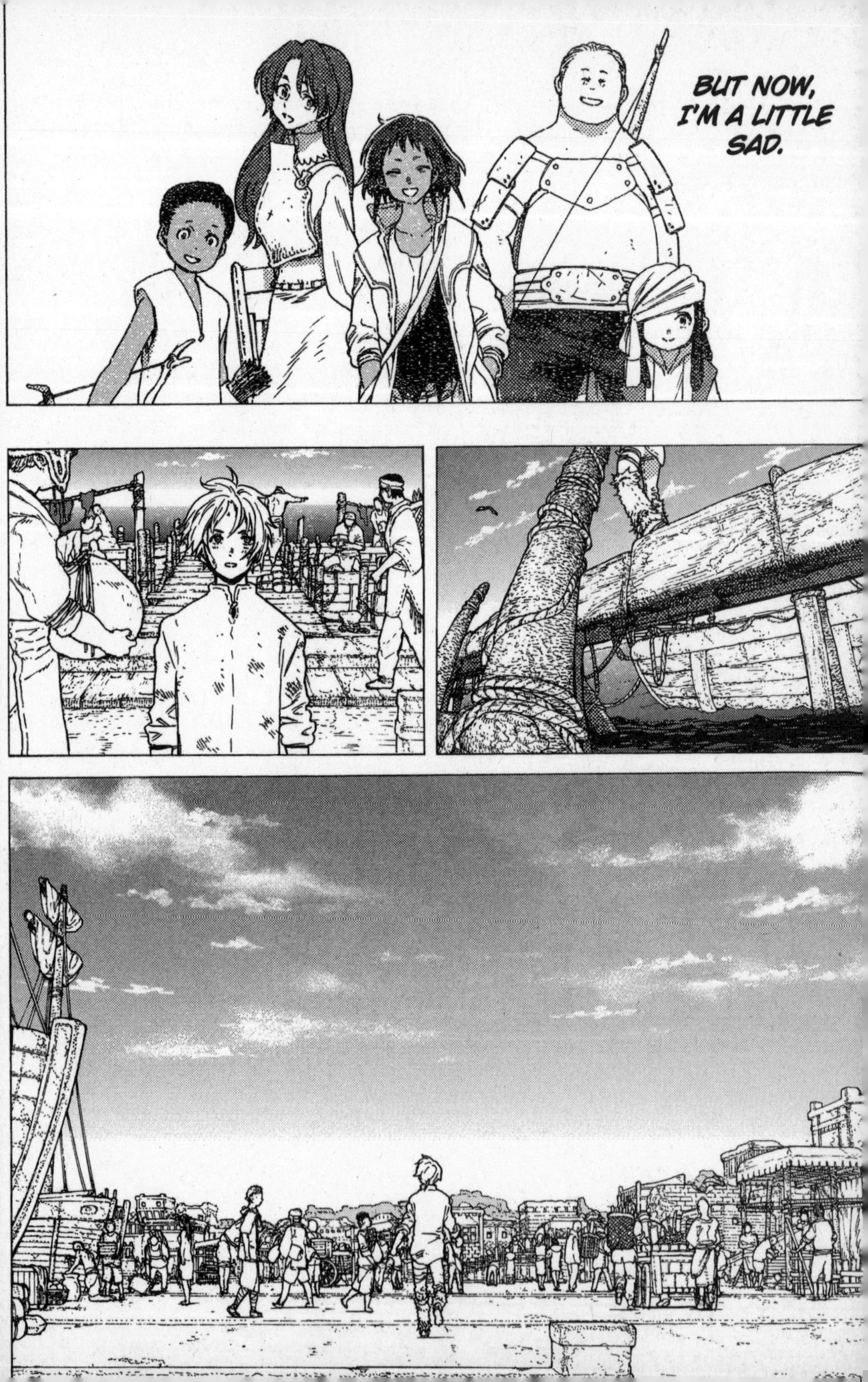
BUT NOW, I'M A LITTLE SAD.

TO TONARI

We successfully managed to secure a place to live,
but there's no one to watch the kids.

But I believe.
I believe we can all make it even without parents.

Have things calmed down on the island?

FROM NAND

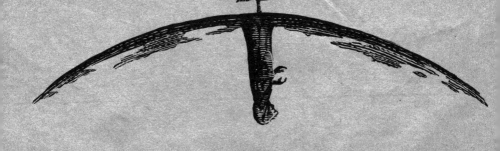

TO NAND

We still haven't finished our reconstruction work.
The Immortal made it off the island, but I think I'll be here
for 15 more years or so.

I think there are a lot more kind people on the island after the Nokker attack.
And, fortunately, I'm still alive even though I'm the island leader.
And some of the adults are even saying they'll protect me.

Another tournament to decide the leader apparently started up on its own,
but everyone had other things to do, so there was no audience for it.
I think everyone's noticed by now.
What this island needs isn't murder; it's cooperation.

The people on the island come to me, wanting to hear about the Immortal.
It seems like a new religion is on the verge of forming here.
Like, Immortalism or something? Makes you laugh, right?
And the guardians Hayase leads are fanning those flames.
They even want my diary. And I know why.

If you stop receiving letters from me,
just assume they killed me.

FROM TONARI

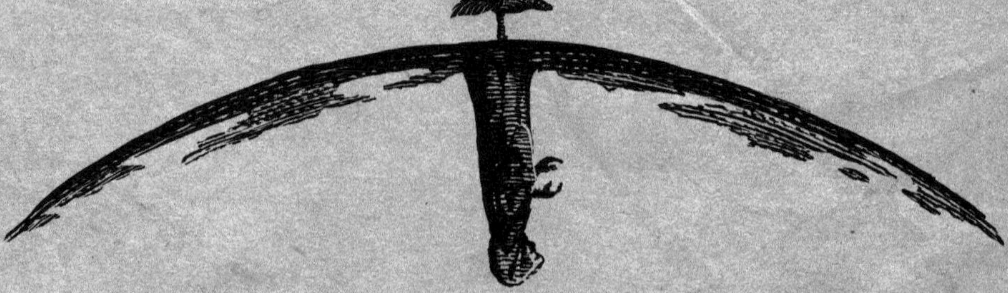

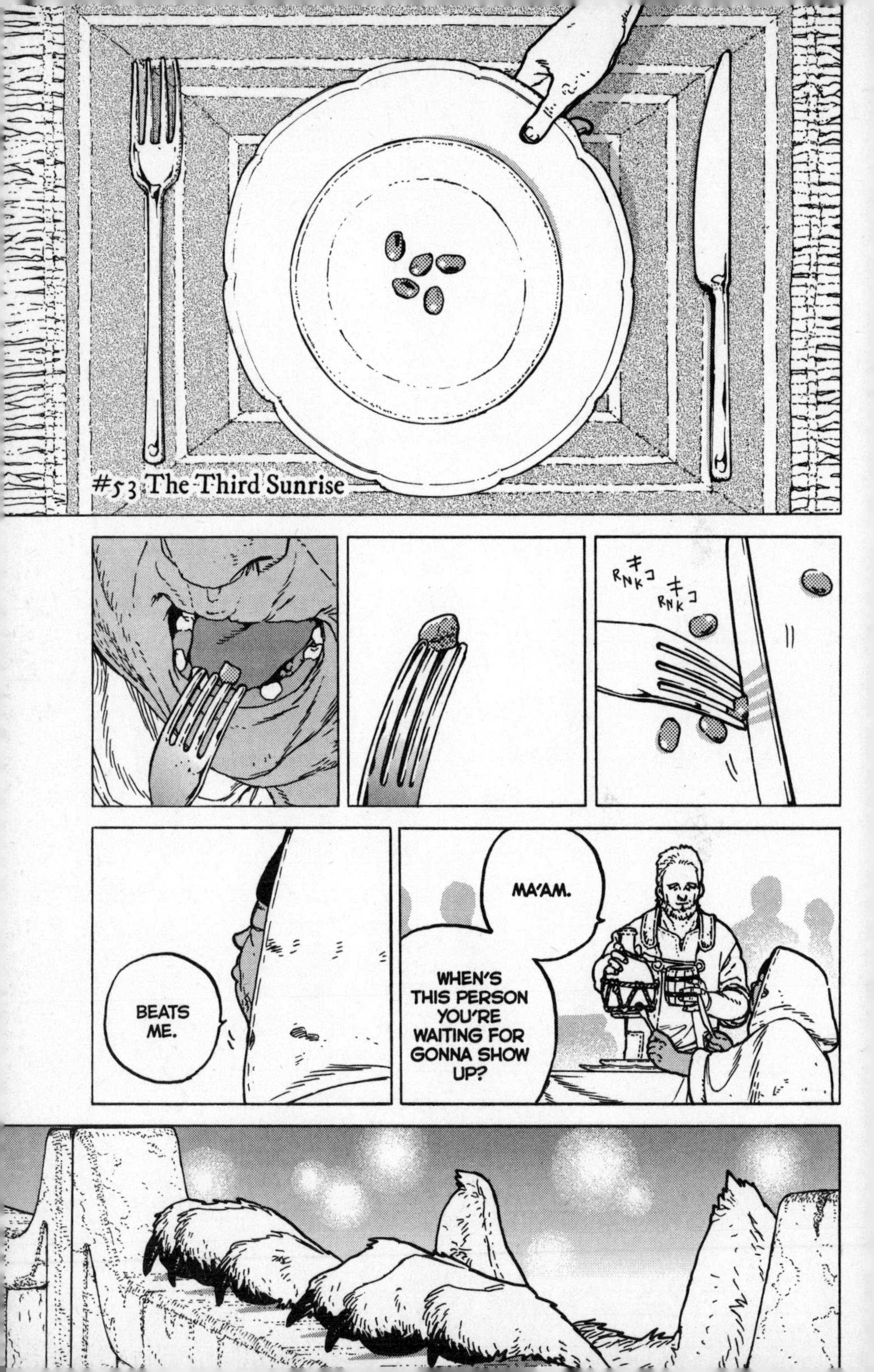
#53 The Third Sunrise
RNK
RNK
MA'AM.
WHEN'S THIS PERSON YOU'RE WAITING FOR GONNA SHOW UP?
BEATS ME.

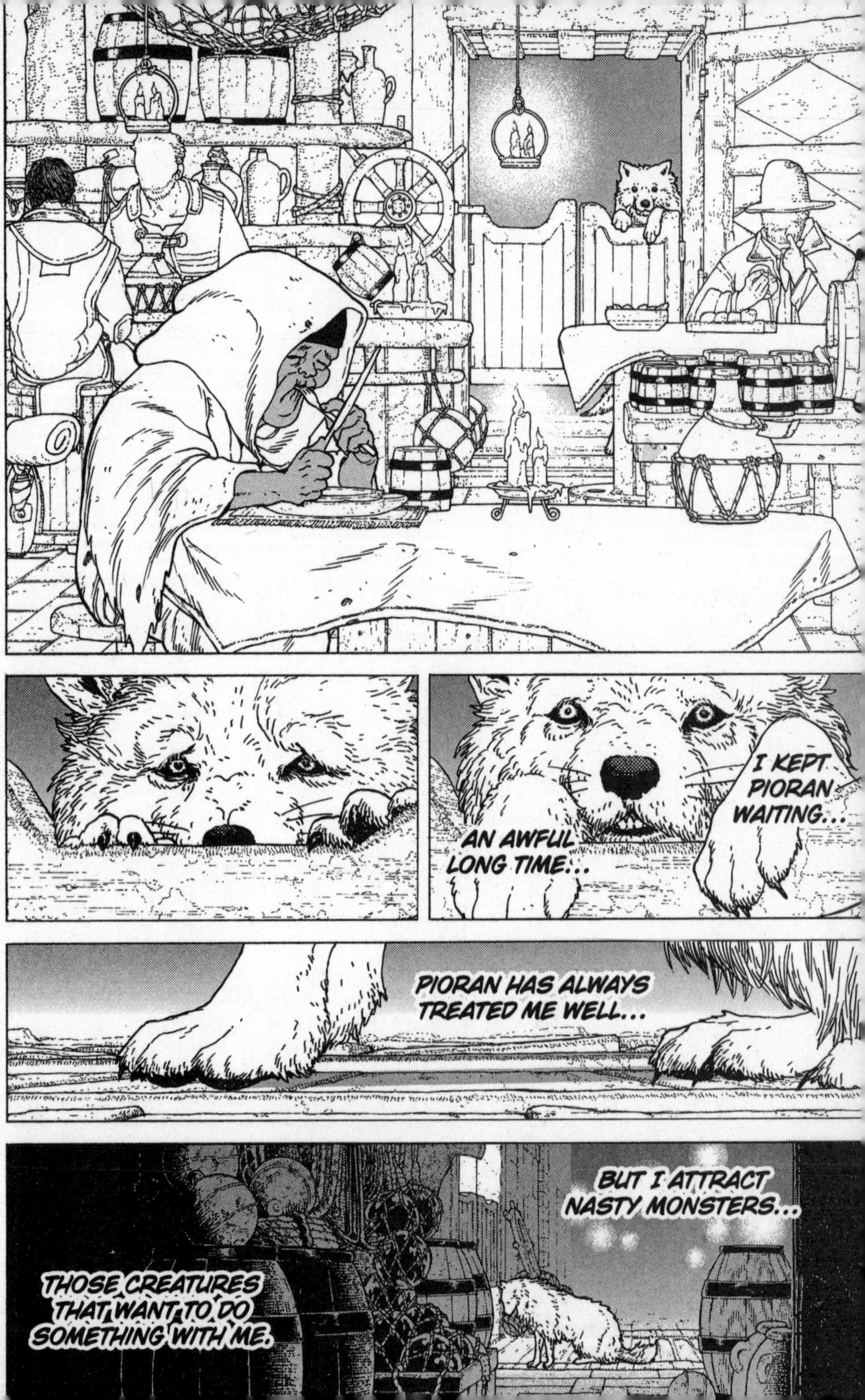
I KEPT PIORAN WAITING...
AN AWFUL LONG TIME...
PIORAN HAS ALWAYS TREATED ME WELL...
BUT I ATTRACT NASTY MONSTERS...
THOSE CREATURES THAT WANT TO DO SOMETHING WITH ME.

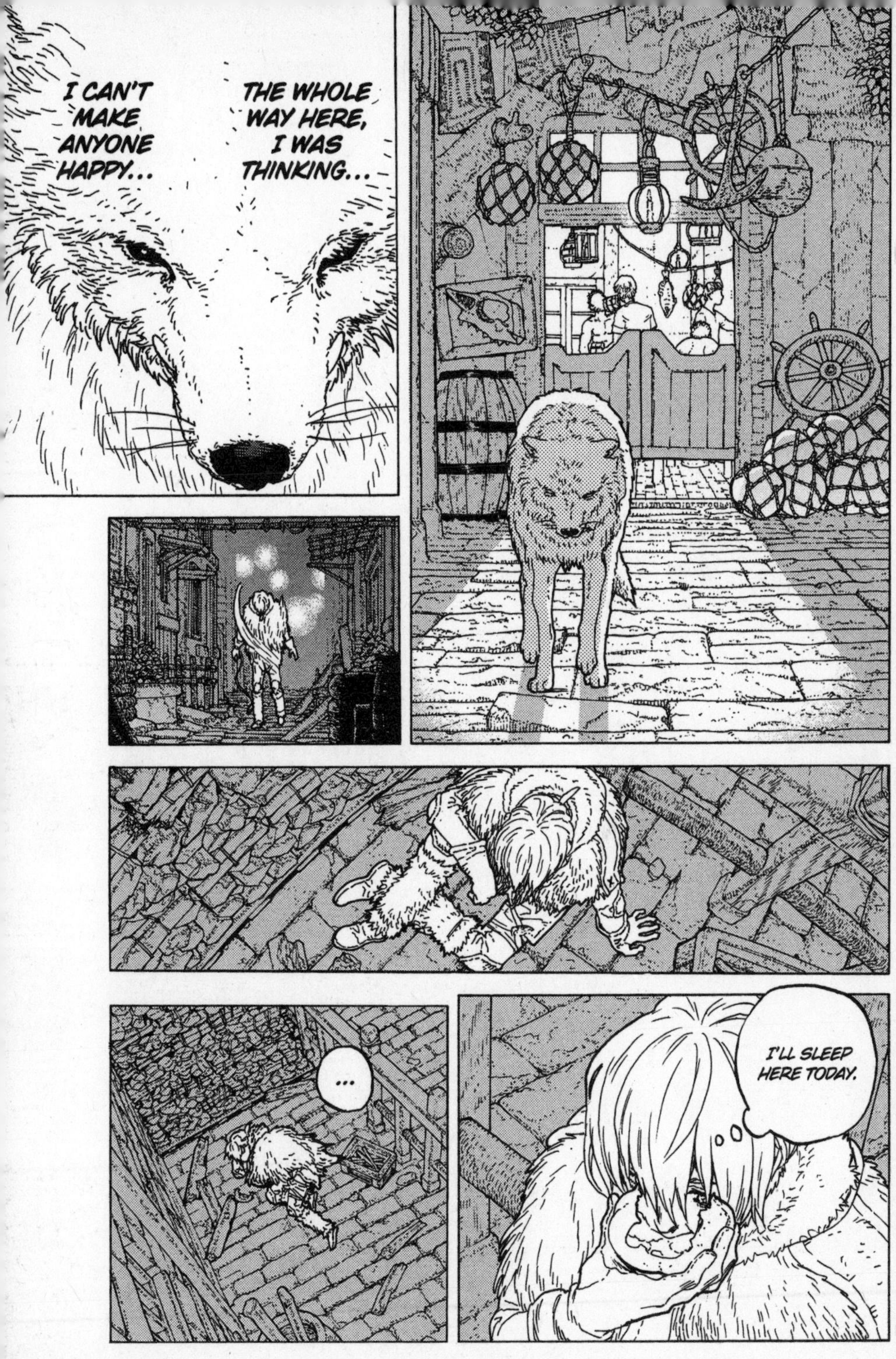
THE WHOLE WAY HERE, I WAS THINKING...
I CAN'T MAKE ANYONE HAPPY...
I'LL SLEEP HERE TODAY.
...

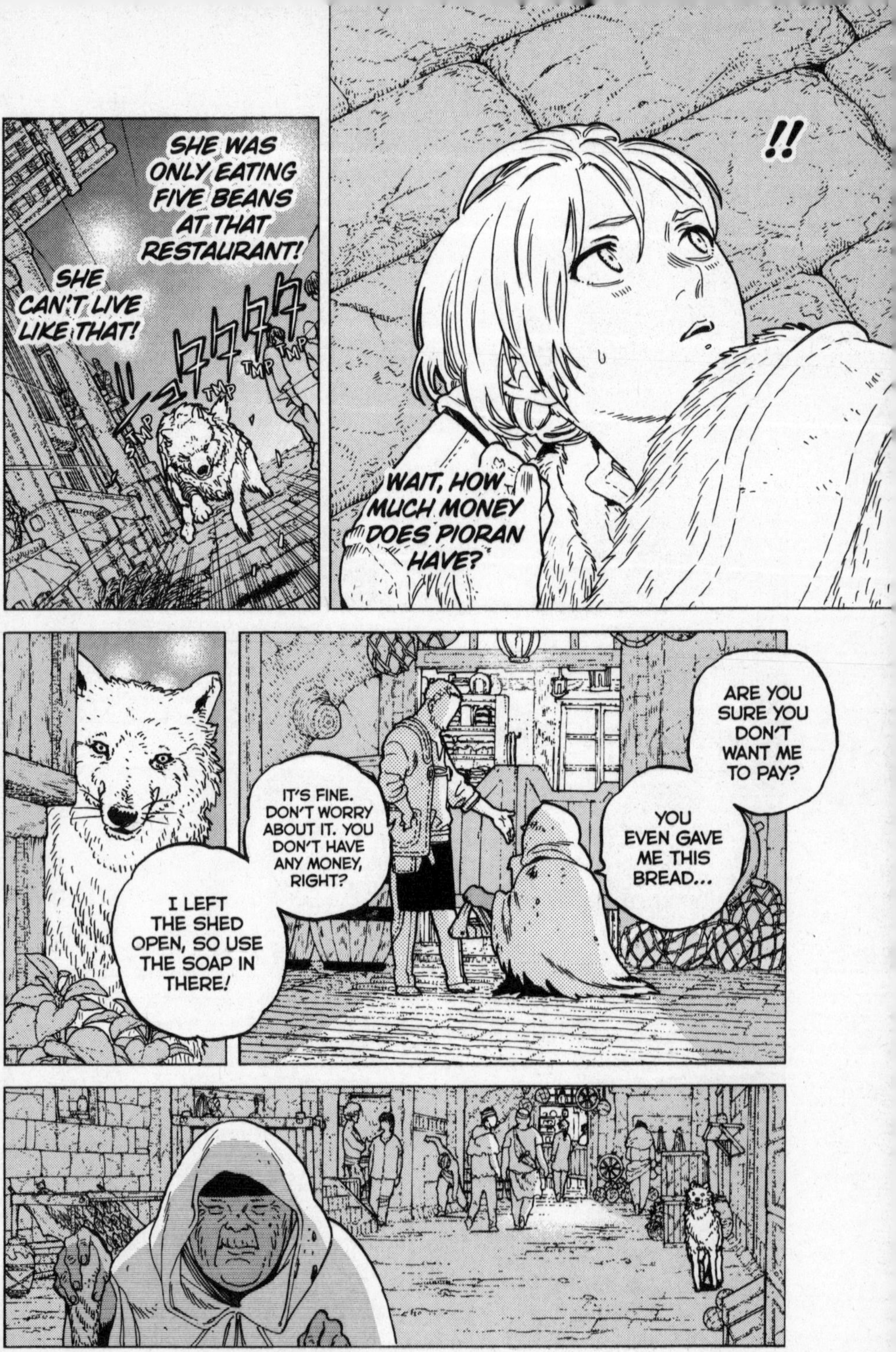
!!
WAIT, HOW MUCH MONEY DOES PIORAN HAVE?
SHE WAS ONLY EATING FIVE BEANS AT THAT RESTAURANT!
SHE CAN'T LIVE LIKE THAT!
TMP TMP TMP TMP
ARE YOU SURE YOU DON'T WANT ME TO PAY?
YOU EVEN GAVE ME THIS BREAD...
IT'S FINE. DON'T WORRY ABOUT IT. YOU DON'T HAVE ANY MONEY, RIGHT?
I LEFT THE SHED OPEN, SO USE THE SOAP IN THERE!

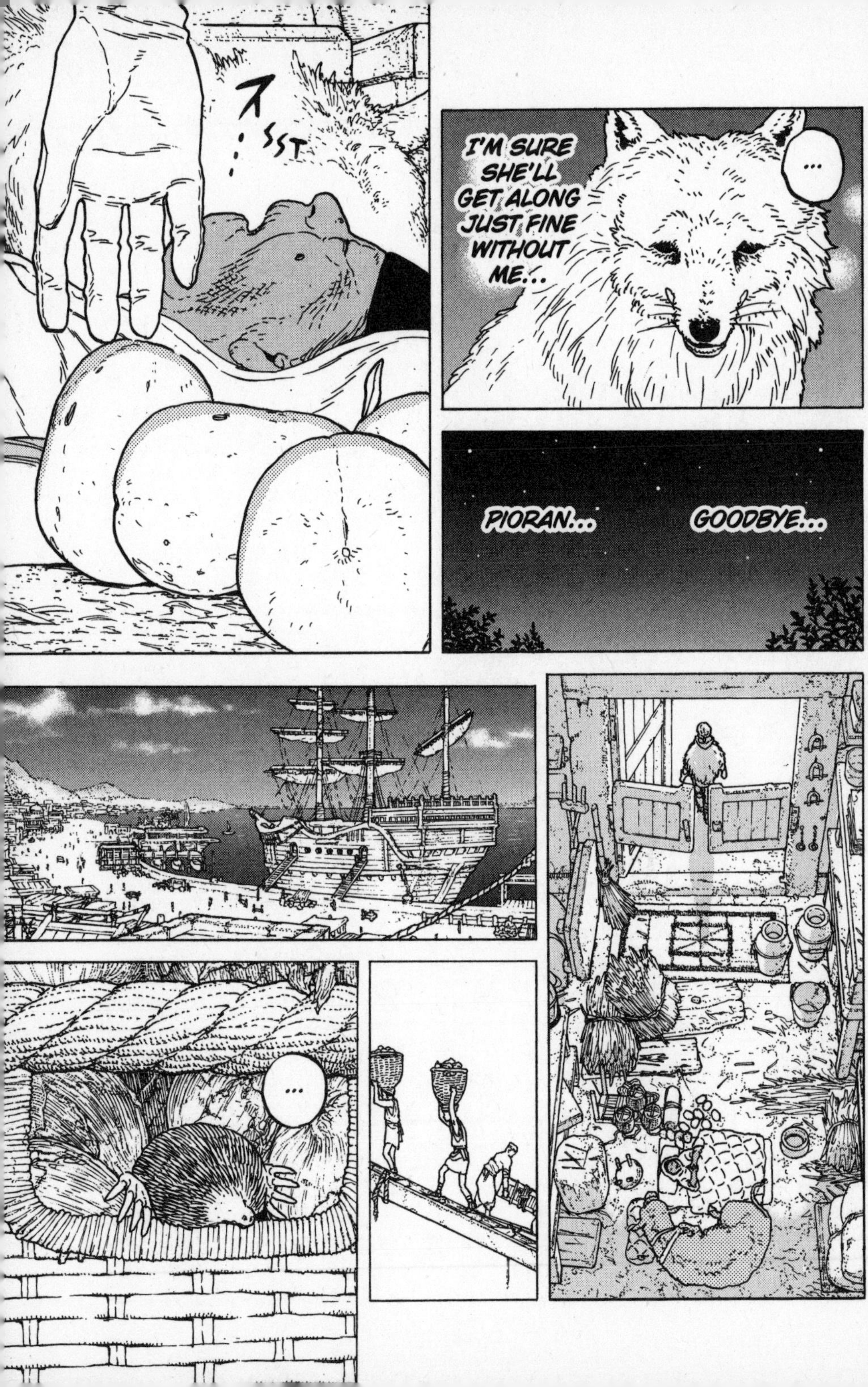
...
I'M SURE SHE'LL GET ALONG JUST FINE WITHOUT ME...
GOODBYE...
PIORAN...
ス
SST
...

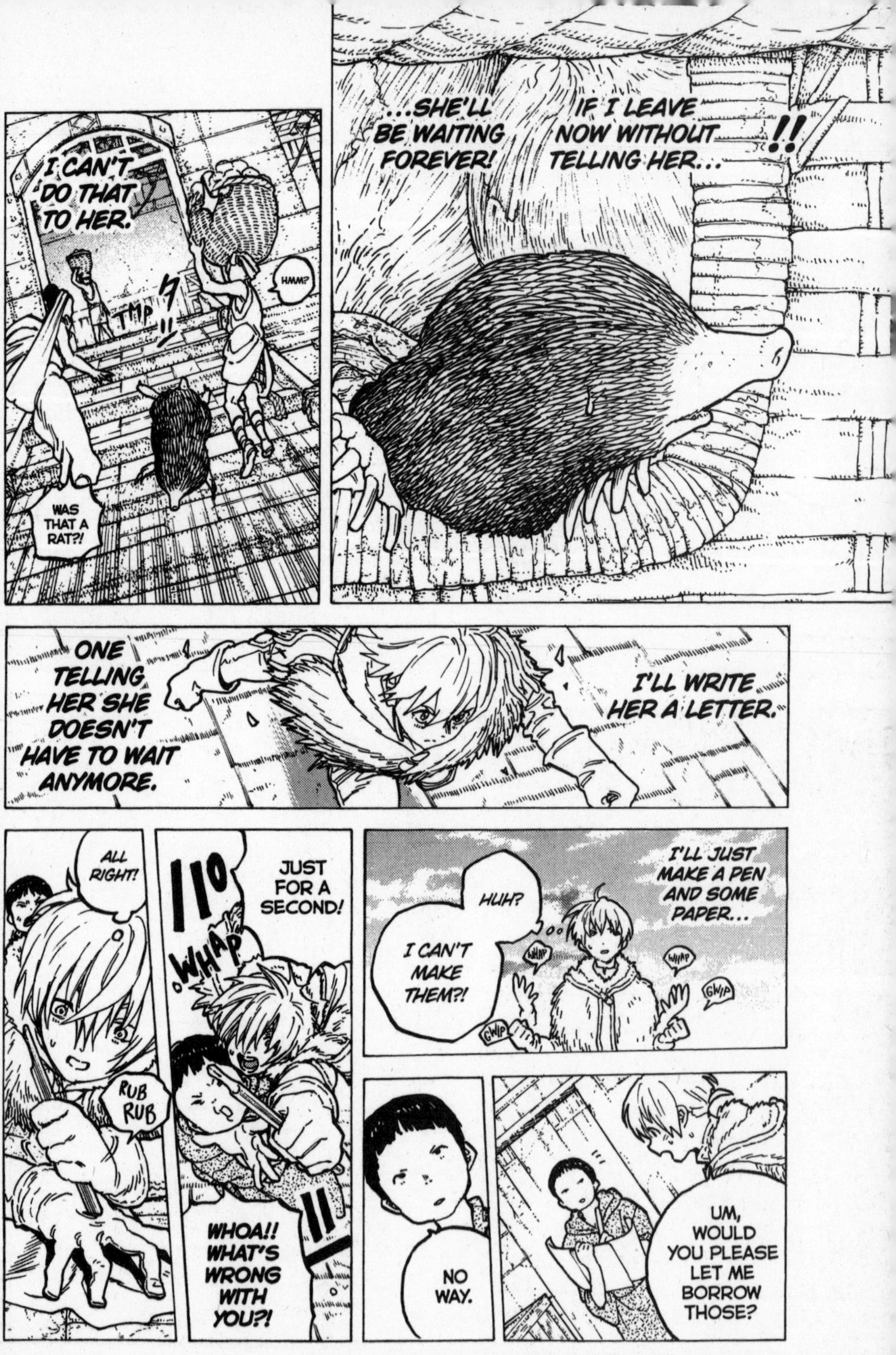
IF I LEAVE NOW WITHOUT TELLING HER...
...SHE'LL BE WAITING FOREVER!
!!
I CAN'T DO THAT TO HER.
HMM?
TMP
WAS THAT A RAT?!
I'LL WRITE HER A LETTER.
ONE TELLING HER SHE DOESN'T HAVE TO WAIT ANYMORE.
I'LL JUST MAKE A PEN AND SOME PAPER...
HUH?
I CAN'T MAKE THEM?!
WHAP
WHAP
GWIP
GWIP
UM, WOULD YOU PLEASE LET ME BORROW THOSE?
NO WAY.
JUST FOR A SECOND!
WHAP
WHOA!! WHAT'S WRONG WITH YOU?!
ALL RIGHT!
RUB RUB

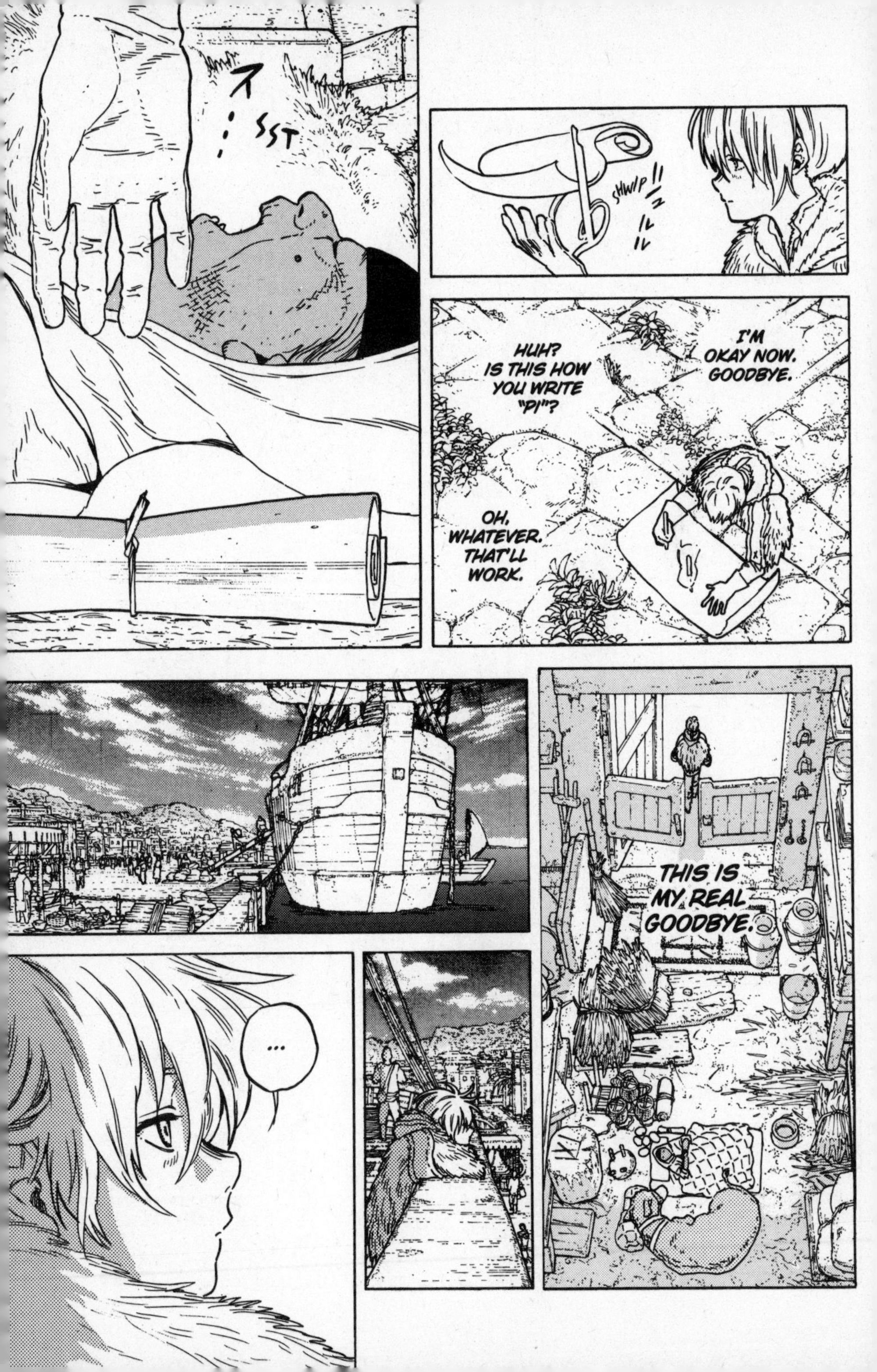
SHWIP!!
I'M OKAY NOW. GOODBYE.
HUH? IS THIS HOW YOU WRITE "PI"?
OH, WHATEVER. THAT'LL WORK.
SST
THIS IS MY REAL GOODBYE.
...

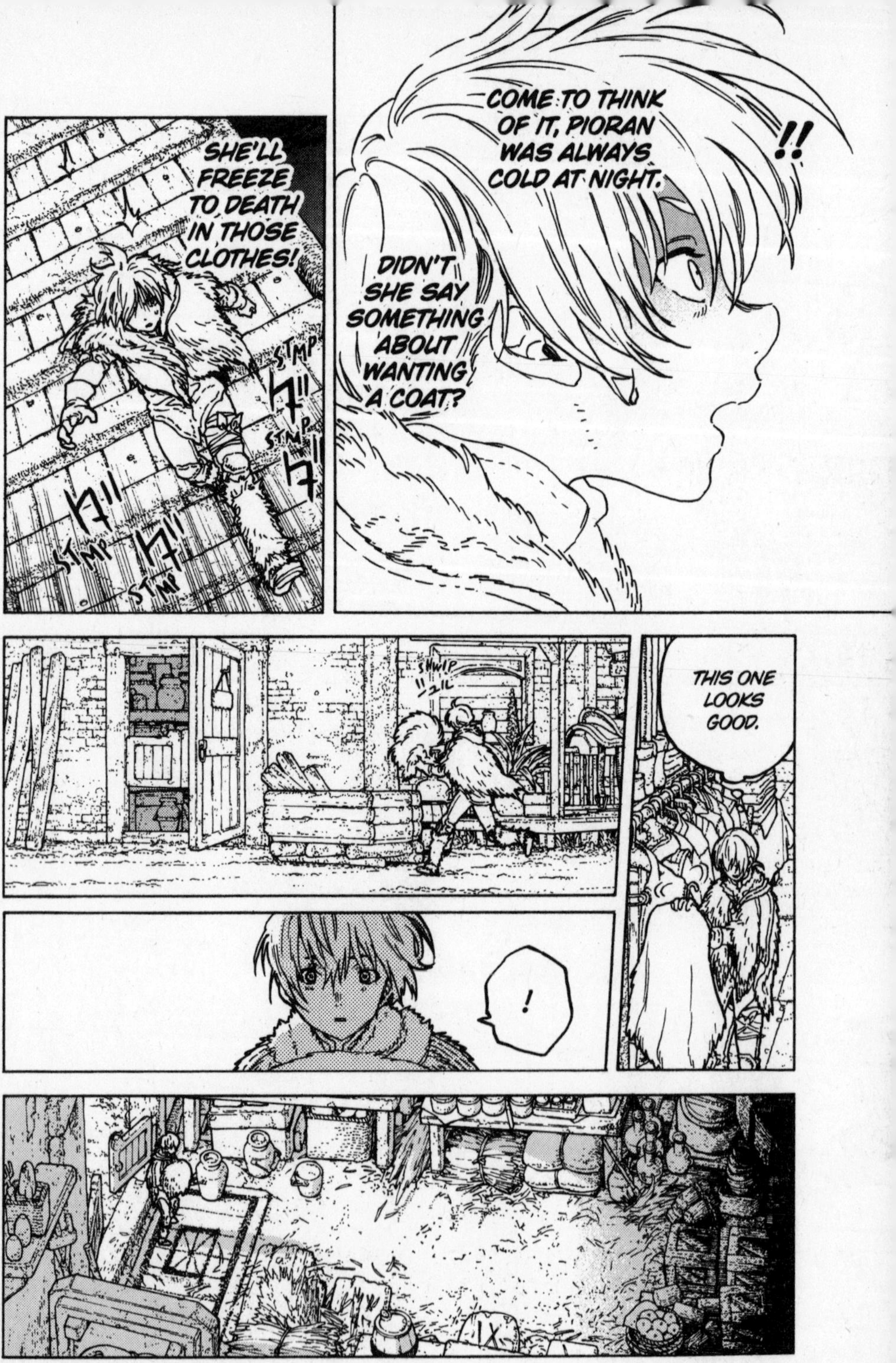

COME TO THINK OF IT, PIORAN WAS ALWAYS COLD AT NIGHT.
!!
DIDN'T SHE SAY SOMETHING ABOUT WANTING A COAT?
SHE'LL FREEZE TO DEATH IN THOSE CLOTHES!
STMP
STMP
STMP
STMP
THIS ONE LOOKS GOOD.
SHWIP
!

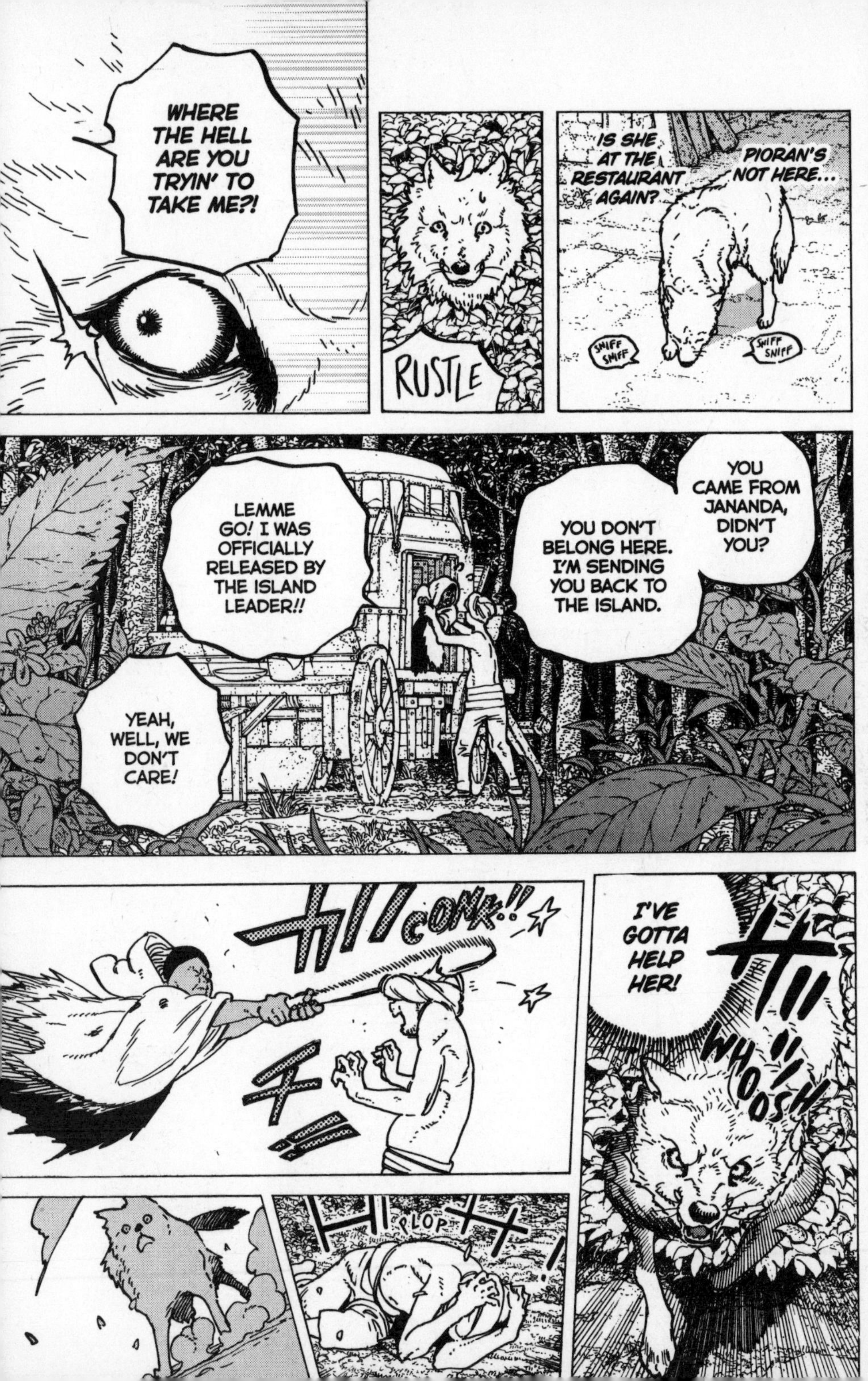
PIORAN'S NOT HERE...
IS SHE AT THE RESTAURANT AGAIN?
SNIFF SNIFF
SNIFF SNIFF
RUSTLE
WHERE THE HELL ARE YOU TRYIN' TO TAKE ME?!
YOU CAME FROM JANANDA, DIDN'T YOU?
YOU DON'T BELONG HERE. I'M SENDING YOU BACK TO THE ISLAND.
LEMME GO! I WAS OFFICIALLY RELEASED BY THE ISLAND LEADER!!
YEAH, WELL, WE DON'T CARE!
I'VE GOTTA HELP HER!
WHOOSH
CONK!!
PLOP

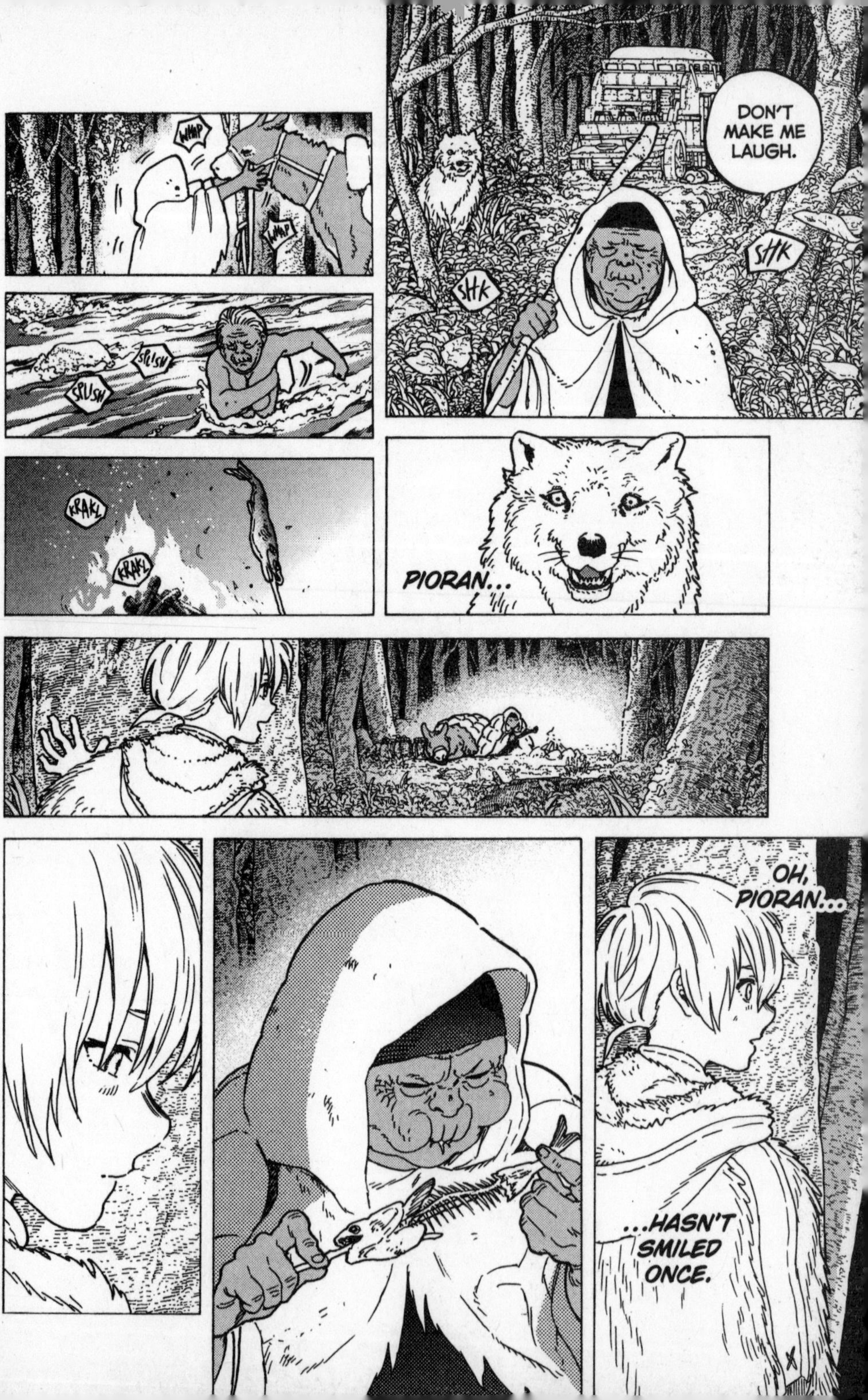
DON'T MAKE ME LAUGH.
SHK
SHK
WHAP
WHAP
SPLISH
SPLISH
PIORAN...
KRAKL
KRAKL
OH, PIORAN...
...HASN'T SMILED ONCE.

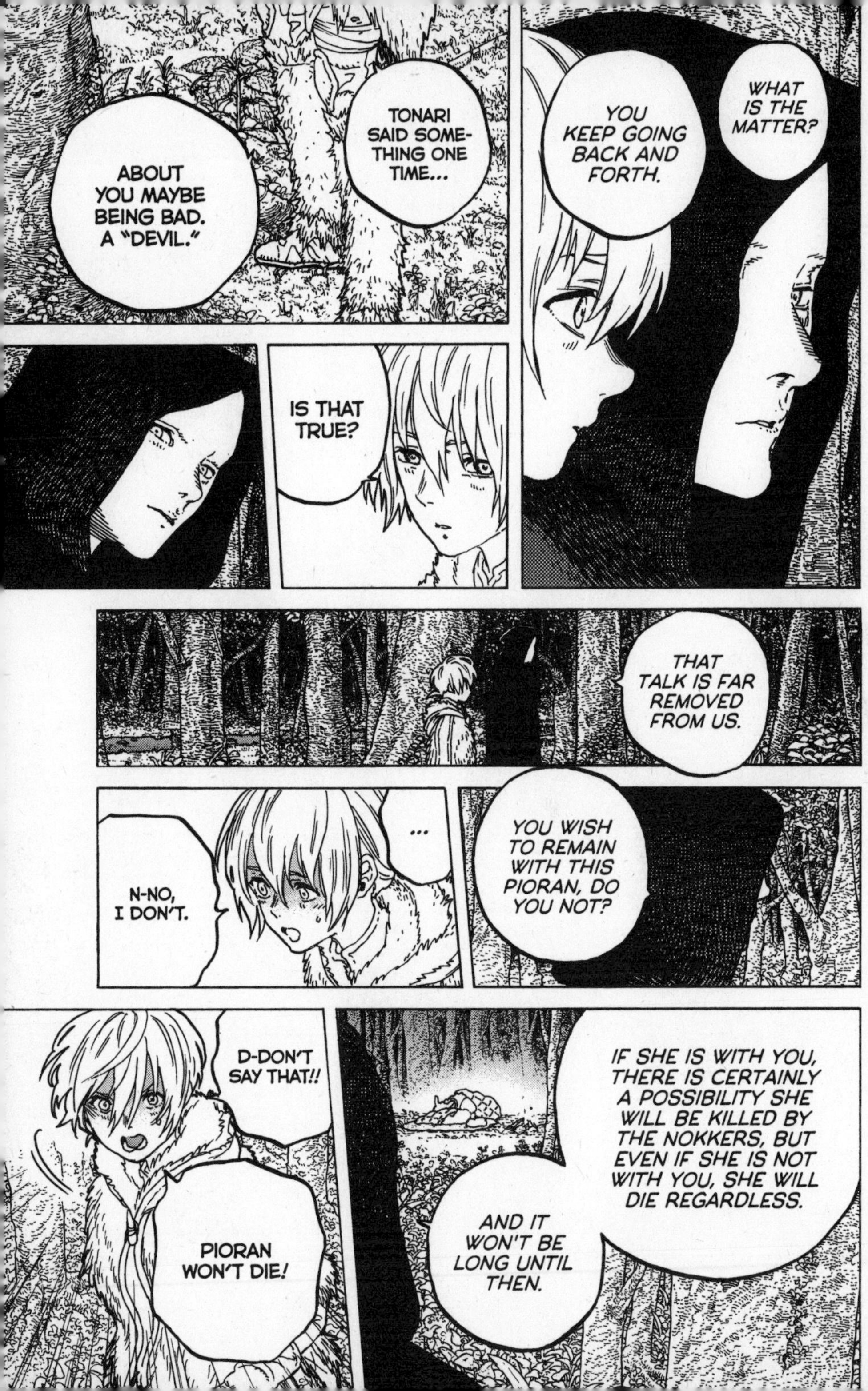
WHAT IS THE MATTER?
YOU KEEP GOING BACK AND FORTH.
TONARI SAID SOMETHING ONE TIME...
ABOUT YOU MAYBE BEING BAD. A "DEVIL."
IS THAT TRUE?
THAT TALK IS FAR REMOVED FROM US.
YOU WISH TO REMAIN WITH THIS PIORAN, DO YOU NOT?
...
N-NO, I DON'T.
IF SHE IS WITH YOU, THERE IS CERTAINLY A POSSIBILITY SHE WILL BE KILLED BY THE NOKKERS, BUT EVEN IF SHE IS NOT WITH YOU, SHE WILL DIE REGARDLESS.
AND IT WON'T BE LONG UNTIL THEN.
D-DON'T SAY THAT!!
PIORAN WON'T DIE!

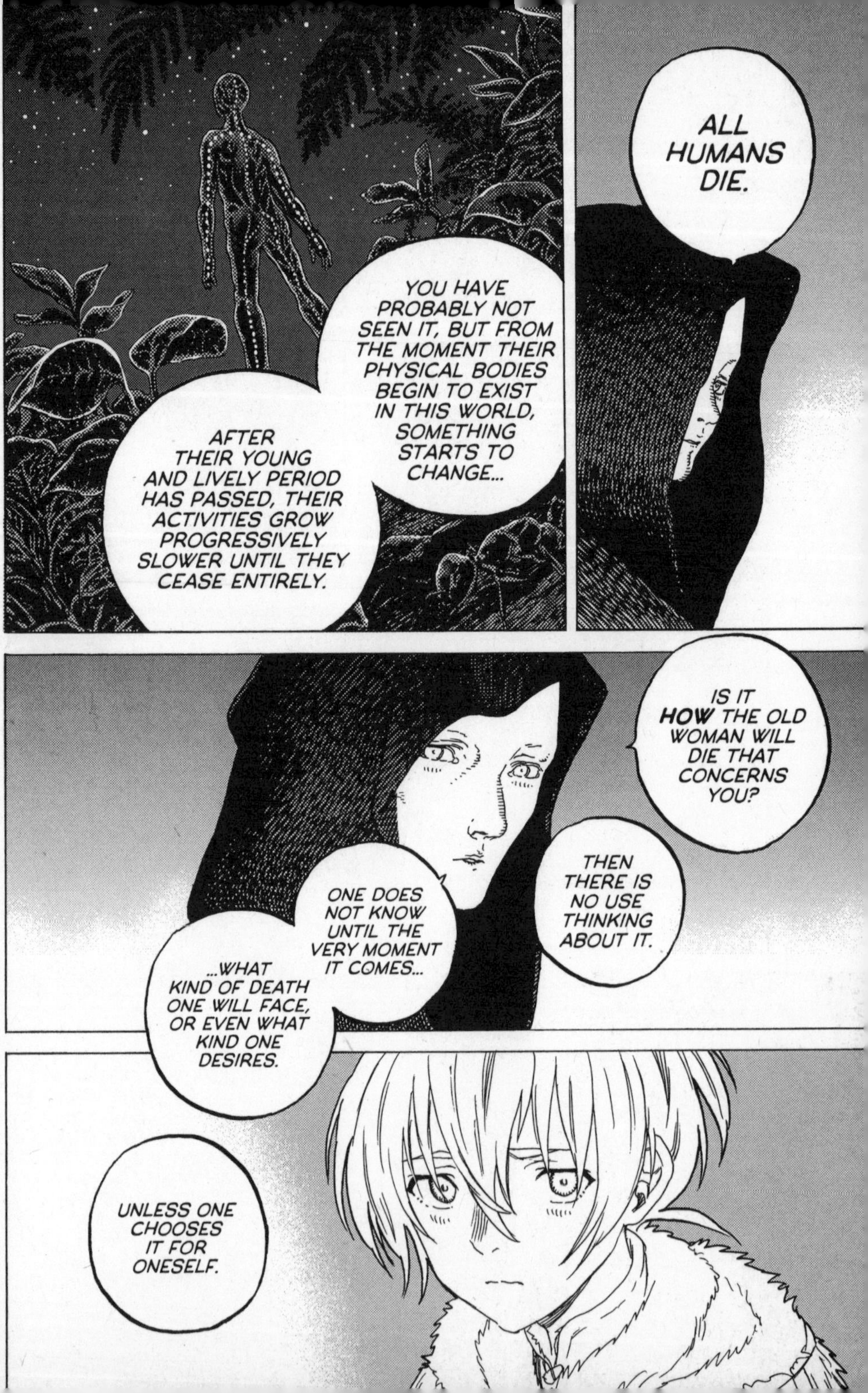
ALL HUMANS DIE.
YOU HAVE PROBABLY NOT SEEN IT, BUT FROM THE MOMENT THEIR PHYSICAL BODIES BEGIN TO EXIST IN THIS WORLD, SOMETHING STARTS TO CHANGE...
AFTER THEIR YOUNG AND LIVELY PERIOD HAS PASSED, THEIR ACTIVITIES GROW PROGRESSIVELY SLOWER UNTIL THEY CEASE ENTIRELY.
IS IT **HOW** THE OLD WOMAN WILL DIE THAT CONCERNS YOU?
THEN THERE IS NO USE THINKING ABOUT IT.
ONE DOES NOT KNOW UNTIL THE VERY MOMENT IT COMES...
...WHAT KIND OF DEATH ONE WILL FACE, OR EVEN WHAT KIND ONE DESIRES.
UNLESS ONE CHOOSES IT FOR ONESELF.

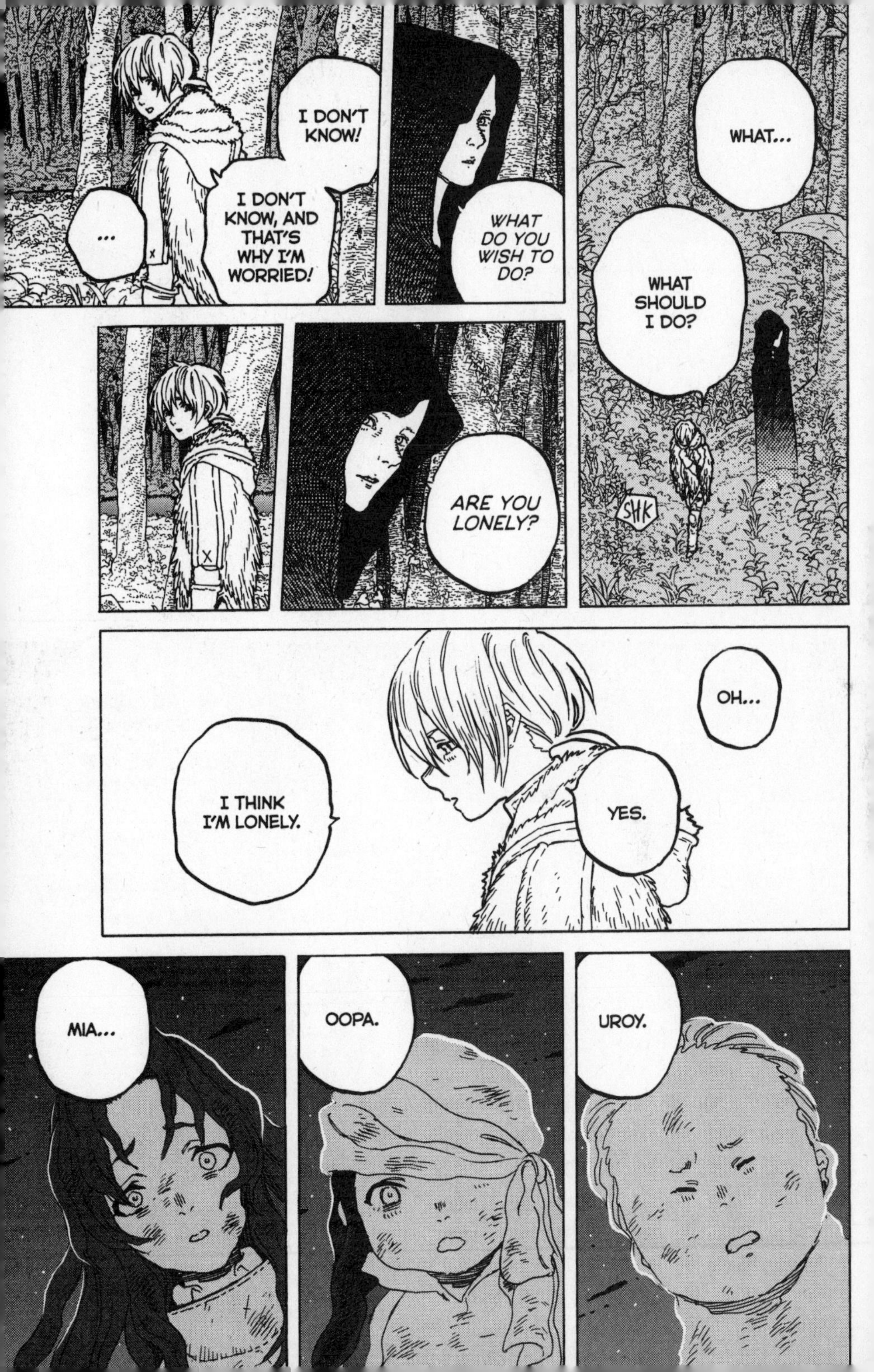
WHAT...
WHAT SHOULD I DO?
SHK
WHAT DO YOU WISH TO DO?
I DON'T KNOW!
I DON'T KNOW, AND THAT'S WHY I'M WORRIED!
...
ARE YOU LONELY?
OH...
YES.
I THINK I'M LONELY.
UROY.
OOPA.
MIA...

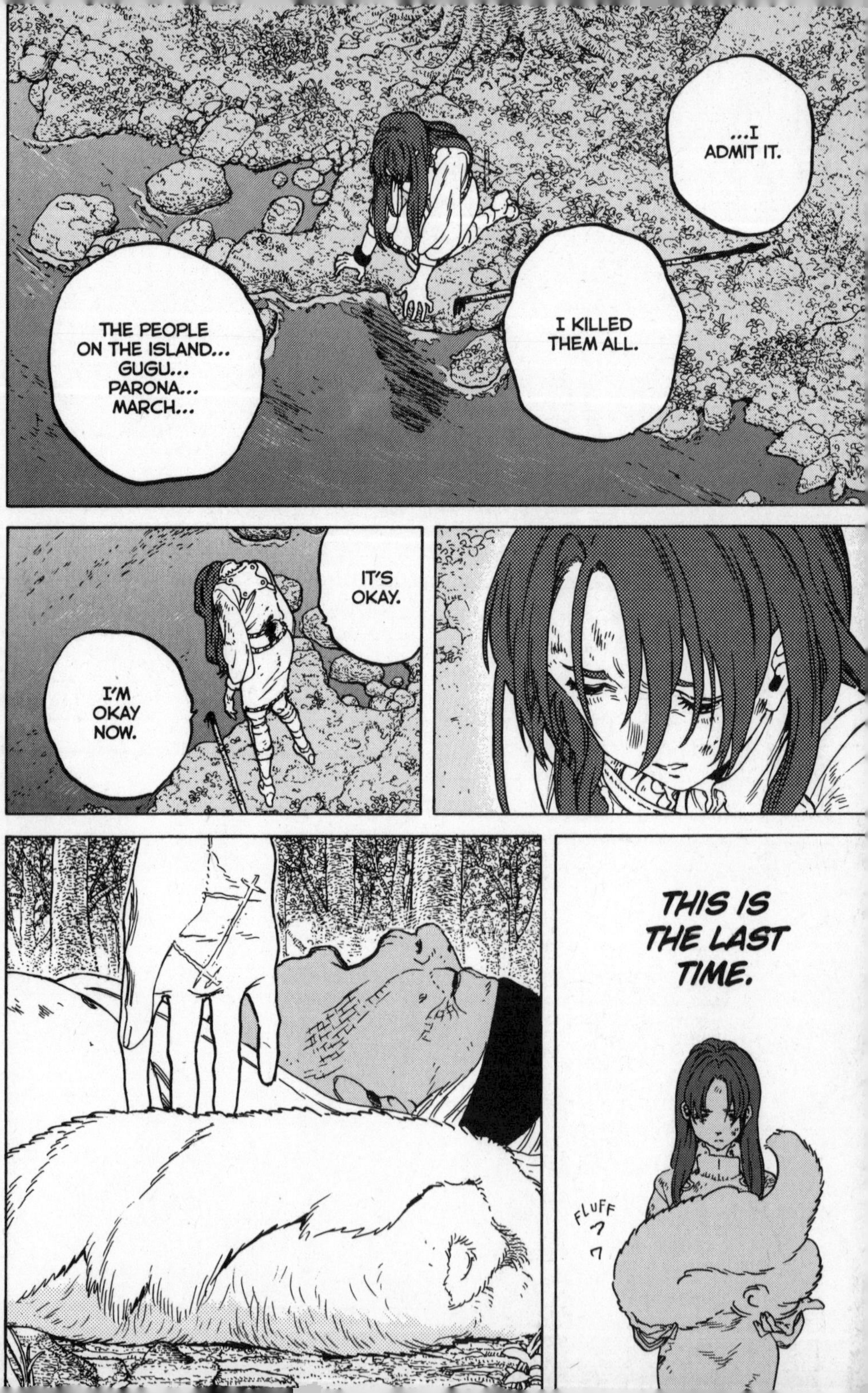
...I ADMIT IT.
I KILLED THEM ALL.
THE PEOPLE ON THE ISLAND... GUGU... PARONA... MARCH...
IT'S OKAY.
I'M OKAY NOW.
THIS IS THE LAST TIME.
FLUFF

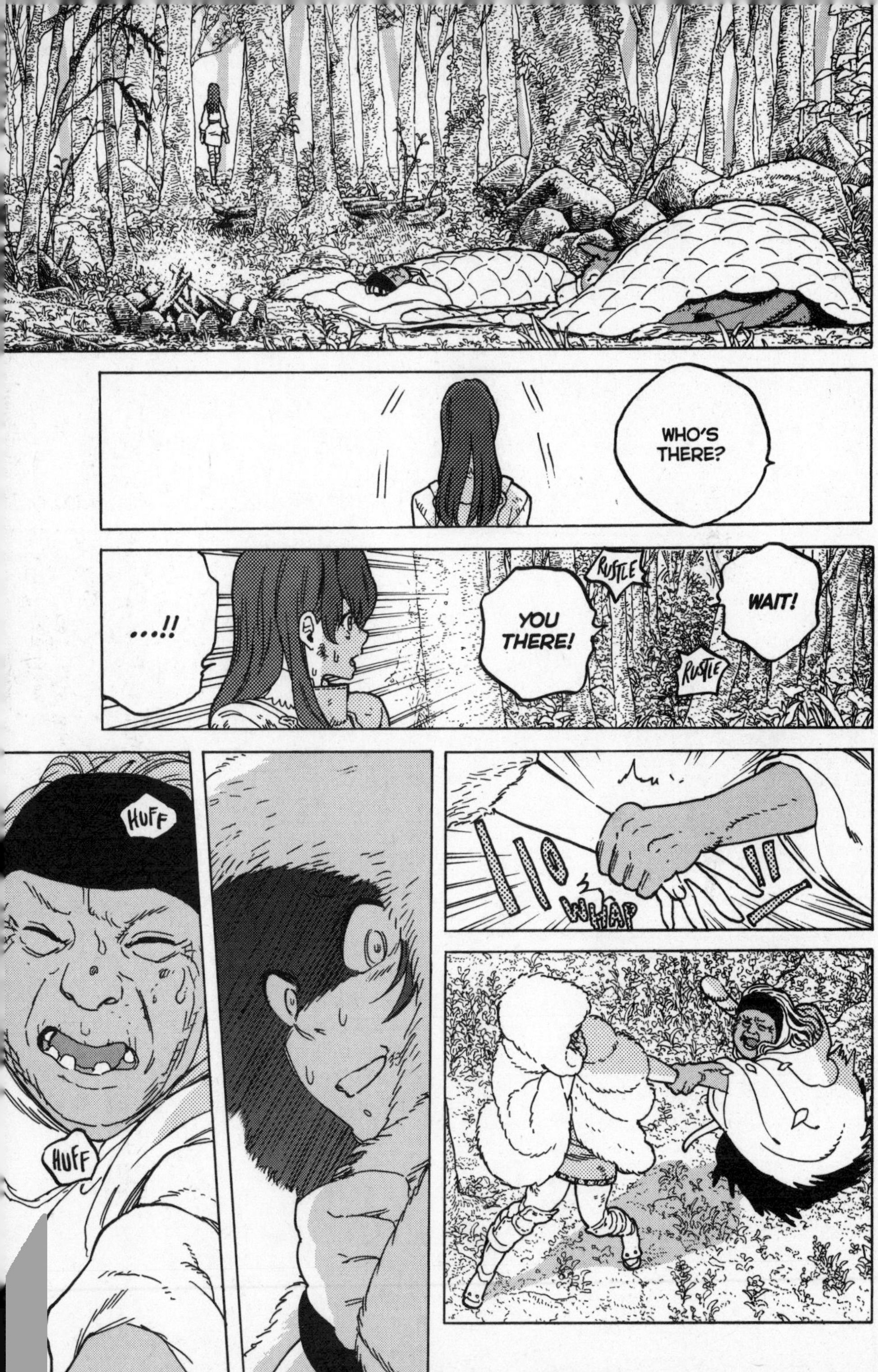
WHO'S THERE?
WAIT!
RUSTLE
YOU THERE!
RUSTLE
...!!
WHAP
HUFF
HUFF

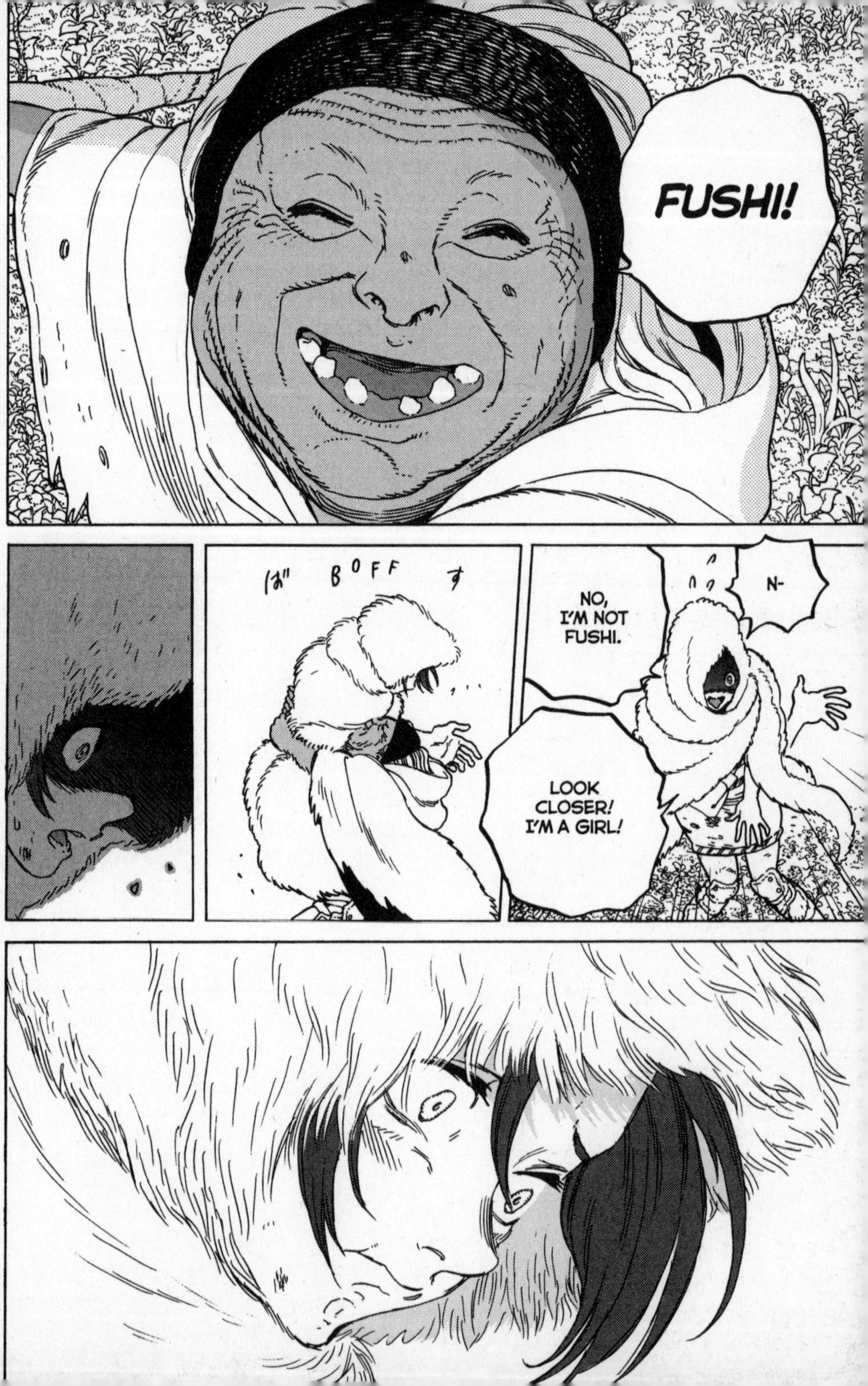
FUSHI!
N-
NO, I'M NOT FUSHI.
LOOK CLOSER! I'M A GIRL!
BOFF

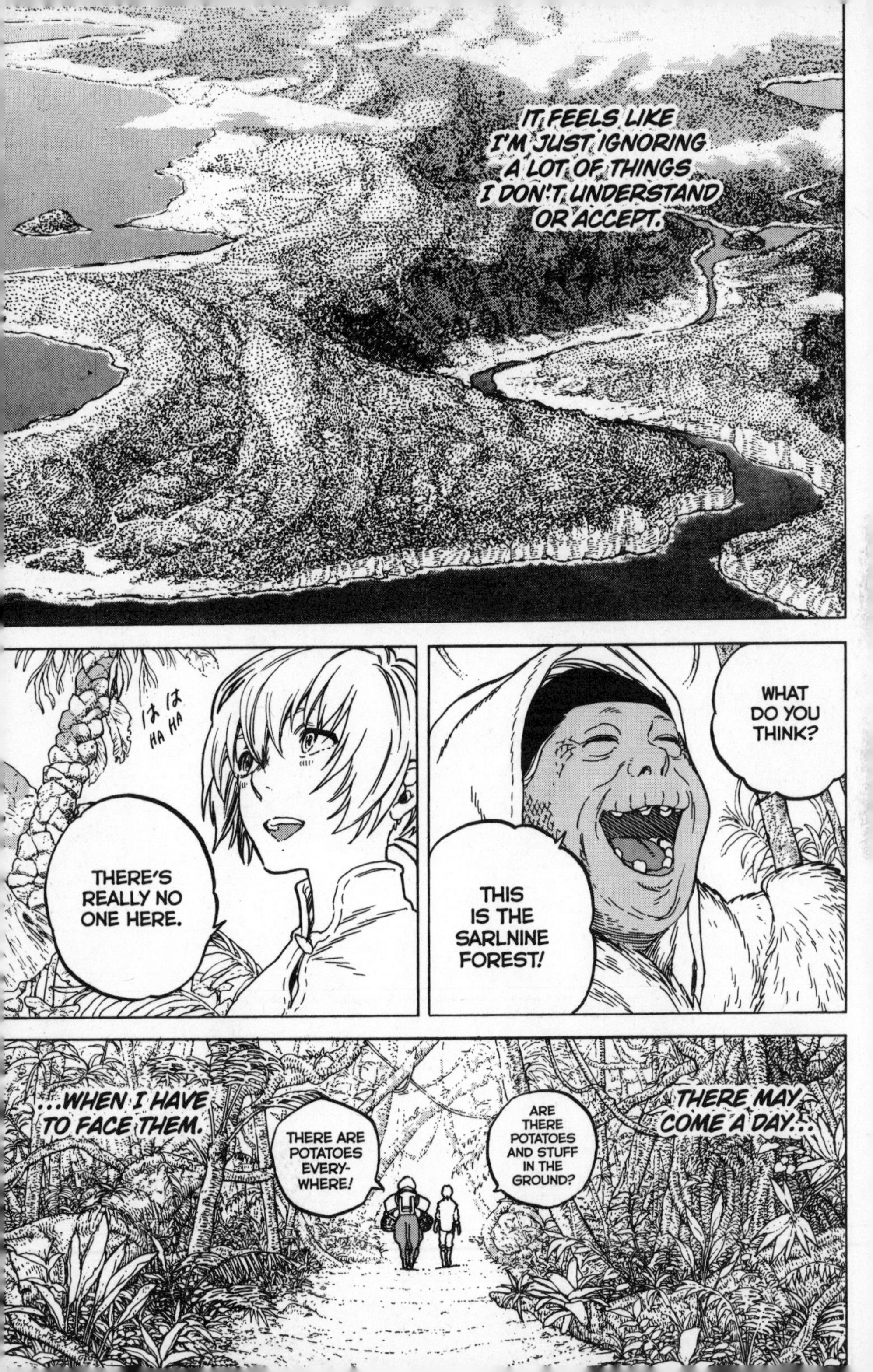
IT FEELS LIKE I'M JUST IGNORING A LOT OF THINGS I DON'T UNDERSTAND OR ACCEPT.
WHAT DO YOU THINK?
THIS IS THE SARLNINE FOREST!
はは
HA HA
THERE'S REALLY NO ONE HERE.
THERE MAY COME A DAY...
ARE THERE POTATOES AND STUFF IN THE GROUND?
THERE ARE POTATOES EVERY-WHERE!
...WHEN I HAVE TO FACE THEM.

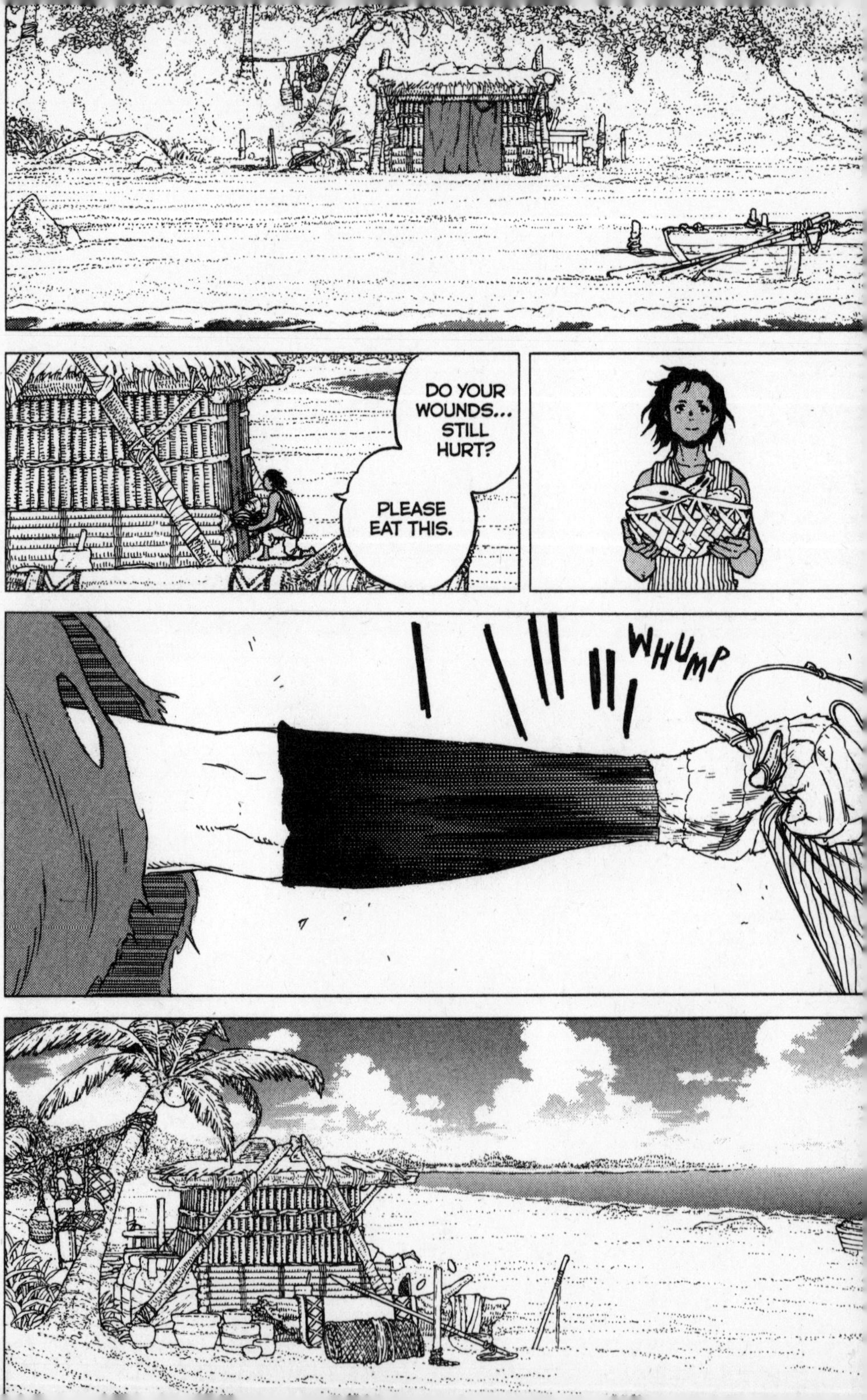
DO YOUR WOUNDS... STILL HURT?
PLEASE EAT THIS.
WHUMP

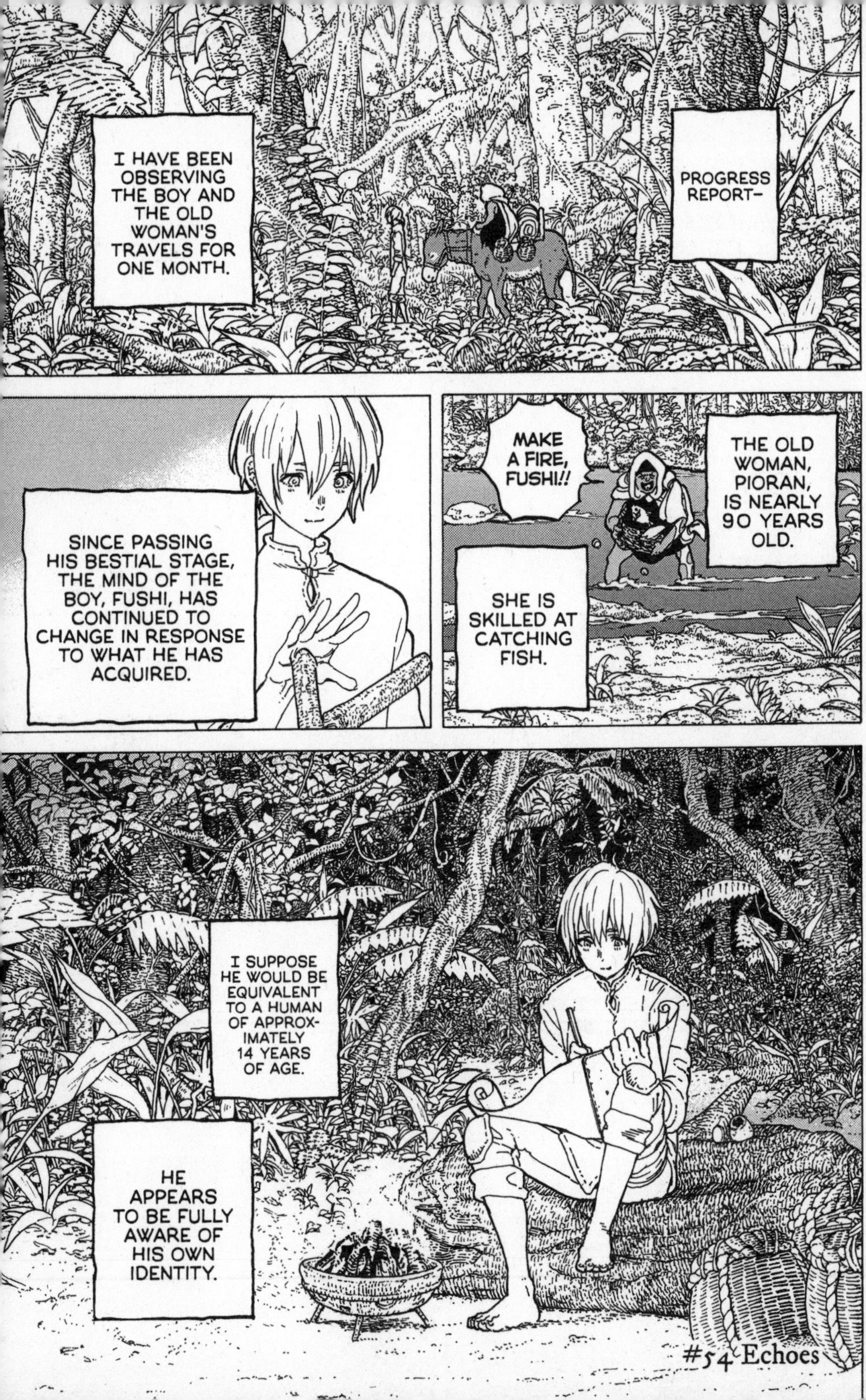
PROGRESS REPORT—
I HAVE BEEN OBSERVING THE BOY AND THE OLD WOMAN'S TRAVELS FOR ONE MONTH.
THE OLD WOMAN, PIORAN, IS NEARLY 90 YEARS OLD.
MAKE A FIRE, FUSHI!!
SHE IS SKILLED AT CATCHING FISH.
SINCE PASSING HIS BESTIAL STAGE, THE MIND OF THE BOY, FUSHI, HAS CONTINUED TO CHANGE IN RESPONSE TO WHAT HE HAS ACQUIRED.
I SUPPOSE HE WOULD BE EQUIVALENT TO A HUMAN OF APPROX-IMATELY 14 YEARS OF AGE.
HE APPEARS TO BE FULLY AWARE OF HIS OWN IDENTITY.
#54 Echoes

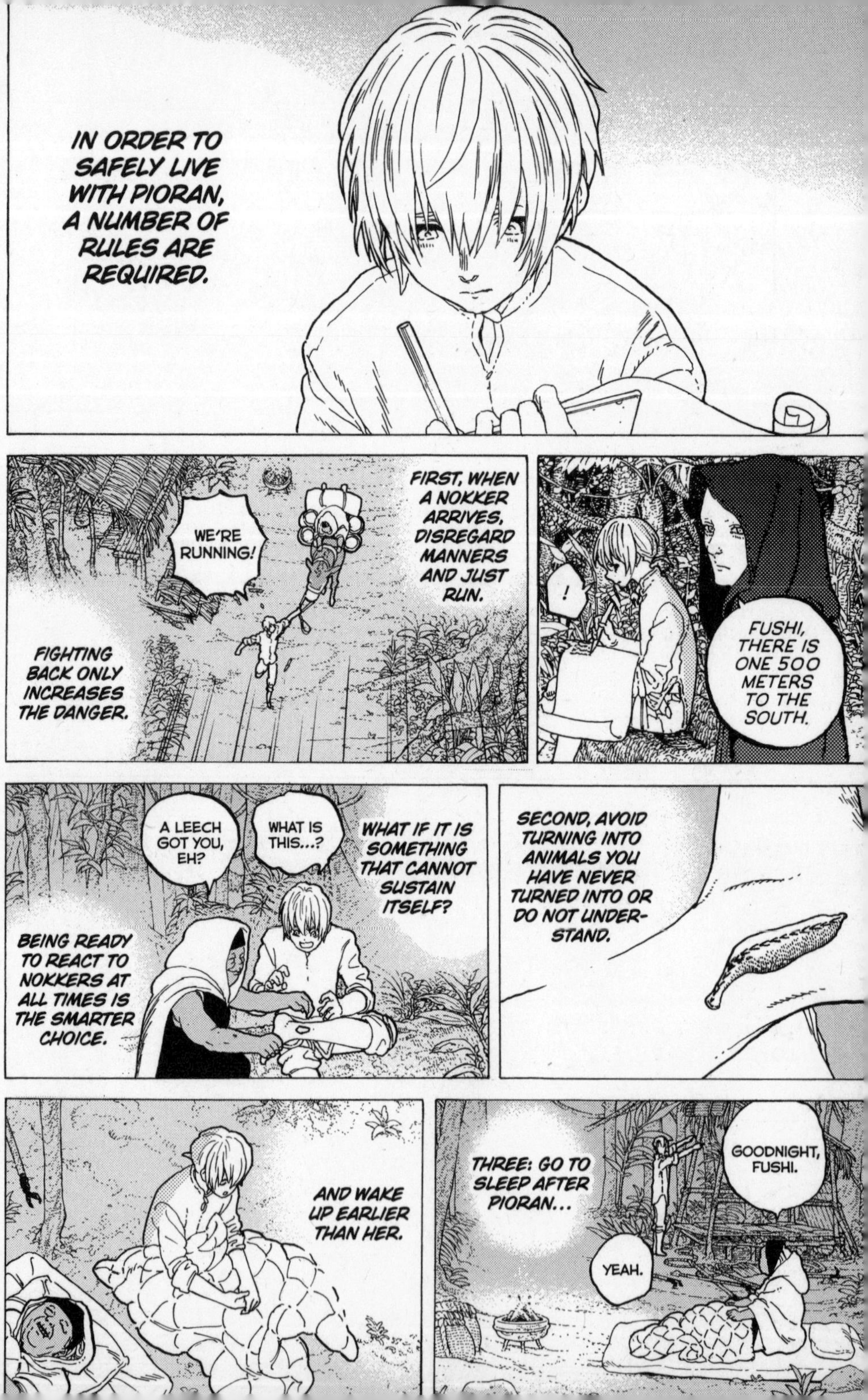
IN ORDER TO SAFELY LIVE WITH PIORAN, A NUMBER OF RULES ARE REQUIRED.
!
FUSHI, THERE IS ONE 500 METERS TO THE SOUTH.
FIRST, WHEN A NOKKER ARRIVES, DISREGARD MANNERS AND JUST RUN.
WE'RE RUNNING!
FIGHTING BACK ONLY INCREASES THE DANGER.
SECOND, AVOID TURNING INTO ANIMALS YOU HAVE NEVER TURNED INTO OR DO NOT UNDER-STAND.
WHAT IF IT IS SOMETHING THAT CANNOT SUSTAIN ITSELF?
WHAT IS THIS...?
A LEECH GOT YOU, EH?
BEING READY TO REACT TO NOKKERS AT ALL TIMES IS THE SMARTER CHOICE.
GOODNIGHT, FUSHI.
THREE: GO TO SLEEP AFTER PIORAN...
YEAH.
AND WAKE UP EARLIER THAN HER.

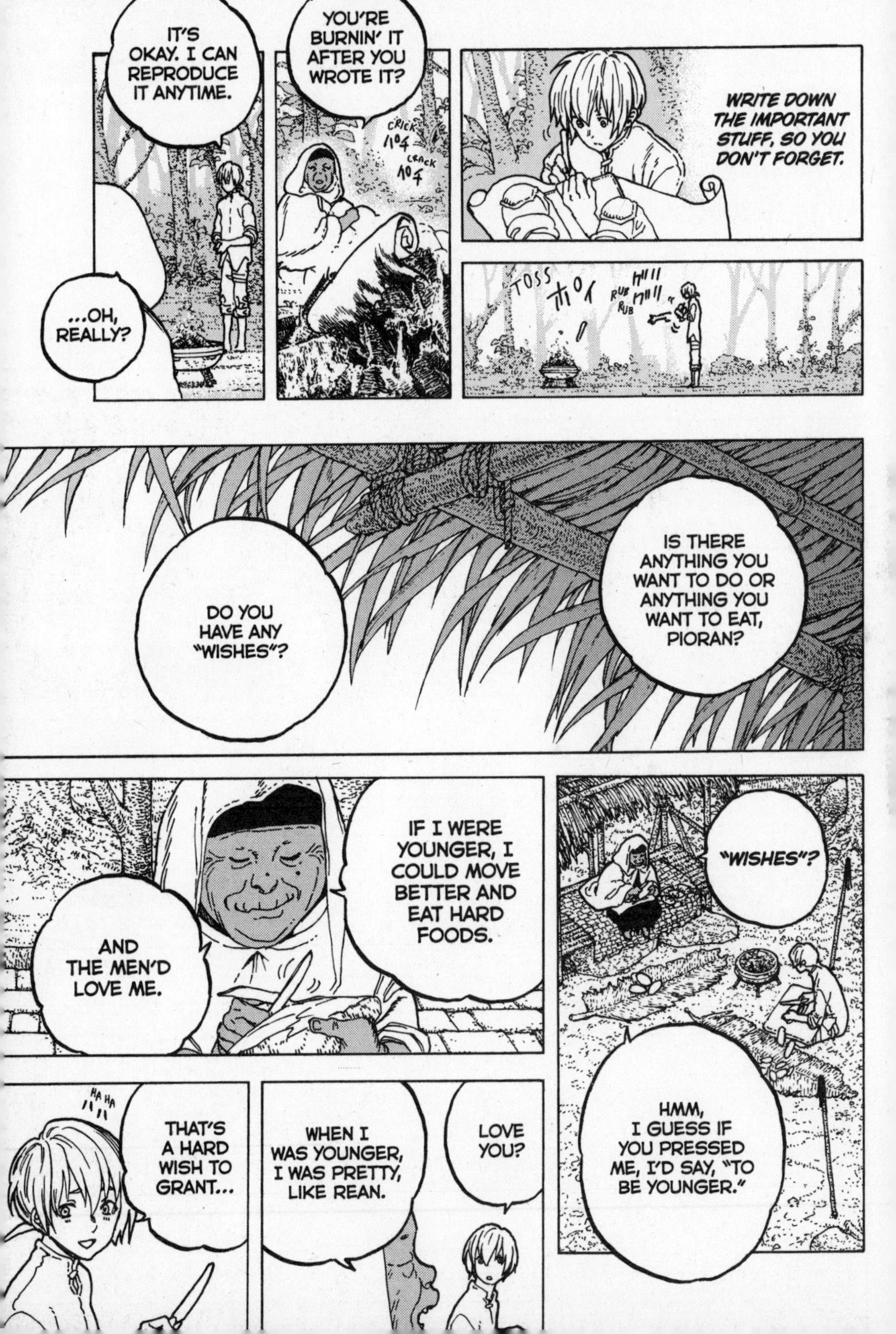
WRITE DOWN THE IMPORTANT STUFF, SO YOU DON'T FORGET.
TOSS
RUB RUB
YOU'RE BURNIN' IT AFTER YOU WROTE IT?
CRICK
CRACK
IT'S OKAY. I CAN REPRODUCE IT ANYTIME.
...OH, REALLY?
IS THERE ANYTHING YOU WANT TO DO OR ANYTHING YOU WANT TO EAT, PIORAN?
DO YOU HAVE ANY "WISHES"?
"WISHES"?
HMM, I GUESS IF YOU PRESSED ME, I'D SAY, "TO BE YOUNGER."
IF I WERE YOUNGER, I COULD MOVE BETTER AND EAT HARD FOODS.
AND THE MEN'D LOVE ME.
LOVE YOU?
WHEN I WAS YOUNGER, I WAS PRETTY, LIKE REAN.
HA HA
THAT'S A HARD WISH TO GRANT...

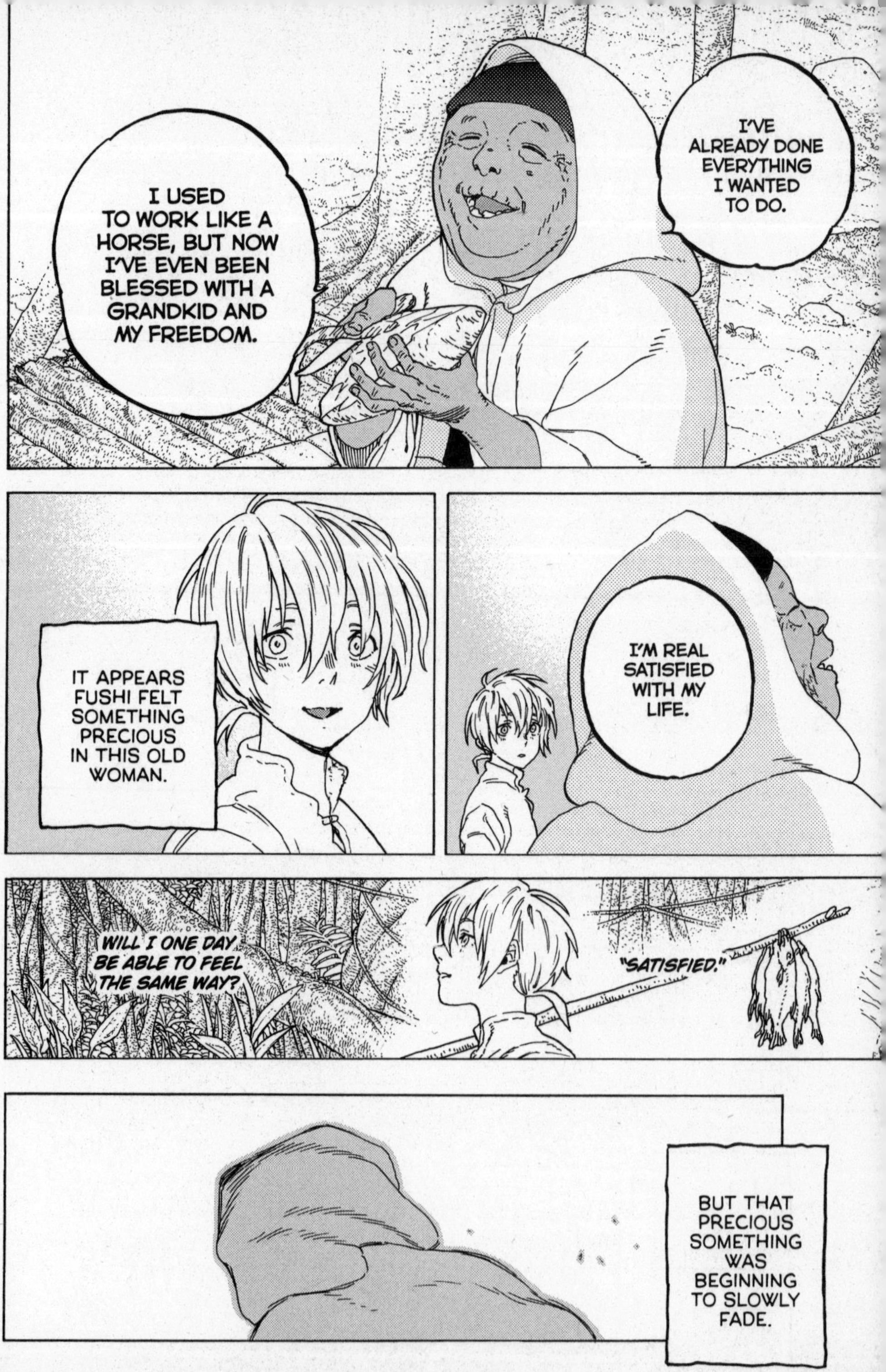
I'VE ALREADY DONE EVERYTHING I WANTED TO DO.
I USED TO WORK LIKE A HORSE, BUT NOW I'VE EVEN BEEN BLESSED WITH A GRANDKID AND MY FREEDOM.
I'M REAL SATISFIED WITH MY LIFE.
IT APPEARS FUSHI FELT SOMETHING PRECIOUS IN THIS OLD WOMAN.
"SATISFIED."
WILL I ONE DAY BE ABLE TO FEEL THE SAME WAY?
BUT THAT PRECIOUS SOMETHING WAS BEGINNING TO SLOWLY FADE.

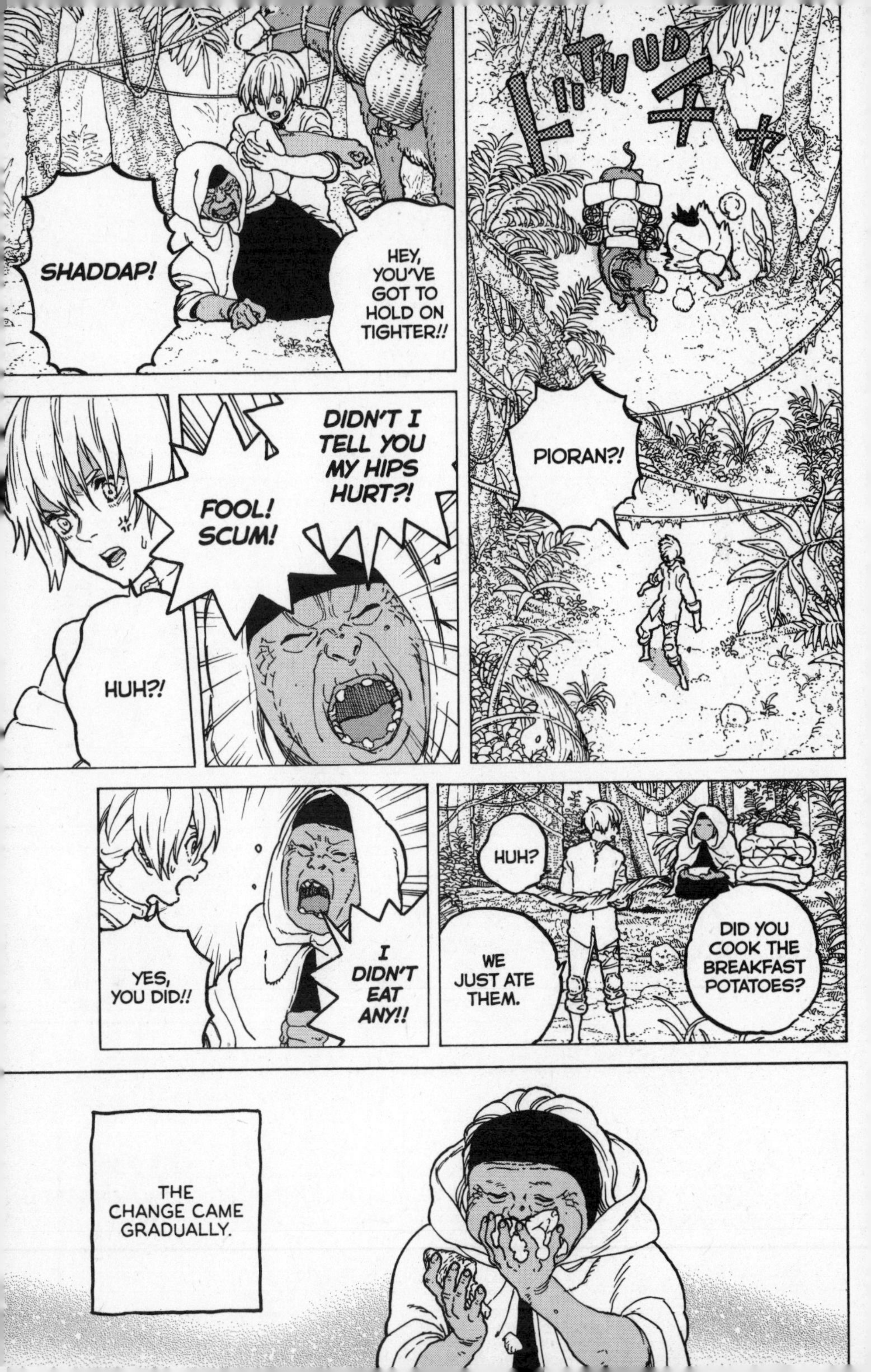
THUD
PIORAN?!
HEY, YOU'VE GOT TO HOLD ON TIGHTER!!
SHADDAP!
DIDN'T I TELL YOU MY HIPS HURT?!
FOOL! SCUM!
HUH?!
DID YOU COOK THE BREAKFAST POTATOES?
HUH?
WE JUST ATE THEM.
I DIDN'T EAT ANY!!
YES, YOU DID!!
THE CHANGE CAME GRADUALLY.

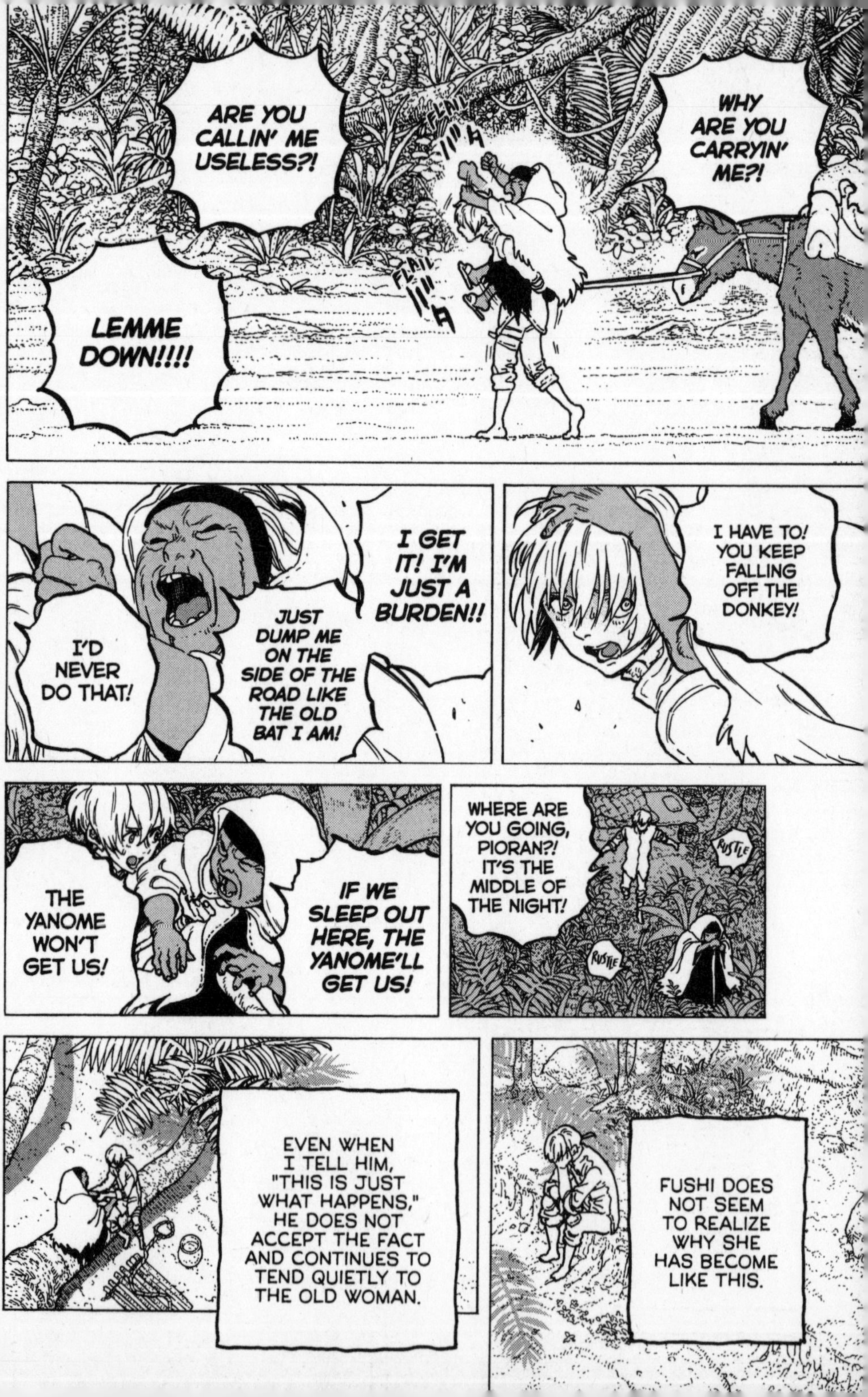
WHY ARE YOU CARRYIN' ME?!
FLAIL
ARE YOU CALLIN' ME USELESS?!
FLAIL
LEMME DOWN!!!!!
I HAVE TO! YOU KEEP FALLING OFF THE DONKEY!
I GET IT! I'M JUST A BURDEN!!
JUST DUMP ME ON THE SIDE OF THE ROAD LIKE THE OLD BAT I AM!
I'D NEVER DO THAT!
WHERE ARE YOU GOING, PIORAN?! IT'S THE MIDDLE OF THE NIGHT!
RUSTLE
RUSTLE
IF WE SLEEP OUT HERE, THE YANOME'LL GET US!
THE YANOME WON'T GET US!
FUSHI DOES NOT SEEM TO REALIZE WHY SHE HAS BECOME LIKE THIS.
EVEN WHEN I TELL HIM, "THIS IS JUST WHAT HAPPENS," HE DOES NOT ACCEPT THE FACT AND CONTINUES TO TEND QUIETLY TO THE OLD WOMAN.

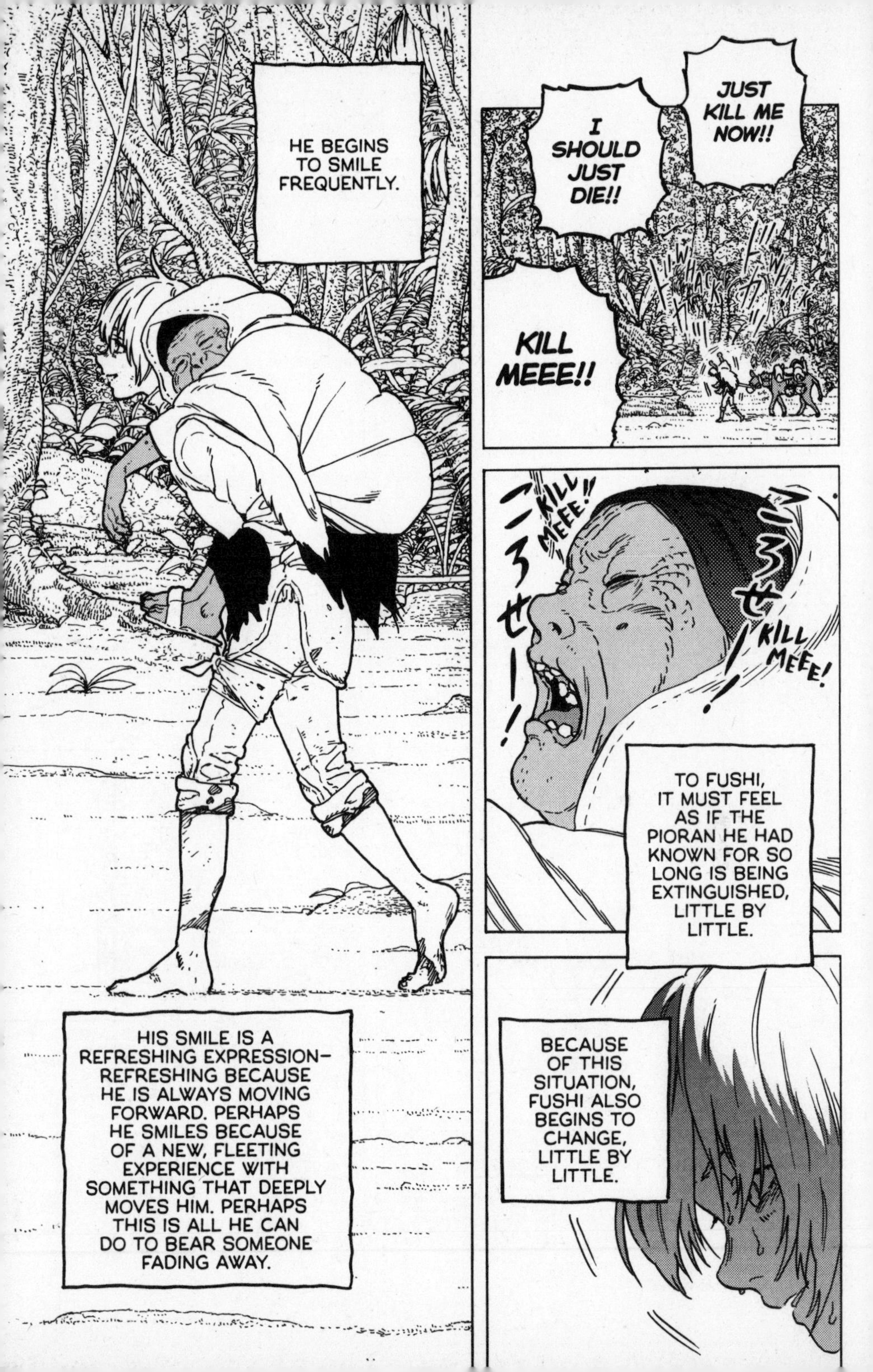
JUST KILL ME NOW!!
I SHOULD JUST DIE!!
WHACK
WHACK
KILL MEEE!!
ころせ!!
KILL MEEE!
ころせー!!
KILL MEEE!!
TO FUSHI, IT MUST FEEL AS IF THE PIORAN HE HAD KNOWN FOR SO LONG IS BEING EXTINGUISHED, LITTLE BY LITTLE.
BECAUSE OF THIS SITUATION, FUSHI ALSO BEGINS TO CHANGE, LITTLE BY LITTLE.
HE BEGINS TO SMILE FREQUENTLY.
HIS SMILE IS A REFRESHING EXPRESSION—REFRESHING BECAUSE HE IS ALWAYS MOVING FORWARD. PERHAPS HE SMILES BECAUSE OF A NEW, FLEETING EXPERIENCE WITH SOMETHING THAT DEEPLY MOVES HIM. PERHAPS THIS IS ALL HE CAN DO TO BEAR SOMEONE FADING AWAY.

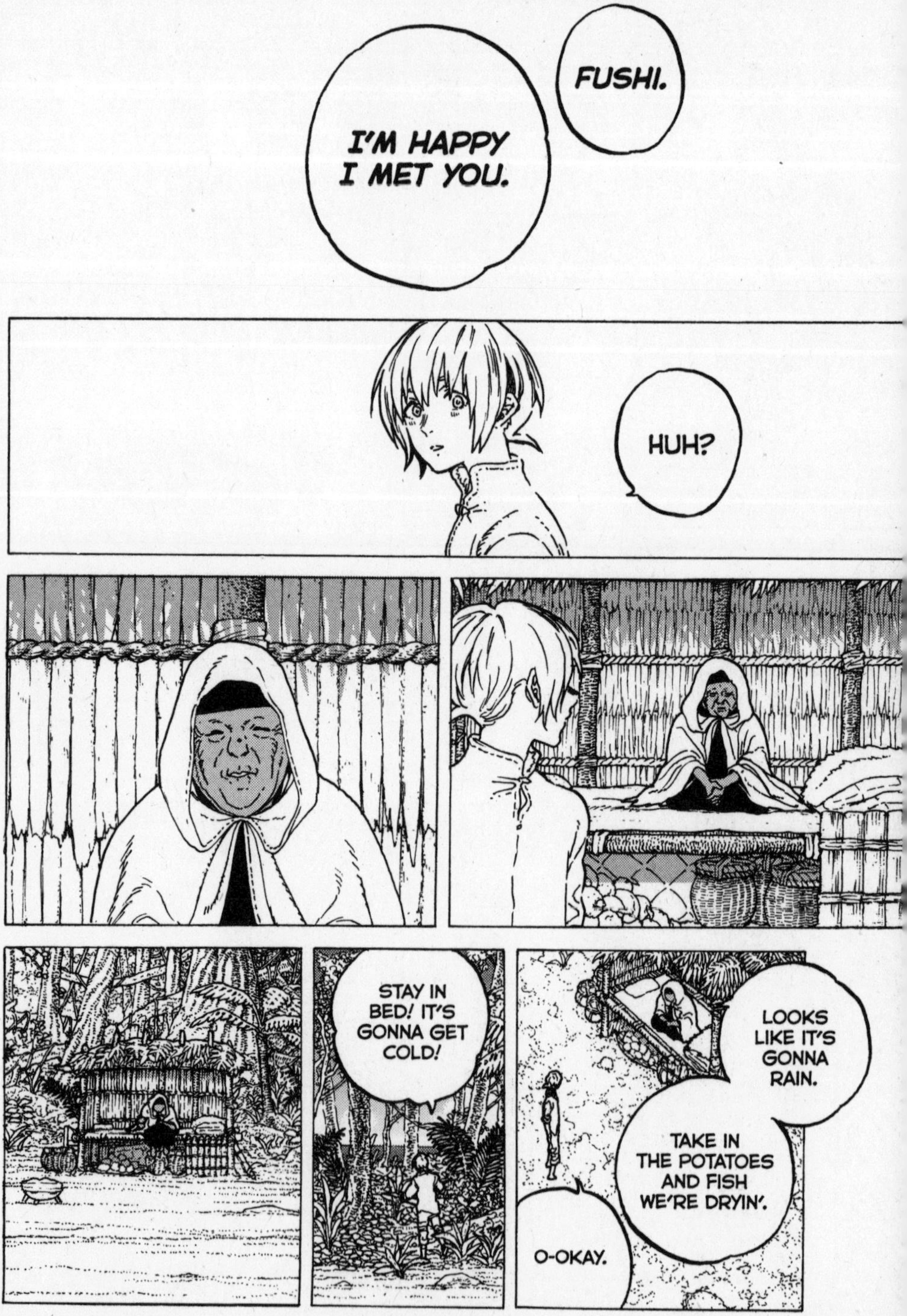
FUSHI.
I'M HAPPY I MET YOU.
HUH?
LOOKS LIKE IT'S GONNA RAIN.
TAKE IN THE POTATOES AND FISH WE'RE DRYIN'.
O-OKAY.
STAY IN BED! IT'S GONNA GET COLD!

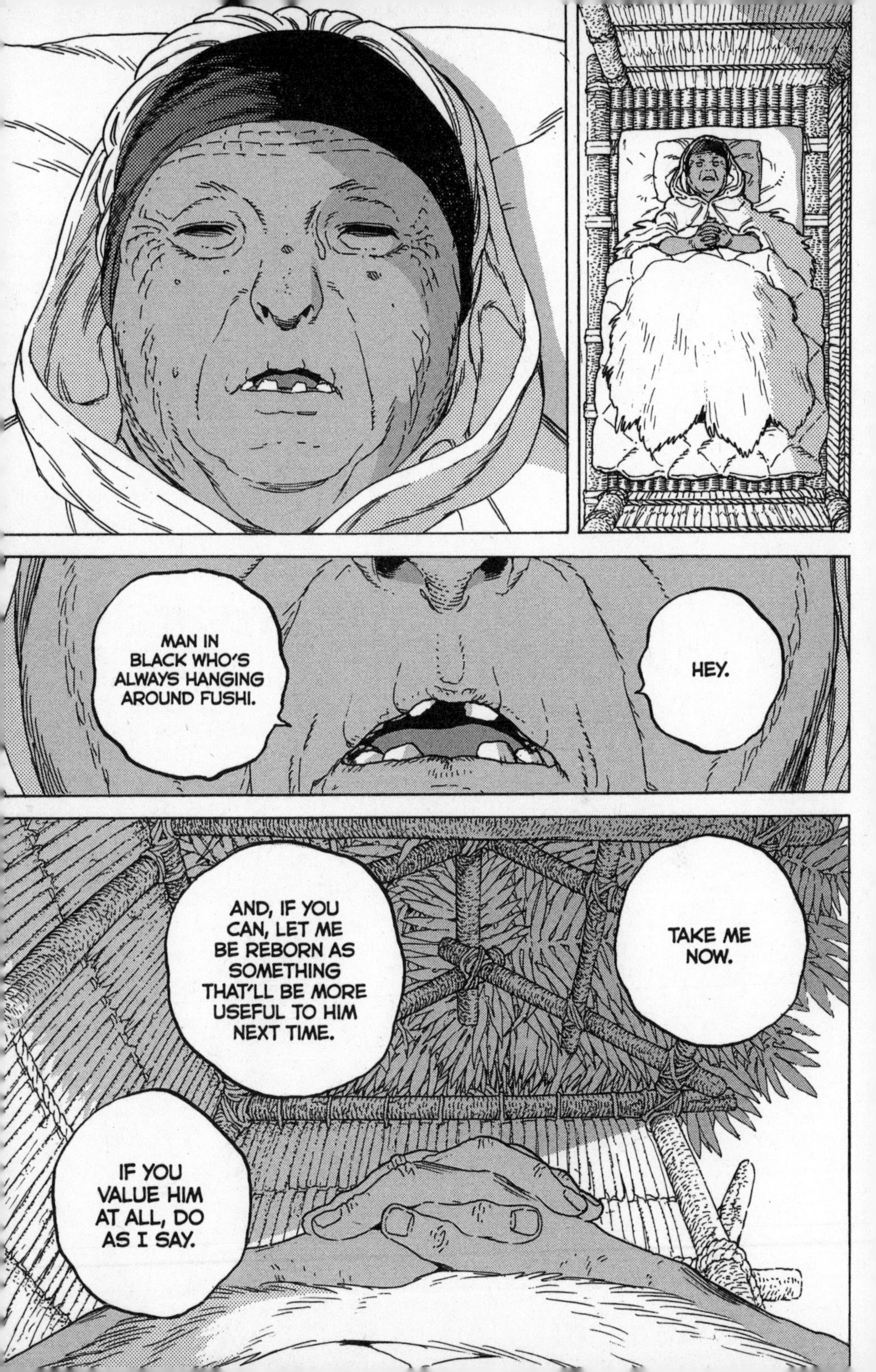
HEY.
MAN IN BLACK WHO'S ALWAYS HANGING AROUND FUSHI.
TAKE ME NOW.
AND, IF YOU CAN, LET ME BE REBORN AS SOMETHING THAT'LL BE MORE USEFUL TO HIM NEXT TIME.
IF YOU VALUE HIM AT ALL, DO AS I SAY.

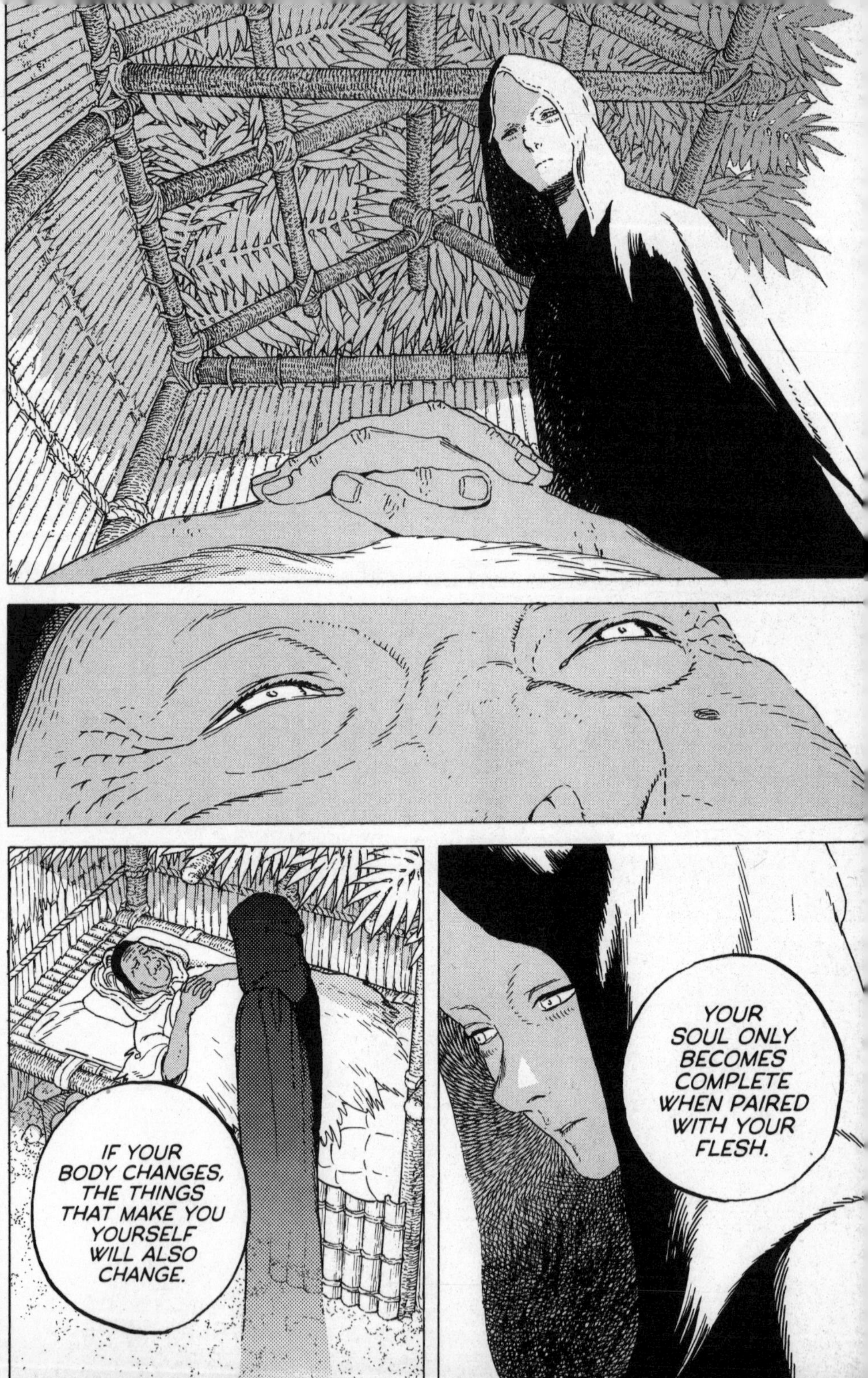
YOUR SOUL ONLY BECOMES COMPLETE WHEN PAIRED WITH YOUR FLESH.
IF YOUR BODY CHANGES, THE THINGS THAT MAKE YOU YOURSELF WILL ALSO CHANGE.

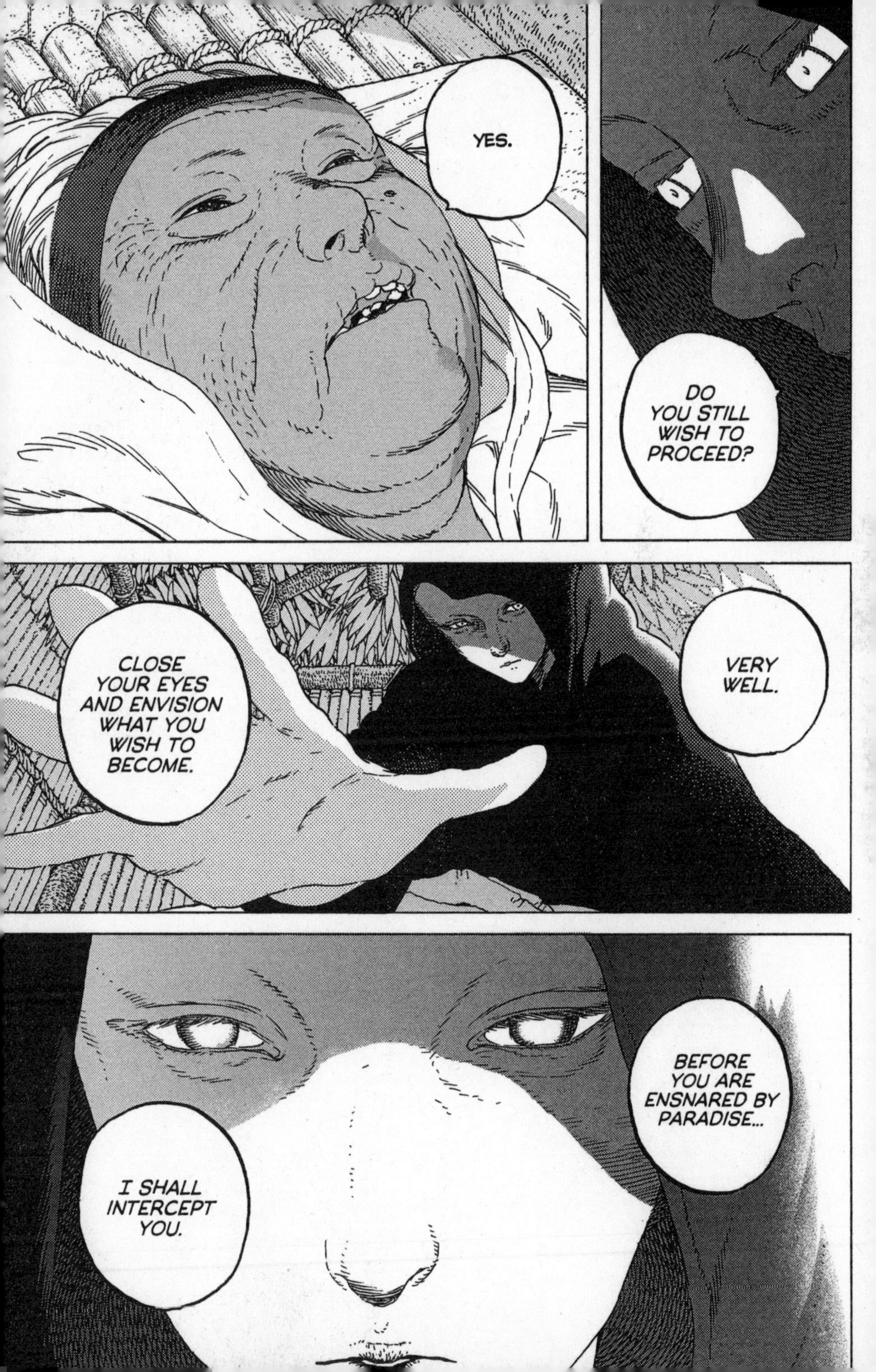
DO YOU STILL WISH TO PROCEED?
YES.
VERY WELL.
CLOSE YOUR EYES AND ENVISION WHAT YOU WISH TO BECOME.
BEFORE YOU ARE ENSNARED BY PARADISE...
I SHALL INTERCEPT YOU.

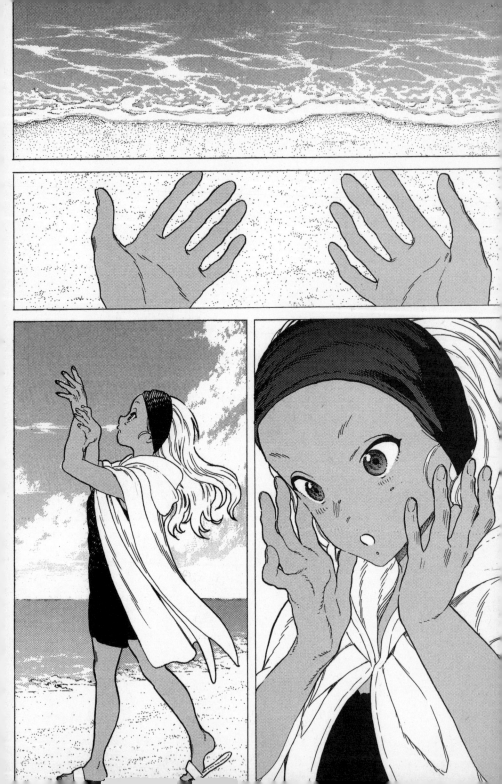

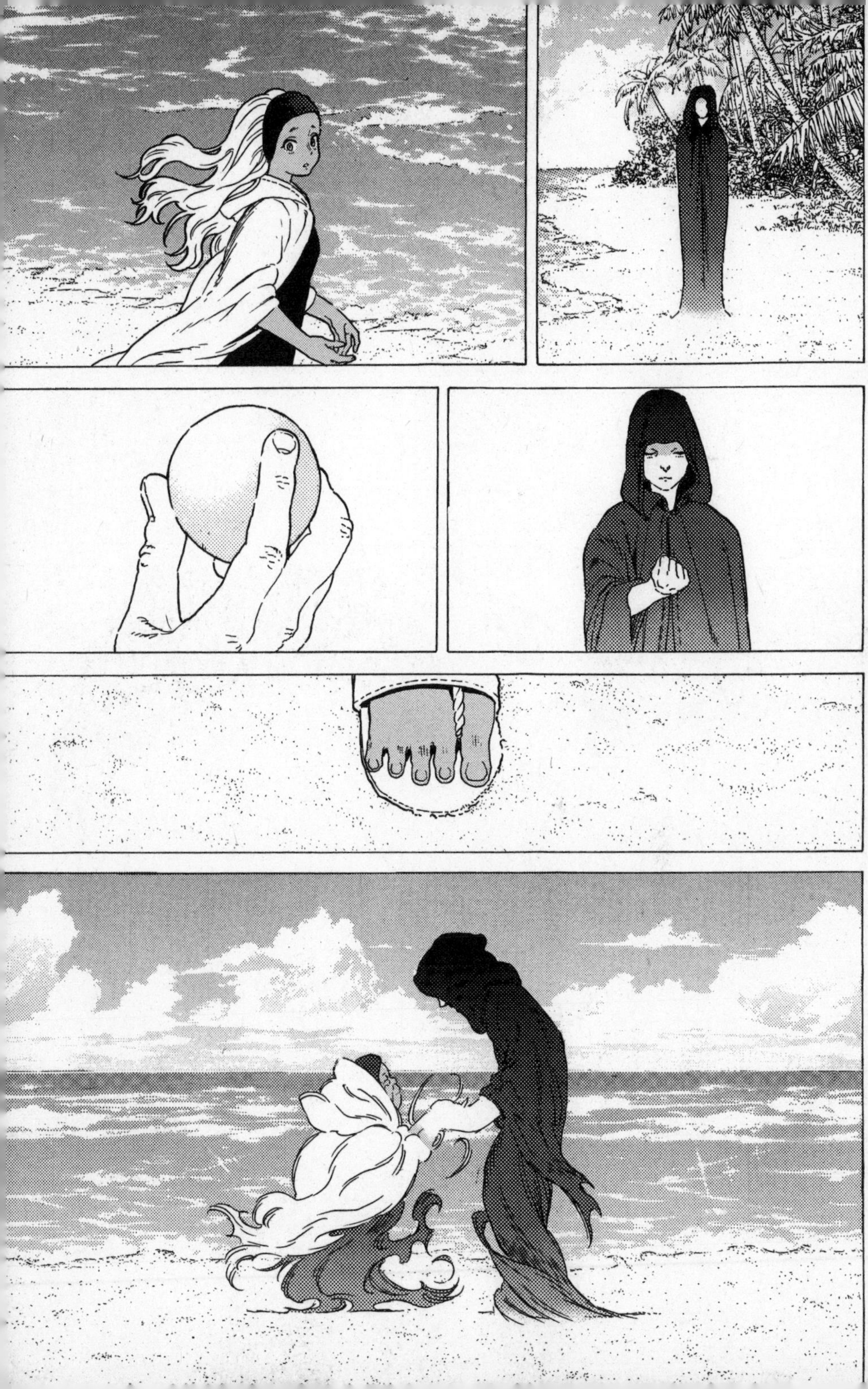

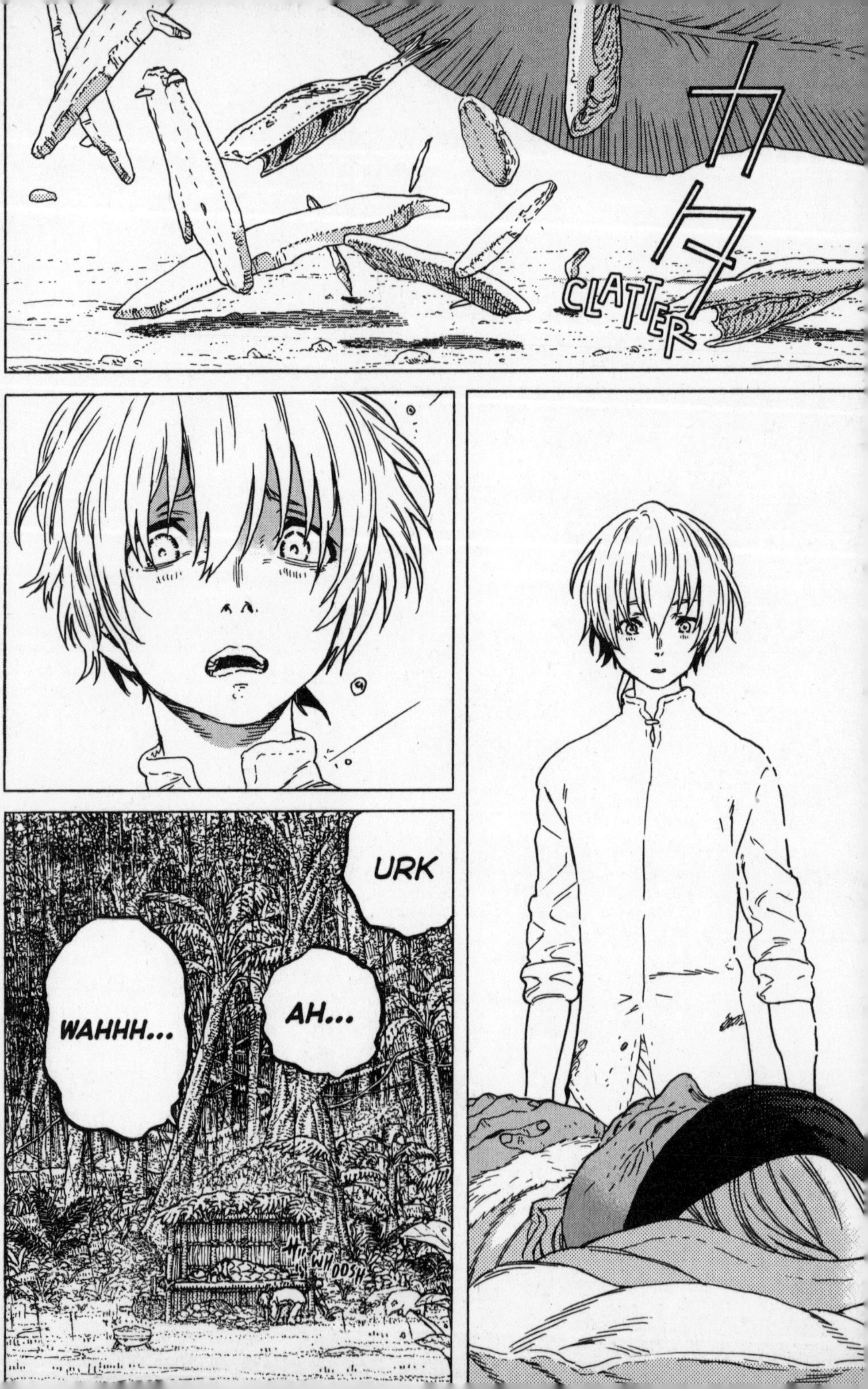
カタ
CLATTER
URK
AH...
WAHHH...
WHOOSH

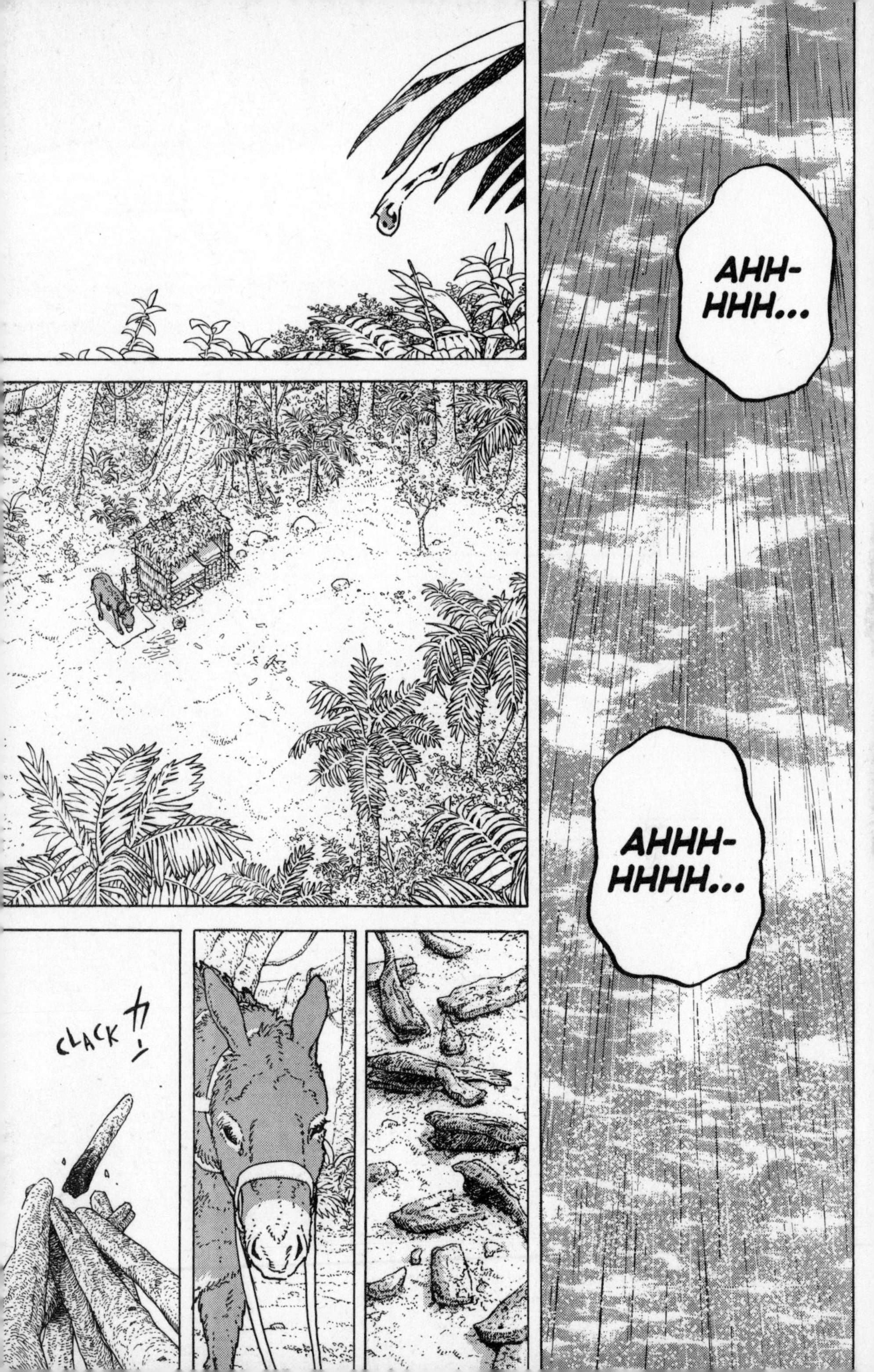
AHH-HHH...
AHHH-HHHH...
CLACK カ!

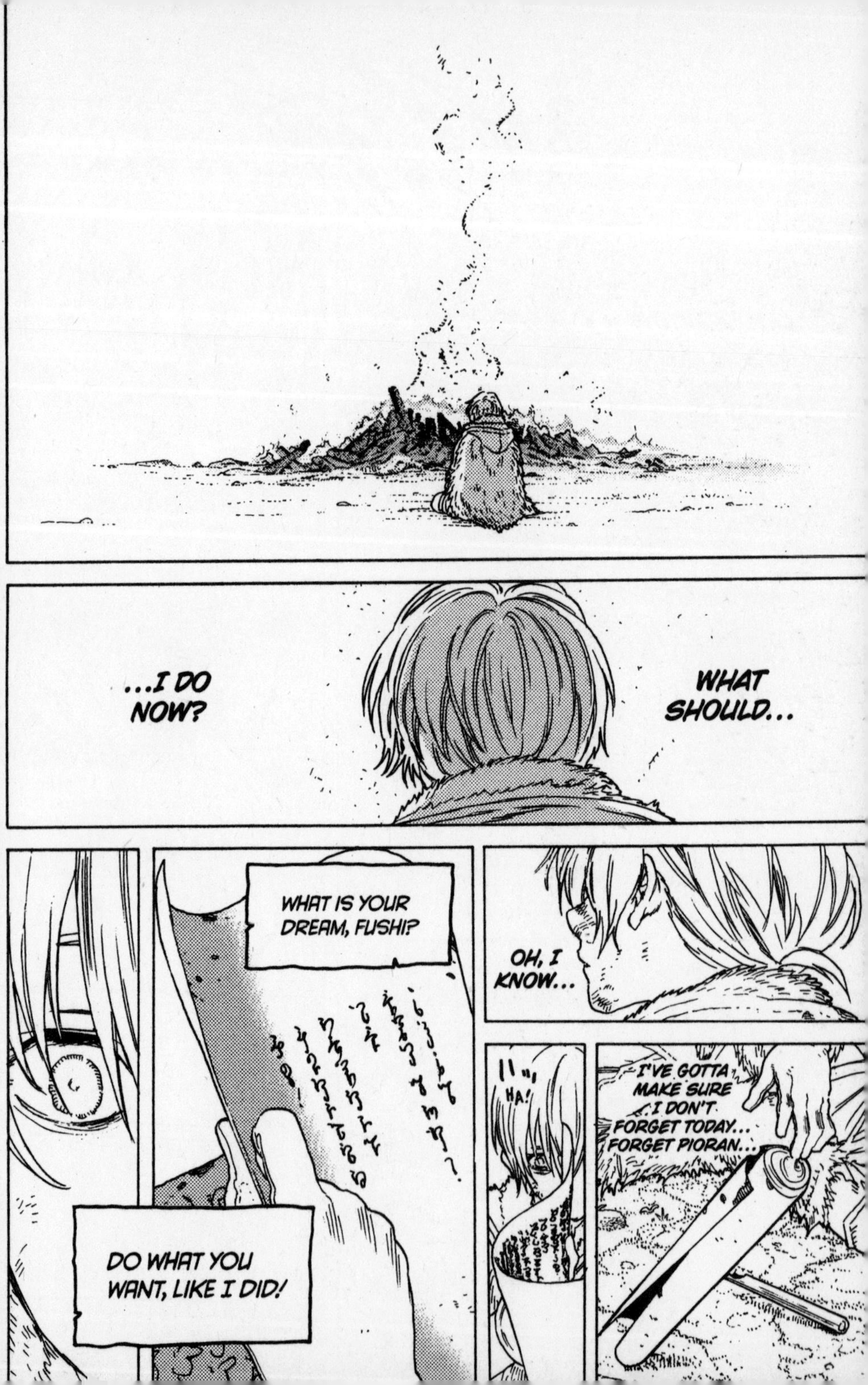
WHAT SHOULD...
...I DO NOW?
OH, I KNOW...
I'VE GOTTA MAKE SURE I DON'T FORGET TODAY... FORGET PIORAN...
HA!
WHAT IS YOUR DREAM, FUSHI?
DO WHAT YOU WANT, LIKE I DID!

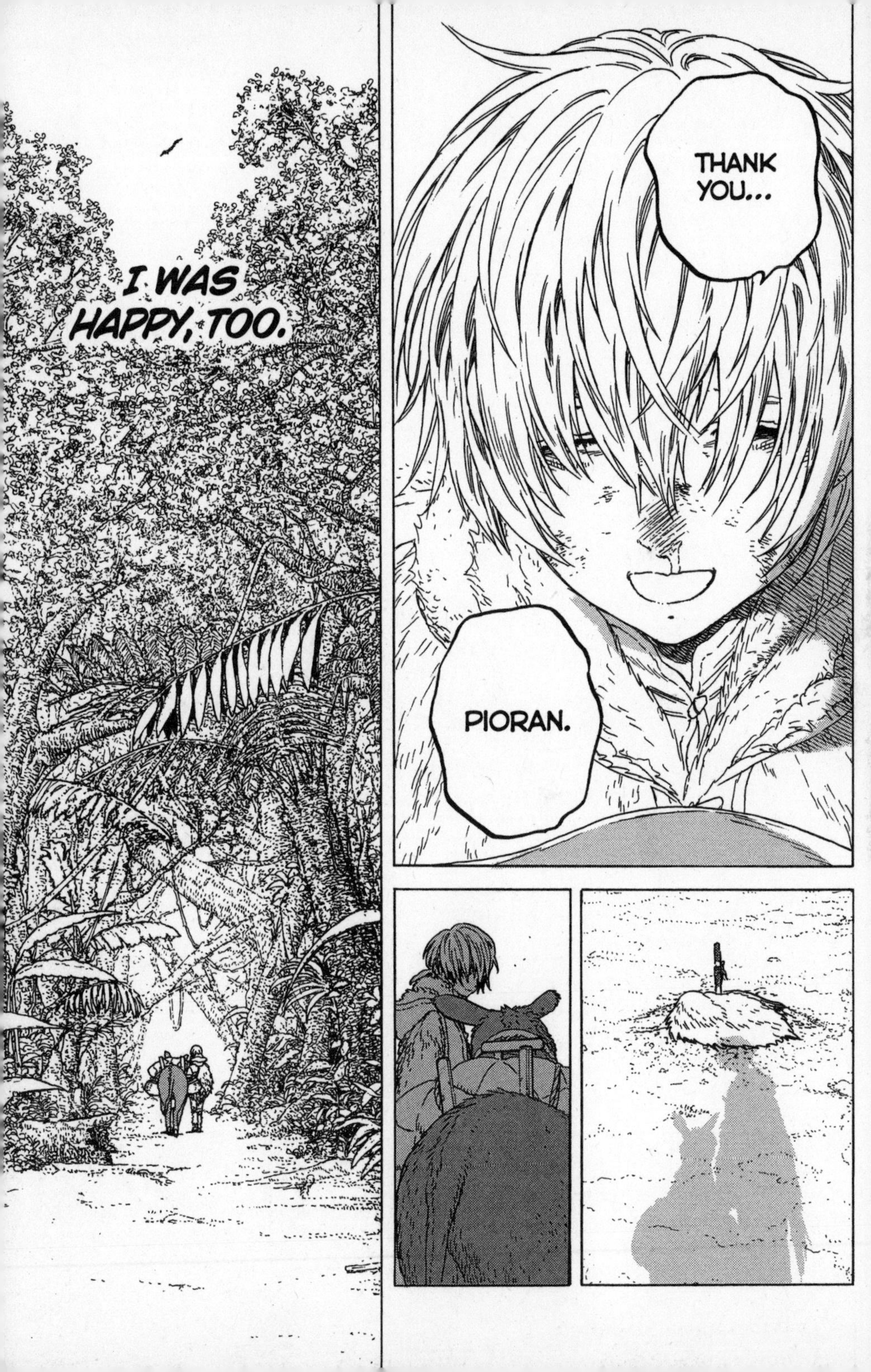
THANK YOU...
PIORAN.
I WAS HAPPY, TOO.

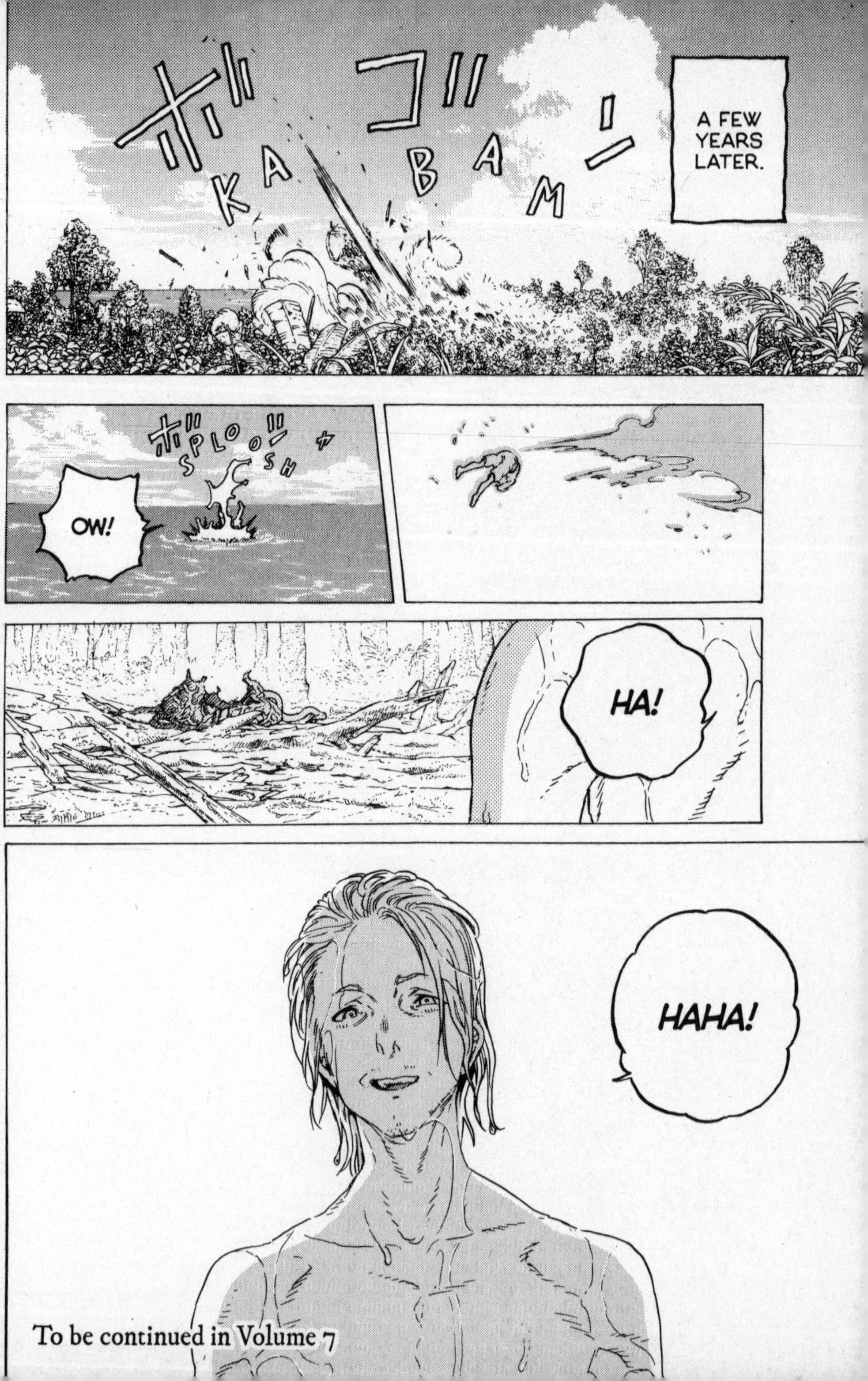
A FEW YEARS LATER.
KABAM
SPLOOSH
OW!
HA!
HAHA!
To be continued in Volume 7

TO YOUR ETERNITY

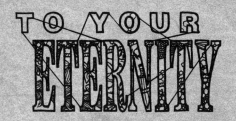

NEXT VOLUME PREVIEW

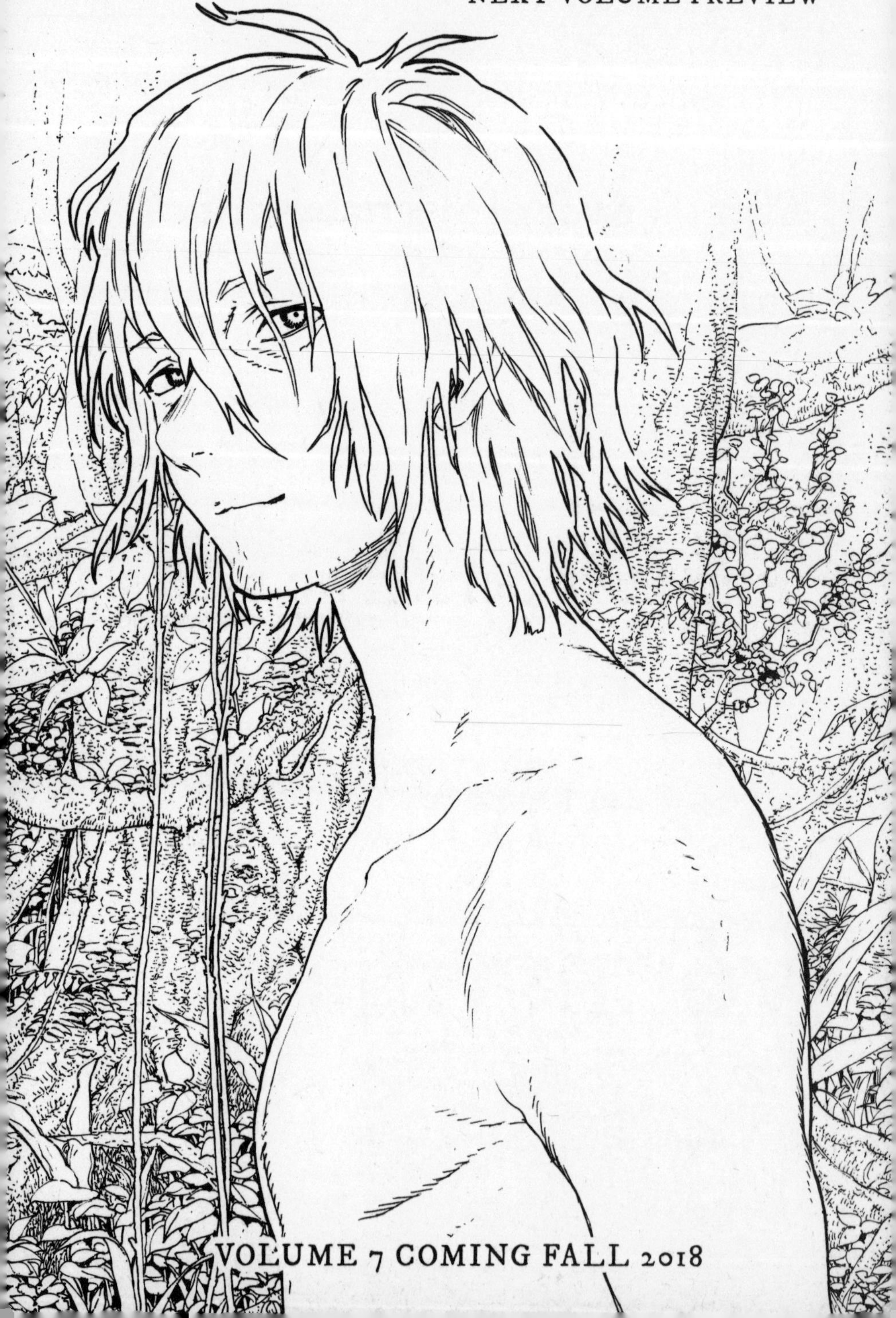

VOLUME 7 COMING FALL 2018

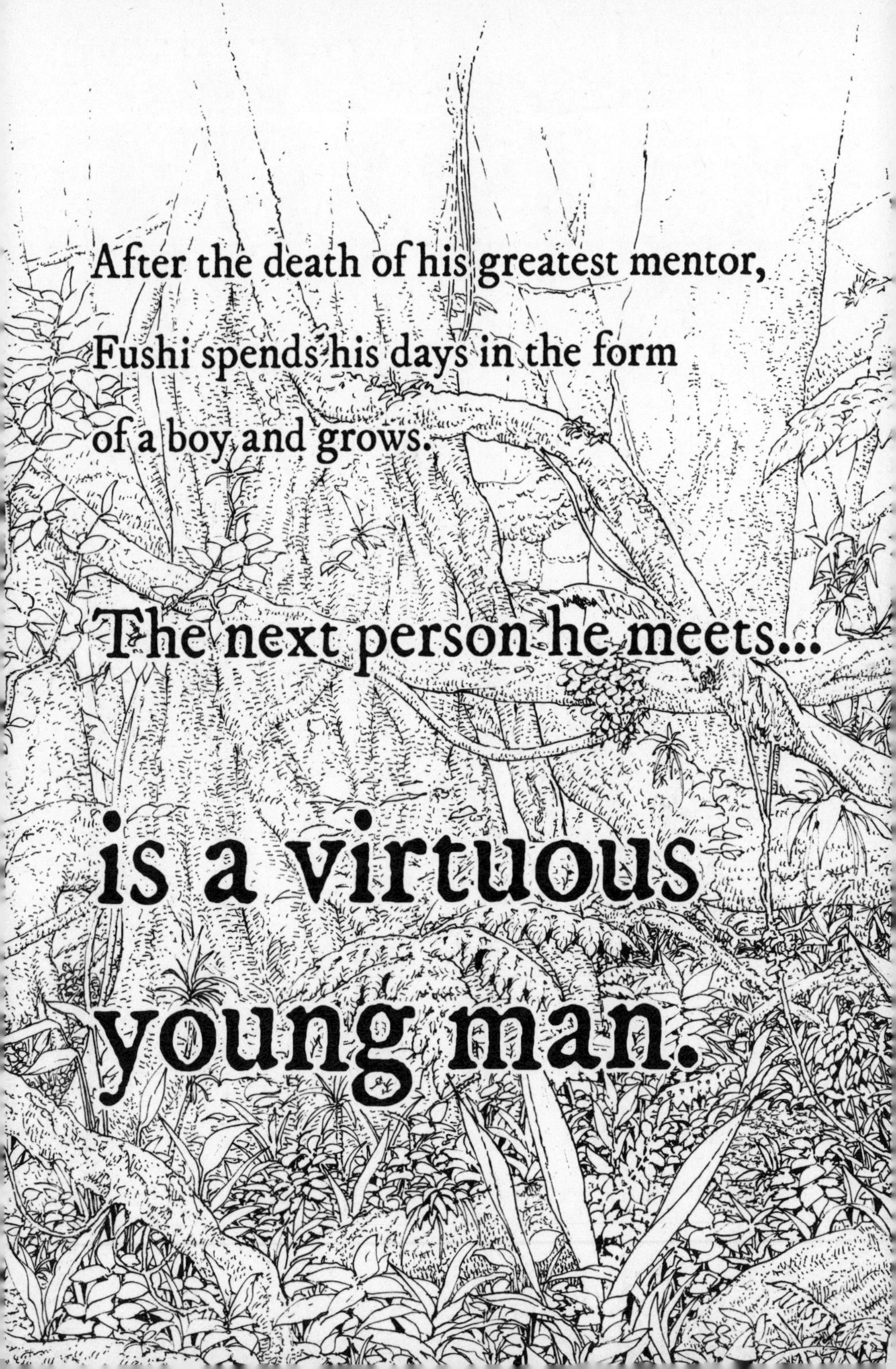
After the death of his greatest mentor,
Fushi spends his days in the form
of a boy and grows.
The next person he meets...
is a virtuous
young man.

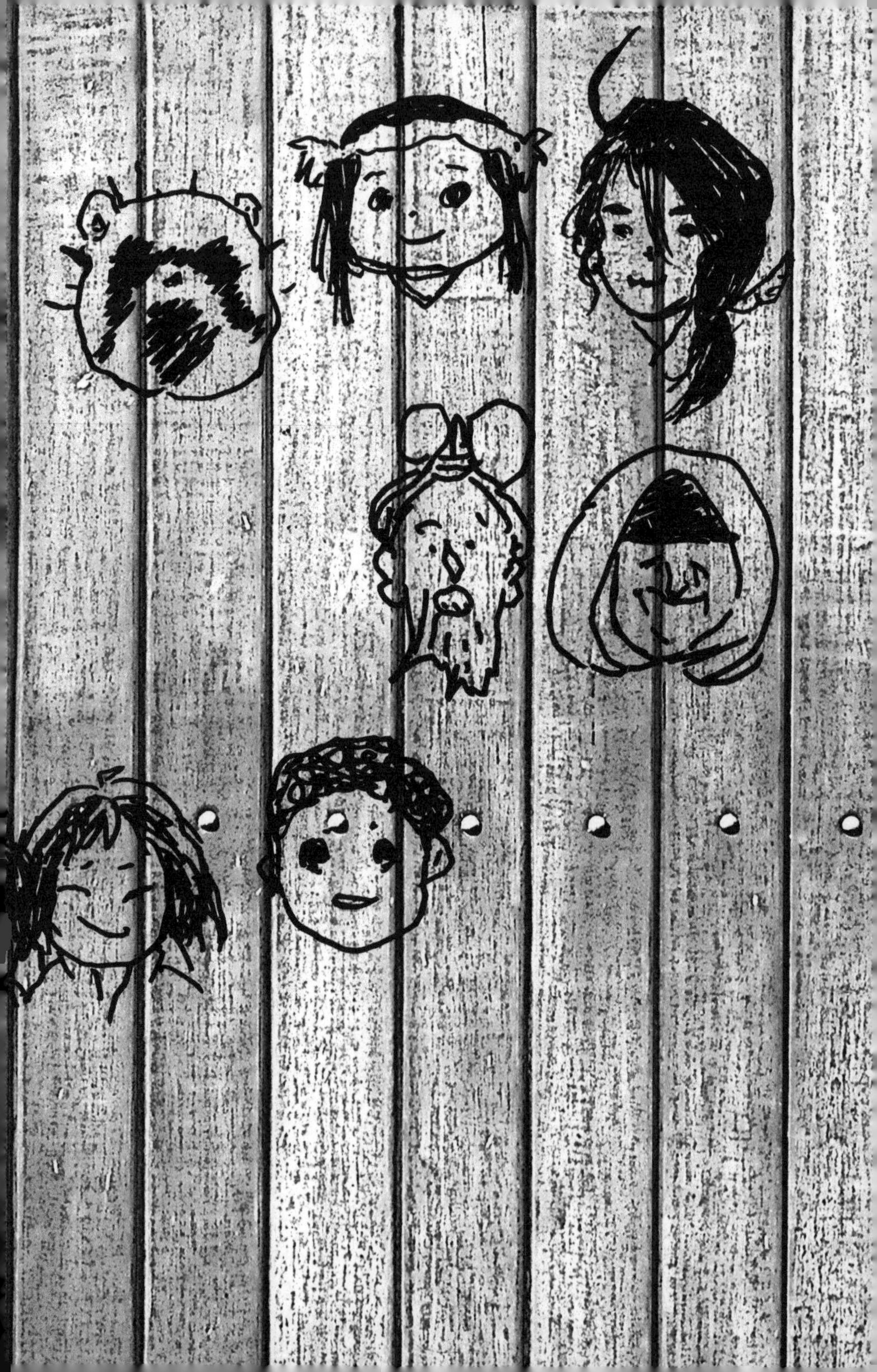

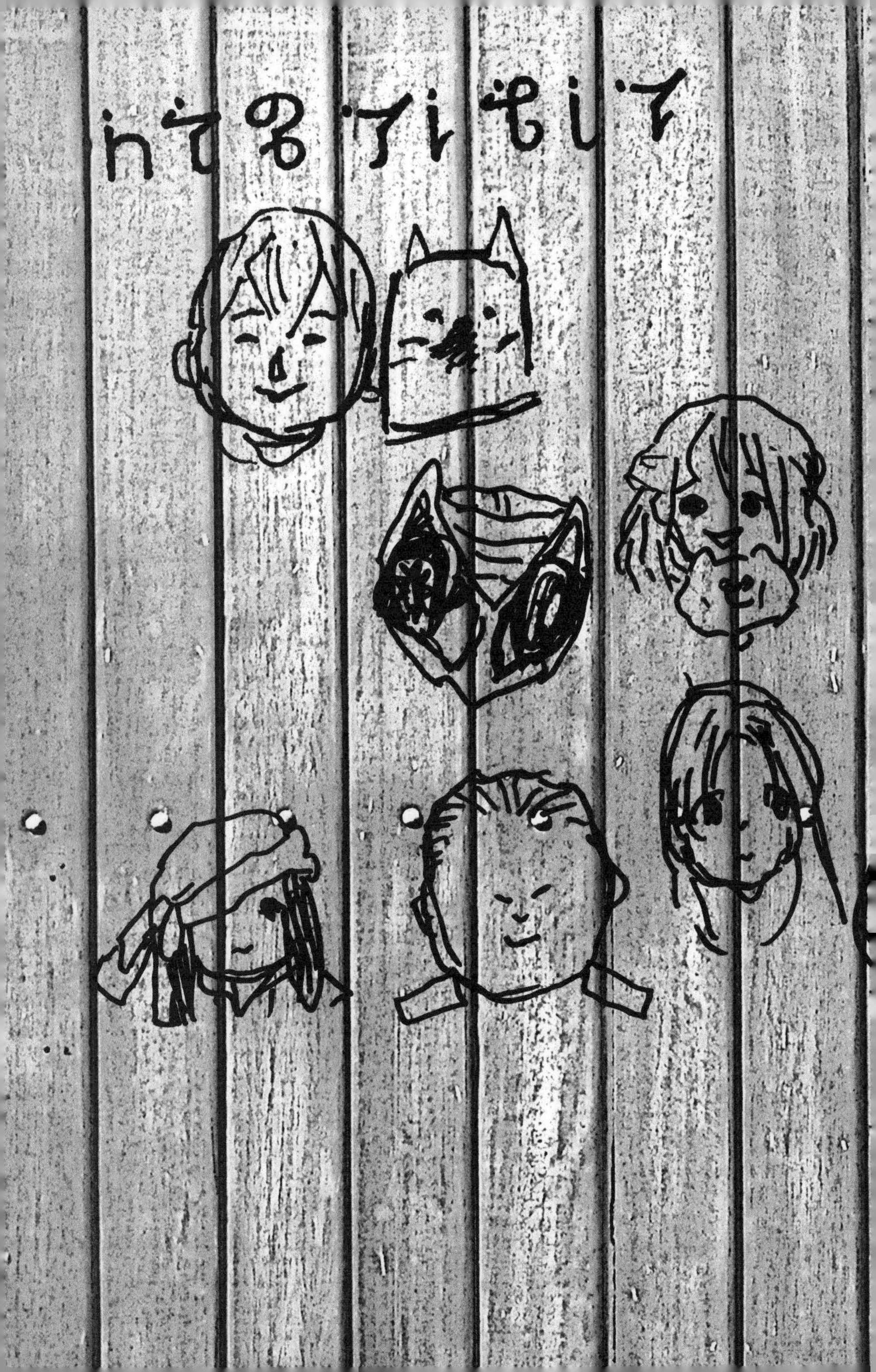

A Kodansha Comics Trade Paperback Original.

To Your Eternity volume 6 copyright © 2018 Yoshitoki Oima
English translation copyright © 2018 Yoshitoki Oima

Published in the United States by Kodansha Comics,
an imprint of Kodansha USA Publishing, LLC, New York.

Publication rights for this English edition arranged through Kodansha Ltd., Tokyo.

First published in Japan in 2018 by Kodansha Ltd., Tokyo,
as *Fumetsu no Anata e* volume 6.

Cover Design: Tadashi Hisamochi (hive&co., Ltd.)
Title Logo Design: Shinobu Ohashi

ISBN 978-1-63236-576-7

Printed in the United States of America.

www.kodanshacomics.com

9 8 7 6 5 4 3 2 1

Translation: Steven LeCroy
Lettering: Darren Smith
Editing: Haruko Hashimoto, Alexandra Swanson
Editorial Assistance: YKS Services LLC/SKY Japan, INC.
Kodansha Comics Edition Cover Design: Phil Balsman